European Perspectives on Exercise and Sport Psychology

Stuart J.H. Biddle, PhD
University of Exeter
Exeter, England

Human Kinetics

For Fiona, Jack and Greg

Library of Congress Cataloging-in-Publication Data

European perspectives on exercise and sport psychology / Stuart J.H.
  Biddle, editor.
      p.   cm.
  Includes bibliographical references and index.
  ISBN 0-87322-826-X
  1. Sports--Europe--Psychological aspects.   2. Exercise-
-Psychological aspects.   I. Biddle, Stuart.
  GV706.4.E87   1995
  796'.01'094--dc20   94-32258

ISBN: 0-87322-826-X

Developmental Editor: Julia Anderson; **Assistant Editors:** Jacqueline Blakley and Karen
Bojda; **Copyeditor:** Kenneth Walker; **Proofreader:** Denelle Eknes; **Indexer:** Barbara E.
Cohen; **Typesetting and Text Layout:** Angela K. Snyder; **Text Designer:** Judy Henderson;
Illustrator: Studio 2D; **Cover Designer:** Jack Davis; **Printer:** Braun-Brumfield

Printed in the United States of America

10   9   8   7   6   5   4   3   2   1

Human Kinetics
P.O. Box IW14, Leeds LS16 6TR, United Kingdom
(44) 1132 781708

United States: P.O. Box 5076, Champaign, IL 61825-5076
1-800-747-4457 (in U.S. only)

Canada: Human Kinetics, Box 24040, Windsor, ON N8Y 4Y9
1-800-465-7301 (in Canada only)

Australia: Human Kinetics, 2 Ingrid Street, Clapham 5062, South Australia
(08) 371 3755

New Zealand: Human Kinetics, P.O. Box 105-231, Auckland 1
(09) 523 3462

Contents

Chapter 15   Future Directions in Exercise and
**   Sport Psychology   324**

Paul Kunath

Preface

The motivation for this book arose from a desire to see a greater representation of European work in the international literature on exercise and sport psychology. Having studied in both Britain and the USA, I have a healthy respect for the North American perspective. The North Americans dominate the English language literature in exercise and sport psychology, and they are to be congratulated on their contribution to the many advances made in the short history of our subject. But it is unhealthy to rely on, or be dominated by, one perspective.

I make the point in the introduction to the book that there are probably as many similarities as differences between North American and European exercise and sport psychology. I was motivated, however, to produce a forum for the dissemination of ideas and research from authors working in Europe. This motivation stems from my experience with the European Federation of Sport Psychology (FEPSAC— Fédération Européene de Psychologie des Sports et des Activités Corporelles), first as a member of the managing council from 1987 and subsequently as president from 1991. The twice-yearly meetings of the managing council have taken me to many European countries, where I have met and had discussions with sport and exercise psychologists, physical educators, coaches and students. One is immediately struck by the common issues and problems in the different countries. For example, qualifications and accreditation, codes of conduct and ethics, motivation for a physically active and healthy lifestyle, mental training for elite performance, the personality debate, psychological measurement, and other topics are often discussed and reveal many similarities whether one is in Greece, France, Sweden, Great Britain or even the USA. However, each country will bring its own 'system' to bear on such issues. Human behaviour is shaped by its culture and shapes its own culture. To this end, a book focusing on European perspectives helps to bring forward other views on common topics of interest. The book has been organised around key themes in European exercise and sport psychology in recent years: exercise participation, sport performance, and motivation and social psychology in both sport and physical education settings.

Part I, 'Psychology of Exercise Participation', reviews key areas of the rapidly developing field of exercise psychology and includes chapters on motivation, mental health, and exercise promotion. Part II, 'Psychology of Sport Performance', examines alternative perspectives on personality, new developments in the study of anxiety, the emerging field of sport psychophysiology and mental training interventions. The increasing importance of motivation is studied in Part III, 'Motivation and Social Psychology in Sport and Physical Education'. Intrinsic motivation, goal orientations, and cognitions and emotions are topical areas covered in depth in Part III, as well as the important yet neglected study of sport crowds. In Part IV, discussion centres on research issues and future directions for European exercise and sport psychology.

This book is intended for senior undergraduates studying exercise and sport psychology, although selected chapters will also be appropriate to supplement the reading of post-graduate students.

There are numerous fine scholars in European exercise and sport psychology, many of whom are little known outside their own countries or beyond publications in their own languages. A collection of chapters in English by scholars from many countries will, I hope, broaden awareness of the work of such scholars and of perspectives from the various countries. Although I requested authors to report research of their own so that we can have a flavour of 'European research', I did not impose a standard format or length. A criticism sometimes levelled at edited books is that the coverage is uneven or that there is overlap between chapters. Although both apply here to a certain degree, it was my intention to let the authors tell their own stories from their own perspectives without excessive idiosyncratic editorial constraints. In my opinion this is a strength, not a source of criticism. Comprehensive coverage of the field of exercise and sport psychology was not intended.

The integration of European sport and exercise psychologists has been a fundamental aim of FEPSAC. The idea of a European federation began in December 1968 at the first European Congress, held in Varna, Bulgaria. The second European Congress, in Vittel, France in June 1969 saw the creation of FEPSAC and the election of its first president, Ema Geron (then from Bulgaria, now Israel). Currently there are over 20 member countries, and this number is increasing as the former states of the USSR join as independent countries.

The aims of FEPSAC are to contribute to the scientific study of sport, sport psychology and related fields; to organise and co-ordinate scientific work and the exchange of information and documentation; and to establish and promote scientific collaboration between European sport and exercise psychologists through meetings, symposia and scientific congresses. FEPSAC now publishes a biannual bulletin, a directory of European sport psychologists, annual reports from member countries and supports the publication of books (e.g., Hackfort & Spielberger, 1989, as well as the current volume).

Acknowledgments

I am very grateful to the following for making the hard work of editing this book that little bit more manageable, enjoyable and rewarding:

The members of the FEPSAC Managing Council. This book is a FEPSAC-sponsored initiative, and the Council of 1987-1991, as well as the present Council, have played an important role in shaping the structure and content of the book and in providing contacts with possible authors. The Council for 1991-1995 is as follows:

Stuart Biddle (Great Britain)   President

Laszlo Nadori (Hungary)   Vice-President

Erwin Apitzsch (Sweden)   Secretary General

Erwin Hahn (Germany)   Treasurer

Alberto Cei (Italy)

Marc Durand (France)

Jarmo Luikkonen (Finland)

Roland Seiler (Switzerland)

Yves Vanden Auwelle (Belgium)

The external reviewers who helped the editor review the chapters. I am very grateful for the time and effort taken by the reviewers: Yuri Hanin (Research Centre for Olympic Sports, Jyväskylä, Finland), Lew Hardy (University College of North Wales, UK), Jarmo Luikkonen (University of Jyväskylä, Finland), Hubert Ripoll (Université de Poitiers, France), Andy Smith (Kerland Sports Services, UK), and Adrian Taylor (University of Brighton, UK).

The authors themselves for their friendly co-operation and hard work. The delays that we have experienced have been almost entirely my fault!

The staff of Human Kinetics for their work, including those at HK (Europe) in Leeds during the early stages, Rainer Martens for his advice and guidance on book structure and content, and latterly Julia Anderson for her excellent work as developmental editor.

Fiona for her love and support, and Jack and Greg for providing the best 'perspective' of all and for not waking too often during pre-breakfast 'prime writing time'!

Introduction

Given the extensive use of American students as subjects in published psychological research, it is not surprising that some people suggest that psychological knowledge is no more than the psychology of American psychology students! Unfortunately sport and exercise psychology also has a restricted focus. My own review of papers published on motivation between 1979 and 1991 in two key sport and exercise psychology journals—the *International Journal of Sport Psychology* (*IJSP*) and the *Journal of Sport and Exercise Psychology* (*JSEP*)—revealed that the majority of studies were restricted to children, youth or young adults (see Biddle, 1994 and chapter 1). Similarly, Duda and Allison (1990) have reported on the lack of information on ethnic and racial background of subjects in studies published in *JSEP*, a lack that reflects the ethnocentric nature of exercise and sport psychology research, at least as published in that journal. In short, key English language journals in our field appear to be gathering and reporting research findings from populations of limited representativeness.

The most widely used language for international academic exchange and communication is English, and exercise and sport psychology is no exception. Consequently, there is a danger that the content of English language publications may become the accepted knowledge of the subject, at least internationally. For this reason, I became interested in assembling authors to provide a European perspective on exercise and sport psychology, albeit in English. The English language literature in this field is dominated by North American authors. This is true both of journal articles and of textbooks. Judging by their citations, North American authors often fail to acknowledge authors outside their own country. For example, Cox, Qiu, and Liu (1993), in their overview of sport psychology, provide a brief historical perspective. Although they state that their chapter focuses on North America, they also say that 'whereas the history of sport psychology in Western Europe, England, Australia and North America has been well documented in English (Singer, 1989; Wiggins, 1984), the same is not true for Eastern Europe and much of Asia' (p. 5). However, the two references they cite to support the documentation of developments in Western Europe, England and Australia are overviews of the subject in the USA (Singer) and in North America (Wiggins)!

Is There a Distinct European Perspective on Exercise and Sport Psychology?

Europe has provided a strong influence on the history of psychology and its various subdisciplines. For example, social psychological theory is rich in European influence, not only from scholars who lived in Europe, but also from those who moved out of Europe to work in the United States (e.g., Heider and Lewin). Indeed, Graumann (1988), in his excellent historical analysis of social psychology, suggests that 'the situation of social psychology in postwar Europe can hardly be understood without the dialectics of the transatlantic exchange' (p. 16). Graumann's chapter is contained in an edited volume on social psychology, subtitled 'A European Perspective' (Hewstone, Stroebe, Codol, & Stephenson, 1988). In the preface to this volume, the editor stated that our 'European perspective' refers to the geographical location of our contributors, the literature they cite, and to a lesser extent to their conception of social psychology. There are undoubtedly more similarities than differences between European and North American social psychology.

This comment applies equally to exercise and sport psychology. There are differences, but equally there are many similarities. One factor is that many scholars in Europe have studied in North America, whereas few American scholars have studied in Europe, because of language difficulties. Consequently, many researchers in exercise and sport psychology in countries such as Great Britain, Israel or Greece have experienced the North American system of education at first hand at the level of the master's or doctor's degree and have been exposed to North American literature in the process.

Despite the similarities in exercise and sport psychology in Europe and North America (and such similarities probably also exist with other geographical regions like Australasia and South America), it is important for the development of our field to communicate the findings from different countries as widely as possible. We study human behaviour, and it is influenced by the society and culture we live in. Consequently, we cannot rely on research findings from one geographical area to explain all of human behaviour. We need more 'cultural' research in exercise and sport psychology, studying the cultural basis of psychological phenomena in sport and physical activity. In addition, we need more 'cross-cultural' research to find out how psychological factors and behaviours vary in different cultures (see Bond, 1983; Lonner & Berry, 1986).

How Perspectives Differ Between Countries

Although there are probably as many similarities between countries as there are differences, historical, cultural and other factors shape the development and focus of exercise and sport psychology in the various European countries. For example, with the development of the delivery of psychological services in sport in Great Britain, British sport psychologists have spent some time working on issues of professional conduct and accreditation (Biddle, 1989; Biddle, Bull, & Seheult, 1992). In Eastern European countries, recent changes in the political structure have led to a greater awareness of aspects of psychology that contribute to physical activity other than elite sport. Hosek (1991), writing about current trends in what was then Czechoslovakia, said that less emphasis used to be given to the psychology of handicapped participants, school physical education, exercise, recreation and rehabilitation when elite sport was the dominant interest during the Socialist era. Much of this interest was stimulated by strong financial support from the government. Kantor and Ryzonkin (1993) state that in the former USSR 'the major effort of research . . . is focused on the psychological preparation of individual athletes and of teams for competition' (p. 46). They also say that 'noncompetitive sport psychology is the least developed area of contemporary sport psychology in the former USSR; however, now there is great interest in this specialty' (p. 48).

The political structure shaped much of the development of sport psychology in many of the Eastern European countries, the emphasis being strongly on elite performance. In Estonia, however, research has had a broader base. For example, research dissertations were produced in 1963 on the role of music in artistic movement experiences, in 1971 on physical education students and in 1972 on the development of preschool children (Oja, 1992).

Research in Western European countries parallels much research in North America. For example, my own review of material presented at British conferences shows a great deal of similarity to that found in North American journals (Biddle, 1989). The decline in interest in motor learning research in Britain has been offset by an increase in two other areas: exercise psychology and aspects of applied sport psychology. Recent conferences of the British Association of Sport and Exercise Sciences have seen a strong emphasis on exercise and well-being as well as on research on motivation. The latter topic also features a great deal in France where research on intrinsic motivation and goal orientations is taking place (see Famose, Sarrazin, Cury, & Durant, 1993; Ripoll & Thill, 1993; Thill, 1989 and chapter 10).

Germany produces a great deal of excellent research in exercise and sport psychology and, according to Hackfort (1993), 'research in top-level sports is of great interest to the public but certainly not the only area in which German sport psychologists are engaged' (p. 40). However, in Spain the emphasis appears to be more on elite sport psychology (De Diego & Sagredo, 1993). The German perspective, however, is broad and includes most areas of contemporary exercise and sport psychology. Published in German journals (e.g., *Betrifft: Psychologie und Sport* and *Sportpsychologie*), much of this excellent work is lost to non-German readers. For example, the research on exercise, sport and mental well-being by Abele and Brehm, some of it published in English, is a significant advance on the traditional perspectives on exercise and mental health in the North American and British literature. (See Abele, Brehm, & Grall, 1991; Abele & Brehm, 1993; Hackfort's 1994 critique of research into health and well-being.)

Also in Germany there is great emphasis on Kuhl's (1985) Action Control Theory and related perspectives (see Hackfort, 1993; Nitsch, 1989; as well as chapter 14). Although this perspective is not well known in some other countries, a few researchers have adopted it, including some in North America (e.g., Kendzierski, 1990).

Finally, are we able to find evidence of different levels of 'activity' in different European countries in exercise and sport psychology? One indicator of this might be the number of sport and exercise psychologists in the country. However, data are sparse or unreliable on this. In the second edition of *The World Sport Psychology Sourcebook* (Salmela, 1992), 27 European countries have a total of 713 entries in the 'Who's Who' section. The numbers range from one for each of Ireland, Liechenstein,

Lithuania and Luxembourg, to 44 for the former Soviet Union, 47 for France, 48 for Great Britain, and 186 for Germany.

The first edition of the Fédération Européene de Psychologie des Sports et des Activités Corporelles (FEPSAC) *Directory of European Sport Psychologists* (FEPSAC, 1993) includes 297 entries. The response to a reasonably detailed questionnaire, including questions about research and professional interests, was largely from sport psychologists living in Western Europe. Thus this information source does not provide a pan-European view. In terms of research interests listed, the areas of stress and anxiety, motivation, and exercise and health were particularly popular (see Figure 1). Among the special skills listed by the European sport psychologists, counselling was more frequently cited than teaching or research (see Figure 2).

When respondents were asked to indicate, in rank order, their 'main regular clients', the category they listed most frequently as the top rank was 'top sports competitors' (see Figure 3). This reflects the current concentration of applied sport psychology at the higher, rather than the lower, end of the performance spectrum. However, when asked the same question about their educational (teaching) work in exercise and sport psychology, the picture was more varied (see Figure 3).

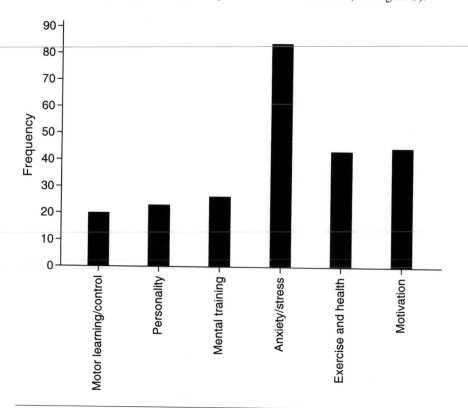

Figure 1.   Most frequently cited areas of research interests of European sport psychologists.
Note. Data from *Directory of European Sport Psychologists*, 1993, FEPSAC.

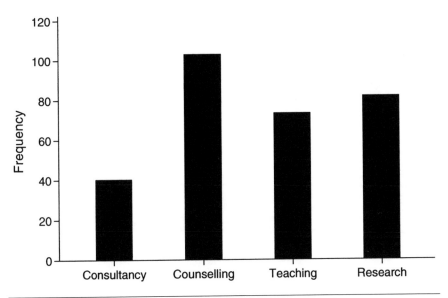

Figure 2.   Frequency of special skills of European sport psychologists.
Note. Data from *Directory of European Sport Psychologists*, 1993, FEPSAC.

Defining Key Terms

In attempting to cover current perspectives of work in Europe, this book deals with both sport psychology and exercise psychology, as well as physical education contexts. Exercise psychology is clearly a rapidly expanding area, as can be seen by the increasing use of the word 'exercise' when referring to research into physical activity. This is true in European research, as well as in journals published in North America, such as *Research Quarterly for Exercise and Sport* and the *Journal of Sport and Exercise Psychology*. Indeed, the latter journal changed its name in 1988 by adding the word *exercise* to its title so as to reflect the field better. For the same reason I did not limit the title of this book to the term 'sport psychology'. I felt that this would not have given due credit to the book's wider content.

Exercise is operationally defined here as physical activity, usually of a structured and planned nature, that has the goal of maintaining or improving physical or psychological fitness. In other words, exercise has a strong health-related connotation. Sport, on the other hand, refers to rule-bound, structured and competitive gross motor activities characterised by prowess, chance and strategy. Finally, physical education is discussed in the specific context of school curriculum time devoted to the physical activities of sport, dance and exercise.

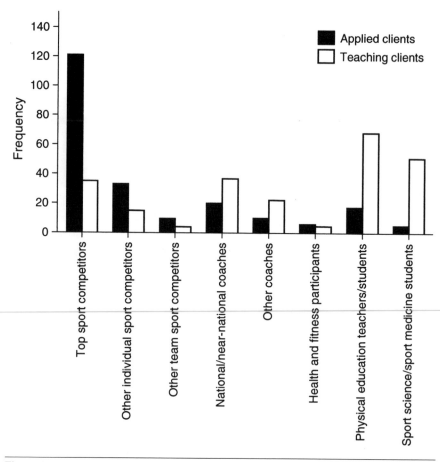

Figure 3. Clients ranked first for applied sport psychology work and teaching by European sport psychologists.
Note. Data from *Directory of European Sport Psychologists*, 1993, FEPSAC.

Conclusion

There probably is no single European perspective on exercise and sport psychology. However, the diversity and richness of research and professional activity in exercise and sport psychology across the European continent, much of which is published in languages other than English, deserve greater visibility and recognition. We need to take this work into account if we are to truly understand human behaviour in sport and physical activity.

References

Abele, A., & Brehm, W. (1993). Mood effects of exercise versus sports games: Findings and implications for well-being and health. *International Review of Health Psychology*, **2**, 53-80.

Abele, A., Brehm, W., & Grall, T. (1991). Sportliche Aktivitat und Wohlbefinden. In A. Abele & P. Becker (Eds.), *Wohlbefinden* (pp. 279-296). Weinheim, Germany: Beltz.

Biddle, S.J.H. (1989). Applied sport psychology: A view from Britain. *Journal of Applied Sport Psychology*, **1**, 23-34.

Biddle, S.J.H. (1994). Motivation and participation in exercise and sport. In S. Serpa, J. Alves, & V. Pataco (Eds.), *International perspectives on sport and exercise psychology* (pp. 103-126). Morgantown, WV: F.I.T.

Biddle, S.J.H., Bull, S.J., & Seheult, C.L. (1992). Ethical and professional issues in contemporary British sport psychology. *The Sport Psychologist*, **6**, 66-76.

Bond, M.H. (1983). A proposal for cross-cultural studies of attribution. In M. Hewstone (Ed.), *Attribution theory: Social and functional extensions* (pp. 144-157). Oxford, England: Blackwell.

Cox, R.H., Qiu, Y., & Liu, Z. (1993). Overview of sport psychology. In R.N. Singer, M. Murphey, & L.K. Tennant (Eds.), *Handbook of research on sport psychology* (pp. 3-31). New York: Macmillan.

De Diego, S., & Sagredo, C. (1993). Sport psychology in Spain: A reality. In J.R. Nitsch & R. Seiler (Eds.), *Proceedings of the 8th European Congress of Sport Psychology: Vol. I. Motivation, emotion, stress* (pp. 357-361). Sankt Augustin, Germany: Academia Verlag.

Duda, J.L., & Allison, M.T. (1990). Cross-cultural analysis in exercise and sport psychology: A void in the field. *Journal of Sport and Exercise Psychology*, **12**, 114-131.

Famose, J-P., Sarrazin, P., Cury, F., & Durant, M. (1993). Study of the effects of perceived ability, motivational goal and competitive context upon the selection of task difficulty in a free choice situation. In S. Serpa, J. Alves, V. Ferreira, & A. Paulo-Brito (Eds.), *Proceedings of the 8th World Congress of Sport Psychology* (pp. 656-659). Lisbon, Portugal: International Society of Sport Psychology/Sociedade Portuguesa de Psicologia Desportiva/Faculdade de Motricidade Humana.

Fédération Européene de Psychologie des Sports et des Activités Corporelles. (1993). *Directory of European sport psychologists*. Lund, Sweden: Author.

Graumann, C.F. (1988). Introduction to a history of social psychology. In M. Hewstone, W. Stroebe, J-P. Codol, & G.M. Stephenson (Eds.), *Introduction to social psychology* (pp. 3-19). Oxford, England: Blackwell.

Hackfort, D. (1993). Contemporary areas of research in sport psychology in Germany. In R.N. Singer, M. Murphey, & L.K. Tennant (Eds.), *Handbook of research on sport psychology* (pp. 40-43). New York: Macmillan.

Hackfort, D. (1994). Health and wellness: A sport psychology perspective. In S. Serpa, J. Alves, & V. Pataco (Eds.), *International perspectives on sport and exercise psychology* (pp. 165-183). Morgantown, WV: F.I.T.

Hewstone, M., Stroebe, W., Codol, J-P., & Stephenson, G.M. (Eds.) (1988). *Introduction to social psychology*. Oxford, England: Blackwell.

Hosek, V. (1991). Current trends of sport psychology in Czechoslovakia. *FEPSAC Bulletin*, **3**(1), 8-10.

Kantor, E., & Ryzonkin, J. (1993). Sport psychology in the former USSR. In R.N. Singer, M. Murphey, & L.K. Tennant (Eds.), *Handbook of research on sport psychology* (pp. 46-49). New York: Macmillan.

Kendzierski, D. (1990). Decision making versus decision implementation: An action control approach to exercise adoption and adherence. *Journal of Applied Social Psychology*, **20**, 27-45.

Kuhl, J. (1985). Volitional mediators of cognition-behaviour consistency: Self-regulatory processes and action versus state orientation. In J. Kuhl & J. Beckmann (Eds.), *Action control: From cognition to behaviour* (pp. 101-128). New York: Springer-Verlag.

Lonner, W.J., & Berry, J.W. (Eds.) (1986). *Field methods in cross-cultural research*. Beverly Hills, CA: Sage.

Nitsch, J. (1989). Future trends in sport psychology and sport sciences. In C.K. Giam, K.K. Chook, & K.C. Teh (Eds.), *Proceedings of the 7th World Congress in Sport Psychology* (pp. 200-204). Singapore: Singapore Sports Council.

Oja, S. (1992). The origin and development of sport psychology in Estonia. *FEPSAC Bulletin*, **4**(1), 5-11.

Ripoll, H., & Thill, E. (1993). Contemporary areas of research in sport psychology in France: Overview and perspectives. In R.N. Singer, M. Murphey, & L.K. Tennant (Eds.), *Handbook of research on sport psychology* (pp. 34-39). New York: Macmillan.

Salmela, J.H. (1992). *The world sport psychology sourcebook* (2nd ed.). Champaign, IL: Human Kinetics.

Singer, R.N. (1989). Applied sport psychology in the United States. *Journal of Applied Sport Psychology*, **1**, 61-80.

Thill, E. (1989). *Motivation et strategies de motivation en milieu sportif*. Paris: Presses Universitaires de France.

Wiggins, D. (1984). The history of sport psychology in North America. In J. Silva & R. Weinberg (Eds.), *Psychological foundations of sport* (pp. 9-22). Champaign, IL: Human Kinetics.

I
PART

PSYCHOLOGY OF EXERCISE PARTICIPATION

Interest in exercise psychology is on the increase. It is also spreading to countries previously strongly focused on elite performance. For example, the change in political conditions in East European countries has led to greater interest in 'sport for all' and exercise promotion. This is consistent with the World Health Organization's Health for All targets for the year 2000 for European countries. Targets associated with healthy public policy, knowledge and motivation for healthy behaviour, positive health behaviour, and research strategies all have important implications for sport and exercise psychology.

This section of the book addresses the three main areas of exercise psychology: antecedent factors likely to be associated with participation in exercise, the psychological consequences of exercise, and the psychological issues associated with the promotion of physical activity and exercise. Chapters on the key areas of motivation (chapter 1, by Stuart Biddle) and attitudes (chapter 2, by George Doganis and Yannis Theodorakis) contribute to the understanding of psychological antecedents in exercise. In particular it is important to expand our horizons and adopt more of a life-span perspective on such factors or likely 'determinants' of participation.

The issues of psychological, or mental health, outcomes of exercise are addressed in both normal populations (see chapter 3, by Nanette Mutrie and Stuart Biddle) and abnormal or clinical populations (see chapter 4, by Egil Martinsen). Many familiar with this area of research will know that the literature points to favourable psychological outcomes from exercise, but at the same time the research methods adopted have rarely been satisfactory. The challenge ahead seems to be associated with the development of stronger research designs in this area, as well as broadening the approach from negative to more positive aspects of mental health. The research has concentrated a great deal on anxiety and depression. Perhaps the time is right to spend more time on studying positive affect, well-being, enjoyment and self-esteem.

The area of promoting exercise can be lost in the increasing amount of research on antecedents and consequences of exercise. The chapter on exercise promotion (chapter 5, by R. Andrew Smith and Stuart Biddle) attempts to integrate some theoretical approaches with more applied guidelines and strategies. This should also be a growth area for the future.

1

CHAPTER

Exercise Motivation Across the Life Span

Stuart J.H. Biddle

GREAT BRITAIN

Few subjects in sport and exercise are as universal and central as human motivation. Whether the participant is an elite marathon runner striving for greater speed after 30 km of hard racing or a recreational exerciser who has dropped out of a fitness class after a few sessions, motivation is deemed important. For this chapter the subject of motivation will focus on participation in exercise and physical activity. In this context, *physical activity* is defined as all human musculoskeletal movement resulting in energy expenditure; it includes all aspects of movement, such as walking and manual labour. *Exercise* refers to structured forms of physical activity usually engaged in to gain, maintain or improve fitness (Caspersen, Powell, & Christenson, 1985). Although this could include sport, I will be referring not to motivation in elite high-performance sport but to participation in exercise and physical activity at a recreational, or health-related, level.

Physical activity is considered important in contemporary European society. For example, the World Health Organization (WHO, 1985) published its targets for the European regional strategy for Health for All for the year 2000, including these:

ensure equality in health, by reducing the present gap in health status between countries and groups within countries;

add life to years, by ensuring the full development and use of people's . . . capacity to derive full benefit from and to cope with life in a healthy way;

add health to life, by reducing disease and disability;

add years to life, by reducing premature deaths, and thereby increasing life expectancy. (p. 23)

Current research evidence strongly supports the efficacy of exercise and physical activity in the last three of these aims (Bouchard, Shephard, Stephens, Sutton, & McPherson, 1990). In addition, more specific objectives particularly relevant to physical activity were included in Target 15 on 'knowledge and motivation for healthy behaviour' and Target 16 on 'positive health behaviour'.

Target 15 points to the need to help people 'change habits that have become routine' (p. 62). Such habits will include physical inactivity in many cases. Similarly, WHO (1985), in statements associated with Target 16, suggest that 'positive health behaviour constitutes a conscious effort by individuals to actively maintain their health' (p. 64). However, they contend that 'positive health behaviour is by far the most challenging field for a health promotion policy' (p. 65). Clearly these targets and associated statements make implicit and explicit reference to motivation and the problems of changing health behaviours. This is also reflected in national documents on health promotion. For example, a consultation paper for England, produced by the British government (Department of Health, 1991), stated that

There is considerable emphasis in this document on the need for people to change their behaviour. . . . The reason is simple. We live in an age where many . . . main causes of premature death and unnecessary disease are related to how we lead our lives. (pp. iv-v)

Society faces a difficult problem. Although it is acknowledged that exercise and physical activity contribute significantly to an individual's healthy lifestyle, many people appear to face considerable difficulties when they attempt to start or maintain such activities. The study of human motivation, therefore, appears to be an area of more than academic interest.

Recent reviews of research on motivational determinants of people's involvement in exercise and physical activity show that much of it has centred on children and young adults (see Biddle & Mutrie, 1991). For obvious reasons, greater attention has been given to the young and active. The difficulties of studying nonparticipants, or those outside places where research is more convenient to conduct, such as schools, universities and sports clubs, have resulted in a biased profile of research on motivation and exercise (Biddle, 1994).

This bias is more than just a problem for researchers. First, the greatest challenge in exercise and public health promotion is to motivate nonexercisers to start regular exercise. However, this subpopulation has rarely been studied (Sallis & Hovell, 1990). Second, a great deal of discussion has centred on the importance of promoting physical activity in childhood so that such positive habits will persist in later life. However, very little is known about such 'tracking effects', even at a cross-sectional level (see chapter 5). A life-span perspective is important for a fuller understanding of the processes involved in exercise motivation. In particular, there is a need to study older adults (over 50 years of age) as this age-group is almost totally missing from contemporary research in exercise psychology, although a few studies have appeared recently in the European literature (Ashford & Rickhuss, 1992; Codina, Jimenez, & Rufat, 1991).

Defining Motivation

The study of human motivation has remained at the heart of psychology since the earliest days of the discipline (Weiner, 1992). The roots of motivation research are firmly European (e.g., Freud, Lorenz), although recent dominant perspectives have been influenced greatly by North Americans (e.g., Bandura, Weiner). For Weiner (1992) the subject matter of the field of motivation concerns why people think and behave as they do. His elaboration on the components of motivation broadly agrees with Maehr and Braskamp (1986) who contend that

> Most motivational talk arises from observations about variation in five behavioral patterns, which we label direction, persistence, continuing motivation, intensity, and performance. (p. 3)

In the context of exercise, *direction* refers to the extent to which an individual might choose exercise in preference to other behaviours; *persistence* refers to concentration of attention on a task, or duration of exercise; *continuing motivation* is the extent to which the individual returns on a regular basis to exercise; intensity is the effort put into exercise. Finally, inferences about motivation can be made from performance.

Historically, human motivation has been viewed from the perspectives of 'people as machines' (e.g., drive theory), personality (e.g., achievement motivation theory), and social cognition (e.g., self-efficacy and attribution theories) (Weiner, 1991, 1992). Contemporary motivation theory is no longer based on the notions of drives or instincts but more on social perception and cognitive perspectives espoused in approaches such as attribution theory and achievement goal orientations (see Roberts, 1992a; Weiner, 1992). To use Weiner's (1992) metaphorical approach, psychologists have moved from 'the machine metaphor' to 'Godlike metaphors' whereby humans are seen to act as evaluating judges of their own behaviour through cognitive and emotional processes.

This chapter will review the current state of knowledge of the role of motivation in exercise across an individual's life span. Research will be reviewed in two main areas: descriptive findings and findings based on more theoretical foundations or models. Emphasis will be placed on European research, but, where appropriate, other relevant research will be discussed.

Descriptive Research on Children and Youth

Much of the research on sport and exercise motivation has been atheoretical or descriptive in nature. Such studies have often simply asked participants or nonparticipants why they have chosen their preferred course of action. In addition, many studies have ascertained reasons for ceasing participation.

Much of the research on children's participation motivation tends to focus on competitive sport rather than more diverse aspects of exercise and physical activity. However, this is not surprising, because children are less likely to participate in fitness pursuits currently favoured by adults.

Motives for Participation

Research in Wales on youth and young adults 16 to 24 years of age (Heartbeat Wales, 1987) found that nonparticipants would find the following to be incentives to become active in sport: improved fitness or weight loss, having more free time, and maintainance of good health. Figure 1.1 illustrates these and other incentives across the life span, allowing comparison between age-groups.

Figure 1.1 shows that incentives decline with age, although the relative strength of the main incentives remains fairly constant within each age-group. Similarly, Ashford, Biddle, and Goudas (1993) found, in a survey of 336 participants in six English leisure centres, that subjects 16 to 25 years of age were significantly less interested in the motives associated with sociopsychological well-being than subjects over 25 years. Younger subjects appeared to be more motivated by the pursuit of physical development, either through skills and competition or fitness. Ashford and Rickhuss (1992) also found age-group differences in sport participation motives. Sports mastery motives were rated significantly higher by younger children (aged 6-9 years), whereas social status was an important motive for youth aged 10 to 14 years.

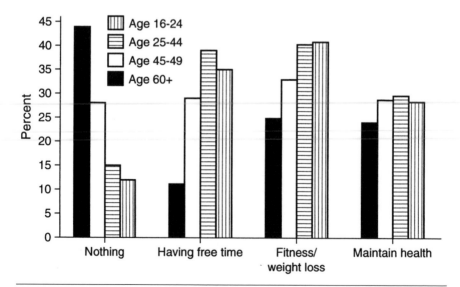

Figure 1.1   Age differences in selected incentives for taking up sport reported by nonparticipants in Heartbeat Wales (1987) survey.
Note. Data compiled from Heartbeat Wales (1987, p. 40).

A study in Finland (Telama & Silvennoinen, 1979) of over 3,000 youths aged 11 to 19 years, showed clear differences in motivation for physical activity as a function of age and gender. Boys of all ages and younger subjects of both sexes were more interested in achieving success in competition, but by late adolescence very few girls showed interest in this factor. This pattern was reversed for motives associated with relaxation and recreation. Also of interest, given the current focus on children's exercise and fitness (Armstrong & Biddle, 1992), was that fitness motivation was strongest among subjects who often thought about sport and took part in sports club activities. This fitness motive was unimportant for those 18 to 19 years old and for those uninterested or inactive in sport. This has important implications for the way we promote fitness in youth and illustrates the need to distinguish between sport and exercise.

Another study from Finland (Saarinen, 1987) found that boys 16 to 17 years old rated fitness, experiencing success and developing skills as the most important motives for physical activity. Girls likewise rated the factors of fitness and experiencing success highest but also strongly endorsed the motive of recreation. In a large study in Italy by Buonamano, Cei, and Mussino (1993), on over 2,500 participants in youth sports, enjoyment was reported as the main reason for participation by 49.2% of the sample. This was followed by physical (health or fitness) motives (32%), social reasons (8.9%), competition (4.2%), skill motives (2.9%), and social visibility or status (2.8%). A factor analysis of the questionnaire used by Buonamano et al. (1993) revealed factors of success and status, fitness and skill, extrinsic rewards, team factors, friendship and fun, and energy release.

German research (Brettschneider, 1992) has shown that the participation of adolescents in sport has increased in recent years. Activities now featuring more often compared with the 1950s are 'new individual sports such as bodybuilding, jogging and surfing as well as the Eastern movement forms and the different forms of aerobic dancing' (Brettschneider, 1992, p. 541). Similarly, Brettschneider (1992) reports on research on 2,000 adolescents and young adults in which distinctive profiles of adolescent lifestyle could be seen. For example, 5% of the group were categorised as a 'no sports group' since they preferred other leisure-time pursuits. Another 4% were motivated by body image and general image promotion, whereas 13% were characterised by individuality and self-expression and 'are disposed to health-related hedonism' (p. 548). Such typologies were confirmed by both quantitative and qualitative data.

The findings reported so far might have important implications for physical education curricula if one objective is to educate children and youth for an active lifestyle as adults. However, our own research (Biddle & Brooke, 1992) has shown that 12-year-old British children have a strong intrinsic interest in physical education and sport. For example, using the Motivational Orientation in Sport Scale (Weiss, Bredemeier, & Shewchuk, 1985), we found that all five dimensions of intrinsic motivation were rated above the scale midpoint, thus showing moderate to high intrinsic motivation in physical education and sport. Indeed, these scores were much higher than those reported for a comparable scale constructed for classroom settings. However, boys were found to have higher intrinsic motivation than girls for physical education and sport. In a related study, we found that such differences were also related to the higher activity levels of boys than girls (Biddle & Armstrong, 1992). Similarly, data from children in Northern Ireland (Van Wersch, Trew, & Turner, 1992) have shown that interest in physical education remains relatively constant in boys from age 11 to 19 years, whereas during the same period girls' interest declines sharply. Interest was assessed by questionnaire items pertaining to attitude, behaviour, motivation and perceptions of fun in the physical education setting.

North American research (Canada Fitness Survey, 1983; Gould & Petlichkoff, 1988; Wankel & Kreisel, 1985) confirms reports from Europe that children are motivated for a variety of reasons. Reviews by Biddle (1992c), Biddle and Fox (1988) and Gould and Petlichkoff (1988) concluded that children are motivated for diverse reasons, including fun and enjoyment, learning and improving skills, being with friends, success and winning, and physical fitness and health. The latter factor might also include weight control and body appearance for older youth. However, more research is needed to understand the differences in motives across activities, levels of participation and developmental stages, although the research so far shows some similarity in motives across settings and groups.

Reasons for Ceasing Participation

Various surveys are available on the reasons children and youth give for nonparticipation or ceasing involvement in sport and exercise (Canada Fitness Survey, 1983; Heartbeat Wales, 1987). However, one of the problems is that many studies classify those who cease activity as 'dropouts', yet it is possible that they have switched their interest to another activity. Indeed, White and Coakley (1986), in a study of adolescents in southeast England, stated that the terms 'nonparticipant' and 'dropout' were inappropriate descriptors for young people who no longer participated in organised sport.

> Our data strongly suggest that changes in participation patterns and leisure activity priorities were normal among the young people we interviewed. As they discovered new things about themselves and their abilities, they were likely to change their activity patterns to fit their new discoveries. This meant that 'dropping out' of sport was often a developmentally constructive decision. (White & Coakley, 1986, p. 11)

Gould and Petlichkoff (1988) make the important distinction between sport-specific dropout (ceasing participation in one sport) and domain-general dropout (ceasing sport participation altogether). This distinction may need to be incorporated into future studies.

As with motives for participation, there appear to be numerous reasons why children and youth cease their involvement. For example, White and Coakley (1986) conducted 60 in-depth interviews with 13- to 23-year-olds, half of whom had decided to participate in one of five different sports initiatives in their local town (see also Coakley & White, 1992). The others had either ceased involvement or had decided not to participate at all. The decision to participate or not appeared to be influenced by perceptions of competence, by external constraints (such as money and friends of the opposite sex), degree of support from significant others, and past experiences, including school physical education. Negative memories of school physical education included feelings of boredom and incompetence, lack of choice and negative evaluation from peers. These results are supported by Saarinen (1987) with Finnish school students. Here it was found that those who had had negative experiences in school physical education also expressed a negative attitude to physical activity outside school. Such attitudes centred on an overemphasis on competition and performance results, and the compulsory nature of the programme, with its lack of personal choice of activities.

Similarly, Heartbeat Wales (1987) found that youngsters aged 12 to 17 years did not participate in physical activity for the practical reasons of time, money and facilities, whereas Gould (1987) summarised the reasons for childrens' nonparticipation as conflicts of interest, lack of playing time, lack of fun, limited improvement in skills or no success, boredom, and injury. Competitive stress and dislike of the coach have also been cited in sport settings. Children, therefore, appear to have multiple motives for involvement and noninvolvement in sport, although less research is available on more diverse physical activity settings.

Descriptive Research on Adults

The literature on children and youth has focused mainly on participation in competitive sport, whereas research on adults has focused generally on reasons for participation or nonparticipation in exercise and recreation (Biddle, 1992c).

Motives for Participation

Ashford, Biddle, and Goudas (1993) studied participants in 14 activities in six English public sports centres. Subjects were divided into 5-year age-groups from 16 to 19 years up to 65 years and over. Fifteen motives for participation were rated on a questionnaire. A factor analysis produced four clear factors, two being related to performance ('assertive achievement' and 'sports mastery and performance'), with two related to fitness and health ('physical well-being' and 'sociopsychological well-being'). Males rated higher than females on the two performance factors. Also, as reported earlier, younger subjects were less interested than older participants in the factor of sociopsychological well-being. This supports findings in the literature on the relationship between exercise and mental health, which suggest that the beneficial psychological effects of exercise are more pronounced in older subjects (North, McCullagh, & Tran, 1990; Stephens, 1988). Similarly, research in Portugal (Serpa, 1986) has also shown that motivation to participate in exercise ('leisure sport') is strongly health-oriented, the main motives being associated with psychological well-being.

An instrument to assess motivation for exercise has been developed in Britain by Markland and Hardy (1993). The 'Exercise Motivations Inventory' (EMI) consists of 12 subscales labelled stress management, weight management, re-creation, social recognition, enjoyment, appearance, personal development, affiliation, ill-health avoidance, competition, fitness and health pressures. An initial study revealed that men aged 18 to 25 years reported that they exercised more for competition and social recognition and less for weight management than women of the same age. The most strongly endorsed factors for women were re-creation, fitness, enjoyment and weight management, whereas for men they were re-creation, competition, fitness and personal development.

The English 'Allied Dunbar National Fitness Survey' (ADNFS, 1992) was an ambitious study of over 4,000 people aged 16 to 74 years from 30 parliamentary constituencies. Home interviews took place with 1,840 men and 2,109 women for up to 1.5 hours. Physical measures were taken subsequently, mostly in mobile laboratories. The physical tests involved anthropometry, blood pressure, lung function, joint flexibility, muscle function and cardiorespiratory response to exercise.

The home interview included questions on involvement in physical activities as well as health, lifestyle and health-related behaviours, barriers and motivation to exercise, social background, personal attributes, and general attitudes. The most important motivational factors for physical activity were 'to feel in good shape physically', 'to improve or maintain health' and 'to feel a sense of achievement'. Physical appearance was also an important factor for women.

Participants in the ADNFS also rated highly the importance of exercise for health. The level of importance declined slightly across the age groups of 16 to 34 years, 35 to 54 and 55 to 74. Surprisingly, however, relatively little is known about changes in motives through the adult life cycle, although Mihalik, O'Leary, McGuire, and Dottavio (1989) did study 6,720 subjects from the cross-sectional Nationwide Recreation Survey in the USA. They found that there was a decline in participation of 29- to 36-year-olds, which was attributed to changes in job and family circumstances. However, motivational factors in changes in activity patterns through the life cycle have yet to be systematically investigated. Initial results reported by Ashford and Rickhuss (1992) suggest that British adults aged 23 to 39 are more interested in sport and exercise for reasons of physical fitness, 'getting exercise' and fun, whereas adults aged 40 years and over report health improvement as a strong motive, alongside getting exercise and fun. Physical fitness was less important for this age group.

British research has also shown interesting differences in the motivation of subjects within the same type of activity. Schlackmans (1986) studied nearly 2,000 women in 10 English towns. Exercise and fitness classes were studied, which included traditional keep-fit, jazz-dance, and 'aerobics' (aerobic exercise-to-music). Through qualitative analyses, six main types of participants were identified. These were 'sporty socialisers', 'weight conscious', 'keen exercisers', 'modern mothers', 'social contact' and 'get out of the house'. These are outlined in Table 1.1.

The study by Schlackmans (1986) shows that motivation for exercise is diverse and not just related to factors associated with the exercise itself. A number of social and environment factors are also important and should be recognised by those

Table 1.1   Clusters of Participant Groups in Women's Exercise Classes

Group (% of exercise market)

Sporty socialisers (25%)
  (a) interested in social aspects of participation
  (b) physically quite fit
  (c) good at other sports
  (d) interested in their own exercise progress

Weight conscious (18%)
  (a) exercise as a means to weight loss
  (b) self-perception of being overweight
  (c) less likely to take part in other sports

Keen exercisers (17%)
  (a) interested in physical fitness benefits
  (b) not interested in social aspects of participation
  (c) good at sport
  (d) perceive themselves to be quite fit

Modern mothers (16%)
  (a) keen on sport
  (b) perceive themselves to be quite fit
  (c) interested in their exercise progress

Social contact (15%)
  (a) older than 'modern mothers' group
  (b) women who live alone or had children who have left home
  (c) exercise seen mainly as a means for social contact

Get out of the house (8%)
  (a) youngest group
  (b) little interest in social or physical benefits
  (c) class used as a means of getting away from the house

Note. Data from Schlackmans (1986, pp. 21-24).

wishing to promote exercise participation. For example, some individuals may use exercise as the most convenient way of meeting people or 'getting out of the house'. Exercise may serve a purpose unrelated to fitness, health or other such factors.

One salient dimension that is likely to affect motives for participation is the intensity of the exercise. For example, the anxiety-reducing effects of exercise, so keenly promoted in the popular and research literature, have been shown to be much less likely at higher levels of exercise intensity (see Steptoe & Bolton, 1988; Steptoe & Cox, 1988). This suggests that motives other than, or in addition to, psychological well-being might be found in studies of vigorous exercise. Clough, Shepherd, and Maughan (1988), for example, investigated the reasons for participation of 500 runners taking part in a marathon in Scotland. They found that 70 stated reasons for running could be reduced to six main factors after factor analysis. These factors were well-being, social, challenge, status, addiction and health fitness. Similarly, Barrell, High, Holt, and MacKean (1988) also found challenge, well-being, social factors and fitness to be important motives for participation in marathons and half-marathons in England. These studies suggest that psychological well-being motivates those participating in more vigorous exercise, but, as expected, the motive of challenge is also prominent. Perhaps motivation for these runners is associated with the interaction between challenge and the well-being associated with meeting, or trying to meet, that challenge.

Reasons for Ceasing Participation

Dropping out of exercise should not be seen as an all or none phenomenon (Sonstroem, 1988) but as an ongoing process of change. For example, Sallis and Hovell (1990) have proposed a process model of exercise in which at least two different routes could be taken by adults who cease participation. One route is to become sedentary; the other is to cease participation temporarily, but to return at a later date. Motivational factors affecting these routes may be different (Biddle, 1992a, 1992b; Biddle & Smith, 1991; Sallis & Hovell, 1990; also see chapter 5). Indeed, why some adults resume participation after a period of inactivity is poorly understood.

The English National Fitness Survey (ADNFS, 1992) reported the reasons given for stopping regular participation in moderate to vigorous sport, exercise and active recreation. The three most frequently cited reasons were associated with work, loss of interest and the need for time for other things. The factors of marriage or change in partnership and having or looking after children were also important factors, but more so for women. Reported barriers preventing adults from taking more exercise were classified into five main types: physical, emotional, motivational, time and availability. Time barriers appeared to be the most important for both men and women, although women were likely to report emotional barriers to exercise more than men. These barriers referred to perceptions of not being 'the sporty type' or being too embarrassed about involvement in physical activity. Predictably, the physical and emotional barriers increased across the age-groups, while time barriers decreased, at least for those over 55 years of age.

Other surveys and interview studies have been conducted in Britain on why adults cease participation in sport. Studies in Australia and North America have also identified reasons for nonparticipation in exercise and fitness programmes (see Biddle & Mutrie, 1991).

In the Heartbeat Wales (1987) survey lack of time and loss of interest were cited frequently as reasons for ceasing participation in sport. In an interview study of 250 adults in the north of England, Boothby, Tungatt, and Townsend (1981) found that the most frequently stated reasons for stopping sport participation were loss of interest, lack of facilities, physical problems (such as low fitness or disability), moving away from an area and lack of spare time. Similar results were obtained by Lee and Owen (1985) in a study of adults ceasing participation in aerobic exercise programmes in Australia.

Perceived lack of time is frequently cited as the major reason for nonparticipation. Owen and Bauman (no date) reported on just over 5,000 sedentary Australians and found that the reason 'no time to exercise' was much more likely to be reported by those in the 25 to 54 age-group compared with those over 55 years. This confirms the results from the ADNFS (1992). The barrier of time in the Australian study was not reported as often by those with higher education levels. Those who had children, however, reported a perceived lack of time more than others. Again, these data show the need to study motives and barriers in a wider social context.

A final comment on nonparticipation concerns the growing interest of some European researchers in sport retirement and career transition (Dupont & Schilling, 1992; Patriksson, 1991; Strahlman, 1991). This has implications not only for sport, but also for participation in health-related exercise after competition has ceased. We need to develop our understanding of the effects of prolonged or intense involvement, such as motivational effects, on activities pursued in later life. This clearly is an avenue for future work.

Theoretical Approaches

Some authors (e.g., Klint & Weiss, 1987) have suggested that the study of participation motives at a descriptive level needs to progress towards a more theoretical approach. Similarly, Gould and Petlichkoff (1988) have proposed that reported motives ('surface level' motivation) are underpinned by more theoretical explanations of why people do or do not participate. Certainly the understanding of exercise motivation will be furthered by our ability to provide theoretically-based models. However, the current state of knowledge gleaned from surface participation motives is important for practical applications in exercise promotion. We now know in what ways children, youth and adults are motivated to participate, although information on changes through the life span is sparse (see Ashford & Rickhuss, 1992; Brodkin & Weiss, 1990). Nevertheless, we do not understand fully *why* people are motivated in these ways, *how* these motivations are derived or developed, or *what* the underlying processes are, whether psychological or otherwise. This is where the development and testing of theoretical models become important.

It is likely that the distinction between descriptive individual motive constructs and more theoretically driven models of motivation is one of time proximity. For example, the participation motives reviewed so far could be viewed as proximal, or immediate, motivational determinants whereas integrated theoretical models of, say, goal orientations or perceived competence might be more distal (remote) factors in the motivational chain.

The diversity of the theoretical approaches to exercise motivation makes them difficult to summarise. However, Gould and Petlichkoff (1988) suggest three broad headings under which to conceptualise theories for sport motivation in children: achievement orientations, competence motivation and cognitive-affective stress. While the competence- or achievement-oriented models are wholly appropriate and important, they provide but one perspective on the issue of exercise motivation.

The purpose of this section, therefore, is to provide an overview of theoretical perspectives currently popular in exercise psychology, as well as other perspectives that might be important for future research. Discussion will centre on competence perceptions, goal orientations and attributions, self-confidence, decision-making theories, and enjoyment. Related approaches, as well as those listed here, are dealt with in this volume (see chapters 2, 10-12). In addition, extensive discussion of expectancy-value models and health-related behaviour theories can be found in Biddle and Mutrie (1991).

The excellent historical picture of human motivation theory drawn by Weiner (1991, 1992) has shown that the same trends have been mirrored in the sport psychology literature (Biddle, 1994; Roberts, 1992b). Early attempts at explaining sport motivation (exercise was rarely a topic in the early days of sport psychology) were characterised by a recognition of drive theory and relatively mechanistic views of humans. For example, Butt (1976) states that 'motivation may be seen as evolving from two major sources: a biologically-based fund of energy, and all secondary or environmental influences, each with positive and negative pulls' (p. 3). This approach is not widely researched in the contemporary literature, although Butt herself has persisted (Butt & Cox, 1992). Similarly, Alderman (1974) said 'motivated behaviour is the sum total of instincts and needs, motives and drives, conscious and unconscious forces, and a function of what one expects to gain from participation in sport' (p. 202). Both Butt and Alderman recognise other factors in human motivation, but their approach gives greater emphasis to mechanistic factors ('Man as machine'; Weiner, 1992) than contemporary approaches favour. Psychology and sport psychology have witnessed a paradigmatic shift towards cognitive and social cognitive approaches ('Man as Godlike'; Weiner, 1992). This shift emphasises the importance of individuals' perceptions within the context of sport and exercise, and how cognitions and emotions affect and interact reciprocally with behaviour.

This is confirmed through a content analysis I conducted of two main sport and exercise psychology journals, the *International Journal of Sport Psychology* and the *Journal of Sport (and Exercise) Psychology* (*JSEP*; the word 'exercise' was added in 1988). The content analysis (Biddle, 1994) involved entering details of 224 articles on motivation into a computer data base. Articles between 1979 and 1991 were considered because 1979 was the first year of publication of *JSEP*. These were then sorted by fields for analysis. The most frequently studied topics were attributions, self-confidence, achievement motivation (including goal orientations), group cohesion and goal-setting. Attribution research showed a decline in the number of papers from the period 1980-85 to 1986-91, although a shift of focus towards goal orientations could partly account for this. The areas of self-confidence, achievement motivation and goal-setting showed increases across time. The content analysis also revealed a bias towards the study of younger participants, with only 6% of studies involving adults over 50 years of age. Similarly, many studies used what appeared to be convenience samples of students. Coaches, officials or physical education teachers were rarely the subject of investigation.

Finally, the methods adopted in these sport and exercise motivation studies reflected a strong bias in favour of survey (50%) and experimental (30.8%) methods. Qualitative methods (0.89%) and longitudinal designs (1.3%) were rare. Such results are further evidence of the narrow approaches adopted in research on sport and exercise motivation and highlight the need for a life-span approach utilising a wide variety of methods, theories and samples.

Harter's Competence Motivation Theory

Attempts at explaining human behaviour through individuals' desire to seek situations where they can display competence are not new in psychology. White's (1959) seminal paper on 'effectance' (competence) motivation argued against the mechanistic explanations of the time in favour of a more cognitive approach. This was followed by a comprehensive interpretation of competence motivation by Susan Harter in the USA (see Harter, 1978; Harter & Connell, 1984). Many sport psychologists have followed the lead of Harter and tested her theory, or parts of the theory, in physical activity settings (see Ommundsen & Vaglum, 1991; Weiss, 1987). The concept of perceived competence underpins many currently favoured approaches, such as attributions, goal orientations and intrinsic motivation.

Harter's theory suggests that individuals are motivated in achievement domains where their competence can be demonstrated, particularly if they also feel intrinsically motivated in that area and see themselves as having an internal perceived locus of control. Successful mastery attempts under such conditions are associated with positive emotion and low anxiety.

Harter has specified at least three achievement domains: cognitive, physical and social. However, self-perception domains are likely to become more differentiated with age. Harter's measures of self-perception and competence reflect this. For example, Harter and Pike (1983) have developed a pictorial scale for young children reflecting the domains of perceived competence and social acceptance, whereas the 'Self-Perception Profile for Children' (Harter, 1985) assesses the specific domains of scholastic competence, social acceptance, athletic competence, physical appearance and behavioural conduct. This is expanded further to 12 domains in the 'Self-Perception Profile for College Students' (Neemann & Harter, 1986) and 11 domains for the 'Adult Self-Perception Profile' (Messer & Harter, 1986).

Harter's theory predicts that those high in perceived physical competence will be more likely to participate in physical activity. Such a relationship has been found, although it is not strong, probably due to the influence of other variables (Roberts, 1992b).

Ommundsen and Vaglum (1991) studied a representative sample of 223 Norwegian boys from a soccer league in Oslo. In testing Harter's theory, they found that higher perceptions of ability in soccer were related to higher levels of enjoyment. In addition, enjoyment was also predicted by perceived coach and parental behaviours, and perceived soccer-related self-esteem. These findings support the view that socialisation factors are also important in competence perceptions and motivation (see Brustad, 1992).

The strength and attraction of Harter's theory centre on the development of psychometrically sound and developmentally-based instruments for the testing of her model. However, in sport and exercise psychology the following points can be offered in discussion and critique of the theory:

1. The complete model has not been tested. Only parts of the model, such as motivational orientation, or domain-specific perceptions of competence, have been tested against behaviour and related variables.
2. Harter's theory has been tested almost exclusively on children and youth in North American volunteer sport settings. Little work has been done on the testing of Harter's scales in European populations (see Biddle & Brooke, 1992), nor has the cross-cultural validity of the theory received a great deal of attention (Ommundsen & Vaglum, 1991; Ponkko, 1992).
3. The focus of research into competence motivation has generally been on sport rather than more diverse settings of health-related exercise. It remains to be seen how relevant Harter's model is to such settings.
4. Harter's scale for the assessment of perceived competence adopts a comparative, or ego, orientation where children are asked to rate themselves relative to others. There appears to be a need, therefore, to also include mastery, or self-related, judgements of competence (Roberts, 1992b).

Attributions and Achievement Goals

The study of attribution theories in sport psychology was dominant in the 1980s, and such approaches are still popular in the 1990s (see Biddle, 1993; and chapters 11-12). From a motivational standpoint, much has been written about attributions which will not be repeated here (for extensive reviews see Weiner, 1986, 1992). It is sufficient for now just to say that attributions given after participation in exercise may have important behavioural and motivational implications, although much of the research has centred on competitive sport of young adults and youth, and little on health-related exercise for older adults (Biddle, 1993).

One approach related to theories of attribution that has received a great deal of attention recently is that of achievement goal orientations (Duda, 1992, 1993; Roberts, 1992b). Such an approach might prove to be an important step towards finding a theoretically integrating framework for exercise motivation (see chapters 10 and 12).

Dissatisfied with traditional approaches to achievement motivation, Maehr and Nicholls (1980) suggested that achievement could only be considered in the light of the personal meaning individuals attached to achievement. Subsequent research by Maehr, Nicholls and others established that two main goals for educational achievement could be identified: mastery or task goals, and ego goals. Individuals adopting the mastery or task perspective define success in terms of personal improvement and task mastery, whereas those adopting the ego orientation define success as winning or demonstrating superior ability relative to others. Research has shown that these two goal orientations are largely uncorrelated and thus individuals can be high in both, low in both or high in one and low in the other.

Extensive research in the USA, led by Joan Duda (see Duda, 1992 and 1993 for reviews), has revealed that 'conceptually coherent relationships have emerged with respect to the interdependencies between goal perspectives and motivational processes, achievement-related behaviours, and values and beliefs in the sport domain' (Duda, 1992, p. 84). For example, our own research with 11- to 12-year-old children in England has revealed consistent relationships between goal orientations and motivational variables. Duda, Fox, Biddle, and Armstrong (1992) found that a task orientation in sport, measured by Duda's Task and Ego Orientation in Sport Questionnaire (TEOSQ), was associated with a focus on cooperation and the belief that success in sport results from effort. An ego orientation, however, was accompanied by an emphasis on work avoidance and the view that success in sport is related to ability. Factor analysis revealed a 'task dimension' (task orientation, cooperation and effort belief) and an 'ego dimension' (ego orientation, work avoidance, ability and deception beliefs). The task dimension was quite strongly correlated with sport enjoyment whereas the ego dimension was slightly related to sport boredom. However, Fox, Goudas, Biddle, Duda, and Armstrong (1994) have shown that the children with the most positive motivational profile and greatest involvement in physical activity are those high in both task and ego orientation. The group with high task and low ego scores had the second most positive profile.

Given the orthogonal relationship of the task and ego constructs, it might be more important to investigate the differences between the four groups (high task/high ego, low task/low ego, etc.), rather than look at correlations between each goal and selected variables. Nevertheless, taken overall, a task orientation does appear to have certain motivational advantages (see chapter 12), but the above cautionary note about the need to look at both goals in combination is still valid. For example, we have shown that intrinsic motivation after physical fitness testing in children is highest in the group with a high task and low ego orientation (Goudas, Biddle, & Fox, 1994).

Research by Jean Whitehead in England has shown that children are likely to have more than two achievement goal orientations. Developing the work of Ewing (1981) in the USA, she confirmed that children may have goals of ability (ego), mastery (task) and social approval, but she also found other goals. Whitehead (1992) considered that the goals could be grouped into three categories: personal progress (goals of breakthrough and mastery), beating others (victory, ability), and pleasing others (social approval, teamwork). Clearly, the goals of task and ego are likely to be too restrictive to explain the achievement behaviours of sport or exercise participants, particularly the latter, for whom achievement may not be too important. However, it remains to be seen whether task and ego goals are the most important from a motivational perspective.

Papaioannou suggests (see chapter 12) that it is also necessary to study the motivational climate of physical activity settings in conjunction with individual goal orientations (Ames, 1992). For example, in a study of English adolescents, Lloyd and Fox (1992) found that girls in a 6-week aerobic fitness programme, taught as part of their normal physical education curriculum, reported higher levels of enjoyment and motivation to continue participation when placed in a class emphasising a mastery, as opposed to a competitive, climate, regardless of their initial level of ego orientation. Similarly, we have found that intrinsic motivation towards physical education was significantly enhanced by perceptions of the class's mastery climate beyond the motivation accounted for by perceived competence. Pupils perceiving their class to be high in both mastery and performance climate had the highest intrinsic motivation and perceived competence (Goudas & Biddle, 1994).

Self-Confidence and Self-Efficacy

The important variable of self-confidence in exercise has been studied mainly in terms of Bandura's (1977, 1986) self-efficacy theory. This theory is recognised as an important milestone in cognitive motivational research in exercise and sport psychology (Biddle, 1994). Our own review of research on self-confidence and health-related exercise identified nine studies (Biddle & Mutrie, 1991), and more have been published since. This review will not be repeated here. In summary, we found that much of the early work was on male patients in rehabilitation from chronic heart disease, that some evidence showed that self-efficacy could generalise to a limited extent from one exercise mode to another, and that generalised expectancies predict behaviour less effectively than do specific perceptions of efficacy.

In summarising our findings, we identified the following key needs in the study of self-efficacy and exercise (Biddle & Mutrie, 1991):

1. The need to study how self-efficacy influences behaviour in diverse exercise and physical activity settings, such as habitual 'free-living' activity
2. The need for more integration between theories of efficacy and attribution (see McAuley, 1992)
3. The need for further research on the nature and extent of gender differences in self-efficacy
4. The need to study self-efficacy in situations of prolonged effort
5. The need to study the longevity of self-efficacy
6. The need to study the relation of self-efficacy to other theoretical constructs

Self-efficacy is a popular area of motivational research in sport and exercise (Biddle, 1994), but further work is required to place it alongside other perspectives and to expand the exercise contexts that have been studied so far.

Decision-Making Theories

Motivated behaviour involves making decisions. Two theoretical perspectives based specifically on decision-making principles are Subjective Expected Utility Theory (Edwards, 1954) and Action Control Theory (Kuhl, 1985).

Edwards's theory suggests that exercise behaviour is based on the value or importance attached by the subject to the outcomes of exercise and the subject's estimate of the probability that such outcomes will occur. To this extent it is rooted firmly in expectancy-value theories of motivation (see Weiner, 1992). In addition, however, the theory states that the behaviour chosen will be influenced by the subject's perception of the alternative courses of action available and the values and probabilities he or she attaches to these. This is an important point often missing from the literature on exercise psychology—the choice to exercise is made in the context of other possible health and nonhealth behaviours (Smith & Biddle, 1990).

Related to the notion of competing alternatives is Kuhl's Action Control Theory. Action control perspectives have been favoured a great deal by German sport psychologists (see Hackfort, 1989; Kunath & Schellenberger, 1991), but have attracted less attention elsewhere (see chapter 14).

Kuhl (1985) states that 'action control . . . will be used here . . . to denote those processes which *protect* a current intention from being replaced should one of the competing tendencies increase in strength before the intended action is completed' (p. 102). Kendzierski (1990; Kendzierski & LaMastro, 1988) studied both Subjective Expected Utility and Action Control Theories in the context of exercise. In her 1988 study, Subjective Expected Utility Theory was found to predict interest in weight training, but not actual participation. Her 1990 study investigated both theories. Specifically, she classified individuals on Kuhl's 'action control scale', which assesses whether the individual is action oriented or state oriented. Those who plan for the future and focus on it are classified as action oriented. State-oriented individuals are those who focus more on the present or past. The results showed that Subjective Expected Utility Theory predicted intention to exercise but not adherence, but the correlation between intention and behaviour was stronger for action-oriented individuals. However, Kuhl (1985) suggests that state-oriented individuals may have cognitions related to a 'catastatic' mode of control (change-preventing) or a 'metastatic' mode of control (change-inducing). 'As long as an individual is in a catastatic mode of control, the enactment of action-oriented intentions seems to be more difficult than when the individual is in a metastatic mode of control' (Kuhl, 1985, p. 102).

Decision-making theoretical perspectives may prove to be important for the study of exercise motivation through the life span. Perceptions of control and planning strategies require some investigation in the future.

Enjoyment in Exercise

A number of researchers have noted the importance of enjoyment as a factor in exercise motivation (Biddle & Mutrie, 1991; Scanlan & Simons, 1992). However, currently enjoyment is still a relatively elusive construct that does not have a strong theoretical or empirical base. I have included it in this section of the chapter, however, as it has started to feature quite prominently in the literature, and no discussion of motivation would be complete without some mention of enjoyment.

Although there can be little doubt that enjoyment is important for exercise motivation, it has been studied mainly in the sports context with children (see Wankel & Kreisel, 1985). Much more needs to be known about adults through the life span and the potential sources of exercise enjoyment. For example, Ashford et al. (1993) found that the best predictor of enjoyment for participants in English sport centres was the motive factor of sociopsychological well-being. However, this factor accounted for only 8.5% of the variance in enjoyment ratings.

Perhaps the nearest we have to a theory of enjoyment is that of Csikszentmihalyi's (1975) 'flow' model. This suggests that high levels of enjoyment and intrinsic satisfaction ('flow') are more likely to be experienced under conditions of optimal challenge; that is to say when personal abilities match the challenge at hand. An imbalance could create anxiety or boredom (see chapter 12).

There is little doubt that the construct of enjoyment has high ecological validity in motivation. However, the proximal and distal determinants of enjoyment in exercise through the life span require investigation (see Csikszentmihalyi & Csikszentmihalyi, 1988).

Conclusion

In this chapter I have argued for the importance of studying motivation towards exercise from a life-span perspective. However, the current state of knowledge is biased towards the younger end of the age scale. If significant effects on public health are to accrue from physical activity and exercise, we need to know more about the motivation of older adults and changes between stages of the life span.

The chapter has tackled motivation from two angles: descriptive research and perspectives based on integrated theories or models. Many researchers have criticised the descriptive approach and called for greater emphasis on theoretically-based explanations of motivated behaviour. Although I have some sympathy with this view, I also believe that it is important to know the 'surface' motives of individuals adopting, maintaining or ceasing participation in exercise. It is an approach that is likely to have high ecological validity and relevance to psychological factors close to the behaviour itself (proximal determinants). Nevertheless, further research efforts are also needed to establish conceptually coherent models of exercise motivation. These are likely to provide a better explanation of more distal determinants, although the temporal importance and relationship of these factors remain to be clarified.

Acknowledgment

I would like to thank Dr Marios Goudas (University of Exeter) and Dr Basil Ashford (Staffordshire University) for their helpful and insightful comments on an earlier draft of this chapter.

References

Alderman, R.B. (1974). *Psychological behaviour in sport*. Philadelphia: W.B. Saunders.

Allied Dunbar National Fitness Survey. (1992). *Allied Dunbar National Fitness Survey main findings*. London: Sports Council and Health Education Authority.

Ames, C. (1992). Achievement goals, motivational climate and motivational processes. In G.C. Roberts (Ed.), *Motivation in sport and exercise* (pp. 161-176). Champaign, IL: Human Kinetics.

Armstrong, N., & Biddle, S.J.H. (1992). Health-related physical activity in the National Curriculum. In N. Armstrong (Ed.), *New directions in physical education: Vol. II. Towards a national curriculum* (pp. 71-110). Champaign, IL: Human Kinetics.

Ashford, B., Biddle, S.J.H., & Goudas, M. (1993). Participation in community sports centres: Motives and predictors of enjoyment. *Journal of Sports Sciences*, **11**, 249-256.

Ashford, B., & Rickhuss, J. (1992). Life-span differences in motivation for participating in community sport and recreation. *Journal of Sports Sciences*, **10**(6), 626. (Abstract)

Bandura, A. (1977). Self-efficacy: Toward a unifying theory of behavioral change. *Psychological Review*, **84**, 191-215.

Bandura, A. (1986). *Social foundations of thought and action: A social cognitive theory*. Englewood Cliffs, NJ: Prentice Hall.

Barrell, G., High, S., Holt, D., & MacKean, J. (1988). Motives for starting running and for competing in full and half marathon events. In *Sport, Health, Psychology and Exercise Symposium proceedings* (pp. 226-241). London: The Sports Council/Health Education Authority.

Biddle, S.J.H. (1992a). Adherence to physical activity and exercise. In N. Norgan (Ed.), *Physical activity and health* (pp. 170-189). Cambridge, England: Cambridge University Press.

Biddle, S.J.H. (1992b). Exercise psychology. *Sport Science Review*, **1**(2), 79-92.

Biddle, S.J.H. (1992c). Sport and exercise motivation: A short review of antecedent factors and psychological outcomes of participation. *Physical Education Review*, **15**, 98-110.

Biddle, S.J.H. (1993). Attribution research and sport psychology. In R.N. Singer, M. Murphey, & L.K. Tennant (Eds.), *Handbook of research on sport psychology* (pp. 437-464). New York: Macmillan.

Biddle, S.J.H. (1994). Motivation and participation in exercise and sport. In S. Serpa, J. Alves, & V. Pataco (Eds.), *International perspectives on sport and exercise psychology* (pp. 103-126). Morgantown, WV: FIT.

Biddle, S.J.H., & Armstrong, N. (1992). Children's physical activity: An exploratory study of psychological correlates. *Social Science and Medicine*, **34**, 325-331.

Biddle, S.J.H., & Brooke, R. (1992). Intrinsic versus extrinsic motivational orientation in physical education and sport. *British Journal of Educational Psychology*, **62**, 247-256.

Biddle, S.J.H., & Fox, K.R. (1988). The child's perspective in physical education: II. Children's participation motives. *British Journal of Physical Education*, **19**(2), 79-82.

Biddle, S.J.H., & Mutrie, N. (1991). *Psychology of physical activity and exercise: A health-related perspective*. London: Springer-Verlag.

Biddle, S.J.H., & Smith, R.A. (1991). Motivating adults for physical activity: Towards a healthier present. *Journal of Physical Education, Recreation and Dance*, **62**(7), 39-43.

Boothby, J., Tungatt, M.F., & Townsend, A.R. (1981). Ceasing participation in sports activity: Reported reasons and their implications. *Journal of Leisure Research*, **13**, 1-14.

Bouchard, C., Shephard, R.J., Stephens, T., Sutton, J.R., & McPherson, B.D. (Eds.) (1990). *Exercise, fitness, and health: A consensus of current knowledge*. Champaign, IL: Human Kinetics.

Brettschneider, W.-D. (1992). Adolescents, leisure, sport and lifestyle. In T. Williams, L. Almond, & A.C. Sparkes (Eds.), *Sport and physical activity* (pp. 536-550). London: Spon.

Brodkin, P., & Weiss, M.R. (1990). Developmental differences in motivation for participation in competitive swimming. *Journal of Sport and Exercise Psychology*, **12**, 248-263.

Brustad, R.J. (1992). Integrating socialisation influences into the study of children's motivation in sport. *Journal of Sport and Exercise Psychology*, **14**, 59-77.

Buonamano, R., Cei, A., & Mussino, A. (1993, July). *Participation motivation in Italian youth sport*. Paper presented at the 8th World Congress of Sport Psychology, Lisbon, Portugal.

Butt, D.S. (1976). *Psychology of sport*. New York: Van Nostrand Reinhold.

Butt, D.S., & Cox, D.N. (1992). Motivational patterns in Davis Cup, university and recreational tennis players. *International Journal of Sport Psychology*, **23**, 1-13.

Canada Fitness Survey. (1983). *Canadian youth and physical activity*. Ottawa, ON: Author.

Caspersen, C.J., Powell, K.E., & Christenson, G.M. (1985). Physical activity, exercise and physical fitness: Definitions and distinctions for health-related research. *Public Health Reports*, **100**, 126-131.

Clough, P.J., Shepherd, J., & Maughan, R.J. (1988). Motivations for running. In *Sport, Health, Psychology and Exercise Symposium proceedings* (pp. 242-246). London: The Sports Council/Health Education Authority.

Coakley, J.J., & White, A. (1992). Making decisions: Gender and sport participation among British adolescents. *Sociology of Sport Journal*, **9**, 20-35.

Codina, N., Jimenez, M.J., & Rufat, M.J. (1991, September). *Benefits of sport activities in old age: A psychosocial view*. Paper presented at the 8th European Congress of Sport Psychology, Köln, Germany.

Csikszentmihalyi, M. (1975). *Beyond boredom and anxiety*. San Francisco: Jossey-Bass.

Csikszentmihalyi, M., & Csikszentmihalyi, I.S. (Eds.) (1988). *Optimal experience: Psychological studies of flow in consciousness*. Cambridge, England: Cambridge University Press.

Department of Health. (1991). *The health of the nation: A consultative document for health in England*. London: Her Majesty's Stationery Office.

Duda, J.L. (1992). Motivation in sport settings: A goal perspective approach. In G.C. Roberts (Ed.), *Motivation in sport and exercise* (pp. 57-91). Champaign, IL: Human Kinetics.

Duda, J.L. (1993). Goals: A social-cognitive approach to the study of achievement motivation in sport. In R.N. Singer, M. Murphey, & L.K. Tennant (Eds.), *Handbook of research on sport psychology* (pp. 421-436). New York: Macmillan.

Duda, J.L., Fox, K.R., Biddle, S.J.H., & Armstrong, N. (1992). Children's achievement goals and beliefs about success in sport. *British Journal of Educational Psychology*, **62**, 313-323.

Dupont, J.B., & Schilling, G. (1992, July). *Career transition for professional athletes and dancers*. Paper presented at the Olympic Scientific Congress, Benalmadena, Málaga, Spain.

Edwards, W. (1954). The theory of decision making. *Psychological Bulletin*, **51**, 380-417.

Ewing, M.E. (1981). *Achievement orientations and sport behaviour of males and females*. Unpublished doctoral dissertation, University of Illinois, Urbana.

Fox, K.R., Goudas, M., Biddle, S.J.H., Duda, J.L., & Armstrong, N. (1994). Children's task and ego goal profiles in sport. *British Journal of Educational Psychology*, **64**, 253-261.

Goudas, M., & Biddle, S.J.H. (1994). Perceived motivational climate and intrinsic motivation in school physical education classes. *European Journal of Psychology of Education*, **9**, 241-250.

Goudas, M., Biddle, S.J.H., & Fox, K.R. (1994). Achievement goal orientations and intrinsic motivation in physical fitness testing with children. *Pediatric Exercise Science*, **6**, 159-167.

Gould, D. (1987). Understanding attrition in children's sport. In D. Gould & M. Weiss (Eds.), *Advances in pediatric sport sciences: Vol. II. Behavioural issues* (pp. 61-85). Champaign, IL: Human Kinetics.

Gould, D., & Petlichkoff, L. (1988). Participation motivation and attrition in young athletes. In F.L. Smoll, R.A. Magill, & M.J. Ash (Eds.), *Children in sport* (3rd ed., pp. 161-178). Champaign, IL: Human Kinetics.

Hackfort, D. (1989). Action regulation and self presentation in sports. In C.K. Giam, K.K. Chook, & K.C. Teh (Eds.), *Proceedings of the 7th World Congress in Sport Psychology* (pp. 205-206). Singapore: Singapore Sports Council.

Harter, S. (1978). Effectance motivation reconsidered: Toward a developmental model. *Human Development*, **21**, 34-64.

Harter, S. (1985). *Manual for the Self-Perception Profile for Children*. Denver: University of Denver.

Harter, S., & Connell, J.P. (1984). A model of children's achievement and related self-perceptions of competence, control and motivational orientation. In J.G. Nicholls (Ed.), *Advances in motivation and achievement: Vol. III. The development of achievement motivation* (pp. 219-250). Greenwich, CT: JAI Press.

Harter, S., & Pike, R. (1983). *Procedural manual to accompany the Pictorial Scale of Perceived Competence and Social Acceptance for Young Children*. Denver: University of Denver.

Heartbeat Wales. (1987). *Exercise for health: Health-related fitness in Wales*. Cardiff, Wales: Author.

Kendzierski, D. (1990). Decision making versus decision implementation: An action control approach to exercise adoption and adherence. *Journal of Applied Social Psychology*, **20**, 27-45.

Kendzierski, D., & LaMastro, V.D. (1988). Reconsidering the role of attitudes in exercise behaviour: A decision theoretic approach. *Journal of Applied Social Psychology*, **18**, 737-759.

Klint, K.A., & Weiss, M.R. (1987). Perceived competence and motives for participating in youth sports: A test of Harter's competence motivation theory. *Journal of Sport Psychology*, **9**, 55-65.

Kuhl, J. (1985). Volitional mediators of cognition-behaviour consistency: Self-regulatory processes and action versus state orientation. In J. Kuhl & J. Beckmann (Eds.), *Action control: From cognition to behaviour* (pp. 101-128). New York: Springer-Verlag.

Kunath, P., & Schellenberger, H. (Eds.) (1991). *Tatigkeits-orientierte sportpsychologie: Eine einfuhrung fur sportstudenten und praktiker*. Frankfurt, Germany: Verlag Harri Deutsch.

Lee, C., & Owen, N. (1985, March). Reasons for discontinuing regular physical activity subsequent to a fitness course. *The ACHPER National Journal*, 7-9.

Lloyd, J., & Fox, K.R. (1992). Achievement goals and motivation to exercise in adolescent girls: A preliminary intervention study. *British Journal of Physical Education Research Supplement*, **11**, 12-16.

Maehr, M.L., & Braskamp, L.A. (1986). *The motivation factor: A theory of personal invest-ment.* Lexington, MA: Lexington Books.

Maehr, M.L., & Nicholls, J.G. (1980). Culture and achievement motivation: A second look. In N. Warren (Ed.), *Studies in cross-cultural psychology* (Vol. 2, pp. 221-267). New York: Academic Press.

Markland, D., & Hardy, L. (1993). The Exercise Motivations Inventory: Preliminary develop-ment and validity of a measure of individuals' reasons for participation in regular physical exercise. *Personality and Individual Differences,* **15**, 289-296.

McAuley, E. (1992). Self-referent thought in sport and sport activity. In T. Horn (Ed.), *Advances in sport psychology* (pp. 101-118). Champaign, IL: Human Kinetics.

Messer, B., & Harter, S. (1986). *Manual for the Adult Self-Perception Profile.* Denver: University of Denver.

Mihalik, B.J., O'Leary, J.T., McGuire, F.A., & Dottavio, F.D. (1989). Sports involvement across the life span: Expansion and contraction of sports activities. *Research Quarterly for Exercise and Sport,* **60**, 396-398.

Neemann, J., & Harter, S. (1986). *Manual for the Self-Perception Profile for College Students.* Denver: University of Denver.

North, T.C., McCullagh, P., & Tran, Z.V. (1990). Effect of exercise on depression. *Exercise and Sport Sciences Reviews,* **18**, 379-415.

Ommundsen, Y., & Vaglum, P. (1991). Soccer competition anxiety and enjoyment in young boy players: The influence of perceived competence and significant others' emotional involvement. *International Journal of Sport Psychology,* **22**, 35-49.

Owen, N., & Bauman, A. (no date). *Determinants of physical inactivity and of reasons for inactivity.* Unpublished manuscript, University of Adelaide, Adelaide, Australia.

Patriksson, G. (1991, September). *Retirement from elite sport: Psychological aspects.* Paper presented at the 8th European Congress of Sport Psychology, Köln, Germany.

Ponkko, A. (1992, July). *The perceived competence of 5-6 year old kindergarten children and its connections to motor ability and experiences from sports.* Paper presented at the Olympic Scientific Congress, Benalmadena, Málaga, Spain.

Roberts, G.C. (Ed.) (1992a). *Motivation in sport and exercise.* Champaign, IL: Human Kinetics.

Roberts, G.C. (1992b). Motivation in sport and exercise: Conceptual constraints and conver-gence. In G.C. Roberts (Ed.), *Motivation in sport and exercise* (pp. 3-29). Champaign, IL: Human Kinetics.

Saarinen, P. (1987). Not all students take an interest in sports. In *Proceedings of the 7th Congress of the European Federation of Sport Psychology* (pp. 563-566). Leipzig, Germany: Deutsche Hochschule für Korperkultur.

Sallis, J.F., & Hovell, M.F. (1990). Determinants of exercise behaviour. *Exercise and Sport Sciences Reviews,* **18**, 307-330.

Scanlan, T.K., & Simons, J.P. (1992). The construct of sport enjoyment. In G.C. Roberts (Ed.), *Motivation in sport and exercise* (pp. 199-215). Champaign, IL: Human Kinetics.

Schlackmans. (1986). *Women's fitness and exercise classes: Vol. I. Summary and conclusions.* London: Author.

Serpa, S. (1986). Motivation and 'gymnastique de maintien.' In L-E. Unestahl (Ed.), *Contem-porary sport psychology: Proceedings from the 6th World Congress of Sport Psychology* (pp. 261-262). Orebro, Sweden: Veje.

Smith, R.A., & Biddle, S.J.H. (1990, September). *Exercise adherence: A theoretical perspec-tive.* Paper presented at the annual conference of the British Association of Sports Sciences, Cardiff, Wales.

Sonstroem, R.J. (1988). Psychological models. In R.K. Dishman (Ed.), *Exercise adherence: Its impact on public health* (pp. 125-153). Champaign, IL: Human Kinetics.

Stephens, T. (1988). Physical activity and mental health in the United States and Canada: Evidence from four population surveys. *Preventive Medicine, 17*, 35-47.

Steptoe, A., & Bolton, J. (1988). The short-term influence of high and low intensity physical exercise on mood. *Psychology and Health, 2*, 91-106.

Steptoe, A., & Cox, S. (1988). Acute effects of aerobic exercise on mood. *Health Psychology, 7*, 329-340.

Strahlman, O. (1991, September). *Motivation-related issues on sport retirement.* Paper presented at the 8th European Congress of Sport Psychology, Köln, Germany.

Telama, R., & Silvennoinen, M. (1979). Structure and development of 11 to 19 year olds' motivation for physical activity. *Scandinavian Journal of Sports Sciences, 1*, 23-31.

Van Wersch, A., Trew, K., & Turner, I. (1992). Post-primary school pupils' interest in physical education: Age and gender differences. *British Journal of Educational Psychology, 62*, 56-72.

Wankel, L.M., & Kreisel, P.S.J. (1985). Factors underlying enjoyment of youth sports: Sport and age group comparisons. *Journal of Sport Psychology, 7*, 51-64.

Weiner, B. (1986). *An attributional theory of motivation and emotion.* New York: Springer-Verlag.

Weiner, B. (1991). Metaphors in motivation and attribution. *American Psychologist, 46*, 921-930.

Weiner, B. (1992). *Human motivation: Metaphors, theories and research.* Newbury Park, CA: Sage.

Weiss, M.R. (1987). Self-esteem and achievement in children's sport and physical activity. In D. Gould & M.R. Weiss (Eds.), *Advances in pediatric sport sciences: Vol. II. Behavioural issues* (pp. 87-119). Champaign, IL: Human Kinetics.

Weiss, M.R., Bredemeier, B.J., & Shewchuk, R.M. (1985). An intrinsic/extrinsic motivation scale for the youth sport setting: A confirmatory factor analysis. *Journal of Sport Psychology, 7*, 75-91.

White, A., & Coakley, J.J. (1986). *Making decisions: The response of young people in the Medway towns to the 'Ever Thought of Sport?' campaign.* London: Greater London and South East Region Sports Council.

White, R. (1959). Motivation reconsidered: The concept of competence. *Psychological Review, 66*, 297-333.

Whitehead, J. (1992, July). *Toward the assessment of multiple goal perspectives in children's sport.* Paper presented at the Olympic Scientific Congress, Benalmadena, Málaga, Spain.

World Health Organization. (1985). *Targets for Health for All.* Copenhagen: Author.

2

CHAPTER

The Influence of Attitude on Exercise Participation

George Doganis
Yannis Theodorakis

GREECE

Participation in sport, exercise and physical activities is a central issue in the sport and exercise sciences. Scientific knowledge revolves around the factors preceding the behaviour (leading to participation), during actual participation and following participation (consequences). Today, a European perspective necessitates the adoption of a broad definition of participation in sport and exercise, as this is the inheritance of the Sport for All campaign conducted in Europe since 1966. According to the Council of Europe,

> sport . . . is to be understood in the modern sense of free, spontaneous physical activity engaged in during leisure time; its functions . . . being recreation, amusement and relaxation. Sport in this sense includes sports proper and various other activities provided that they demand some effort. (Marchand, 1990, p. 3)

Therefore, participation in sport and exercise refers to all major forms of participation, either formal or informal—physical activities, recreation and competitive sport. Nevertheless, certain countries in Europe (e.g., France, Germany) still seem to adopt a view of Sport for All that apparently contrasts with competitive sport (Marchand,

1990). But today, as Rittner claims (in Riiskjaer, 1986), sport undergoes a transformation characterised by differentiation. This in turn challenges the formal pyramid model of sport and leads to a health- and fun-related view of sport that is associated with a new morality, new activities, new lifestyles and new social contexts.

Because participation in any form of physical activity is voluntary and consequently subject to human decision-making processes, the factors associated with these processes have attracted the interest of social and psychological researchers. Inevitably, the topic of attitudes and their relation to participation has been one of the most popular among such investigators. However, as Martens (1975) states, attitudes were popular among physical education researchers for the wrong reasons. Martens says many researchers began studying attitudes because they (wrongly) thought that this kind of research would be simple to carry out. A second misperception was that merely assessing attitudes towards physical activities would result in significant practical implications. This simplistic approach is attributed to the lack of awareness of developments in attitude theory and measurement that emphasised the process of attitude formation and change and the subsequent effect of attitudes on actual behaviour.

The significance of the study of attitudes for understanding exercise behaviour seems obvious. Fox and Biddle (1987) refer to physical education and suggest that reconsidering the role of attitudes should be focused on two priorities: positive attitudes towards exercise and 'fitness independence'. In addition, according to Slava, Laurie, and Corbin (1984), children's participation in sport declines as children grow older. The authors suggest that physical education teachers must provide the knowledge children need to build positive attitudes towards physical activity, and in doing so convince them of the importance of a lifetime engagement in physical activities.

Any consideration of attitudes assists in building a programme of physical activity that is consistent with the motivation and interest of the participant (Fox & Biddle, 1988). In addition, according to Sidney and Shephard (1976), through observed attitudes one could provide the basis for the outline of an attractive exercise programme. It is therefore crucial for those involved in sport and exercise to investigate the variables that contribute to the adoption of physical activity and a healthy lifestyle.

It seems that in East European countries, ideological issues were perceived as influencing the formation of attitudes towards exercise. According to Bierstedt (1985), the society's ideological evaluation of sport plays an important role in establishing attitudes to physical activity and sport. This view reflects the philosophy in formerly Communist countries, where it was perceived that attitude formation towards sport is subject to propaganda influences. This point is also raised by Kunicki (1985), who in discussing barriers to participation in recreational activities in Poland states that ideology could turn into a serious barrier if it is not constructed properly, is not cohesive, is incorrectly introduced into the minds of the populace and differs significantly from practical life.

The purpose of this chapter, therefore, is threefold: to examine issues regarding the nature of attitudes, to present the major theoretical approaches associated with attitudes and exercise participation, and to summarise relevant research. Special reference will be made to European investigations.

The Nature of Attitude

The word 'attitude' has been defined in a variety of ways. Starting from the older definitions given by the pioneers in this area, we run into a number of contradictions. Thurstone's (1931) definition, considering attitude as the feeling towards a psychological object, seems both simple and confining. In contrast, Allport (1935) added many elements in his definition of attitudes. He primarily stressed its dynamic character, considering that attitude 'is a mental and neural state of readiness organized through experience, exerting a directive or dynamic influence upon the individual's response to all objects and situations with which it is related' (p. 11). Krech and Crutchfield (1948) stressed the cognitive and affective elements of attitude, defining it as 'an enduring organisation of motivational, emotional, perceptual and cognitive processes with respect to some aspect of the individual's world' (cited in Fishbein & Ajzen, 1975, p. 9). The element of predisposition is stressed by Sarnoff (1960), who considers attitude simply 'as a disposition to react favourably or unfavourably to a class of objects' (p. 252). Attitudes have also been defined as the degree of positive or negative encountering of certain psychological objects such as symbols, slogans, persons, ideas, institutions, and so forth. An individual who is affected positively ('likes') is said to hold a favourable attitude towards an object. If he or she is affected negatively (does not 'like') he or she is said to have a negative attitude towards that object (Edwards 1957). Similarly, Fishbein and Ajzen (1975), define attitude as 'a learned predisposition to respond in a consistently favorable or unfavorable manner with respect to a given object' (p. 6). Thus they stress the element of predisposition and at the same time emphasize that attitudes are learned, a point also underlined by Allport who pointed out that attitudes are organised by experiences. Finally, Fishbein and Ajzen (1975) state that the elements differentiating attitudes from other similar concepts, such as habits, traits, drives, and so forth, are that attitudes manifest themselves simultaneously in terms of predispositions, are learned, but mainly are characterised by the element of evaluation.

Attitudes are central to much research in social psychology, for it is believed that individuals tend to act in accordance with their own attitudes (Cooper & Croyle, 1984). To understand the relationship between attitudes and behaviour, one has to consider the elements comprising an attitude. These are

1. the cognitive element of the individual's beliefs, convictions, ideas or knowledge about an object, person or concept, assisting him or her in making differentiations and drawing conclusions;
2. the affective element, which expresses the appreciation, wish or feelings of the individual towards an object or person; and
3. the behavioural element, including the predisposition to act.

In other words, the attitude includes the person's intention to act in a certain way towards an object or a person (Bootzin, Bower, & Zajonc, 1986; Buss, 1978; Martens, 1975). According to Triandis (1971), attitudes involve what people think about the object of the attitude, what they feel about it, and how they would like to behave towards it.

Traditionally, the affective element of attitudes involves feelings, emotions or drives, while the cognitive element consists of beliefs, inferences or thoughts related to the object (McGuire, 1969). An individual after a car accident may feel badly (affective element) when thinking of the accident, but he or she may recognise (cognitive element) that one cannot move in the city without a car and continue to drive one (Triandis, 1971). The dissonance between attitudes and behaviour has repeatedly been stressed in the literature, which most often cites the classic work of LaPiere (1934). The attitudes of an individual do not always predict specific behaviours (Bootzin, Bower, & Zajonc, 1986).

A number of theories concerning attitudes have been formulated. Learning theorists postulate that an attitude is 'a learned, implicit anticipatory response' (Doob, 1947, p. 136). In contrast, cognitive theorists (e.g., Chein, 1948) treat attitudes as a filter through which we perceive reality, that is, the cognitive process transforms the incoming stimuli. Finally behaviourists (e.g., Bem, 1972) claim that attitudes are the outcome of behaviour—people form attitudes by observing their own behaviour.

Attitude Formation

Attitudes are learned either from direct experience or from other people. Direct experience is most relevant to the development of the cognitive and affective components; other people are most relevant to the behavioural component (Triandis, 1971). According to Fishbein and Ajzen (1975), attitudes are formed as soon as the corresponding beliefs are formed. This implies that usually the individual maintains a neutral attitude towards objects he or she does not know at all or has little information about. The individual must have information in order to form a positive or negative attitude, to have the corresponding beliefs and to have also positively or negatively evaluated the characteristics of these beliefs. Therefore, belief formation is of paramount importance for attitude formation. Fishbein and Ajzen (1975) classify beliefs into two major categories: the 'descriptive beliefs' and the 'inferential beliefs'.

Descriptive beliefs are primarily formed by direct observation and direct experience, and are shaped by interaction with other individuals. Additionally, these beliefs are formed by the effect of external sources, such as newspapers, books, journals, radio, television, friends, and so forth. Inferential beliefs rely on the descriptive beliefs and are further shaped by personal factors and an inferential process that necessitates repetition, judgement and, possibly, attempts to understand the effect of new information or attempts to change a belief as a result of new information.

Beliefs are related to a number of other features. For instance, a schoolgirl may believe that if she becomes involved in rhythmic gymnastics she will improve her health and develop an attractive body. At the same time, however, she may believe that she will not have enough time to learn a foreign language and that she will regularly be feeling excessively tired. To understand the attitude of an individual towards participation in a physical activity, therefore, we must examine the way he or she estimates and evaluates the sum of such related beliefs. Furthermore, all beliefs are not equally important in the formation of an attitude. Maybe the first two or three beliefs are dominant and form the attitude. However, it is difficult to determine which beliefs are considered dominant by the individual. The suggestion made by some investigators that five to nine beliefs be studied is made with caution and only as a rule of thumb (Fishbein & Ajzen, 1975).

Attitude-Behaviour Consistency

The three-dimensional structure of attitudes (affective, cognitive and behavioural) has already been mentioned. Rosenberg (1968) notes that different individuals may hold attitudes that are similar on the affective dimension, but different on the cognitive dimension. When the cognitive and the affective elements are highly correlated, there is a stronger relationship between attitudes and behaviour. Fishbein (1967) notes that it is common in research on attitudes to examine only the affective aspect of attitudes. Ostrom (1969) states that the cognitive element covers the beliefs about the object of the attitude, about its characteristics and about its relation to other objects. In similar work, based on a further analysis of data from Fishbein and Ajzen (1974), Bagozzi and Burnkrant (1979) employed factor analysis and showed that both the cognitive and affective elements correlated with behaviour.

Having expressed an intention, an individual will proceed to act when the following conditions are met:

1. The intention does not alter in the meantime.
2. Attitudes towards the behaviour do not change.
3. Personal and social beliefs do not alter.
4. The conditions under which the behaviour is to be performed are appropriate in the light of any previous events, experiences, knowledge, and so forth.

These four conditions are related to time. That is, the longer the time interval between attitude and behaviour, the larger their inconsistency (Davidson & Jaccard, 1979; Norman, 1975; Schwartz, 1978), as new information or events may alter the person's intention (Fishbein & Ajzen, 1975). Therefore, the time interval between an attitude measure and the behaviour to be predicted should be short, in order to improve prediction. For example, Zuckerman and Reis (1978) used three time intervals (5 days, 2 weeks and 3 months) and found that the best prediction was made from the 5-day interval.

Schwartz (1978) showed that the importance of the relationship between attitudes towards a specific behaviour and behaviour itself was affected by the general stability of the individual's attitudes; the more stable the attitudes, the more feasible the prediction of behaviour over long time intervals. In three studies, Norman (1975) examined both the affective and cognitive elements of attitudes, and he found that the students who showed higher cognitive-affective consistency were more likely to behave according to their attitudes.

In a recent review, Fazio (1990) claims that the relationship between attitudes and behaviour is not always evident from the reported findings. This relationship is determined by a number of factors, such as the way attitudes are formed, the consistency between the cognitive and affective elements, the stability of attitudes, the latitude of rejection, and so forth.

It appears that two types of theories provide insights into the relationship between attitudes and behaviour. In the 'Spontaneous Processing Model', the decision to behave is spontaneous because the attitude is automatically recalled from memory. This model focuses on the speed of attitude recall from memory, the so-called 'accessibility'. The power of the attitude varies, depending on the individual's evaluation of the attitude in question (Fazio & Zanna, 1978; Fazio & Williams, 1986; Fazio, Powell, & Herr, 1983). The second type of theory is called by Fazio (1990) a 'Deliberative Processing Model', which views behaviour as organised, planned and decided through deliberate cognitive procedures.

A number of studies have dealt with mediating variables that seem to have a systematic impact on the relationship between attitudes and behaviour, as well as the prediction of behaviour. Such variables are: accessibility (Fazio & Williams, 1986; Fazio et al., 1983; Fazio, Chen, McDonel, & Sherman, 1982; Tourangeau, Rasinski, Bradburn, & D'Andrade, 1989), affective-cognitive consistency (Millar & Tesser, 1989; Norman, 1975; Rosenberg, 1968), attitude importance (Krosnick, 1988a, 1988b), attitude strength and role-identity (Theodorakis, 1992a), confidence (Felson & Bohrnstedt, 1980), degree of intention formation (Bagozzi & Yi, 1989), importance of the message (Meyerowitz & Chaiken, 1987), information (Davidson, Yantis, Norwood, & Montano, 1985; Jaccard & Wood, 1988), intention certainty (Nederhof, 1989), involvement (Nederhof, 1989; Verplanken, 1989), knowledge (Block & Beckett, 1990; Wilson, Kraft, & Dunn, 1989), latitude of rejection (Fazio & Zanna, 1978), personal experience (Borgida & Campbell, 1982), and vested interest (Sivacek & Crano, 1982).

Sport, Exercise and Attitude Formation

The formation of attitudes towards participation in physical activity and exercise has attracted very little attention. The work of Pease and Anderson (1986) showed that the formation of such attitudes takes place earlier than the age of 10 to 12 years. In agreement are the findings of McIntosh and Albinson (1982) who report that children in Canada have formed their attitudes towards physical education and activity by the age of 13 or 14 years.

Other investigations deal with the modification or change in attitudes as a result of participation in organised exercise programmes. For example, parents seem to play an important role in the formation of their children's attitudes towards physical education (Edwards & Crawford, 1990), the teacher affects children's attitudes (Edwards & Crawford, 1990; Figley, 1985; Patterson & Faucette, 1990), laboratory experiences lead to the reinforcement of attitudes (Connor, Smith, Fryer, Erickson, Fryer, & Drake, 1986; Corbin & Chevrette, 1981; Laurie, 1981), experience and knowledge in general strengthen attitudes (Barrell & Holt, 1982; James, Erickson, & Johnson, 1977; Hall, 1978; Theodorakis, Goudas, & Kouthouris, 1992), and the practical experience of physical education teachers with individuals with special needs leads to the adoption of more positive attitudes towards these individuals (Stewart, 1990). Educational health programmes, besides increasing knowledge, have been shown to alter children's attitudes and lead to corresponding behaviour at home (Connor et al., 1986). These investigations show that practical experience, acquired skills and competence, as a result of participation in organised exercise programmes, contribute to the formation of positive or negative attitudes or to their modification.

According to Martens (1975), attitude change may involve the cognitive, affective or behavioural components. The cognitive component is expressed by beliefs and, according to the theory of attitudes, it precedes and shapes the affective component. Therefore, a systematic intervention modifying the beliefs related to an attitude constitutes the initial step in reinforcing or modifying an attitude or a behaviour (Ajzen & Fishbein, 1980). Greenockle, Lee, and Lomax (1990) note that the techniques of intervention for modifying attitude or behaviour in relation to exercise are more effective in younger people. This is supported by McIntosh and Albinson (1982) and Pease and Anderson (1986).

Major Theoretical Approaches to Attitude and Exercise Participation

In Kenyon's model of attitudes towards physical activity (Kenyon, 1968a, 1968b), physical activities are perceived as multidimensional psychological and social phenomena. His work was based on the assumption that all physical activities could be classified into specific categories which seem to produce different kinds of satisfaction for each individual. In his scale of attitude to physical activities, Kenyon discriminated six domains, as follows: Social, Catharsis, Fitness and Health, Vertigo, Aesthetic, and Ascetic, although others have also been suggested (e.g., chance). According to Fox and Biddle (1988), it would be more accurate if this scale were named an 'incentive inventory', as it does not actually assess attitudes towards physical activities but attitudes to various reasons for participation.

Based on Kenyon's scale for adults, a scale was developed for children (Children's Attitudes Toward Physical Activity; CATPA). This scale was the result of a series of studies by Schutz, Smoll, and co-workers (Schutz & Smoll, 1977, 1984; Schutz, Smoll, Carre, & Mosher, 1985; Schutz, Smoll, & Wood, 1981a, 1981b; Simon & Smoll, 1974; Smoll & Schutz, 1980). However, in addition to the descriptive profiling advocated by Kenyon and others, a number of social and sport and exercise psychologists have proposed a more theoretical approach to the study of attitudes. Brief consideration will be given to a selection of such theories or models.

Physical Estimation and Attraction

Positive emotional and psychological benefits are commonly believed to result from physical exercise (Sonstroem & Morgan, 1989). According to the Physical Estimation and Attraction model developed by Sonstroem, the self-perception of athletic ability (estimation) and the attraction of the activity (attraction) are variables that could lead individuals to an active lifestyle or could predict athletic behaviour (Sonstroem, 1976). However, the model only succeeded in predicting initial participation (Sonstroem & Kampper, 1980); in the work of Dishman and Gettman (1980) and Dishman, Ickes, and Morgan (1980), the model did not predict adherence. It is worth pointing out, however, that investigations have shown relationships between self-perceptions of athletic ability and attraction, and between self-esteem and level of physical fitness (Neale, Sonstroem, & Metz, 1969; Sonstroem, 1974, 1976). Sonstroem (1988) pointed out that there is a need for more specific attitude and self-esteem scales in order to explain exercise behaviour better.

In more recent work a model for examining the interaction between exercise and self-esteem has been developed (Sonstroem & Morgan, 1989). This model contains dimensions of competence and self-acceptance. Also, Fox and Corbin (1989) have developed the 'Physical Self-Perception Profile' to assess more specific perceptions of physical self-worth. In particular, they focus on perceived body attractiveness, sport competence, physical strength and physical conditioning, and validity has now been demonstrated in a European context (Page, Ashford, Fox, & Biddle, 1993).

Social Learning Theory

A social learning theory approach—Social Cognitive Theory—was developed by Bandura (1977, 1986). Central to this is the concept of 'self-efficacy'. This is defined as an individual's belief that he or she can successfully execute the behaviour required to produce the desired outcome. The theory is particularly useful in explaining exercise behaviour as it incorporates the judgements made by the individual regarding the gains from regular exercise and the perceived ability to exercise, two significant variables for explaining behaviour in exercise settings.

Bandura (1990) stresses the importance of beliefs by stating that 'among the mechanisms of agency, none is more central or pervasive than people's beliefs about their capabilities to exercise control over events that affect their lifes' (p. 128). The usefulness of the model has been confirmed in a number of studies. For a general review on sport and social learning theory, see Bandura (1990).

Interpersonal Behaviour

According to Triandis (1971), behaviour is a function of attitudes, norms, habits and expectancies about reinforcement. Triandis (1977) considers habit as a fundamental factor mediating the relationship between attitudes and behaviour, because a number of well-learned skills are performed almost automatically. He notes that a behaviour is not only affected by thoughts, feelings, intentions or social norms, but also by the behavioural habits of the individual (Triandis, 1971). Despite the significant contribution of the theory to the understanding of attitudes, it has not been used much in studies dealing with exercise.

Reasoned Action Theory

According to the Theory of Reasoned Action (Ajzen & Fishbein, 1980; Fishbein & Ajzen, 1974, 1975), in order to answer questions such as 'why do individuals exercise?', 'how can we increase exercise participation?', or 'why do individuals prefer to participate in basketball rather than tennis?', one must consider that each question is focused on a different type of behaviour, not on general exercise behaviour per se. The basic assumption of the theory is that the implementation of a behaviour depends on the intention of the individual to proceed to action. Intention is determined by two variables. The first, named 'attitudes toward behaviour', refers to the degree of positive or negative appraisal of the behaviour. The second—'subjective norm'— refers to the social pressures for the implementation of the behaviour.

Planned Behaviour Theory

The Theory of Planned Behaviour (Ajzen, 1988; Ajzen & Madden, 1986; Schifter & Ajzen, 1985) is an extension of the Reasoned Action theory and aims at explaining behaviours when, irrespective of the individual's intention to perform an act, there are usually impeding barriers. In the extended theory, the main addition is the inclusion of the variable of 'Perceived Behavioural Control', a variable expressing the extent to which an individual finds it easy or difficult to proceed to an act, the number of opportunities and resources available, or the factors facilitating or hindering behaviour (see Figure 2.1). In general, the more positive the attitudes, the greater the social pressures exerted, and at the same time the more one perceives one is in

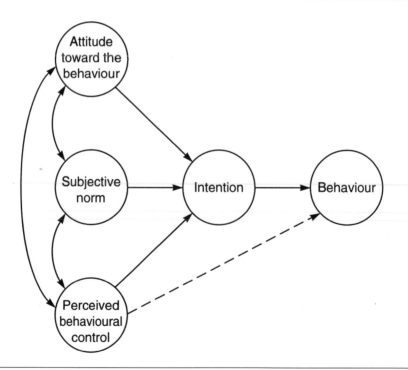

Figure 2.1   Theory of Planned Behaviour.
Note. From *Attitudes, Personality, and Behavior* (p. 133) by I. Ajzen, 1988, Milton Keynes, England: Open University Press. Copyright 1988 by Open University Press. Reprinted by permission.

control of the act, the more probable that the individual will have a positive intention to participate in the target behaviour (Schifter & Ajzen, 1985).

Research on Attitude and Physical Activity

A large number of studies have used Kenyon's 'Attitudes Toward Physical Activity' (ATPA) scale (Kenyon 1968a, 1968b). However, the results of these studies are inconclusive and have contributed little to the explanation of the relationship between attitudes and exercise behaviour. Additionally, attitudes are not always treated as independent variables; in some studies they have been used as dependent variables. This dual approach reflects the basic theoretical dilemma of whether attitudes are a cause or an effect of behaviour.

Studying the relationship between attitudes and participation, Smoll, Schutz, and Keeney (1976) found that children participated in physical activities to which they held more positive attitudes. Other results were reported by Tolson and Chevrette (1974), who found that attitudes are affected by the exercise programme, and by Schutz et al., (1985), who reported a moderate relationship between attitudes and behaviour.

On the other hand, no relation between attitude and behaviour was reported in a number of investigations using Kenyon's ATPA scale (Dishman & Gettman, 1980; Dishman et al., 1980; Godin & Shephard, 1986a; Onifade, 1985), Schutz et al.'s (1985) CATPA scale (Long & Haney, 1986), and the 'Richardson-Thurstone Attitude Questionnaire' (Booth, McVetey, Orban, & Richards, 1989). When Godin and Shephard (1986a) used Kenyon's scale and a scale based on Ajzen's Theory of Reasoned Action, they found that Kenyon's scale failed to predict exercise behaviour. In a similar study in Greece with primary school pupils (Theodorakis, Doganis, Bagiatis, & Goudas, 1991), these results were confirmed. This investigation led to the conclusion that although Kenyon's model is a general attitude scale, it contributes satisfactorily to the explanation of the exercise behaviour only in conjunction with Reasoned Action theory.

Other investigators have attempted to modify attitude scales in order to make them more sport- or activity-specific. Hallinan, Snyder, Drowatzky, and Ashby (1990) modified Kenyon's scale for use in basketball and tennis. Schutz et al., (1981a) constructed the 'Children's Attitudes Toward Specific Sport' (CATSS) scale and found that children's attitudes towards physical activity were similar to the attitudes held for the sport in which they were participating and that the two scales (CATPA and CATSS) were equivalent.

The value of CATPA has been questioned by Brustad (1991) who raises two psychometric concerns. First, its validity is questioned because the six factors were generated from adult populations, not from children. Second, the tendency of the scale to measure trait-like aspects of children's attitudes is criticised. Besides, Schutz et al., (1981b) do not suggest the use of the scale for research on attitude-behaviour relationships and individual differences.

In conclusion, as Martens (1975) stresses in referring to Kenyon's scale, merely to know the attitudes of an individual or a group may not be particularly useful. It is more important to know how these attitudes are formed and what their contribution is to actual behaviour.

Direct Measures of Attitude: European Research

Although much of the initial work on attitude assessment was done in North America, some important research has been done in Europe. For example, in the German version of Kenyon's scale (Singer, Eberspaecher, Rehs, & Boes, 1978), all recreational and competitive sport groups, irrespective of gender, scored higher on the subscale 'exercise and health' than on other subscales. In England, Birtwistle and Brodie (1991) studied the relationship between children's attitudes to physical activity and a number of health-related fitness measures. They found a linear relationship between health-related fitness profiles and attitudes to physical activity. Furthermore they reported that the best predictor of children's attitude score was the suppleness component of fitness, which had a linear relationship with four of the seven CATPA subdomains.

Biddle and Bailey (1985), using ATPA, reported significant gender differences in attitudes and motives for participation in groups of adult fitness class participants in England. However, they did not find any association between motives and attitudes. Also, Smith and Biddle (1991) found that adherers and nonadherers to fitness club attendance differed little in beliefs and attitudes.

We have carried out three investigations in Greece aiming at adapting and validating Schutz et al.'s (1985) version of the CATPA, but with the addition of three more subscales used by Long and Haney (1986). In the first study (Theodorakis, Doganis, & Bagiatis, 1989), discriminant analysis showed that the following subscales differentiated males and females taking part in fitness programmes: health and exercise, aesthetic experience, body shaping, and emotional release. In the second study (Theodorakis, Doganis, & Bagiatis, 1992), the sample consisted of women taking part either in fitness programmes, ballet or top-level sport. The results showed that the samples were discriminated according to the type of physical activity. Factor analysis confirmed the structural validity of the scale, consisting of nine subscales which were the same as in other investigations carried out in other countries (Long & Haney, 1986; Martin & Williams, 1985; Schutz et al., 1981b).

The third study attempted to construct a new scale: 'Attitudes Toward Exercise' (Theodorakis, 1992b). In a female sample, of the nine dimensions of the scale, those with the highest scores were: exercise and health, catharsis, and body shaping. A number of other studies are in agreement with the high scoring on the subdomains associated with health and exercise (e.g., Schutz et al., 1985; Shephard, Montelpare, Berridge, & Flowers, 1986; Singer et al., 1978). The scale was moderately successful in predicting participation in an exercise programme.

In Finland, attitudes of secondary school students towards physical activity were studied by Heinila (1987) using Kenyon's ATPA scale. Finnish adolescents were found to be disposed towards health and fitness, and all dimensions of Kenyon's scale were consistent across the two age-groups used, 13 to 16 and 17 to 19 years of age. Heinila also found that attitudes towards physical activities and sport were partly a function of gender.

In a comparative study, Curry and Weiss (1989) investigated what they called 'motivation for sport participation' in American and Austrian student athletes. Motivation was measured by a modified version of Kenyon's ATPA inventory. Employing factor analysis, they found three factors in the modified scale: competition, fitness and social. The American sample scored higher on the competition factor and the Austrian students higher on the fitness dimension. On the social factor Austrian males and American females scored highest.

Indirect Measures of Attitude: European Research

While the majority of European studies have used standard tools for the measurement of attitudes (ATPA, CATPA), some have employed either indirect (values, meaning, perceptions, etc.) or nonstandardised measures of attitudes. In Scotland, in a 3-year project on leisure lifestyles involving 10,000 young people aged 9 to 20 years, Shucksmith, Hendry, and Love (1991) found that those participating in competitive sport held more positive attitudes than nonparticipants towards sport, leisure, friendship and school. In contrast to participants, more nonparticipants thought leisure time was boring and sport was too costly to allow participation; they did not like organised leisure and preferred a clear distinction between work and leisure.

In England, Williams (1988) studied the role of attitudes of adolescents towards aspects of physical education and their role in patterns of participation in physical activities outside school. She explored four domains of attitudes towards physical education: health, leisure, competition and outdoor physical education. She reported that the attitude to health was the most favourable and the attitude to competition was the least favorable. In general, participants had more favourable attitudes than nonparticipants, the most pronounced differences being on competition. This implies that those who hold negative attitudes towards competition are less likely to participate in physical activities outside school.

In the former Soviet Union, Novikov (1987) examined the lifestyle of students and attitudes they had towards physical culture ('role of physical culture in student life'). Physical culture was rated 'essential' by 50.6%, 'valuable' by 36.9% and 'desirable' by 7.9%.

Stoljarov, Gendin, Sergeev, and Falaleev (1985) investigated the attitudes of 2,000 Siberian school students to health and sport. In the students' 'system of values', health and physical perfection were rated fourth in importance, after satisfaction with work, authority and respect, and happy private life. There was a correlation between attitudes towards health, 'physical perfection' and frequency of participation in physical activities during free time. In addition, Sergeev, Stolyarov, and Gendin (1988) examined what they called 'the value-orientational attitude' of parents towards the physical education of their children. They reported that parents perceived physical activity as being good primarily for health and physical fitness, as ensuring the harmonious development of the child, and as positively affecting character and willpower. They concluded that 'the strongest influence on the sport/physical culture activity of children is exerted by the attitude of parents toward physical development of their children and by the extent of the parents' own activities in the field of sport/ physical culture' (p. 162).

Mrazek and Schafer (1988) used the techniques of association analysis and semantic differential to study the meaning of sport for adolescents in Germany and the USA in order to see if it was related to sport activity. They stated that associations and semantic differentials 'are clearly directed toward the cognitive and emotional level of the idea of sport' (p. 120). They also reported that in the USA adolescents spent more hours per week in sport than Germans, while there were no differences in the expressed interest in sport. In explaining actual paticipation in both samples, they stated that the term 'sport' was 'very concrete, positive, undifferentiated and more or less stereotyped' (p. 111) in the USA, but in Germany it seemed to be connected with effort and ascetic behaviour; that is, it was perceived as being more serious. Finally, American adolescents regarded sport as more comfortable, exciting and 'stronger' than Germans, who thought sport was more versatile and more 'tiring and necessary'.

In Yugoslavia, Momirovic, Hosek, and Poduska (1988) used regression analysis to study the relationship between social attitudes to self-management, clericalism-nationalism, authoritarianism, conformism and social hostility to involvement in sports and athletic achievements. They found a low but significant multiple correlation between involvement and achievement in sport and high self-management orientation and low social hostility. They attribute this low correlation partly to the retardation of the educational role of sport in schools, which, they claim, cannot produce even minimal positive changes in attitude.

Attitude and Exercise Adherence

A large number of studies, mostly conducted outside Europe, have investigated factors related to adherence patterns in physical activity and exercise. Attitudes towards physical activities and exercise appear to be central in the interests of the researchers. In essence, these studies have attempted to examine the perceived personal and social factors leading either to adherence to, or attrition from, exercise programmes. For example, Wankel (1985), in a study of joggers, found that attitudes towards the exercise programme, the initial goals of participation and social support, were the variables differentiating those who continued from those who ceased participation. Those who continued wished to develop their skills, were more curious, wanted to satisfy their competitive drive and develop social relationships and create friendships. Additionally, they had more support from their families in continuing their participation.

Conversely, McCready and Long (1985) found only a small relationship between adherence, attitudes towards physical activity and locus of control. Of the attitude scale subdomains, only 'social continuation' and 'catharsis' were related to exercise adherence. A number of demographic and related variables, such as age, free time, occupation, exhaustion from work, social support, attraction and expected success were related to participation.

Noland and Feldman (1985) noted that 'attitudes toward physical activities' was the most important factor in predicting adherence of 20- to 30-year-old women to exercise, followed by barriers and the 'chance' dimension of locus of control. Granzin and Olsen (1989), in the USA, studied the relationship of three categories of predictor variables and voluntary commitment to physical fitness. They found that the attitude variables most strongly related to voluntary commitment were favourable self-perceptions of athletic ability, being influenced by friends to exercise and the perceived benefits of exercise regarding mental ability.

Shephard (1985) summarises the results of a large-scale study in Canada on participants over the age of 10 years. Specifically, motives, beliefs and problems of participation were studied. He reported that individuals take part in exercise in order to feel better, have an attractive or fit body, to develop social relationships, to improve their health, to control stress and to learn new things. He found the factors influencing participation to be time, facilities, family interests, friends, organisation and money. Furthermore, barriers to taking exercise were related to perceived lack of time, to facilities and to programme content.

After reviewing the literature, Dishman (1986) summarised the available information on nonadherence to exercise programmes as follows:

1. Self-motivation predicts adherence to exercise but not dropout.
2. Barriers, such as facilities, distance from home, lack of free time, and so forth, have a negative effect on adherence.
3. Support from programme leaders, spouses and family has a positive effect.
4. Intention and perceived ability have a positive effect on adherence but do not predict dropout.

The subject of perceived barriers to participation in exercise programmes has attracted the interest of a large number of investigators around the world. In Europe, Thomas (1985) refers to the problems faced by young mothers in England that prevent them taking part in exercise: fatigue from daily tasks or work, little free time, lack of transport, children, working hours, lack of self-confidence, embarrassment in wearing exercise clothes because of body shape or fat and lack of support from the family. The attitudes they express towards exercise concern body vitalisation, health, weight control, return of 'lost youth', feeling better, enjoyment and relaxation.

In a review article on social barriers to physical recreation in Poland, Kunicki (1985) identifies three categories of barriers: ideological, cultural and psychological. He refers to attitudes as personality traits and concludes that he is pessimistic about the prospects for the introduction of more active recreation in Poland, because of the existing barriers and negative mental attitudes.

In Norway, Fasting and Sisjord (1985) examined the qualitative and quantitative dimensions of leisure and their relationship with participation in physical activities. They found that the most significant barrier to participation among women was perceived lack of freedom (the number of hours their spouse was away from home in the evenings). Active women had spouses who spent more evenings at home than passive women.

Using Attitude to Predict Exercise Participation

While much earlier research was mainly concerned to identify the factors associated either with participation patterns and adherence to physical activity and exercise programmes or with attrition from them, a number of relatively recent investigations have focused mainly on the prediction of either intention to participate or actual exercise participation. Many of these studies were based on theoretical models aiming at predicting behaviour from a number of variables. Most of them were conducted outside Europe.

In general, the reported coefficients of prediction are not high. Additionally, both the types of observed behaviours and the time scale of prediction are limited. The studies are concerned with questions such as whether someone will jog or not during the next few weeks, whether someone will exercise during the next month, whether students or high school pupils will participate in physical activities. Most studies use self-reported measures of behaviour and not more objective ones. Finally, it is worth pointing out that in this area of research, European studies based on a sound theoretical background have been surprisingly rare. Therefore, reference will be made mainly to studies conducted outside Europe.

Research on prediction of intention to exercise has focused on attitudes. Ferguson, Yesalis, Pomrehn, and Kirkpatrick (1989) found that 37% of the variance in exercise intention was explained by the perceived benefits of exercise (attitudes), current exercise behaviour, self-esteem and gender. The unique contribution of this study is the inclusion of a scale measuring children's knowledge about exercise, which correlated with exercise intentions. Their conclusion is that the development of positive attitudes towards exercise at an early age may play an important role in physical activity participation.

A number of other studies have focused on prediction of intention to participate in physical activities from attitudes and social factors. The Reasoned Action model was effective in predicting exercise behaviour in studies by Bentler and Speckart (1981), Riddle (1980), Godin, Valois, Shephard, and Desharnais (1987), and Theodorakis et al. (1991). Other studies found attitude generally to be a stronger predictor of intention than social influences (Dzewaltowski, 1989; Godin & Shephard, 1986a, 1986b; Godin, Cox, & Shephard, 1983; Godin et al., 1987; Riddle 1980; Young & Kent, 1985). However, Greenockle et al. (1990) showed that the social norm was a stronger predictor of intention than attitude.

Only a few studies have been conducted on Planned Behaviour theory in exercise and sport. Godin, Vezina, and Leclerc (1989) reported that the use of the factor 'barriers' significantly contributed to the prediction of intention of pregnant women to take part in exercise after childbirth. Wankel, Craig, and Stephens (1990) showed that individuals who exercised more had a stronger intention and more positive attitudes, more support from significant others, and thought they were more in control of their behaviour than those who exercised less. Ajzen and Driver (1991) applied Planned Behaviour theory to leisure participation, and their results showed the usefulness of the theory. In another study (Theodorakis, 1992a), intention was found effective in predicting participation of young swimmers in the team's training, but 'perceived behavioural control' had little effect on behaviour.

In a study in Greece (Theodorakis, 1992b), the relationship between attitude and exercise was examined through the variables 'intention', 'perceived behavioural control' and two new variables, 'self-identity' and 'attitude strength'. Also, 'attitudes toward exercise', 'locus of control for exercise behaviour' and 'body cathexis' were examined as mediator variables. Participation was recorded over a 2-month period and served as a behavioural criterion measure. Results showed the effectiveness of the variables of intention and perceived behavioural control in predicting exercise participation, and that self-identity and attitude strength significantly increased the predictive power of the model. Attitudes towards exercise, locus of control for exercise behaviour and body cathexis also had a moderate effect.

Past behaviour has also been found to be helpful in predicting exercise behaviour (Anderson, Lorenz, & Pease 1986; Godin et al., 1987). Other studies have shown that past experiences assist in predicting intention to participate in physical activities (Godin & Shephard, 1986a; Godin et al., 1983).

In two studies by Dzewaltowski and colleagues (Dzewaltowski, 1989; Dzewaltowski, Noble, & Shaw, 1990), Bandura's social cognitive theory showed some effectiveness in predicting participation in exercise programmes. Adherence to exercise in physical fitness programmes has also been predicted from self-efficacy theory (Desharnais, Bouillon, & Godin, 1986; Garcia & King, 1991). In addition, researchers have examined self-efficacy in relation to sport performance (Feltz, 1988; Fitzsimmons, Landers, Thomas, & Mars, 1991; Martin & Gill, 1991; McAuley, 1985), and in relation to exercise participation (McAuley, 1992; McAuley & Jacobson, 1991). Similarly, Valois, Desharnais, and Godin (1988) showed that the Triandis model (Triandis, 1977), was effective in predicting exercise participation.

Other models have been used in an effort to predict exercise behaviour, such as Health Locus of Control (Dishman & Steinhardt, 1990), the Health Belief Model (Slenker, Price, Roberts, & Jurs, 1984), and Protection Motivation Theory (Wurtele & Maddux, 1987). Finally, Kendzierski and Lamastro (1988) demonstrated that Edwards's subjective expected utility theory predicted interest in, but not adherence to, a weight lifting exercise programme.

Conclusion

The new trends in research on the relationship between attitudes and exercise behaviour have adopted sound theoretical models derived from social psychological paradigms, and the old approaches have gradually been abandoned. The apparent distance between expressed positive attitudes towards participation in exercise and actual participation should stimulate scientists to adopt those research paradigms that are more promising in explaining the complex interplay between actual exercise behaviour and the variables associated with it. Of course, there is still much to be done in Europe as the new sociopolitical changes taking place urge all scientists in the field of exercise and sport to work towards the integration of a multicultural society, according to the 'sport for all' philosophy.

The contribution of scientific investigations to the explanation and understanding of exercise and sport participation is potentially great. Attitudes are important variables providing insights into the interplay between personal wishes, beliefs and opinions, and sociocultural conditions. Therefore, their role in assisting in the improvement of participation rates and the quality of exercise programmes is self-evident.

Particular attention should be paid to the identification of environmental and cultural barriers, and the role of 'significant others' in participation. Alternative suggestions for exercise programmes should always exist, and furthermore it is essential to provide ideas on time organisation and exercise during holidays. The minimisation of barriers and inequalities (facilities, illness, transportation, etc.), and the maximisation of facilitating factors (attractive programmes, alternative schedules, individualised exercise programmes, etc.) should always be provided for.

At a macrolevel, information about the benefits of regular exercise is essential, while at a microlevel inadequate knowledge and criticism from 'significant others' about the usefulness of regular exercise contribute negatively and affect attitudes.

References

Ajzen, I. (1988). *Attitudes, personality, and behavior*. Milton Keynes, England: Open University Press.

Ajzen, I., & Driver, B.L. (1991). Prediction of leisure participation from behavioral, normative and control beliefs: An application of the theory of planned behavior. *Leisure Sciences*, **13**, 185-204.

Ajzen, I., & Fishbein, M. (1980). *Understanding attitudes and predicting social behavior*. Englewood Cliffs, NJ: Prentice Hall.

Ajzen, I., & Madden, T.J. (1986). Prediction of goal-directed behavior: Attitudes, and perceived behavioral control. *Journal of Experimental Social Psychology*, **22**, 453-474.

Allport, G.W. (1935). Attitudes. In M. Fishbein (Ed.), *Readings in attitude theory and measurement* (pp. 3-13). New York: Wiley.

Anderson, D.F., Lorenz, F.O., & Pease, D.G. (1986). Prediction of present participation from children's gender, past participation and attitudes: A longitudinal analysis. *Sociology of Sport Journal*, **3**, 101-111.

Bagozzi, R.P., & Burnkrant, R.E. (1979). Attitude organization and the attitude-behavior relationship. *Journal of Personality and Social Psychology*, **37**, 913-929.

Bagozzi, R.P., & Yi, Y. (1989). The degree of intention formation as a moderator of the attitude-behavior relationship. *Social Psychology Quarterly*, **52**, 266-279.

Bandura, A. (1977). Self-efficacy: Toward a unifying theory of behavioral change. *Psychological Review*, **84**, 191-215.

Bandura, A. (1986). *Social foundations of thought and action*. Englewood Cliffs, NJ: Prentice Hall.

Bandura, A. (1990). Perceived self-efficacy in the exercise of personal agency. *Journal of Applied Sport Psychology*, **2**, 128-163.

Barrell, G.V., & Holt, D. (1982). Attitude changes of specialist students of physical education towards physical activity during teacher-training courses. *Perceptual and Motor Skills*, **54**, 477-478.

Bem, D.J. (1972). Self perception theory. In L. Berkowitz (Ed.), *Advances in experimental social psychology* (Vol. 6, pp. 1-62). New York: Academic Press.

Bentler, P.M., & Speckart, G. (1981). Attitudes "cause" behaviors: A structural equation analysis. *Journal of Personality and Social Psychology*, **40**, 226-238.

Biddle, S.J.H., & Bailey, S. (1985). Motives for participation and attitudes toward physical activity of adult participants in fitness programmes. *Perceptual and Motor Skills*, **61**, 831-834.

Bierstedt, H. (1985). The athletic activities of citizens of the GDR: Some sociological aspects of their structure and social conditions. *International Review for Sociology of Sport*, **20**, 39-51.

Birtwistle, G.E., & Brodie , D.A. (1991). Canonical relationships between two sets of variables representing the CATPA subdomains and health related fitness. *International Journal of Physical Education*, **28**(1), 21-25.

Block, K.K., & Beckett, K.D. (1990). Verbal descriptions of skill by specialists and nonspecialists. *Journal of Teaching in Physical Education*, **10**, 21-37.

Booth, F.B., McVetey, S.D., Orban, A.R.W., & Richards, G. (1989). Attitudes and exercise behaviours among selected health science students at the University of Ottawa. *Journal of Human Movement Studies*, **16**, 139-148.

Bootzin, R.R., Bower, G.H., & Zajonc, R.B. (1986). *Psychology today*. New York: Random House.

Borgida, E., & Campbell, B. (1982). Belief relevance and attitude-behavior consistency: The moderating role of personal experience. *Journal of Personality and Social Psychology*, **42**, 239-247.

Brustad, R. (1991). Children's perspectives on exercise and physical activity: Measurement issues and concerns. *Journal of School Health*, **61**(5), 228-230.

Buss, A.H. (1978). *Psychology behavior in perspective*. New York: Wiley.

Chein, I. (1948). Behavior therapy and the behavior of attitudes: Some critical comments. *Psychological Review*, **55**, 175-188.

Connor, M.A., Smith, L.G., Fryer, A., Erickson, S., Fryer, S., & Drake, J. (1986). Future fit: A cardiovascular health education and fitness project in an after-school setting. *Journal of School Health*, **56**, 329-333.

Cooper, J., & Croyle, T.R. (1984). Attitudes and attitude change. *Annual Review of Psychology*, **35**, 395-426.

Corbin, C.B., & Chevrette, J.M. (1981). Attitudes of freshmen before and after a lecture-laboratory physical education course. *Physical Educator*, **38**, 138-139.

Curry, T., & Weiss, O. (1989). Sport identity and motivations for sport participation: A comparison between American college athletes and Austrian student sport club members. *Sociology of Sport Journal*, **6**, 257-268.

Davidson, A.R., Yantis, S., Norwood, M., & Montano, D.A. (1985). Amount of information about the attitude object and attitude-behavior consistency. *Journal of Personality and Social Psychology*, **49**, 1184-1198.

Davidson, R.A., & Jaccard, J.J. (1979). Variables that moderate the attitude-behavior relation: Results of a longitudinal study. *Journal of Personality and Social Psychology*, **37**, 1364-1376.

Desharnais, R., Bouillon, J., & Godin, G. (1986). Self-efficacy and outcome expectation as determinants of exercise adherence. *Psychological Reports*, **59**, 1155-1159.

Dishman, R.K. (1986). Exercise compliance: A new view for public health. *Physician and Sportsmedicine*, **14**(5), 127-145.

Dishman, R.K., & Gettman, L. (1980). Psychobiologic influences on exercise adherence. *Journal of Sport Psychology*, **2**, 295-310.

Dishman, R.K., Ickes, W., & Morgan, W.P. (1980). Self-motivation and adherence to habitual physical activity. *Journal of Applied Social Psychology*, **10**, 115-132.

Dishman, R.K., & Steinhardt, M. (1990). Health locus of control predicts free living, but not supervised physical activity: A test of exercise-specific control and outcome-expectancy hypotheses. *Research Quarterly for Exercise and Sport*, **61**, 383-394.

Doob, L.W. (1947). The behavior of attitudes. *Psychological Review*, **54**, 135-156.

Dzewaltowski, D.A. (1989). Toward a model of exercise motivation. *Journal of Sport and Exercise Psychology*, **11**, 251-269.

Dzewaltowski, D.A., Noble, J.M., & Shaw, J.M. (1990). Physical activity participation: Social cognitive theory versus the theories of reasoned action and planned behavior. *Journal of Sport and Exercise Psychology*, **12**, 388-405.

Edwards, A.L. (1957). *Techniques of attitude scale construction*. New York: Appleton-Century-Crofts.

Edwards, C., & Crawford, G.M. (1990). Contemporary American physical education: A fitness critique. *International Journal of Physical Education*, **27**, 35-39.

Fasting, K., & Sisjord, M. (1985). Gender roles and barriers to participation in sports. *Sociology of Sport Journal*, **2**, 345-351.

Fazio, R.H. (1990). Multiple processes by which attitudes guide behavior: The mode model as an integrative framework. In L. Berkowitz (Ed.), *Advances in experimental social psychology* (Vol. 23, pp. 75-109). New York: Academic Press.

Fazio, R.H., Chen, J.M., McDonel, E.C., & Sherman, S.J. (1982). Attitude accessibility, attitude-behavior consistency, and the strength of the object-evaluation association. *Journal of Experimental Social Psychology*, **18**, 339-357.

Fazio, R.H., Powell, M.C., & Herr, P.M. (1983). Toward a process model of the attitude-behavior relation: Accessing one's attitude upon mere observation of the attitude object. *Journal of Personality and Social Psychology*, **44**, 723-735.

Fazio, R.H., & Williams, C.J. (1986). Attitude accessibility as a moderator of the attitude behavior relations: An investigation of the 1984 presidential election. *Journal of Personality and Social Psychology*, **51**, 505-514.

Fazio, R.H., & Zanna, M.P. (1978). Attitudinal qualities relating to the strength of the attitude-behavior relationship. *Journal of Experimental Social Psychology*, **14**, 398-408.

Felson, R.B., & Bohrnstedt, G.W. (1980). Attributions of ability and motivation in a natural setting. *Journal of Personality and Social Psychology*, **39**, 799-805.

Feltz, D. (1988). Gender differences in the causal elements of self-efficacy on a high avoidance motor task. *Journal of Sport and Exercise Psychology*, **10**, 151-166.

Ferguson, K.J., Yesalis, C.E., Pomrehn, P.R., & Kirkpatrick, M.B. (1989). Attitudes, knowledge, and beliefs as predictors of exercise intent and behaviour in schoolchildren. *Journal of School Health*, **59**(3), 112-115.

Figley, G.E. (1985). Determinants of attitudes toward physical education. *Journal of Teaching in Physical Education*, **4**, 229-240.

Fishbein, M. (1967). A consideration of beliefs and their role in attitude measurement. In M. Fishbein (Ed.), *Readings in attitude theory and measurement* (pp. 389-400). New York: Wiley.

Fishbein, M., & Ajzen, I. (1974). Attitudes towards objects as predictors of single and multiple behavioral criteria. *Psychological Review*, **81**, 59-84.

Fishbein, M., & Ajzen, I. (1975). *Belief, attitude, intention and behavior*. Reading, MA: Addison-Wesley.

Fitzsimmons, P., Landers, D., Thomas, J., & Mars, H. (1991). Does self-efficacy predict performance in experienced weightlifters? *Research Quarterly for Exercise and Sport*, **62**, 424-431.

Fox, K., & Biddle, S.J.H. (1987). Health-related fitness testing in schools: I. Philosophical and psychological implications. *Bulletin of Physical Education*, **23**(1), 29-39.

Fox, K., & Biddle, S.J.H. (1988). The child's perspective in physical education: III. A question of attitudes? *British Journal of Physical Education*, **19**, 107-111.

Fox, K., & Corbin, C. (1989). The Physical Self-Perception Profile: Development and preliminary validation. *Journal of Sport and Exercise Psychology*, **11**, 408-430.

Garcia, A., & King, A. (1991). Predicting long-term adherence to aerobic exercise: A comparison of two models. *Journal of Sport and Exercise Psychology*, **13**, 394-410.

Godin, G., Cox, H.M., & Shephard, R.J. (1983). The impact of physical fitness evaluation on behavioural intentions towards regular exercise. *Canadian Journal of Applied Sport Sciences*, **8**, 240-245.

Godin, G., & Shephard, R.J. (1986a). Importance of type of attitude to the study of exercise behavior. *Psychological Reports*, **58**, 991-1000.

Godin, G., & Shephard, R.J. (1986b). Psychosocial factors influencing intentions to exercise of young students from grades 7 to 9. *Research Quarterly for Exercise and Sport*, **57**, 44-52.

Godin, G., Valois, P., Shephard, R.J., & Desharnais, R. (1987). Prediction of leisure time exercise behavior: A path analysis (Lisrel V) model. *Journal of Behavioral Medicine*, **10**, 145-158.

Godin, G., Vezina, L., & Leclerc, O. (1989). Factors influencing intentions of pregnant women to exercise after giving birth. *Public Health Reports*, **104**, 188-196.

Granzin, K., & Olsen, J. (1989). Identifying those ready to make a voluntary commitment to fitness. *Journal of Sport Management*, **3**, 116-128.

Greenockle, K.M., Lee, A., & Lomax, R. (1990). The relationship between selected student characteristics and activity patterns in a required high school physical education class. *Research Quarterly for Exercise and Sport*, **61**, 59-69.

Hall, D. (1978). Changing attitudes, changing behaviors. *Journal of Physical Education and Recreation*, **49**(4), 20-21.

Hallinan, C.J., Snyder, E., Drowatzky, J.A., & Ashby, A.A. (1990). Values held by prospective coaches toward women's sport participation. *Journal of Sport Behavior*, **13**, 167-180.

Heinila, L. (1987). *Attitudes toward sport and physical activity among boys and girls in Finnish urban secondary schools*. Paper presented at the Jyvaskyla Congress on Movement and Sport in Womens' Lives, University of Jyvaskyla, Jyvaskyla, Finland.

Jaccard, J., & Wood, G. (1988). The effects of incomplete information on the formation of attitudes toward behavioral alternatives. *Journal of Personality and Social Psychology*, **54**, 580-591.

James, W.T., Erickson, C., & Johnson, D. (1977). Changing habits by changing attitudes. *Journal of Physical Education and Recreation*, **48**(7), 13.

Kendzierski, D., & Lamastro, V. (1988). Reconsidering the role of attitudes in exercise behavior: A decision theoretical approach. *Journal of Applied Social Psychology*, **18**, 737-759.

Kenyon, G.S. (1968a). A conceptual model for characterizing physical activity. *Research Quarterly*, **39**, 96-104.

Kenyon, G.S. (1968b). Six scales for assessing attitudes toward physical activity. *Research Quarterly*, **39**, 566-574.

Krech, D., & Crutchfield, R.S. (1948). *Theory and problems in social psychology*. New York: McGraw-Hill.

Krosnick, J.A. (1988a). Attitude importance and attitude change. *Journal of Experimental and Social Psychology*, **24**, 240-255.

Krosnick, J.A. (1988b). The role of attitude importance in social evaluation: A study of policy preferences, presidential candidate evaluations, and voting behavior. *Journal of Personality and Social Psychology*, **55**, 196-210.

Kunicki, B. (1985). Social barriers in physical recreation. *International Review for Sociology of Sport*, **20**(3), 167-177.

LaPiere, T.R. (1934). Attitudes versus actions. *Social Forces*, **13**, 230-237.

Laurie, D.R. (1981). Knowledge, attitudes and reported behavior before and after a lecture-laboratory physical fitness class. *Physical Educator*, **38**, 55.

Long, B.C., & Haney, C.J. (1986). Enhancing physical activity in sedentary women: Information, locus of control, and attitudes. *Journal of Sport Psychology*, **8**, 8-23.

Marchand, J. (1990). *Sport for all in Europe*. London: Council of Europe/Her Majesty's Stationery Office.

Martens, R. (1975). *Social psychology and physical activity*. New York: Harper & Row.

Martin, C.J., & Williams, L.R.T. (1985). A psychometric analysis of an instrument for assessing children's attitudes toward physical activity. *Journal of Human Movement Studies*, **11**, 89-104.

Martin, J.J., & Gill, D. (1991). The relationships among competitive orientation, sport-confidence, self-efficacy, anxiety and performance. *Journal of Sport and Exercise Psychology*, **13**, 149-159.

McAuley, E. (1985). Modeling and self-efficacy: A test of Bandura's model. *Journal of Sport Psychology*, **8**, 283-295.

McAuley, E. (1992). The role of efficacy cognitions in the prediction of exercise behavior in middle-aged adults. *Journal of Behavioral Medicine*, **15**, 65-88.

McAuley, E., & Jacobson, L. (1991). Self-efficacy and exercise participation in sedentary adult females. *American Journal of Health Promotion*, **5**, 185-191.

McCready, M.L., & Long, B.C. (1985). Locus of control, attitudes toward physical activity, and exercise adherence. *Journal of Sport Psychology*, **7**, 346-359.

McGuire, W.J. (1969). The nature of attitudes and attitude change. In G. Lindzey & E. Aronson (Eds.), *The handbook of social psychology* (pp. 136-314). Cambridge, MA: Addison-Wesley.

McIntosh, D.K., & Albinson, A. (1982). Physical education in Ontario secondary schools: A follow-up study. *Canadian Association for Health Education and Recreation Journal*, **48**, 14-17.

Meyerowitz, B.E., & Chaiken, S. (1987). The effect of message framing on breast self-examination: Attitudes, intentions, and behavior. *Journal of Personality and Social Psychology*, **52**, 500-510.

Millar, G.M., & Tesser, A. (1989). The effects of affective-cognitive consistency and thought on the attitude-behavior relation. *Journal of Experimental Social Psychology*, **25**, 189-202.

Momirovic, K., Hosek, A., & Poduska, S. (1988). The status of sports activity in the structure of social attitudes. *International Review for Sociology of Sport*, **23**(4), 361-369.

Mrazek, J., & Schafer, G. (1988). The meaning of "sport" in the Federal Republic of Germany and the USA. *International Review of Sociology of Sport*, **23**(2), 109-122.

Neale, D.C., Sonstroem, R.J., & Metz, K.F. (1969). Physical fitness, self-esteem, and attitudes toward physical activity. *Research Quarterly*, **40**(4), 743-749.

Nederhof, J.A. (1989). Self-involvement, intention certainty and attitude-intention consistency. *British Journal of Social Psychology*, **28**, 123-133.

Noland, M.P., & Feldman, R.H. (1985, October). An empirical investigation of leisure exercise behavior in adult women. *Health Education*, pp. 29-34.

Norman, R. (1975). Affective-cognitive consistency, attitudes, conformity and behavior. *Journal of Personality and Social Psychology*, **32**, 83-91.

Novikov, B. (1987). The influence of physical culture on the personality of Soviet students. *International Review for Sociology of Sport*, **22**, 331-339.

Onifade, S.A. (1985). Relationship among attitude, physical activity behavior and physical activity belief of Nigerian students toward physical activity. *International Journal of Sport Psychology*, **16**, 183-192.

Ostrom, T.M. (1969). The relationship between the affective, behavioral, and cognitive components of attitude. *Journal of Experimental Social Psychology*, **5**, 12-30.

Page, A., Ashford, B., Fox, K.R., & Biddle, S.J.H. (1993). Evidence of cross-cultural validity for the Physical Self-Perception Profile. *Personality and Individual Differences*, **14**, 585-590.

Patterson, P., & Faucette, N. (1990). Children's attitudes toward physical activity in classes taught by specialist versus nonspecialist P.E. teachers. *Journal of Teaching in Physical Education*, **9**, 324-331.

Pease, D.G., & Anderson, D.F. (1986). Longitudinal analysis of children's attitudes toward sport team involvement. *Journal of Sport Behavior*, **9**, 3-10.

Riddle, K.P. (1980). Attitudes, beliefs, behavioral intentions, and behaviors of women and men toward regular jogging. *Research Quarterly for Exercise and Sport*, **51**, 663-674.

Riiskjaer, S. (1986). Alterations in the sports involvement. *Scandinavian Journal of Sports Science*, **8**(3), 117-122.

Rosenberg, M.J. (1968). Hedonism, inauthenticity, and other goals toward expansion of a consistency theory. In R.P. Abelson, G. Aronson, W. McGuire, & P. Tannenbaum (Eds.), *Theories of cognitive consistency: A sourcebook* (pp. 73-102). Chicago: Rand McNally.

Sarnoff, I. (1960). Psychoanalytic theory and social attitudes. *Public Opinion Quarterly*, **24**, 251-279.

Schifter, D.E., & Ajzen, I. (1985). Intention, perceived control, and weight loss: An application of the theory of planned behavior. *Journal of Personality and Social Psychology*, **49**, 843-851.

Schutz, R.W., & Smoll, F.L. (1977). Equivalence of two inventories for assessing attitudes toward physical activity. *Psychological Reports*, **40**, 1031-1034.

Schutz, R.W., & Smoll, F.L. (1984). The stability of attitudes toward physical activity during childhood and adolescence. In B. McPherson (Ed.), *Sport and aging: Olympic Scientific Congress proceedings* (pp. 187-197). Champaign, IL: Human Kinetics.

Schutz, R.W., Smoll, F.L., Carre, F.A., & Mosher, R.E. (1985). Inventories and norms for children's attitudes toward physical activity. *Research Quarterly for Exercise and Sport*, **56**, 256-265.

Schutz, R.W., Smoll, F.L., & Wood, T.M. (1981a). Physical activity and sport: Attitudes and perceptions of young Canadian athletes. *Canadian Journal of Applied Sport Sciences*, **6**, 32-39.

Schutz, R.W., Smoll, F.L., & Wood, T.M. (1981b). A psychometric analysis of an inventory for assessing children's attitudes toward physical activity. *Journal of Sport Psychology*, **4**, 321-344.

Schwartz, S.H. (1978). Temporal instability as a moderator of the attitude-behavior relationship. *Journal of Personality and Social Psychology*, **36**, 715-724.

Sergeev, M.I., Stolyarov, V.I., & Gendin, A.M. (1988). The role of the family in the physical education of pre-school children. *International Review of Sociology of Sport*, **23**, 153-166.

Shephard, R.J. (1985). Motivation: The key to fitness compliance. *Physician and Sportsmedicine*, **13**(7), 88-101.

Shephard, R.J., Montelpare, W., Berridge, M., & Flowers, J. (1986). Influence of exercise and of lifestyle education upon attitudes to exercise of older people. *Journal of Sports Medicine and Physical Fitness*, **26**, 175-179.

Shucksmith, G., Hendry, L., & Love, G. (1991). Describing young peoples' leisure and lifestyles: Report of phase 1 (1985-1989) of a research project. *Scottish Journal of Physical Education*, **19**(2), 4-6.

Sidney, K.H., & Shephard, R.J. (1976). Attitudes toward health and physical activity in the elderly: Effects of a physical training program. *Medicine and Science in Sports*, **8**, 246-252.

Simon, J.A., & Smoll, F.L. (1974). An instrument for assessing children's attitudes toward physical activity. *Research Quarterly*, **45**, 407-415.

Singer, R., Eberspaecher, H., Rehs, H-J., & Boes, K.L. (1978). Experience with a German version of the Kenyon scale (ATPA). In U. Simri (Ed.), *Proceedings of International Symposium on Psychological Assessment in Sport* (pp. 171-179). Netanya, Israel: Wingate Institute of Physical Education and Sport.

Sivacek, J., & Crano, W.D. (1982). Vested interest as a moderator of attitude-behavior consistency. *Journal of Personality and Social Psychology*, **43**(2), 210-221.

Slava, S., Laurie, D.R., & Corbin, C.B. (1984). Long-term effects of a conceptual physical education program. *Research Quarterly for Exercise and Sport*, **55**, 161-168.

Slenker, S.E., Price, J.H., Roberts, S.M., & Jurs, S.J. (1984). Joggers versus nonexercisers: An analysis of knowledge, attitudes and beliefs about jogging. *Research Quarterly for Exercise and Sport*, **55**, 371-378.

Smith, R.A., & Biddle, S.J.H. (1991). Exercise adherence in the commercial sector. In *Proceedings of the 4th Annual Conference of European Health Psychology Society* (pp. 154-155). Leicester, England: British Psychological Society.

Smoll, F.L., & Schutz, R.W. (1980). Children's attitudes toward physical activity: A longitudinal analysis. *Journal of Sport Psychology*, **2**, 137-147.

Smoll, F.L., Schutz, R.W., & Keeney, J.K. (1976). Relationships among children's attitudes, involvement, and proficiency in physical activities. *Research Quarterly*, **47**, 797-803.

Sonstroem, R. (1974). Attitude testing examining certain psychological correlates of physical activity. *Research Quarterly*, **45**, 93-103.

Sonstroem, R. (1976). The validity of self-perceptions regarding physical and athletic ability. *Medicine and Science in Sports*, **8**, 126-132.

Sonstroem, R. (1988). Psychological models. In R.K. Dishman (Ed.), *Exercise adherence: Its impact on public health* (pp. 125-154). Champaign, IL: Human Kinetics.

Sonstroem, R., & Kampper, P.K. (1980). Prediction of athletic participation in middle school males. *Research Quarterly*, **51**, 685-694.

Sonstroem, R., & Morgan, W.P. (1989). Exercise and self-esteem: Rationale and model. *Medicine and Science in Sports and Exercise*, **21**, 329-337.

Stewart, C.C. (1990). Effect of practical types in preservice adapted physical education curriculum on attitudes toward disabled populations. *Journal of Teaching in Physical Education*, **10**, 76-83.

Stoljarov, V., Gendin, A., Sergeev, M., & Falaleev, A. (1985). The place of health, physical culture and sport activity in the life and value orientation of Soviet school students. *International Review of Sociology of Sport*, **20**(1), 63-74.

Theodorakis, Y. (1992a). Prediction of athletic participation: A test on planned behavior theory. *Perceptual and Motor Skills*, **74**, 371-379.

Theodorakis, Y. (1992b). *Social psychological factors in predicting adult female participation in physical fitness programmes.* Unpublished doctoral dissertation, Aristotle University of Thessaloniki, Greece.

Theodorakis, Y., Doganis, G., & Bagiatis, K. (1989). Attitudes toward physical activity in males and females. *Sport Psychology*, **2**, 43-52.

Theodorakis, Y., Doganis, G., & Bagiatis, K. (1992). Attitudes toward physical activity in female physical fitness programme participants. *International Journal of Sport Psychology*, **23**, 262-273.

Theodorakis, Y., Doganis, G., Bagiatis, K., & Goudas, M. (1991). Preliminary study of the ability of reasoned action model in predicting exercise behavior of young children. *Perceptual and Motor Skills*, **72**, 51-58.

Theodorakis, Y., Goudas, M., & Kouthouris, H. (1992). Change of attitudes toward skiing after participation in a skiing course. *Perceptual and Motor Skills*, **75**, 272-274.

Thomas, J. (1985). Why doesn't mum go out to play? *Physical Education Review*, **8**, 7-13.

Thurstone, L.L. (1931). The measurement of social attitudes. *Journal of Abnormal and Social Psychology*, **26**, 249-269.

Tolson, H., & Chevrette, J.M. (1974). Changes in attitudes toward physical activity as a result of individualized exercise prescription. *Journal of Psychology*, **87**, 203-207.

Tourangeau, R., Rasinski, A.K., Bradburn, N., & D'Andrade, R. (1989). Belief accessibility and context effects in attitude measurement. *Journal of Experimental Social Psychology*, **25**, 401-421.

Triandis, H.C. (1971). *Attitude and attitude change.* New York: Wiley.

Triandis, H.C. (1977). *Interpersonal behavior.* Monterey, CA: Brooks.

Valois, P., Desharnais, R., & Godin, G. (1988). A comparison of the Fishbein and Ajzen and the Triandis attitudinal models for the prediction of exercise intention and behavior. *Journal of Behavioral Medicine*, **11**, 459-472.

Verplanken, B. (1989). Involvement and need for cognition as moderators of beliefs-attitude-intention consistency. *British Journal of Social Psychology*, **28**, 115-122.

Wankel, L.M. (1985). Personal and situational factors affecting exercise involvement: The importance of enjoyment. *Research Quarterly for Exercise and Sport*, **56**, 275-282.

Wankel, L.M., Craig, C.L., & Stephens, T. (1990, June). *Social psychological factors associated with different patterns of physical activity involvement.* Paper presented at the World Congress On Sport For All, Tampere, Finland.

Williams, A. (1988). Physical activity patterns among adolescents: Some curriculum implications. *Physical Education Review*, **11**, 28-39.

Wilson, D.T., Kraft, D., & Dunn, S.D. (1989). The disruptive effects of explaining attitudes: The moderating effect of knowledge about the attitude object. *Journal of Experimental Social Psychology*, **25**, 379-400.

Wurtele, K.S., & Maddux, E.J. (1987). Relative contributions of protection motivation theory components in predicting exercise intentions and behavior. *Health Psychology*, **6**, 453-466.

Young, R.A., & Kent, A.T. (1985). Using the theory of reasoned action to improve the understanding of recreation behavior. *Journal of Leisure Research*, **17**, 90-106.

Zuckerman, M., & Reis, T.H. (1978). Comparison of three models for predicting altruistic behavior. *Journal of Personality and Social Psychology*, **36**, 498-510.

3
CHAPTER

The Effects of Exercise on Mental Health in Nonclinical Populations

Nanette Mutrie
Stuart J.H. Biddle

GREAT BRITAIN

The Allied Dunbar National Fitness Survey (ADNFS) (1992) showed that physical activity was positively related to perceptions of health and well-being among the English population. However, there is more evidence concerning the effects of exercise on the mental health of clinical populations than there is for nonclinical groups (see chapter 4). One reason for this is that mood states in clinical populations tend to be easier to measure and are of direct interest to those who are trying to help their patients return to a healthier psychological state. Another reason for the lack of information on how exercise affects mental health in nonclinical populations is our preoccupation in the 1970s and 1980s with measuring physiological variables related to exercise participation. There is no doubt of the importance to disease prevention of physiological improvements via exercise (see Bouchard, Shephard, Stephens, Sutton, & McPherson, 1990), but the issue of psychological benefit may be equally important. Unless some positive feeling is associated with exercise, the likelihood of ceasing participation, and thus losing any potential physiological gain, is increased (see Biddle & Mutrie, 1991, and chapter 1).

The importance of psychological outcomes from exercise participation is emphasised when the issue of mental health is considered. In excess of 20% of the adult population in the United Kingdom are likely to suffer a mental illness in their lifetime (Department of Health, 1992), and Chamove (1988) has suggested that physical activity plays a role in preventing abnormal psychological states. In addition, in the unknown percentage of the population who are not clinically mentally ill but experience dysphoria, can exercise play a role in creating more positive moods? Finally, there is another segment of the population who do not report any unhappiness or dissatisfaction in life but who may use various strategies to maintain this harmonious state. Exercise may have a role as a coping strategy for this segment of the population.

Exercise and Mental Health: A Current Consensus?

Although the belief that physical activity can be beneficial for mental health is not new (see Ryan, 1984), there has been a great deal of recent research on mental health and exercise (Biddle & Mutrie, 1991). For nonclinical populations the emphasis has been on changes in anxiety, depression, self-esteem and reactivity to stress associated either with participation in acute or chronic exercise, or with levels of habitual physical activity (Biddle, 1992a). The increased level of interest and research activity in this field has led to the publication of position and consensus statements from the International Society of Sport Psychology (ISSP, 1992) and the American National Institute of Mental Health (NIMH) (Morgan & Goldston, 1987). The position statement of the International Society of Sport Psychology draws almost exclusively on North American research and concurs with the NIMH consensus statements. These included the following:

- Exercise is associated with reduced state anxiety.
- Exercise is associated with reductions in mild to moderate depression.
- Long-term exercise is associated with reductions in traits such as neuroticism and anxiety.
- Exercise results in the reduction of various stress indices.
- Exercise has beneficial emotional effects across all ages and in both sexes (International Society of Sport Psychology, 1992; Morgan & Goldston, 1987).

Summary evidence for such statements can be found in numerous studies, although the statement that exercise has beneficial emotional effects on children is not well supported. This is not because studies refute the statement; we simply do not have many studies investigating this age-group (Biddle, 1993; Brown, 1982). This clearly needs to be rectified.

Recently, research on exercise and mental health has become a little easier to interpret with the publication of several meta-analytic reviews. However, these are all North American and rely on the North American literature. These reviews have investigated anxiety (Petruzzello, Landers, Hatfield, Kubitz, & Salazar, 1991), depression (North, McCullagh, & Tran, 1990), self-esteem in children (Gruber, 1986), and stress reactivity (Crews & Landers, 1987). In addition, McDonald &

Hodgdon (1991) have conducted meta-analyses of several areas of mental health in relation to aerobic fitness training, including anxiety, depression, mood, self-concept and personality. Meta-analysis is a technique of quantifying results from several similar studies by calculating an effect size (ES). This demonstrates the strength of the effect of exercise compared with no exercise or other interventions. An ES is represented in standard deviation units. In other words, an ES of 0.5 shows the experimental (exercise) group to be different from the control or other intervention group by one-half of a standard deviation on the measure in question. As a rough rule of thumb, ES's in the 0.2 to 0.3 range are considered low, ES's from 0.4 to 0.7, are considered moderate, and ES's of 0.8 and above are considered large.

All the meta-analyses conclude, in general terms, that exercise has a beneficial effect on mental health. Figure 3.1 shows the ES's of the five meta-analytic reviews cited here. Petruzzello et al. (1991), for example, found that the ES for exercise on

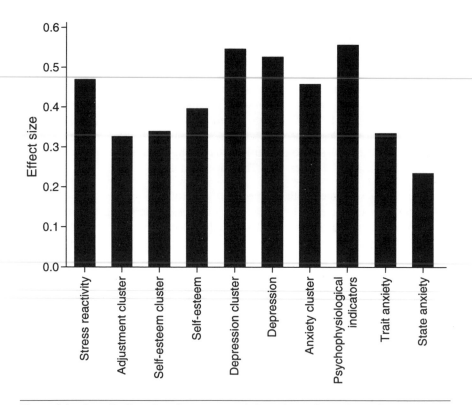

Figure 3.1 Overall effect sizes from meta-analytic reviews of exercise or fitness and psychological indices.

Note. Data on state anxiety, trait anxiety, and psychophysiological indicators from Petruzzello et al. (1991, p. 151), on depression from North et al. (1990, p. 389), on anxiety, self-esteem and adjustment clusters from McDonald and Hodgdon (1991, pp. 185-186), on self-esteem from Gruber (1986, p. 39), and on stress reactivity from Crews and Landers (1987, p. 119).

state anxiety was 0.24 whereas for trait anxiety it was 0.34. A larger ES was found, however, for psychophysiological indices of anxiety (0.56). These results were confirmed by McDonald and Hodgdon (1991) when they studied aerobic exercise and anxiety. They found the mean ES of various measures of anxiety to be 0.47.

North et al. (1990) calculated an overall ES for exercise on depression of 0.53. This was confirmed by McDonald and Hodgdon (1991) with their mean ES of different depression measures of 0.55.

Crews and Landers (1987) found an average ES of 0.48 for the effect of aerobic fitness on psychosocial reactivity to stress. Gruber's (1986) study of self-esteem and exercise in children reported an overall ES of 0.41. In their own meta-analysis, McDonald and Hodgdon (1991) found that aerobic exercise was beneficial across various self-esteem measures (mean ES = 0.35), as well as measures of personality and 'adjustment' (ES = 0.33). In short, Figure 3.1 gives a clear indication that the meta-analyses on exercise and mental health have shown positive results for exercise, although most of the ES's are in the moderate rather than the high range.

Effects of Exercise on Mood and Well-Being

The relationship between mood and exercise is but one aspect of the complex issue of well-being, and good experimental work is necessary to establish whether or not exercise is causally related to positive mood states. Cross-sectional data, such as those provided by ADNFS (1992), suggest either that those who perceive themselves to be in good health are more attracted to exercise or that exercise helps people feel better about themselves. European experimental research that tackles this question is sparse, but two examples will be described.

Does Exercise Promote Positive Mood?

Moses, Steptoe, Mathews, and Edwards (1989) designed an excellent study to establish the effects of three different 10-week exercise programmes on mental well-being in a group of 94 nonclinical subjects in England. The subjects were randomly assigned to either a high intensity aerobic programme (70-75% of maximum heart rate), a moderate intensity aerobic programme (60% of maximum heart rate), or a strengthening-stretching programme which served as an attention-placebo control. There was also a waiting list control group. All three exercise programmes were equated in frequency (one supervised and three home-based sessions) and duration (10 weeks). The analyses of changes in a variety of dependent measures made before and after the 10-week programmes and at a 3-month follow-up found that the greatest physiological gains were made by the high-intensity group, but the greatest psychological gain was made by the moderate intensity group. More specifically, the moderate intensity group showed increases in their perceptions of coping ability but the other two groups did not. In this study, mood was measured by the Profile of Mood States (POMS). The moderate intensity group showed decreases on one of the subscales of POMS (tension-anxiety), but the other groups did not show any change. This pattern of mood change is shown in Figure 3.2.

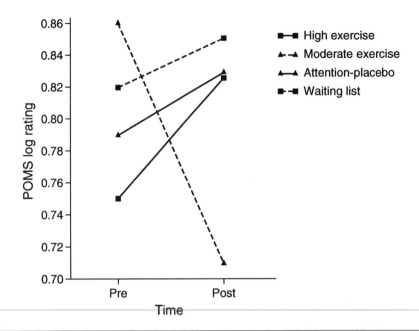

Figure 3.2   Changes in log-transformed POMS tension-anxiety ratings pre- to post-exercise.

Note. From 'The Effects of Exercise Training on Mental Well-Being in the Normal Population: A Controlled Trial' by J. Moses, A. Steptoe, A. Mathews, and S. Edwards, 1989, *Journal of Psychosomatic Research*, **33**, pp. 47-61. Copyright 1989 by Pergamon Press. Reprinted by permission.

Although these results indicate that exercise of moderate intensity caused positive mood changes, other psychological measures (the other five subscales of POMS, a measure of Type A behaviour and perceived self-efficacy) showed no change. This points to a problem which will be addressed later; can the psychological effects of exercise be properly measured? Other British research also suggests that the measurable psychological effect from exercise is limited.

   Mutrie et al. (1991) offered a 12-week supervised exercise programme, with a 6-month follow-up, to a random selection of the population who lived near an exercise facility in Scotland. Eighty-three people, who previously had been sedentary, agreed to undertake the exercise programme that was based in the local facility. The physiological and psychological responses of this group were compared to those of a control group of 60 people who intended to remain sedentary over the same period of time. Both groups were identical on all physiological and psychological measures at the start of the programme. The psychological measures included self-motivation, locus of control and the POMS questionnaire. Among females in this study there were no significant changes over time in any of the psychological measures. Among males, only two of the possible six subscales of the POMS questionnaire showed statistically significant changes. The data from the energetic-tired subscale showed a significant interaction between groups and time such that the exercisers increased their perception of energy more than the controls from baseline to 12 weeks, but with no further change at 6-month follow-up. This pattern is shown in Figure 3.3. The data from the confident-unsure subscale showed a significant main effect for time, with both groups of males increasing perception of confidence over time. This pattern is shown in Figure 3.4.

Considering the number of psychological variables measured, it is surprising that only males showed any positive change and, given that in one case both the groups improved, it is likely that the effect was related to involvement in the study rather than exercise per se.

It may be concluded that there is a limited amount of experimental research on the effects of exercise on mood and well-being, although nonexperimental research

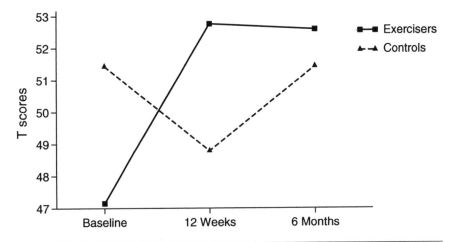

Figure 3.3 Interaction between exercise group, control group and time for males on POMS scores of energetic-tired.
Note. Data from N. Mutrie et al. (1991, pp. 446-447).

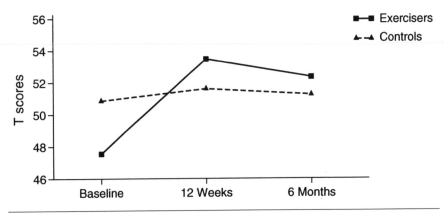

Figure 3.4 Increases in confidence POMS subscale scores reported by male exercisers and control subjects.
Note. Data from N. Mutrie et al. (1991, pp. 446-447).

designs have shown positive effects. What little evidence there is indicates that exercise produces positive change in a very limited range of measures. One reason for such meagre results could be that exercise studies attract people who are already psychologically very healthy and thus have little room for improvement in any of the standard measures. For example, in the population attracted to Mutrie et al.'s (1991) study, all baseline scores on POMS were within one-half of a standard deviation from the standardised mean. Yet subjectively exercisers report feeling better with exercise (Biddle & Mutrie, 1991). Perhaps regular exercisers use their exercise to help them cope with the daily and weekly fluctuations in mood that we all experience, causing the net result from regular activity to be positive mood states.

The literature on exercise deprivation lends some support to this idea. Researchers have asked regular exercisers to stop exercise for a period of days (Tooman cited in Harris, 1987), weeks (Morris, Steinberg, Sykes, & Salmon, 1988) or months (Baekeland, 1970) and have found that deprivation caused a 'feel worse' effect which disappeared once exercise was reinstated.

Further evidence for the idea that exercise helps people maintain a constant positive mood state comes from Germany. Abele and Brehm (1993) have made a useful distinction between physical activities that create an *equilibration* effect on mood and well-being, (that is, these activities return mood to a median level and provide a relaxation function), and activities that create a *disequilibration* effect, (that is, create short-term disturbance and recovery, sometimes seen in people's 'quest for excitement'). These authors suggest that exercise (noncompetitive fitness activities) can have an equilibration effect, while competitive sports activities have a disequilibration effect. Abele and Brehm (1993) present evidence to support their theoretical position from many studies that have not appeared in the English language psychology literature. Their work suggests that alternative measurements of mood must be made and that we must not confine ourselves to exercise studies in assessing the psychological effects of activity (see 'How Measurement Methods Affect Research Results'). Literature on the mood and mental health effects from competitive sport, for example, apart from studies on anxiety, is sparse.

Another way of studying the effect of exercise on mood is to focus on the acute effects of one exercise session rather than the chronic, longer-term, effects of a programme of exercise. Steptoe and Bolton (1988) assigned 40 women to either a high-level exercise bout (15 minutes at 100 watts on a cycle ergometer) or a low-level exercise bout (15 minutes at 25 watts). Mood was assessed by an adapted version of POMS before, during and after the bout of exercise. The purpose of the study—to examine mood responses to two exercise intensities—was disguised. Consideration was given to possible differential responses of those who were fitter compared to those who were less fit; these two fitness groupings were established by making a median split of the whole group's estimated $\dot{V}O_2max$ scores. However, the only significant difference in responses between the two fitness groupings was that the fitter group reported greater mental vigour and exhilaration than the less fit after the high-intensity exercise.

The results indicated that for both fitness groups, tension-anxiety and mental fatigue increased immediately after high-intensity exercise and then declined during the rest of the recovery period. These results are illustrated in Figure 3.5.

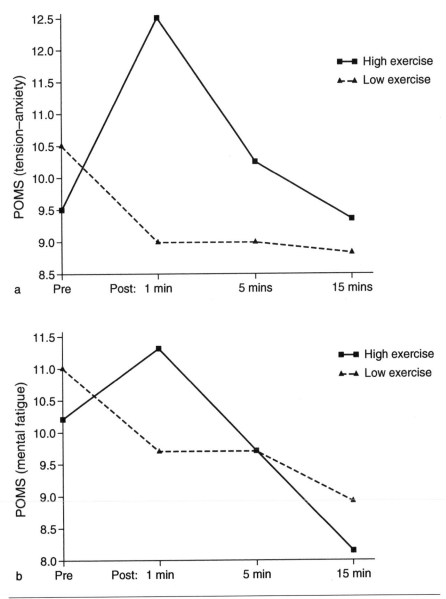

Figure 3.5   (a) Tension-anxiety and (b) mental fatigue score changes in women before exercise to three time periods postexercise.
Note. From 'The Short-Term Influence of High and Low Intensity Physical Exercise on Mood' by A. Steptoe and J. Bolton, 1988, *Psychology and Health*, **2**, pp. 91-106. Copyright 1988 by Harwood Academic Publishers. Reprinted by permission.

How are these results of research on acute effects of exercise linked to the effects of a programme of exercise over a period of time? Several problems exist in trying to interpret the literature. First, are the longer-term mood effects related at all to the acute effects? If a person experiences several positive responses to consecutive bouts of exercise (over a period of days or weeks), will these accumulate into a positive mood change over that period of time? Second, is the intensity of exercise important? Although Steptoe and Bolton (1988) reported increases in two negative mood states immediately after high-intensity exercise, the mood states had returned to levels similar to those associated with the low-intensity exercise after 15 minutes of recovery time. It would also seem that increases in positive mood from high-intensity exercise are available only to those with higher fitness levels. Clearly, further studies on acute effects of exercise on different fitness categories are needed to clarify this complex picture.

The third problem is in the description of exercise intensities. In the studies involving an exercise programme of several weeks duration, intensity is usually described in a relative way, such as a percentage of a subject's maximum heart rate or maximum capacity. However, in Steptoe and Bolton's (1988) acute exercise study, despite excellent design features in other respects, intensity is described in terms of an absolute amount of work. Cycling at 25 watts, even for the lower fitness group in the study, was perceived to be between 'very light' and 'fairly light' on the Borg scale of perceived exertion (Borg & Noble, 1974). This level of exertion can therefore be referred to correctly as low. On the other hand, the higher intensity of exercise elicited perception of exertion ratings of no greater than 14.1, which is within the bandwidth of 12 to 15 recommended by Birk and Birk (1987) to coincide with an intensity sufficient to produce an aerobic training effect (American College of Sports Medicine, 1990) while avoiding the risks of high-intensity work. Thus the higher-intensity workload in Steptoe and Bolton's study (1988) appears only to equate what would be described in relative terms as moderately intense exercise. These problems make it very difficult to draw overall conclusions regarding the acute and chronic effects of exercise in relation to intensity. Thus mood changes after each bout of exercise may play a very small part in explaining the more beneficial psychological outcomes noted by Moses et al. (1989) for a programme of exercise conducted at moderate intensity compared to one of high intensity.

Given the difficulties of drawing general conclusions from research on acute and chronic exercise, it is surprising that one of the recent meta-analytic reviews discussed earlier (McDonald & Hodgdon, 1991) did not differentiate between these two time frames. This aspect of the effects of exercise on mood must be considered in future meta-analyses, and European results must also be considered. These were ignored by McDonald and Hodgdon (1991).

The Relationship Between Exercise and Self-Esteem

Those promoting participation in exercise and sport often claim it will enhance self-esteem. Indeed, this is a common rationale for the teaching of physical education to children (see Fox, 1991, 1992). Sonstroem (1984), in a review of the effects of exercise on self-esteem, concluded that

> the consistently positive results . . . suggest a basis for the belief in the salutary effects of physical training programs. It is concluded that exercise *programs* are associated with significant increases in the self-esteem *scores* of participants. These score increases are particularly pronounced in subjects initially low in self-esteem. . . . These conclusions refer to exercise programs rather than fitness increases, and to increases in self-esteem scores rather than in self-esteem per se. (p. 138)

Until recently, inadequate measurement of self-esteem was a factor preventing substantial progress being made in understanding the potential links between exercise and self-esteem. Often researchers have employed a global measure of self-esteem rather than a multidimensional measure. It has been shown that self-esteem is a global construct underpinned by a multidimensional and hierarchical structure. Global self-esteem is composed of differentiated perceptions of the self, such as physical, social and academic self-perceptions. These in turn are underpinned by increasingly transient perceptions of worth and competence, such as sport ability or physical appearance for the physical subdomain of global self-esteem (see Fox, 1992; Fox & Corbin, 1989; Shavelson, Hubner, & Stanton, 1976).

Such theoretical advances are only now being met with concurrent advances in psychometric assessment. For example, Fox & Corbin (1989) have developed the Physical Self-Perception Profile (PSPP). This is a measure of physical self-worth and four subdomains of this construct: sport competence, body attractiveness, perceived strength and physical condition. These factors were derived initially from research on an American student population but some evidence for cross-cultural validity has been demonstrated with British subjects (Page, Ashford, Fox, & Biddle, 1993). However, the measurement of these constructs with British children has been more problematic (Biddle et al., 1993).

The PSPP should make it possible to investigate how exercise might affect different aspects of self-perceptions and how these might impact self-esteem. For example, participation in exercise may increase positive feelings about physical condition which may, in turn, affect physical self-worth and self-esteem. These relationships are more likely if the domain in question is seen to be important (see Fox, 1992).

Sonstroem, Harlow, Gemma, and Osborne (1991) have tested a model of these proposed relationships between exercise and self-esteem. They found that changes in physical self-efficacy were related to self-esteem, but through the intervening variable of perceived physical competence. However, they present this model 'as an interim research paradigm useful for guiding investigations that subsequently may expand or alter the model' (Sonstroem et al., 1991, p. 361).

The preceding discussion indicates that the area of self-esteem has been perceived as important by researchers and practitioners. Contemporary self-esteem theory, and associated advances in measurement technology, point to a promising future in furthering our understanding of the relationship between exercise and self-esteem.

How Measurement Methods Affect Research Results

An important issue for researchers is how to measure the psychological changes that may be associated with exercise. McDonald and Hodgdon (1991) reported that POMS and the Multiple Affect Adjective Check List (MAACL) were the two most common scales used in exercise studies. In British studies two versions of the POMS have been used. Moses et al. (1989) used the unipolar version (McNair, Lorr, & Droppleman, 1971), which has six mood scales of tension-anxiety, depression-dejection, anger-hostility, vigour-activity, fatigue-inertia and confusion-bewilderment. Five of these scales are negative mood states, the sixth (vigour-activity) being positive. The 'iceberg profile' is a particular configuration of POMS scores first described by Morgan (1980) as comprising lower than average scores on the five negative subscales and higher than average scores on the positive subscale. Some studies (Gondola & Tuckman, 1982; Berger & Owen, 1983) have supported the existence of an iceberg profile for recreational exercisers. However, the authors of the POMS scale were aware of the problem of a 'floor effect' on the negative scales when used with nonclinical populations. If the population in question produced low scores on the negative scales (for example, an absence of depression), then even if they felt better at the retest they could not score any lower. Moses et al. (1989) used log transformations of the raw POMS scores to overcome this effect.

A new bipolar version of POMS has now been introduced (Lorr & McNair, 1984) in which each scale has both a positive and negative pole. The subscales in the bipolar version are energetic-tired, elation-depression, confident-unsure, composed-anxious, agreeable-hostile and clearheaded-confused. Raw scores are transformed to standardised T-scores (mean of 50 and standard deviation of 10; see Lorr & McNair, 1984). Considerable numbers of subjects are required to produce sufficient statistical power to detect changes of half a standard deviation (five T-score points), and the practical significance of such a change is a matter of judgement. In Mutrie and Kelly's (1992) results none of the changes over time resulted in mean scores above 55 on any of the subscales. Thus the bipolar version of POMS may not be the most suitable or sensitive instrument for exercise studies.

Abele and Brehm (1986) have developed a scale, currently only available in German, which measures both evaluative (positive and negative) aspects of mood in conjunction with levels of activation. This scale is required to pursue the idea that different types of activity have different psychological effects (Abele & Brehm, 1993). Their mood inventory (BFS; Befindlichkeitsskalen) consists of the two subscales of evaluation and activation such that scores yield four possible locations, as shown in Figure 3.6.

In the English language, Choi (1992) has developed a scale that has both negative and positive elements that are independent, thus allowing respondents to become, for example, lower in the negative scores while maintaining their positive scores. This scale may prove to be useful in future exercise studies once validity and reliability have been established. Further measures that are sensitive to the psychological benefits reported by exercisers must be designed in order to investigate this issue in nonclinical populations.

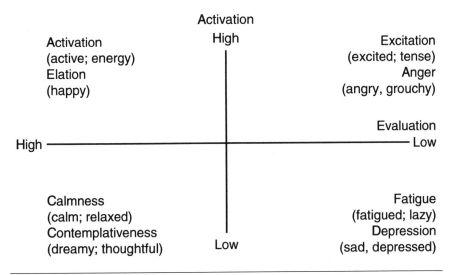

Figure 3.6 Representation of Befindlichkeitsskalen (mood scale) proposed by Abele and Brehm (1993).

Effects of Exercise on Cognitive Functioning

Subjective reports from runners (Mutrie & Knill-Jones, 1986) suggest that over half of those questioned perceived that after running they could think more clearly. This would suggest that running at least, and maybe other forms of activity, can have a positive effect on some form of cognitive functioning. The term cognitive functioning embraces a wide variety of tasks ranging from simple reaction time to complex information processing. Little experimental evidence is available regarding the relationship between different types of cognitive functioning and exercise (in all of its many forms) and thus firm conclusions are not possible at this stage.

Claims that exercise helps children perform better academically have been used in support of daily physical education programmes (see Dwyer, Coonan, Leitch, Hetzel, & Baghurst, 1983; Pollatschek & O'Hagan, 1989). However, the literature on physical activity and cognitive development in children is strongest in the early, preschool years. Research on perceptual-motor development has suggested that the early development of psychomotor function and neuromuscular control could assist academic learning in young children. An increase in cerebral blood flow after physical activity has been documented, and this could assist cognitive functioning. Similarly, activity increases blood flow in the prefrontal somatosensory and primary motor cortices of the brain (see Williams, 1986). However, despite the plausibility of these mechanisms, the studies of cognitive change in children exposed to physical activity interventions have been poorly controlled and open to severe methodological criticism.

Tomporowski and Ellis (1986) reviewed literature on the effects of exercise on cognitive processing and concluded that the evidence was conflicting. The explanation for this seems to lie in the experimental designs used. There is a need for studies to rule out the effects of different fitness levels (as opposed to the effects of exercise) by having subjects work at relative rather than absolute work loads, and it may be that differing intensities and duration of exercise have different effects. In addition, studies are needed to separate two distinct issues: the effect on cognition during exercise and the postexercise effect. Finally, the tests used to measure cognitive functioning must be free from influences of prior experience and learning.

One recent attempt to overcome these methodological deficiencies (Mutrie & Thin, 1992) used a computer task, designed to measure recovery from anaesthesia, as a measure of cognitive functioning. The task involved using a computer 'mouse' to locate targets on a computer screen. Performance was measured by averaging the time the subject took to move the mouse onto each target in 100 trials. Fourteen subjects first had to learn the task, which they performed whilst seated on a cycle ergometer. At another testing session they exercised at 30%, 50% and 70% of their estimated $\dot{V}O_2$max in a randomised order for 7 minutes at each intensity and with rest periods in between. The cognitive task was undertaken towards the end of each exercise bout and again after completing all three intensities. Results showed no decrement in cognitive performance at any of the intensities when compared to baseline results. However, during the postexercise recovery period there was a significant improvement in cognitive performance. Figure 3.7 illustrates these results. These findings lend experimental support to other reports showing that exercise produces cognitive improvements. For example, in a study investigating the effects of a 10.5-mile (16.9km) treadmill run on mood and cognitive functioning, Jones

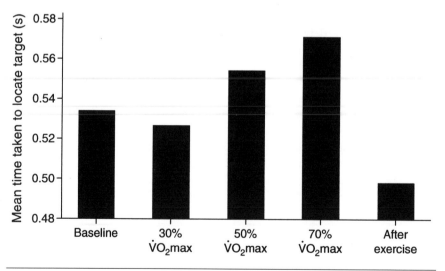

Figure 3.7 Cognitive performance during and after exercise.
Note. Data from Mutrie and Thin (1992, pp. 617-618).

and Cale (1989) found improvements in digit-span performance after the run. However, there are obviously many parameters still to be studied. For example, the state of fatigue of the subject and the motivation to continue performing the task at the best level possible must be investigated further.

As with many areas of exercise psychology, research on cognitive functioning is conducted in a largely atheoretical framework. This reflects the evolutionary stage of the field as it is always necessary to establish whether effects are present before attempting to explain them. However, the critical question of why exercise alters cognitive function remains unanswered. Tomporowski and Ellis (1986) suggested that research to date had focussed on two underlying theories to study the effects of exercise. The first of these is the theory that arousal state (which is influenced by exercise) will affect cognitive performance. In Britain, the work of Jones and Hardy (1989) has furthered our understanding of the arousal-performance relationship and suggests the need for researchers to move beyond the unidimensional model of the inverted-U hypothesis.

The second theoretical model described by Tomporowski and Ellis (1986) suggests that models of attentional processing can supply a framework for understanding the effects of exercise on cognitive functioning. It is certainly true that the experimental paradigm can be seen as an attentional task; the exercise is one task (maintaining pedal frequency, for example) and the cognitive task is another attentional demand. This setup allows for further secondary tasks to be introduced to allow investigation of information processing capabilities during exercise.

These are not the only theoretical frameworks which may be applied to this area, however. The physiological and hormonal effects of exercise can also provide explanations of how exercise affects cognitive performance and must be investigated in future studies.

Gender Differences in Research Data

There was concern that early studies in the area of exercise and mental health had omitted women as subjects (Mutrie, 1987). However, more recent work has included both males and females, and meta-analytic studies support similar (but not identical) effects of exercise on psychological outcomes for males and females (McDonald & Hodgdon, 1991). Conversely, there is some evidence that there may be more psychological benefit from physical activity for women compared to men (Stephens, 1988), although North et al.'s (1990) meta-analysis on exercise and depression contradicts this by showing a slightly more favourable effect for men.

There is still much discussion (Fazey & Ballington, 1992) and concern about the number of women participating in physical activities (ADNFS, 1992), but the issues concerning psychological effects now relate to specific effects of aspects of life experienced by women and not men (e.g., menstruation, the climacteric, pregnancy) and feminist perspectives.

The feminist perspective suggests researchers must be aware that what we have considered to be a 'positive outcome' is probably more closely associated with what we consider to be psychologically healthy for men (Talbot, 1990). The time has come for defining a positive outcome from a female perspective. The feminist perspective also suggests that women can achieve a sense of personal physical and mental empowerment through involvement in sport and exercise (Hall, 1990). This empowerment can be achieved via recognising physical potentials and learning to enjoy movement even when one's body shape is unlike the shape portrayed by the media as 'ideal' or 'desirable' (Packer, 1989).

In addition to the feminist perspective, there are a number of unique issues in women's lives that have become topics in the literature of the exercise sciences. For example, Choi (1992) has shown a positive association between high levels of exercise (at least three times per week) and mood over the course of a menstrual cycle. Her results, which are illustrated in Figure 3.8, show that the high-level exercisers had more positive moods and fewer negative moods than low-level exercisers (exercising less than three times per week), or sedentary women, at three phases of the menstrual cycle.

Cox (1992) has found that, among women attending a hospital menopause clinic, those who exercised regularly (equivalent to 20 minutes three times per week) had significantly higher levels of physical self-worth, an important element in self-esteem (Fox & Corbin, 1989), than women who were sedentary. Similarly, Wallace, Boyer, Dan, and Holm (1986) found that, among women at least 27 weeks pregnant, those who exercised regularly had higher levels of self-esteem than those who did not; in addition, the regular exercisers reported fewer discomforts at each trimester of pregnancy than the non-exercisers.

These associations between more positive psychological states in exercisers during the menstrual cycle, menopause and pregnancy deserve further research attention. The next generation of research must address the issue of whether or not exercise is causally related to these positive states by employing prospective research designs.

Age Differences in Research Data

The benefits of physical activity for older adults have only received attention in the literature during the past decade (Bassey, 1985; Dallosso et al., 1988). A recent English survey (ADNFS, 1992) concluded that regular physical activity could marginalise, or assist in offsetting, the physiological deterioration associated with aging, and a Finnish study suggested that premature mortality may be reduced through physical activity taken in middle age and beyond (Pekkanen et al., 1987). Although recent meta-analytic reviews show that older adults can benefit psychologically as well as younger people, very little information exists on the psychological implications of increased physical activity of older adults (see Netz, Tenenbaum, & Sagiv, 1988). However, work by McMurdo and Burnett (1992), including a randomised control trial on older adults in Scotland, alludes to improvements in life satisfaction and increased opportunities for socialising as important outcomes of exercise participation. Morgan, Dallosso, Bassey, and Fentem (1988) have suggested a positive relationship between customary physical activity (e.g., gardening, shopping, walking, stair-climbing) and psychological well-being, especially for men. The promotion of physical activity for older age-groups, therefore, should not be limited to encouraging

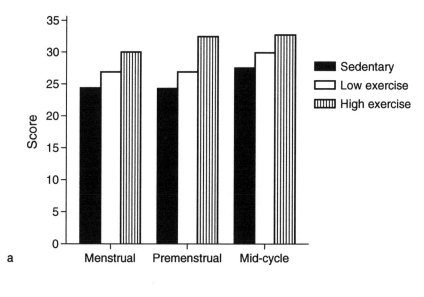

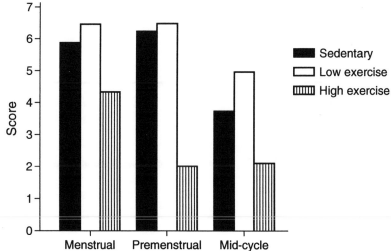

Figure 3.8   (a) Positive and (b) negative affect scores reported by exercisers and sedentary women at three different phases of the menstrual cycle.

Note. From 'The Psychological Benefits of Physical Exercise: Implications for Women and the Menstrual Cycle' by P.Y.L. Choi, 1992, *Journal of Reproductive and Infant Psychology*, **10**, p. 113. Copyright 1992 by Society for Reproductive and Infant Psychology. Reprinted by permission.

people to take part in classes and recognised formal activities, but must include the promotion of 'keeping active' in everyday activities. Psychological outcomes of increased physical activity, especially as they relate to a sense of self-worth, independence and overall well-being, are very important for older age-groups, which face major changes in lifestyle (e.g., retirement or bereavement), and future research will surely address these issues.

Exercise Dependence

So far the discussion has centred on the potential psychological benefits of exercise. However, recent evidence has suggested that some people can approach exercise in what many would see as an unhealthy way. This refers to a dependence on or addiction to exercise.

The term *exercise dependence* was first used by Veale (1987) to describe a state in which exercise has become a compulsive behaviour. Previous literature describing this phenomenon was hampered by lack of an agreed definition. Veale (1987) provided a set of diagnostic criteria to help researchers and clinicians describe this kind of exercise behaviour in a consistent manner. In addition, he distinguished between primary exercise dependence and exercise dependence that is secondary to eating disorders. Exercise dependence is characterised by a frequency of at least one exercise session per day, a stereotypical daily or weekly pattern of exercise, recognition of exercise being compulsive and of withdrawal symptoms if there is an interruption to the normal routine, and reinstatement of the normal pattern within one or two days of a stoppage. The problems that exercise dependence can create range from tiredness and chronic injury to relationship problems and eating disorders (Veale & Le Fevre, 1988).

Exercise scientists must be aware of the potential harm that exercise dependence can cause. The incidence of exercise dependence in the population of exercisers is unknown; thus the significance of the problem in terms of public health is also unknown. Since chronic injury plagues those who are dependent on exercise, sports injury clinic staff should be aware of the criteria for exercise dependence and should know how to help those who could harm themselves, either physiologically or psychologically, because of their compulsive exercise behaviour.

Conclusion

Despite anecdotal evidence the research community has found it difficult to rule out substantial methodological problems in research on positive mental benefits from exercise involvement. Nevertheless, in recent years the weight of evidence has steadily accumulated and led to general conclusions concerning the potential psychological benefits of exercise (see Morgan & Goldston, 1987). On balance one is able to support the psychologically therapeutic effects of exercise, but more work is needed to refine the exact nature of these effects.

Acknowledgment

Thanks are extended to Carol Graybeale and Alistair Thin for assistance with the sections concerning gender-related issues and cognition respectively.

References

Abele, A., & Brehm, W. (1986). Zur Konzeptualisierung und Messung von Befindlichkeit: Die Entwicklung der Befindlichkeitsskalen (BFS). *Diagnostica*, **32**, 209-288.

Abele, A., & Brehm, W. (1993). Mood effects of exercise versus sports games: Findings and implications for well-being and health. In S. Maes, H. Leventhal, & M. Johnston (Eds.), *International review of health psychology* (Vol. 2, pp. 53-80). Chichester, England: Wiley.

Allied Dunbar National Fitness Survey. (1992). *Main findings*. London: Sports Council and Health Education Authority.

American College of Sports Medicine. (1990). The recommended quantity and quality of exercise for developing and maintaining fitness in healthy adults. *Medicine and Science in Sports and Exercise*, **22**, 265-274.

Baekeland, F. (1970). Exercise deprivation. *Archives of General Psychiatry*, **22**, 365-369.

Bassey, E.J. (1985). Benefits of exercise in the elderly. In B. Isaacs (Ed.), *Recent advances in geriatric medicine* (pp. 91-112). London: Churchill Livingstone.

Berger, B.G., & Owen, D.R. (1983). Mood alterations with swimming: Swimmers really do "feel better." *Psychosomatic Medicine*, **45**, 425-433.

Biddle, S.J.H. (1992a). Exercise psychology. *Sport Science Review*, **1**(2), 79-92.

Biddle, S.J.H. (1992b). Sport and exercise motivation: A short review of antecedent factors and psychological outcomes of participation. *Physical Education Review*, **15**, 98-110.

Biddle, S.J.H. (1993). Exercise, children and mental health. *International Journal of Sport Psychology*, **24**, 200-216.

Biddle, S.J.H., & Mutrie, N. (1991). *Psychology of physical activity and exercise: A health-related perspective*. London: Springer-Verlag.

Biddle, S.J.H., Page, A., Ashford, B., Jennings, D., Brooke, R., & Fox, K.R. (1993). Assessment of children's physical self-perceptions. *International Journal of Adolescence and Youth*, **4**, 93-109.

Birk, T.J., & Birk, C.A. (1987). Use of ratings of perceived exertion for exercise prescription. *Sports Medicine*, **4**, 1-8.

Borg, G.A., & Noble, B.J. (1974). Perceived exertion. *Exercise and Sport Sciences Reviews*, **2**, 131-153.

Bouchard, C., Shephard, R.J., Stephens, T., Sutton, J.R., & McPherson, B. (Eds.) (1990). *Exercise, fitness, and health: A consensus of current knowledge*. Champaign, IL: Human Kinetics.

Brown, R.S. (1982). Exercise and mental health in the pediatric population. *Clinics in Sports Medicine*, **1**, 515-527.

Chamove, A.S. (1988). Exercise effects in psychiatric populations: A review. In *Sport, Health, Psychology and Exercise Symposium proceedings* (pp. 8-48). London: Sports Council and Health Education Authority.

Choi, P.Y.L. (1992). The psychological benefits of physical exercise: Implications for women and the menstrual cycle. *Journal of Reproductive and Infant Psychology*, **10**, 111-115.

Cox, K.J.S. (1992). *Exercise, physical self-perception and climacteric symptoms in women.* Unpublished master's thesis, University of Glasgow, Scotland.

Crews, D.J., & Landers, D.M. (1987). A meta-analytic review of aerobic fitness and reactivity to psychosocial stressors. *Medicine and Science in Sports and Exercise*, 19(Suppl. 5), S114-S120.

Dallosso, H.M., Morgan, K., Bassey, E.J., Ebrahim, S.B.J., Fentem, P.H., & Arie, T.H.D. (1988). Levels of customary physical activity among the old and the very old living at home. *Journal of Epidemiology and Community Health*, **42**, 121-127.

Department of Health. (1992). *The health of the nation.* London: Her Majesty's Stationery Office.

Dwyer, T., Coonan, W.E., Leitch, D.R., Hetzel, B.S., & Baghurst, R.A. (1983). An investigation of the effects of daily physical activity on the health of primary school students in South Australia. *International Journal of Epidemiology*, **12**, 308-313.

Fazey, D., & Ballington, N. (1992). Adult female participation in physical activity, perception of competence and attitude towards the participation motives of other women. *Physical Education Review*, **15**(1), 53-60.

Fox, K.R. (1991). Physical education and its contribution to health and well-being. In N. Armstrong & A.C. Sparkes (Eds.), *Issues in physical education* (pp. 123-138). London: Cassell.

Fox, K.R. (1992). Physical education and the development of self-esteem in children. In N. Armstrong (Ed.), *New directions in physical education: Vol. II. Towards a national curriculum* (pp. 33-54). Champaign, IL: Human Kinetics.

Fox, K.R., & Corbin, C.B. (1989). The Physical Self-Perception Profile: Development and preliminary validation. *Journal of Sport and Exercise Psychology*, **11**, 408-430.

Gondola, J.C., & Tuckman, B.W. (1982). Psychological mood states in "average" marathon runners. *Perceptual and Motor Skills*, **55**, 1295-1300.

Gruber, J.J. (1986). Physical activity and self-esteem development in children: A meta-analysis. In G. Stull & H. Eckert (Eds.), *Effects of physical activity on children* (pp. 30-48). Champaign, IL: Human Kinetics.

Hall, M.A. (1990). How should we theorize gender in the context of sport? In M. Messner & D. Sabo (Eds.), *Sport, men, and the gender order* (pp. 223-240). Champaign, IL: Human Kinetics.

Harris, D.V. (1987). Comparative effectiveness of running therapy and psychotherapy. In W.P. Morgan & S.E. Goldston (Eds.), *Exercise and mental health* (pp. 123-130). Washington, DC: Hemisphere.

International Society of Sport Psychology. (1992). Physical activity and psychological benefits: A position statement. *Sport Psychologist*, **6**, 199-203.

Jones, J.G., & Cale, A. (1989). Changes in mood and cognitive functioning during long distance running—an exploratory investigation. *Physical Education Review*, **12**, 78-83.

Jones, J.G., & Hardy, L. (1989). Stress and cognitive functioning in sport. *Journal of Sports Sciences*, **7**, 41-63.

Lorr, M., & McNair, D.M. (1984). *Profile of Mood State manual bi-polar form.* San Diego: Educational and Industrial Testing Services.

McDonald, D.G., & Hodgdon, J.A. (1991). *Psychological effects of aerobic fitness training: Research and theory.* New York: Springer-Verlag.

McMurdo, M.E.T. (1992). Exercise and the elderly. *Scottish Medicine*, **11**(6), 6-7.

McMurdo, M.E.T., & Burnett, L.A. (1992). A randomised controlled trial of exercise in the elderly. *Gerontology*, **38**, 292-298.

McNair, D.M., Lorr, M., & Droppleman, L.F. (1971). *Manual for the Profile of Mood States.* San Diego: Educational and Industrial Testing Service.

Morgan, K., Dallosso, H., Bassey, E., & Fentem, P. (1988). Customary physical activity and psychological well-being among elderly people living at home. In *Sport, Health, Psychology, and Exercise Symposium proceedings* (pp. 135-146). London: Sports Council and Health Education Authority.

Morgan, W.P. (1980). Test of champions: The iceberg profile. *Psychology Today,* **14,** 92-99, 101, 108.

Morgan, W.P., & Goldston, S.E. (Eds.) (1987) *Exercise and mental health.* Washington, DC: Hemisphere.

Morris, M., Steinberg, H., Sykes, E., & Salmon, P. (1988). Temporary deprivation from running produces "withdrawal" syndrome. In *Sport, Health, Psychology and Exercise Symposium proceedings* (pp. 167-171). London: Sports Council and Health Education Authority.

Moses, J., Steptoe, A., Mathews, A., & Edwards, S. (1989). The effects of exercise training on mental well-being in the normal population: A controlled trial. *Journal of Psychosomatic Research,* **33,** 47-61.

Mutrie, N. (1987). The psychological effects of exercise for women. In D. McLeod, R. Maughan, M. Nimmo, T. Reilly, & C. Williams (Eds.), *Exercise benefits, limitations and adaptations* (pp. 270-288). London: Spon.

Mutrie, N., & Kelly, M.P. (1992). A population approach to promoting health via exercise. *Journal of Sports Sciences,* **10,** 554-555. (Abstract)

Mutrie, N., Kelly, M.P., Hughes, A.M., Gilmour, H., Murray, K., Busby, A., Byrne, M., & MacNaughton, S. (1991). Characteristics of intending exercisers: Baseline results from a health promotion project. *Journal of Sports Sciences,* **9**(4), 446-447. (Abstract)

Mutrie, N., & Knill-Jones, R. (1986). Psychological effects of running: 1984 survey of the Glasgow people's marathon. In J.A. Macgregor & J.A. Moncur (Eds.), *Sport and medicine* (pp. 186-190). London: Spon.

Mutrie, N., & Thin, A. (1992). An assessment of the effects of exercise on cognitive functioning. *Journal of Sports Sciences,* **10,** 617-618. (Abstract)

Netz, Y., Tenenbaum, G., & Sagiv, M. (1988). Pattern of psychological fitness as related to pattern of physical fitness among older adults. *Perceptual and Motor Skills,* **67,** 647-655.

North, T.C., McCullagh, P., & Tran, Z.V. (1990). Effect of exercise on depression. *Exercise and Sport Sciences Reviews,* **18,** 379-415.

Packer, J. (1989). The role of stigmatization in fat people's avoidance of physical exercise. *Women and Therapy,* **8**(3), 49-63.

Page, A., Ashford, B., Fox, K.R., & Biddle, S.J.H. (1993). Evidence of cross-cultural validity for the Physical Self-Perception Profile. *Personality and Individual Differences,* **14,** 585-590.

Pekkanen, J., Marti, B., Nissinen, A., Tuomilehto, J., Punsar, S., & Karvonen, M.J. (1987). Reduction in premature mortality by high physical activity: A twenty year follow-up of middle-aged Finnish men. *Lancet,* **1,** 1473-1477.

Petruzzello, S.J., Landers, D.M., Hatfield, B.D., Kubitz, K.A., & Salazar, W. (1991). A meta-analysis on the anxiety-reducing effects of acute and chronic exercise: Outcomes and mechanisms. *Sports Medicine,* **11,** 143-182.

Pollatschek, J.L., & O'Hagan, F.J. (1989). An investigation of the psycho-physical influences of a quality daily physical education programme. *Health Education Research: Theory and Practice,* **4,** 341-350.

Ryan, A.J. (1984). Exercise and health: Lessons from the past. In H.M. Eckert & H.J. Montoye (Eds.), *Exercise and Health*. Champaign, IL: Human Kinetics and the American Academy of Physical Education.

Shavelson, R.J., Hubner, J.J., & Stanton, G.C. (1976). Self-concept: Validation of construct interpretations. *Review of Educational Research*, **46**, 407-441.

Sonstroem, R.J. (1984). Exercise and self-esteem. *Exercise and Sport Sciences Reviews*, **12**, 123-155.

Sonstroem, R.J., Harlow, L.L., Gemma, L.M., & Osborne, S. (1991). Test of structural relationships within a proposed exercise and self-esteem model. *Journal of Personality Assessment*, **56**, 348-362.

Stephens, T. (1988). Physical activity and mental health in the United States and Canada: Evidence from four population studies. *Preventive Medicine*, **17**, 35-47.

Steptoe, A., & Bolton, J. (1988). The short-term influence of high and low intensity physical exercise on mood. *Psychology and Health*, **2**, 91-106.

Talbot, M. (1990). Gender, sports sociology and sports science. In F. Kew (Ed.), *Social scientific perspectives on sport* (BASS Monograph No. 2). Leeds: British Association of Sports Sciences/National Coaching Foundation.

Tomporowski, P.D., & Ellis, N.R. (1986). The effects of exercise on cognitive processes: A review. *Psychological Bulletin*, **99**(3), 338-346.

Veale, D.M.W. (1987). Exercise dependence. *British Journal of Addiction*, **82**, 735-740.

Veale, D.M.W., & Le Fevre, K. (1988). A survey of exercise dependence. In *Sport, Health, Psychology and Exercise Symposium proceedings* (pp. 112-115). London: Sports Council and Health Education Authority.

Wallace, A.M., Boyer, D.B., Dan, A., & Holm, K. (1986). Aerobic exercise, maternal self-esteem and physical discomforts during pregnancy. *Journal of Nurse-Midwifery*, **31**(6), 255-262.

Williams, H.G. (1986). The development of sensory-motor function in young children. In V. Seefeldt (Ed.), *Physical activity and well-being* (pp. 105-122). Reston, VA: American Alliance for Health, Physical Education, Recreation and Dance.

4

CHAPTER

The Effects of Exercise on Mental Health in Clinical Populations

Egil W. Martinsen

NORWAY

Few exercise intervention studies have been performed on psychiatric clinical populations, and only a minority of these reach a satisfactory scientific level. This contrasts with the relatively large number of studies on 'free-living' populations. Psychiatry has paid little attention to exercise. This may reflect the mind-body dualism that has dominated thinking in psychiatry for many years.

Most of the research in this area has been performed in North America. This chapter reviews the research performed in Europe, with an emphasis on Norwegian studies. The focus is on clinical populations—patients meeting the diagnostic criteria for one or more psychiatric disorders, or alternatively subjects having a score above a threshold level on a psychiatric symptom index.

The majority of studies have been performed on patients with nonpsychotic mental disorders, most commonly mild to moderate forms of unipolar depression and anxiety disorders. These disorders are common, and the number of patients greatly exceeds the capacity for professional treatment. Standard forms of treatment are not always effective, and the need for alternative treatment strategies therefore is obvious.

Measurement Techniques Used in Clinical Settings

A series of instruments has been developed to assess the various aspects of mental disorders—symptoms, cognitions, behaviour and level of function—and these are in wide use in clinical studies. Most patients seek therapy to get relief from distressing symptoms, and most scales and inventories are developed to assess their symptom level.

Standardised scales, the psychometric properties of which have been shown to be satisfactory, are used in most clinical studies. Both self-report scales, completed by the patients themselves, and therapist ratings, which therapists complete during clinical interviews, are available. Ideally both self-report and therapist rating scales should be used in a study. In investigations on patients with nonpsychotic mental disorders, however, the scores on self-report and therapist ratings are usually strongly correlated, and self-report may be used alone. In psychotic patients self-report inventories are less reliable, and therapist ratings are necessary.

According to the American College of Sports Medicine (1980), physical exercise may be divided into three main forms: aerobic, muscular strength and endurance, and flexibility, co-ordination and relaxation. Most intervention studies have been performed with aerobic exercise; in a few studies aerobic exercise has been compared with other forms.

Physical work capacity (PWC) is considered to be the most important indicator of physical fitness. It is usually assessed by measuring maximal oxygen consumption during exercise. This may be measured directly during maximal tests or calculated indirectly from submaximal tests. Direct measurements are most accurate if test subjects are able to work to near exhaustion, but they require expensive equipment and trained staff. Indirect calculations are cheaper and easier to perform, but are less accurate (Åstrand & Rodahl, 1985).

Modern criteria-based diagnostic systems in psychiatry have greatly increased diagnostic reliability, thus increasing the probability that independent researchers will agree on the classification of a given patient. The Research Diagnostic Criteria, RDC, (Spitzer, Endicott, & Robins, 1978), the Diagnostic and Statistical Manual of Mental Disorders, DSM-III, (American Psychiatric Association, 1980), and the DSM-III-R (American Psychiatric Association, 1987) are commonly used. Using these diagnostic systems makes it easier to compare results across studies.

In some of the rating scales, such as the Beck Depression Inventory (BDI) (Beck, Ward, Mendelson, Mock, & Erbaugh, 1961), normal ranges of the item scores are given. These instruments may be used to identify cases or patients in population studies. In some exercise intervention studies the scores on such scales are used as the only way of classification, and no formal diagnoses are made. This is not satisfactory. A depressive disorder is only one of many factors that may produce elevated BDI scores. During a normal psychological reaction to events such as bereavement and in the course of other psychiatric disorders many people have elevated BDI scores, but we do not classify all of them as having depressive disorders. When studies use elevated symptom scores as the only basis for classification it is difficult to generalise the results to other populations.

The effects of exercise may vary between gender, between old and young people and among the various social classes. To draw general conclusions, information is needed about these factors.

Nonexperimental studies are useful in the early phases of research in a new field. Exploratory studies without control groups are cheap and easy to perform, and they are useful for generating hypotheses. If no measurable effects are found in exploratory studies, it is no use performing controlled studies on the same topic. If positive effects are found, however, these have to be verified in controlled and preferably randomised studies with adequate sample size.

Exercise Intervention in Depression

Two quasi-experimental and nine experimental exercise intervention studies on clinically depressed patients have been published. Most of these studies have been performed in the USA, and these have been reviewed in detail elsewhere (Martinsen, 1987). This chapter will focus on the remaining, European studies.

Martinsen, Medhus, and Sandvik (1985) studied inpatients at a Norwegian psychiatric clinic specialising in inpatient treatment of individuals with severe neuroses, most commonly unipolar depression and anxiety disorders, and personality disorders. In the treatment, emphasis has traditionally been on psychodynamically-oriented psychotherapy, but the institution has also been open to other forms of treatment, including exercise.

The study was completed within 1 year, and 49 patients took part. Patients were of both genders and were aged between 17 and 60, the mean being 40 years. All patients met the DSM-III criteria for major depression without melancholic or psychotic features, and none of them had severe physical diseases that might interfere with exercise. Patients were randomly assigned to aerobic training or a control condition. Patients in the training group exercised aerobically for 1 hour three times a week for 6 to 9 weeks, most commonly using brisk walks and jogging. Those in the control group attended occupational therapy while the other group exercised. Both activities were performed in small groups of 5 to 10 individuals under supervision from trained staff.

Patients in both groups attended psychodynamically-oriented psychotherapy, individually as well as in groups, for two sessions a week in addition to occupational and milieu therapy. Fourteen patients in the control group and nine in the training group used tricyclic antidepressant agents (TCA) during the study.

Level of depression was assessed by the depression subscale of the Comprehensive Psychopathological Rating Scale (CPRS) (Asberg, Perris, Schalling, & Sedvall, 1978) and by the BDI. Physical fitness was assessed by a submaximal cycle ergometer test, where PWC was calculated according to Åstrand's indirect method. The assessments were performed at the start of the study and every 3 weeks, and were identical for both groups.

Six patients dropped out of the study, four in the training group and two in the control group. Patients in the training group showed a significant increase in PWC, while those in the control group were unchanged. Patients in both groups had significant reductions in depression scores. On both measures the reductions were significantly larger in the training group, as shown in Figure 4.1 (Martinsen et al., 1985).

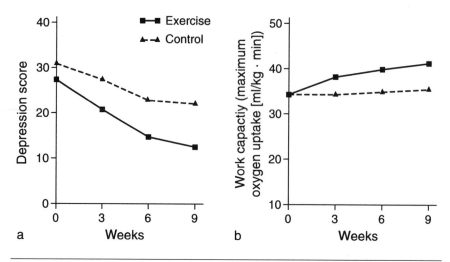

Figure 4.1   (a) Mean depression scores (Beck Depression Inventory) and (b) physical work capacity (maximum oxygen uptake).

Note. From 'Effects of Aerobic Exercise on Depression: A Controlled Study' by E.W. Martinsen, A. Medhus, and L. Sandvik, 1985, *British Medical Journal*, **291**, p. 109. Copyright 1985 by British Medical Association. Reprinted by permission.

For patients in the training group with a small increase in PWC (< 15%), the antidepressant effect was similar to that of the control group. Those with a moderate (15-30%) or large (> 30%) increase in PWC had larger antidepressant effects. Among males in the training group there was a relatively strong correlation between increase in PWC and decrease in BDI (r = 0.43, p < 0.05). Among females this correlation was weak and not statistically significant r = −0.09, p > 0.05). Patients with at least 50% reduction on the BDI from the start to the end of the study were defined as 'responders'. There were 6 responders among the 19 participants in the control group, 3 of each gender. In the training group there were 15 responders, 6 out of 14 females and 9 out of 10 males (Martinsen et al., 1985).

The groups differed in the number of patients using TCA, and this has been used as an argument against the results (Simons, McGowan, Epstein, Kupfer, & Robertson, 1985). All 6 responders in the control group were on TCA, while 5 out of 15 responders in the training group used medication. The difference in use of medication, therefore, cannot explain the results.

The study indicates that exercise is associated with an antidepressive effect in these patients. The study further indicates that these effects are stronger in males and that an increase in aerobic fitness is important, especially in males.

Mutrie (1988) studied 24 subjects with BDI scores above 15 who were referred by general practitioners. No formal diagnoses were made, which is a weakness of this study. Subjects were randomly assigned to aerobic and nonaerobic (stretching and strengthening) exercise, and a waiting list control group. Subjects trained alone three times a week and met with a physical educator every 2 weeks for instruction on how to exercise and for physical tests.

After 4 weeks, subjects in both training groups had larger reductions in BDI scores than the waiting list group, with superior results in the aerobic group. Only the difference between the aerobic group and the waiting list control group reached statistical significance. This is probably due to the small number of subjects in each group. This study indicates that exercise has a therapeutic effect and that aerobic exercise is better than nonaerobic.

Both studies indicate that exercise is associated with an antidepressant effect. Both supervised group exercise for inpatients in Norway, as well as individual home exercise with supervision for outpatients in the UK, seems to be beneficial. This corresponds well to the results of North American studies that have concluded that aerobic exercise is more effective than no treatment, but not significantly different from other forms of treatment, including various forms of psychotherapy. These results were confirmed by a recent meta-analysis by North, McCullagh, and Tran (1990).

There is great variation in the samples used in studies; they include outpatients as well as inpatients, males as well as females, and age-groups from 17 to 60 years of age. The same trend is seen in all studies, indicating that the antidepressant effect associated with exercise is a general effect.

The studies are limited to unipolar depressive disorders without melancholic or psychotic features (or both) commonly regarded as mild to moderate forms of depression. There are no satisfactory studies addressing the value of exercise intervention in psychotic depression, melancholia or in the prevention of bipolar disorders. Clinical experience, however, indicates that exercise has limited value for these disorders (Martinsen, 1987). It may be a supplement to traditional forms of treatment, but should not be the only treatment.

Prevention

Only two investigations have studied whether exercise may prevent the occurrence of depression in vulnerable individuals and prevent relapse for those who have recovered from a depressive episode. Gotestam and Stiles (1990) studied Norwegian soldiers exposed to a stressful real life situation. They found that soldiers actively engaged in sports were significantly less depressed 12 weeks after exposure to the stressful life situation, compared with the physically sedentary ones. Similarly, Martinsen, Sandvik, and Kolbjornsrud (1989) found that previous adult experience with exercise and sports predicted less chance of relapse among nonpsychotic patients treated in hospital and that continuous exercise at follow-up was associated with lower symptom scores.

Exercise and Medication

Two studies have investigated whether exercise may potentiate the effect of antidepressant medication, and vice versa. In the first study, Martinsen (1987) found that exercise and medication had no better effect than exercise alone. In the second study, a nonsignificant trend was found, indicating a better result for the combination of exercise and medication compared with exercise alone (Martinsen, Hoffart, & Solberg, 1989a). No study has yet compared exercise and medication, but Rudolf Bosscher is now directing such a study in Amsterdam.

Using Exercise in Treating Anxiety Disorders

Very few studies have addressed the value of physical exercise in the treatment of patients with anxiety disorders. To my knowledge, no controlled study has yet been published, inside or outside Europe. The first to report on the use of exercise in the treatment of anxiety disorders was the British psychiatrist Orwin, who used physical exercise in the treatment of phobias. He asked patients to run to near exhaustion before being exposed to the anxiety-provoking stimuli. The idea was that the autonomic excitation caused by the exercise would inhibit the situational anxiety. Using this method he reported success in the treatment of eight patients with agoraphobia and one patient with a simple phobia (Orwin, 1974).

Martinsen, Sandvik, and Kolbjornsrud (1989) studied hospitalised patients with DSM-III anxiety disorders. These went through an 8-week specialised treatment programme where the main ingredient was daily sessions of aerobic exercise, and 3 weekly sessions of group psychotherapy. Level of anxiety was assessed by the Symptom Rating Test (SRT) (Kellner & Sheffield, 1973). During the study the level of anxiety was significantly reduced in most diagnostic groups. At one year follow-up, patients with panic disorder with agoraphobia (23 subjects) had lost their gains, but those with generalised anxiety disorder (six subjects) and agoraphobia without panic attacks (two subjects) remained well. Patients with social phobia (five subjects) were almost unchanged at discharge as well as at follow-up. This study included no control group. The patients also received other forms of treatment in addition to exercise, although exercise was the main form of therapy. With this research design one cannot prove whether exercise has a therapeutic effect in anxiety disorders. The results at discharge were relatively similar across diagnostic groups and may simply be due to an unspecific hospitalisation effect.

The most interesting results were those at follow-up, when there was considerable variation among the diagnostic categories. This may reflect the normal variation in the course of the different disorders, but it may also indicate that the various anxiety disorders respond differently to exercise intervention. Generalised anxiety disorder seemed to respond well, but the phobias showed no lasting improvement from this intervention alone.

The results from uncontrolled studies on panic disorder and agoraphobia are conflicting. Orwin reported good results with exercise combined with exposure to the anxiety provoking stimuli, while Martinsen, Sandvik, and Kolbjornsrud reported poor long-term results from a general exercise programme for patients with panic disorder and agoraphobia. There may be a positive effect in generalised anxiety disorder and in simple phobia, but few patients have been studied. So far no controlled exercise intervention study on patients with anxiety disorders has been performed, and our knowledge is very limited.

Studies on free-living populations have shown that exercise intervention is associated with a reduction in state anxiety, probably also in trait anxiety (Morgan & Goldston, 1987), and in neuromuscular tension (de Vries, 1987). Patients with generalised anxiety disorder suffer from chronic anxiety and tension. Maybe patients with this disorder experience the same effect as is seen in free-living populations—a reduction in anxiety and tension.

Psychotherapy research has consistently shown that phobias require specific treatment. Unspecific forms of treatment giving insight or symptom reduction, without specific focussing on the avoided stimuli or situations, are not effective in the long term. Orwin combined exercise with specific exposure to the feared situation and reported success. The patients of Martinsen, Sandvik, and Kolbjornsrud (1989) received general exercise without any exposure. The reason why Orwin had better results may simply be that he combined principles from exposure treatment with exercise.

Exercise Intervention in Other Disorders

For the other psychiatric disorders, the evidence is also weak. Exploratory studies suggest that exercise intervention might be useful in conversion and somatoform pain disorder, alcohol abuse and dependence, and in chronic schizophrenia. In none of these disorders, however, have controlled experiments been published. We have developed interesting hypotheses and have promising clinical experience, but little empirical evidence.

Somatoform Disorders

Delargy, Peatfield, and Burt (1986) reported success by using physical rehabilitation in the treatment of six patients with conversion paralysis. At admission all had been dependent on wheelchairs for an average of 3 years. Within a mean of 41 days all patients were able to walk, and all had maintained these gains at outpatient follow-up for a mean of 10 months. No control group was included.

Martinsen et al. (1989) studied a sample of patients with various DSM-III somatoform disorders: conversion, somatoform pain and somatization disorder, and hypochondriasis. These individuals were taking part in an 8-week inpatient exercise programme. In all groups the scores on the SRT dropped significantly from admission to discharge. At 1-year follow-up, patients with somatoform pain and conversion disorder were still improved, indicating that exercise intervention may have beneficial effects on these disorders. Patients with hypochondriasis and somatization disorders had no long-term gain from this intervention.

These studies indicate that exercise may be of value in somatoform pain and conversion disorder. As no study in this area has yet been published with a control group included, our knowledge is limited.

Alcohol Abuse and Dependence

Exercise is often included in comprehensive treatment programmes of substance abuse and dependence. A few studies indicate that exercise intervention may be useful in the treatment of alcoholics (Taylor, Sallis, & Needle, 1985). In a study without a control group, 11 patients with DSM-III alcohol abuse or dependence were followed during an 8-week inpatient treatment programme and followed up one year after (Martinsen et al., 1989). The level of mental distress assessed by the SRT, was significantly reduced from admission to discharge, and most patients kept their gains at 1-year follow-up. Unfortunately no systematic assessment of drinking behaviours was included. Exercise may be beneficial in alcohol abuse and dependence, but no controlled study has yet been performed.

Schizophrenia

Chamove (1988) studied the short-term effect of exercise intervention on 40 long-term schizophrenic patients in two psychiatric hospitals in Scotland. Exercise was introduced at irregular intervals, and patients and nurses performed daily ratings of symptoms and behaviour. Nurses were blind to whether patients had exercised or not. Both the patients themselves and their nurses rated patients as improved on the days they had been exercising. They showed fewer psychotic features, fewer movement disorders, were less irritable, depressed, retarded and tense, and showed more social interest and competence. The less disturbed patients had greatest improvements.

Is Aerobic Exercise Better Than Nonaerobic in Treating Clinical Disorders?

The results from the study by Martinsen et al. (1985) indicated that there was a positive association between increases in physical fitness and reductions of depression scores, and that this relationship seemed to be especially important in males. If one were able to verify this, it would be an important finding theoretically as well as practically. Theoretically, the finding of an association between a physiological parameter (PWC) and a psychological one (level of depression) might assist in the identification of the aetiology of depression and mechanisms of action in antidepressant treatment. In practice, intensive aerobic exercise may be strenuous for psychiatric patients. If the same psychological gains could be achieved by less intensive exercise, this would be easier to perform in practice, and the drop-out rate would probably be lower.

To find out whether there are real differences between forms of treatment, however, these have to be compared in a randomised trial. This was done in a study comparing aerobic and nonaerobic exercise in 99 inpatients of both sexes (mean age 41) with DSM-III-R major depression, dysthymic disorder or depressive disorder not otherwise specified (Martinsen, Hoffart, & Solberg, 1989a). Patients took part in the same general hospital treatment programme as previously described (Martinsen et al., 1985), with exercise as an additional activity.

Patients were randomly assigned to aerobic or nonaerobic exercise for 1 hour three times a week for 8 weeks. Those in the aerobic group mainly performed jogging or brisk walking, while those in the nonaerobic group trained on muscular strength and endurance, relaxation, flexibility and coordination. In both conditions patients trained in small groups under supervision from a professional coach. Level of depression was assessed by a therapist rating [Montgomery Asberg Depression Rating scale, (MADRS) (Montgomery & Asberg, 1979)] and self-rating (BDI). Fitness testing was performed by ergometer cycle tests, PWC being calculated indirectly from submaximal tests and measured directly during maximal tests. The procedures in both groups were identical, with testing every 4 weeks.

Results showed that patients in the aerobic group achieved significant increases in PWC, while those in the nonaerobic group were unchanged. Indirectly calculated and directly measured values of PWC were strongly correlated. In both groups there were significant reductions in depression scores on both measures, but the differences between the groups were small and not statistically significant. There was a tendency towards a positive correlation between increase in PWC and reduction in BDI among males in the aerobic group ($r = 0.26$, $p > 0.1$). In females the correlation was weak and not statistically significant ($r = 0.16$, $p > 0.1$).

The same group of researchers performed a study of identical design on 79 inpatients with DSM-III-R anxiety disorders, most of whom had panic disorder with agoraphobia (Martinsen, Hoffart, & Solberg, 1989b). These were randomly assigned to aerobic and nonaerobic exercise for 1 hour three times a week for 8 weeks. The physiological assessments were similar to those in the depression study. The level of anxiety was assessed by the anxiety subscale of the Comprehensive Psychopathological Rating Scale (CPRS) (Martinsen, Friis, & Hoffart, 1989), the Phobic Avoidance Rating Scale (PARS) (Hoffart, Friis, & Martinsen, 1989) and the Agoraphobic Cognitions Scale (ACS) (Hoffart, Friis, & Martinsen, 1992). Results showed that patients in the aerobic group achieved a significant increase in aerobic fitness, but those in the nonaerobic group were unchanged. In both groups patients showed significant reductions in anxiety scores on all measures. However, the differences between the groups were small and not statistically significant.

Sexton, Maere, and Dahl (1989) studied inpatients at another Norwegian psychiatric institution. This hospital specialised in inpatient treatment of neurotic patients, using an eclectic, multimodal treatment approach. Fifty-two hospitalised patients of both genders aged 18 to 60 with DSM-III diagnoses of anxiety or unipolar depressive disorders and/or substance abuse took part. Patients were randomly assigned to walking or jogging, and exercised in small groups for 30 minutes three times a week for 8 weeks under supervision by a professional instructor. Joggers were instructed to run at about 70% of predicted maximal pulse rate, while walkers were asked to walk at a comfortable speed. PWC was calculated from submaximal cycle ergometer tests, while level of anxiety and depression was assessed by therapists' ratings and self-ratings. The tests were performed at admission and again after 8 weeks and 6 months.

After 8 weeks the joggers had a significantly greater increase in PWC than the walkers. Both groups showed significant reductions in symptom scores, but the differences between groups were small and not statistically significant. Comparison of those with large (>15%) and small (<15%) increases in aerobic capacity showed no association of symptom reduction with aerobic gain. The correlations between physiological and psychological measures were weak and were not statistically significant. After 6 months, however, both joggers and walkers had persistent and significant increases in PWC. The walkers had increased their fitness during this period, while the joggers maintained their level, and the difference between the two was now small and not statistically significant. Both groups had maintained their psychological gains, and there were no significant differences between them. There was a significantly lower drop-out rate among the walkers.

The first study by Martinsen et al. (1985) indicated that increase in fitness was a necessary condition to achieve antidepressant effects, and a positive correlation between an increase in PWC and a reduction in BDI scores was reported. In later studies with larger samples, this tendency was not so strong, but there still was a trend towards a statistically significant correlation between increases in fitness and reductions in depression scores in males.

When aerobic and nonaerobic exercise were compared in controlled experiments, however, similar effects were obtained with both exercise modes. This has been found consistently in several well-designed studies, with only one exception (see Mutrie, 1988). This study had few test subjects ($n = 24$) compared with the others, in which the number of participants varied between 52 and 99. This makes the results of Mutrie's study less reliable.

The conclusion is that an increase in aerobic fitness does not seem to be important since patients without physiological gains have similar psychological effects as those who have experienced improved fitness. This is supported by the American study of Doyne et al. (1987), which found running and weight lifting to be equally effective in the treatment of depression, both being better than a waiting list control group.

Patient Evaluation of Physical Fitness Intervention

In a 1-year follow-up, Martinsen and Medhus (1989) asked patients to evaluate the usefulness of physical fitness training as compared with other, more traditional, forms of therapy. Patients were given a questionnaire, in which all potentially important therapeutic elements were listed: medication, community meetings, contact with other patients, group psychotherapy, physical exercise, individual psychotherapy and contact with the nurses. They were asked to rank which of the elements they had found most useful, by giving 3 points to the most important, 2 to the second and 1 to the third choice. Patients in the training group ranked physical fitness training as the therapeutic element which had helped them most. Patients in the control group ranked individual psychotherapy as most important (see Figure 4.2).

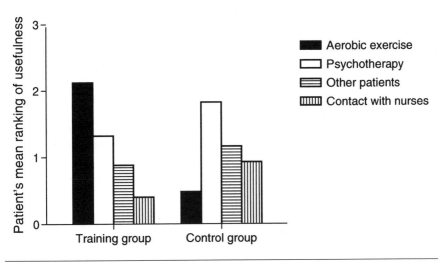

Figure 4.2   Patients' ranking of the most important therapeutic elements. The lowest
rank was scored 1, the next was scored 2, and the highest was scored 3.
Note. From 'Adherence to Exercise and Patients' Evaluation of Physical Exercise in a Comprehensive Treatment Programme for Depression' by E.W. Martinsen and A. Medhus, 1989, *Nordic Journal
of Psychiatry*, **43**, pp. 411-415. Copyright 1989 by Scandinavian University Press. Reprinted by permission of Scandinavian University Press.

Similarly, Sexton et al. (1989) found that patients reported that physical fitness
training had helped them more than traditional forms of therapy, including psychotherapy and medication.

Anstiss (1988) studied 150 patients with DSM-III-R alcohol dependence, who
took part in daily exercise on stationary cycles for 4 weeks. On discharge, 60% of
clients reported that the exercise was of great value, and 29% said it was of considerable value. Most reported that the exercise was enjoyable.

When patients are asked to evaluate the usefulness of exercise, the results are
consistent across studies. Patients appreciate exercise as a useful activity, and many
consider it to be of more help than traditional forms of therapy, including various
forms of psychotherapy and medication. These results, of course, do not prove that
exercise is more effective than other forms of treatment. Nevertheless, the findings
are interesting. In psychiatric treatment, patients tend to be passive receivers, whether
they receive drug therapy or psychotherapy. In exercise treatment, patients have to
be active and take responsibility. They learn a strategy for coping better with their
mental problems, and they know that when exercise works, it is their own efforts
that have made them feel better. In my opinion this is an important aspect of exercise.

Mechanisms Mediating the Psychological Effects of Exercise

Physiological, biochemical and psychological mechanisms have been suggested to
explain how the psychological effects of exercise are mediated. Vigorous exercise

is accompanied by a transient increase in body temperature. Morgan (1984) terms this the 'pyrogen hypothesis' and it is proposed as one possible mechanism mediating the psychological effects of exercise. During endurance exercise the circulating beta-endorphine concentrations increase (Carr et al., 1981). It has also been suggested that an increase in concentrations of monoamines in the brain accompanies exercise (Ransford, 1982).

Among the psychological hypotheses, mastery (White, 1959), self-efficacy (Bandura, 1977) and distraction (Bahrke & Morgan, 1978) are commonly mentioned. Although several hypotheses have been put forward, there is little empirical evidence supporting them. The mechanisms mediating the psychological effects are still largely unknown.

Conclusion

The psychological effects are best documented for the nonbipolar, nonpsychotic depressive disorders. For these patient groups exercise may be considered as a supplement or alternative to the traditional forms of treatment. For the other diagnostic categories the scientific evidence is much weaker. There are indications that a therapeutic effect may be achieved in some anxiety disorders, conversion and somatoform pain disorder, schizophrenia and alcohol abuse and dependence, but the empirical evidence is weak. In the treatment of these disorders exercise may be considered as a potentially useful approach.

The need for treatment in psychiatry can never be fully met by the health professionals. There is, therefore, a great need for simple strategies which individuals may adopt by themselves or with a little help from instructors, to cope more effectively with their own mental problems. Exercise seems to be one such strategy for some patient groups.

Most exercise intervention studies have used aerobic forms of exercise, but there are rather strong indications that similar psychological effects may be achieved with other forms of exercise as well. This has important implications for practical training. For psychological gains, the important thing seems to be participation in exercise, not the acquisition of fitness. Activities that suit the individual, not necessarily aerobic, appear to be the critical factor.

References

American College of Sports Medicine. (1980). *Guidelines for graded exercise testing and exercise prescription* (2nd ed.). Philadelphia: Lea & Febiger.

American Psychiatric Association. (1980). *Diagnostic and statistical manual of mental disorders* (3rd ed.). Washington, DC: American Psychiatric Association.

American Psychiatric Association. (1987). *Diagnostic and statistical manual of mental disorders* (3rd ed., revised). Washington, DC: American Psychiatric Association.

Anstiss, T. (1988). A controlled trial of exercise in alcohol dependency. In *Proceedings of the Sport, Health, Psychology and Exercise Symposium* (pp. 116-118). London: Health Education Authority and Sports Council.

Asberg, M., Perris, C., Schalling, D., & Sedvall, G. (1978). The CPRS: Development and applications of a psychiatric rating scale. *Acta Psychiatrica Scandinavica*, (Suppl. 271).

Åstrand, P.O., & Rodahl, K. (1985). *Textbook of work physiology*. New York: McGraw-Hill.

Bahrke, M.S., & Morgan, W.P. (1978). Anxiety reduction following exercise and meditation. *Cognitive Therapy and Research*, **2**, 323-333.

Bandura, A. (1977). Self-efficacy: Toward a unifying theory of behavioral change. *Psychological Review*, **84**, 191-215.

Beck, A.T., Ward, C.H., Mendelson, M., Mock, J., & Erbaugh, H. (1961). An inventory for measuring depression. *Archives of General Psychiatry*, **4**, 561-571.

Carr, D.B., Bullen, B.A., Skrinar, G.S., Arnold, M.A., Rosenblatt, M., Beitens, I.Z., Martin, J.B., & McArthur, J.W. (1981). Physical conditioning facilitates the exercise-induced secretion of beta-endorphin and beta-lipoprotein in women. *New England Journal of Medicine*, **305**, 560-563.

Chamove, A. (1988). Exercise effects in psychiatric populations: A review. In *Sport, Health, Psychology and Exercise Symposium Proceedings*, (pp. 8-48). London: Health Education Authority and Sports Council.

Delargy, M.A., Peatfield, R.C., & Burt, A.A. (1986). Successful rehabilitation in conversion paralysis. *British Medical Journal*, **292**, 1730-1731.

de Vries, H.A. (1987). Tension reduction with exercise. In W.P. Morgan & S.E. Goldston (Eds.), *Exercise and mental health* (pp. 99-104). Washington, DC: Hemisphere.

Doyne E.J., Ossip-Klein, D.J., Bowman, E.D., Osborn, K.M., McDougall-Wilson, I.B., & Neimeyer, R.A. (1987). Running versus weight-lifting in the treatment of depression. *Journal of Consulting and Clinical Psychology*, **55**, 748-754.

Freemont, J., & Craighead, L.W. (1987). Aerobic exercise and cognitive therapy in the treatment of dysphoric moods. *Cognitive Therapy and Research*, **2**, 241-251.

Gotestam, K.G., & Stiles, T.C. (1990, November). *Physical exercise and cognitive vulnerability: A longitudinal study*. Paper presented at the annual meeting of the Association for the Advancement of Behavior Therapy, San Francisco, CA.

Greist, J.H., Klein, M.H., Eischens, R.R., Gurman, A.S., & Morgan, W.P. (1979). Running as treatment for depression. *Comprehensive Psychiatry*, **20**, 41-54.

Hoffart, A., Friis S., & Martinsen, E.W. (1989). The phobic avoidance rating scale: A psychometric evaluation of an interview-based scale. *Psychiatric Developments*, **1**, 71-81.

Hoffart, A., Friis, S., & Martinsen, E.W. (1992). Assessment of fear among agoraphobic patients: The Agoraphobic Cognitions Scale. *Journal of Psychopathology and Behavioural Assessment*, **14**, 175-187.

Kellner, R., & Sheffield, B.F. (1973). A brief rating scale of distress. *Psychological Medicine*, **3**, 88-100.

Martinsen, E.W. (1987). The role of aerobic exercise in the treatment of depression. *Stress Medicine*, **3**, 93-100.

Martinsen, E.W., Friis, S., & Hoffart, A. (1989). A factor analytical study of the Comprehensive Psychopathological Rating Scale among patients with anxiety and depressive disorders. *Acta Psychiatrica Scandinavica*, **80**, 492-498.

Martinsen, E.W., Hoffart, A., & Solberg, O. (1989a). Comparing aerobic and nonaerobic forms of exercise in the treatment of clinical depression: A randomized trial. *Comprehensive Psychiatry*, **30**, 324-331.

Martinsen, E.W., Hoffart, A., & Solberg, O. (1989b). Aerobic and non-aerobic forms of exercise in the treatment of anxiety disorders. *Stress Medicine*, **5**, 115-120.

Martinsen, E.W., & Medhus, A. (1989). Adherence to exercise and patients' evaluation of physical exercise in a comprehensive treatment programme for depression. *Nordic Journal of Psychiatry*, **43**, 411-415.

Martinsen, E.W., Medhus, A., & Sandvik, L. (1985). Effects of aerobic exercise on depression: A controlled study. *British Medical Journal*, **291**, 109.

Martinsen E.W., Sandvik, L., & Kolbjornsrud, O.B. (1989). Aerobic exercise in the treatment of nonpsychotic mental disorders: An exploratory study. *Nordic Journal of Psychiatry*, **43**, 521-529.

Montgomery, S.A., & Asberg, M. (1979). A new depression scale designed to be sensitive to change. *British Journal of Psychiatry*, **134**, 382-389.

Morgan, W.P. (1984). Physical activity and mental health. In H.M. Eckhert & H.J. Montoye (Eds.), *Exercise and health* (pp. 132-145). Champaign, IL: Human Kinetics.

Morgan, W.P., & Goldston, S.E. (Eds.) (1987). *Exercise and mental health*. Washington, DC: Hemisphere.

Mutrie, N. (1988). Exercise as a treatment for moderate depression in the UK health service. In *Proceedings of the Sport, Health, Psychology and Exercise Symposium* (pp. 96-105). London: Health Education Authority and Sports Council.

North, T.C., McCullagh, P., & Tran, Z.V. (1990). Effect of exercise on depression. *Exercise and Sport Sciences Reviews*, **18**, 379-415.

Orwin, A. (1974). Treatment of situational phobia: A case for running. *British Journal of Psychiatry*, **123**, 95-98.

Ransford, C.P. (1982). A role for amines in the antidepressant effect of exercise. *Medicine and Science in Sports and Exercise*, **14**, 1-10.

Sexton, H., Maere, Å., & Dahl, N.H. (1989). Exercise intensity and reduction in neurotic symptoms. *Acta Psychiatrica Scandinavica*, **80**, 231-235.

Simons, A.D., McGowan, C.R., Epstein, L.H., Kupfer, D.J., & Robertson, R.J. (1985). Exercise as treatment for depression: An update. *Clinical Psychological Reviews*, **5**, 553-558.

Spitzer, R.L., Endicott, J., & Robins, E. (1978). Research diagnostic criteria: Rationale and reliability. *Archives of General Psychiatry*, **35**, 773-782.

Taylor, C.B., Sallis, J.F., & Needle, R. (1985). The relation of physical activity and exercise to mental health. *Public Health Reports*, **100**, 105-109.

White, R.W. (1959). Motivation reconsidered: The concept of competence. *Psychological Review*, **66**, 297-333.

5

CHAPTER

Psychological Factors in the Promotion of Physical Activity

R. Andrew Smith
Stuart J.H. Biddle

GREAT BRITAIN

A great deal has been written about the physical and mental health benefits of participation in sport, exercise and other forms of physical activity. Although many review textbooks are North American (e.g., Bouchard, Shephard, Stephens, Sutton, & McPherson, 1990), literature is also available from Europe (e.g., Macleod, Maughan, Nimmo, Reilly, & Williams, 1987; Norgan, 1992). However, although recognition of nonbiological factors has increased, such reviews are still dominated by the biological *outcomes* of participation, with rather less coverage given to the factors associated with the *promotion* of physical activity. This reflects, to a certain extent, the greater knowledge base and history that exist in the biological sciences in comparison to the sociocultural and psychological sciences concerned with physical activity research. Nevertheless, it does highlight the need for increasing our knowledge and coverage of the likely *antecedents* of participation (see chapter 1). Similarly, it is regrettable that a major European initiative in public health (Normand & Vaughan, 1993) virtually ignores physical activity altogether.

This chapter is a summary of key issues in the promotion of exercise, using psychological research and theory as our foundation. We do not claim that psychology has all the answers—far from it—but we do request that greater recognition be given to the psychological factors likely to be associated with participation. We shall consider strategies for individuals and for groups.

The first half of the chapter will consider behaviour change techniques at different points in the exercise process. The second half of the chapter will consider issues of application relevant to community interventions.

Sallis and Hovell (1990) proposed a 'natural history' model of exercise that includes adoption, maintenance, dropout and resumption (see Figure 5.1). Each stage may have different determinants as well as differentially appropriate strategies for behaviour change. However, little is known about the determinants of exercise adoption or resumption, although more is known about maintenance and dropout (Biddle & Mutrie, 1991; Dishman, 1990; Sallis & Hovell, 1990). This section will consider each of the three phases of adoption, maintenance and resumption, and review likely behaviour change strategies.

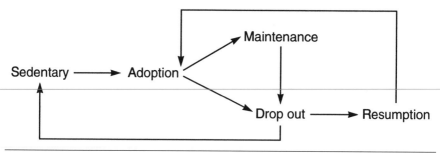

Figure 5.1   A process model of exercise, proposed by Sallis and Hovell (1990).
Note. From 'Determinants of Exercise Behaviour' by J.F. Sallis and M.F. Hovell, 1990, *Exercise and Sport Sciences Reviews*, **18**, p. 309. Copyright 1990 by Williams & Wilkins Co. Reprinted by permission.

Getting Started in Exercise: Adoption

Most public health campaigns on exercise are aimed at getting sedentary individuals to become active, yet surprisingly little is known about why people actually become active. Of course, it is very difficult, if not impossible, to address this question in childhood since very young children are usually active in spontaneous play anyway. As they move through childhood and adolescence they learn new behaviours that reinforce or compete with physical activity as a choice behaviour (Fox, 1991). Despite the difficulty of studying exercise adoption by children, however, factors affecting changes in activity levels or activity choice could possibly be identified.

The factors affecting exercise adoption by adults should be easier to study because a time period of inactivity prior to starting participation can often be identified. However, there are hardly any studies of this phase of the exercise process. Vanden Auweele, Rzewnicki, and Van Mele (1993) studied 265 middle-aged inactive Belgian adults and presented a 'typology of sedentariness'. Using cluster analysis, they found men could be classified into two groups. Sixty percent of the males were characterised by being quite unconcerned about exercise. This might correspond with Prochaska's 'precontemplation' stage of beliefs (see Prochaska & DiClemente, 1986). The second cluster identified by Vanden Auweelle et al. (1993) were males characterised as having thought about what was important to them and having dismissed exercise. They seem to have made a cost-benefit analysis and to have concluded that exercise, on balance, was not worth the effort. Among the women studied, some could also be classified as indifferent to exercise and others were reporting more definite views that physical activity was irrelevant and inappropriate for them.

Vanden Auweelle et al.'s research is an important first step in identifying clusters of sedentary adults. However, as Sallis and Hovell (1990) point out, 'overall, it must be concluded that we understand almost nothing about why some people begin exercising' (p. 313). Despite this state of affairs, it is possible to suggest likely intervention strategies for exercise promotion that could affect the adoption phase, but these suggestions are based on research from other health behaviours or extrapolation of research findings from exercise maintenance studies.

Attitude and Belief Strategies

Many interventions designed to achieve the shift in behaviour from being sedentary to active involve some form of educational strategy centred on changes in beliefs and attitudes. Theories guiding practice include the Theories of Reasoned Action and Planned Behaviour (Ajzen, 1985; Ajzen & Fishbein, 1980), the Health Belief Model (Becker, Haefner, Kasl, Kirscht, Maiman, & Rosenstock, 1977), and other social-psychological models, many based on expectancy-value frameworks (see Biddle & Mutrie, 1991; Godin & Shephard, 1990; as well as chapter 2).

The Theories of Reasoned Action (TRA) and Planned Behaviour (TPB) show that exercise intention and behaviour is associated with beliefs about the outcomes of exercise, the value attached to such outcomes, the beliefs of significant others concerning exercise and the degree to which the individual wishes to comply with such beliefs. In addition, the TPB proposes that the degree of perceived control over exercise will influence intention and behaviour. Interventions based on these models should involve education about the benefits and value of exercise, and the positive and negative influences other people can have on one's behaviour.

Models such as the TRA and TPB can allow for meaningful planning of intervention strategies in the phase of exercise adoption. However, these and similar models are based primarily on social-psychological principles, are unidirectional models, and only predict behaviour from one point in time. Also some studies have predicted intention rather than the behaviour itself (Godin & Shephard, 1986), and some have generalised across several exercise modalities (Dzewaltowski, 1989; see also Godin & Shephard, 1990; Smith & Biddle, 1992). Nevertheless, attitude models are likely to be informative for guiding interventions at the stage of exercise adoption. For example, Owen and Lee (1986) state that 'it is likely that attitudinal theories will have relatively weak predictive power in dealing with long-term maintenance of change, but be more useful in dealing with behavioural intentions and motivation for initial change' (p. 153).

Decision-Making Models

Kendzierski (1990; Kendzierski & LaMastro, 1988) has studied the role of beliefs and attitudes in exercise participation, including adoption. She has used the perspectives of Subjective Expected Utility (SEU) theory as well as Kuhl's Action Control (AC) theory (see also chapter 1). SEU theory, as applied to exercise, would state that decisions are made on the basis of the individual's belief in the value of the exercise outcomes and the probability that such outcomes will occur. However, this is set against beliefs concerning alternative actions, including not exercising. As discussed in chapter 1, Kendzierski and LaMastro (1988) found that SEU theory predicted interest in exercise, but not adherence. They argued that SEU theory might be better used to help explain decisions involving simple choices, whereas adherence to exercise is a complex behaviour. Similarly, Kendzierski (1990) found that SEU predicted exercise intentions but not adherence. She concluded that there was a need to distinguish between decision *making* and decision *implementation*.

Based on decision theories, one strategy used in health behaviour change programmes that could be beneficial in exercise promotion is the decision balance sheet (DBS) procedure. This involves the individual listing potential benefits and costs of participation in exercise (Wankel, 1984). This information can then be used to assist in behavioural planning. An extension of the DBS is a decision matrix in which benefits and costs are listed for adhering and failing to adhere to the behaviour in both the long and the short term. The DBS has been found to be an effective predictor of exercise maintenance (Wankel, Yardley, & Graham, 1985), but its effectiveness for predicting exercise adoption has not been documented.

The practical implications of these approaches for exercise adoption are clear. Individuals contemplating taking up physical activity and exercise may be better placed to plan such a behaviour after consideration of the benefits and costs involved. Self-regulatory skills and behavioural planning are likely to be important factors in exercise participation; therefore decision-based strategies highlighting these issues are likely to be important.

Confidence to Act

Getting started in exercise is likely to be affected by the confidence one has in initiating the appropriate action. Bandura's (1977, 1986) theory of self-efficacy has been prominent in formulations of practical strategies based on self-confidence in exercise (see Biddle & Mutrie, 1991). Bandura (1977) has suggested that information on self-efficacy—beliefs in one's ability to carry out a desired action—is drawn from four main sources. These provide useful points of reference for intervention strategies.

One of the main sources of information on confidence is prior experience and success. For the adoption of exercise, prior success in other activities would appear to be important, although little evidence is available to verify this. In addition, perceptions or definitions of success will be important. Those defining success as self-improvement, or participation, may find greater opportunities for experiencing success than those defining success in social comparative terms.

Other sources of self-confidence include vicarious experience, verbal and social persuasion, and control of physical signs. Vicarious processes could include observing others successfully adopt and maintain an exercise programme. Verbal and social persuasion refers to persuasion from others as well as positive self-talk. Finally, controlling physiological signs of anxiety may help to enhance confidence, although the extent that this is required for health-related exercise is not known. Other formulations on self-confidence (see Corbin, 1984) are also available, and these offer the following guidelines:

- Establish realistic goals.
- Avoid situations where the individual may feel vulnerable to lapses of confidence. This is likely to occur where the activity is seen to be 'inappropriate', such as where it is strongly sex-typed.
- Use immediate and objective feedback.
- Physically guide people through movements that they may initially lack confidence in performing.

Staying With Exercise: Maintenance

Maintaining involvement in exercise has been identified as a problem. Some estimates suggest that about half those who start supervised exercise programmes will cease participation within a few months (Dishman, Sallis, & Orenstein, 1985). 'Self-regulatory' skills for maintaining involvement in physical activity will be discussed in relation to cognitive-behavioural strategies.

Cognitive-Behavioural Strategies

Cognitive-behavioural strategies can cover a large number of practical techniques (see Biddle & Mutrie, 1991; Knapp, 1988; Lee & Owen, 1986). Discussion, therefore, will be selective and deal with the following: initial involvement and definitions of success; self-regulatory skills; reinforcement and exercise consequences.

Initial Involvement.   Most advice about fitness and health-related exercise centres on the biological outcomes of involvement in physical activity. Often, guidelines designed for the improvement of cardiorespiratory fitness have been used for promoting involvement in exercise. However, from the standpoint of behavioural change, improvement in fitness should not be contemplated until some form of comfortable routine has been established. For example, Rejeski and Kenney (1988) propose that adherence is best achieved by progressing from a 'starter phase' to a 'growth phase'. Initial involvement (starter phase) is centred on appropriate behaviour change and gradual changes in physical activity levels, light and enjoyable exercise with minimal risk of injury or discomfort, and the learning of new skills. Fitness improvements could actually be discouraged at this stage. Only later (during the growth phase) should changes in fitness be planned more explicitly (Biddle & Smith, 1991).

This 'stage' approach to exercise maintenance may require individuals to change their definition of exercise 'success' (Fox, 1992). Often, people will define success in physical activities in social comparative terms, particularly if this involves sport. However, from the point of view of behavioural change, success should be defined in individual terms. This might involve looking at changes in behaviour and at self-improvement. Confusion between athletic excellence and exercise involvement is not helpful in the promotion of physical activity for health.

Self-Regulatory Skills. Goal-setting has been used in many different contexts to stimulate and maintain behaviour (Locke & Latham, 1990). There are a number of factors likely to affect the success of goal-setting, including the extent to which the individual participates in the setting of goals, the level of the goal, goal acceptance, commitment and importance, and the feedback available from monitoring achievement of the goal. Most people agree that goal-setting needs to include goals at different time intervals—in other words, short-, medium-, and long-term goals. Individuals could be encouraged to see the goal-setting process as a stairway, moving from short-term goals (first step) to long-term goals (top of the stairway).

For exercise adherence, it may be better to focus, at least in the initial stages, on the behaviour itself. That is to say that the focus should be on *process* goals that target behavioural patterns rather than the outcomes of exercise (*product* goals; see Biddle & Smith, 1991). An example of a process goal might be 'walking to work on Mondays and Fridays', whereby a product goal might be 'walking to work in less than 25 minutes'. Process goals are more likely to stimulate the behaviour, at least initially.

Goal-setting requires regular assessment of progress and self-monitoring, as well as behavioural flexibility if goals are met easily or not at all. Goals can also be incorporated into other strategies such as written contracts or decision balance sheet procedures (Biddle & Mutrie, 1991; Oldridge & Jones, 1983).

Using self-monitoring to create a greater awareness of the desired actions may assist in changing such target behaviours. For example, individuals wishing to become more physically active could use self-monitoring and reinforcement procedures to highlight the changes required. This would involve the individual in monitoring the target behaviour over a period of time, possibly including a baseline period prior to the introduction of any new behaviour change strategy. A typical self-monitoring chart is shown in Figure 5.2.

Associated with the monitoring of the desired behaviour could be a period of monitoring other cues to exercise or competing cues. Cues might include preparation of exercise clothes and planning exercise routines or schedules, whereas competing cues might include television watching, smoking or alcohol use.

Reinforcement and Exercise Consequences. Dishman et al. (1985) stated it was more likely that feelings of enjoyment and well-being would enhance exercise

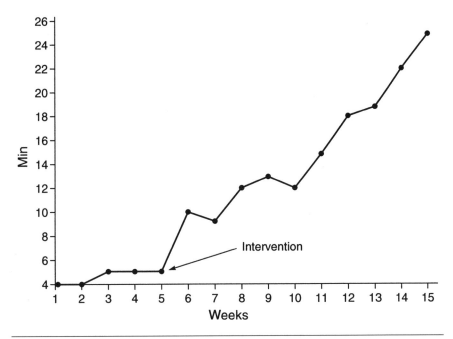

Figure 5.2   A typical self-monitoring chart for behavioural change.

adherence than concerns about health. This suggests that behaviour modification, at least from the point of view of maintaining exercise, should involve a consideration of the psychological outcomes of participation. If participants enjoy exercise or 'feel good' after exercise, this is likely to be a powerful reinforcing and motivating influence. Surprisingly little research has investigated the motivational aspects of the mental health outcomes of exercise (see Biddle, 1992a; Biddle & Mutrie, 1991; Martinsen, 1989; as well as chapters 3 and 4).

Much of the research on exercise and mental health has focused on the effects of exercise on self-esteem, anxiety and depression. Some research is available on the nature of enjoyment in sport and exercise (Wankel, 1985), yet this concept remains elusive. From a practical standpoint of behaviour change, the role of psychological well-being should be viewed from two perspectives: the psychological consequences ('feel good' effect) of exercise and the psychological reactions during exercise.

Much has been written about the likely effects of exercise on mental health and psychological well-being (Morgan & Goldston, 1987). The evidence points to the potential for acute or chronic exercise to reduce anxiety and depression, to elevate levels of self-esteem, and to buffer the effects of psychosocial stress (Biddle, 1992b). Reinforcement of such changes could act as powerful motivators to exercise adherence. However, little is known about the motivating role of such psychological changes.

Available evidence suggests that the way people react to the exercise experience can influence their adherence. For example, maintaining exercise participation is likely to be enhanced if the levels of physical exertion required are comfortable and acceptable. British research by Steptoe and coworkers (Steptoe & Bolton, 1988; Steptoe & Cox, 1988) has shown that more moderate, as opposed to more intense, aerobic exercise is associated with anxiety reduction. Similarly, studies have suggested that those individuals less biologically suited to vigorous exercise regimens, such as those who are overfat, or who are not suited to a particular type of exercise, are more prone to drop out (Dishman & Gettman, 1980; Ingjer & Dahl, 1979). However, more research is required on the factors influencing emotional reactions to exercise.

Two factors likely to relate to adherence in exercise classes are the exercise leader and the group dynamics of the class. Again, little research is available, but it is likely that the exercise leader could have a very important role to play in exercise maintenance through enthusiastic and empathetic leadership, and teaching self-regulatory skills to class members. In addition, group cohesion, particularly related to social factors, is likely to assist in adherence (see Carron, Widmeyer, & Brawley, 1988).

Starting Up Again After Inactivity: Resumption

Little research is available on how or why people start exercising after a period of inactivity. The term 'exercise resumption' has not been used a great deal in the literature, but some parallels are available from the study of other health behaviours in terms of the 'relapse' phenomenon. Nevertheless, while there may be a 'stop-start syndrome' in exercise, the process of relapse usually refers to the resumption of an undesirable high-frequency behaviour (e.g., smoking), whereas exercise is a desirable low-frequency behaviour (see Knapp, 1988; Marlatt, 1985). Despite this, the concept of 'stop-start', or relapse, could be useful for guiding interventions in exercise (Biddle & Mutrie, 1991). Marlatt's relapse model will be used to discuss key factors in exercise resumption.

Central to the relapse prevention model is the individual's coping response. Belief in the ability to cope with a 'high risk' situation—a situation where ceasing exercise is likely—is important in successfully managing the stop-start syndrome. Those more prone to quitting physical activity could have an inadequate coping response and associated feelings of low self-efficacy. Intervention at this stage should involve the development of self-efficacy specifically related to exercise resumption if relapse has occurred, or related to continuing exercise to avoid relapse. Development of self-efficacy has already been discussed and may include the use of other strategies such as goal-setting and decision-making exercises. Interventions may also be required to change negative attributions for the perceived 'failure' of exercise dropout or relapse. For example, attributing the relapse to uncontrollable factors (e.g., 'I'm not good enough to exercise') will produce negative emotion, such as guilt, and an expectation that little can be done to change the situation in the future. Such attributions need changing so that the emphasis is placed on changeable and personally controllable factors.

Strategies for Promoting Community Involvement

The first part of this chapter considered the psychological techniques that may be used to modify an individual's physical activity levels. Although these techniques may have a significant effect on the lifestyle and health of the individual, they are likely to have less of an effect on public health indices recorded by epidemiological research. This is because very few individuals will have the opportunity to take part in a one-on-one counselling programme with a trained exercise leader or take part in small group workshops. Such labour-intensive psychological techniques will remain restricted to small sections of our communities for the foreseeable future. For physical activity to have a significant effect on measures such as the incidence of coronary heart disease, psychological techniques aimed at communities and mass populations must also be used. Unfortunately, there would seem to be an inverse relationship between the size of the target population and the degree of behavioural change achieved.

Before the exercise psychologist can use psychological techniques to promote physical activity in the community they must become part of the health promotion system. In the UK this usually means working alongside the Health Promotion team of a District Health Authority. Our perception of this role is illustrated in Figure 5.3. Here we have represented a community-based strategy to increase physical activity as a 'planning pyramid'. This shows more specialised facilities and programmes, catering for fewer people, at the top of the pyramid, and mass community programmes at the base.

Pyramid I shows the overall physical activity strategy on face 'a'. The other faces of the pyramid could be modifications of 'a' for subpopulations or different geographical regions. Sector 1 of pyramid I represents more technical medical rehabilitation taking place in hospitals and specialised clinics. Personnel are likely to include medical doctors, nurses, physiotherapists and, possibly, sport and exercise scientists. The population here will be small and the exercise advice and 'prescription' precise and 'technical'. Moving down the pyramid, sector 2 shows intervention at the level of recognised health clinics and centres staffed by physiotherapists and exercise scientists. At the lowest level, sector 3, the largest population is targetted and the exercise advice least technical. This represents 'mass' physical activity promotion through health-related exercise classes at leisure centres staffed by exercise leaders and, possibly, qualified physical educators.

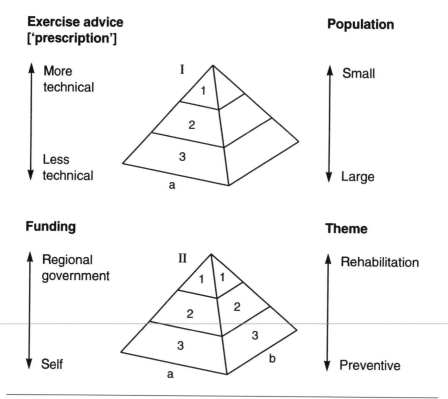

Figure 5.3 Proposed community physical activity intervention 'planning pyramids'.

Pyramid II shows two more focused interventions based on the same principles of staffing and population size as just outlined. Face 'a' depicts interventions targetting coronary heart disease (CHD) while face 'b' is associated with the mental health outcomes of physical activity. For CHD, sector 1 again represents medical and hospital CHD rehabilitation work. Sector 2 might include supervised exercise programmes at recognised centres for rehabilitation, as well as home-based programmes monitored by rehabilitation staff. Sector 3 includes community-based physical activity and exercise interventions for individuals with CHD risk factors, as well as general health-related exercise programmes.

Finally, we depict interventions aimed at mental health on face 'b' of pyramid II. At the top of the pyramid might be exercise aimed at hospitalised clinical patients, while sector 2 could involve community general practitioners (physicians) prescribing physical activity for their patients suffering nonclinical disorders. Interventions in sector 3 might involve community-based physical activity and exercise programmes that emphasise mental well-being and stress management.

These pyramids suggest that the work and expertise of the exercise psychologist can be valuable at all levels through strategy development, technical work in particular settings and training of personnel (e.g., exercise leaders) in the lower sectors of the pyramid. However, at present there are too few exercise psychologists to impact on more than just a small number of such interventions or programmes.

Defining the Target Behaviour

Successful techniques for the promotion of physical activity begin with a clear statement of the behaviour to be promoted. Fishbein and Ajzen's (1975) concept of the relationship between attitudes, social norm and confidence clearly illustrates the need for a specifically stated target behaviour. The first step in defining the target behaviour is to distinguish between the terms physical activity, exercise and sport. Unfortunately, these terms are often used interchangeably although each calls for a different form of promotion and marketing. From a community perspective the target behaviour is most likely to be physical activity, such as walking programmes and lifestyle activity. This target behaviour is selected because it is the least behaviourally challenging and is the stepping stone for a sedentary population to move on to exercise and sport.

The complexity of these behavioural patterns, however, should not be overlooked by health promoters. It is very difficult to define individuals as being 'active' or 'sedentary' because people change! They drop out of, and into, exercise. The complexity of the behavioural patterns we are attempting to promote should caution us against grand objectives for health promotion campaigns. 'Sport for All' may be a valiant battle cry but an unachievable and unrealistic objective we should advise against when defining the target behaviour!

Identifying Target Groups

From an applied perspective, one of the most difficult stages of community health promotion is defining the term 'community'. Different agencies, with differing political agendas, will have different perceptions of the community. Exercise psychology can assist this process by identifying those sections of the community most likely to be sedentary. This can be achieved by a specific research study, or by reference to existing activity and participation figures. Once target groups have been identified, based on estimated activity levels, exercise psychologists can assist in the design of 'barrier profiles' for these groups. These may be relatively unsophisticated, pointing out that most groups will report lack of time as a barrier, or more detailed listing of hypothesised barriers for the particular groups.

Changing Attitude

Since both the sport and the exercise psychology literature have been influenced strongly by social psychological theory, it is not surprising that the notion of attitude change has dominated many promotion campaigns. Unfortunately, some campaigns have been based on a simplistic and atheoretical understanding of the nature of attitude and its relationship to behaviour. Many campaigns have simply listed positive outcomes from participation, such as weight loss, improved aerobic fitness and a 'toned' body. As Fishbein and Ajzen (1975) have demonstrated, these beliefs about outcomes must be supported by positive behavioural evaluations (values). Also, policy makers must be careful not to impose their own value systems on a community that may have a very different list of priorities.

Once the message of the attitude campaign has been defined, preferably taking account of the profile research outlined above, a decision must be made on how to communicate this message. Television advertisements aimed at promoting physical activity are still rare in Europe. Public health services tend not to have a budget capable of meeting such costs. Attitude campaigns tend to be carried by posters and leaflets. An excellent example in the UK has been the 'It doesn't have to be hell to be healthy' campaign. This can be seen as tackling a negative outcome of exercise participation, in line with Fishbein and Ajzen (1975), and helping to overcome a barrier to participation.

The effectiveness of such methods for changing community activity patterns is debatable. However, Aaro (1991) reports on the favourable outcomes of a combined community and mass media physical activity campaign in Norway. He suggests two reasons for such success. First, local action is stimulated by mass media coverage, and, second, the mass media bring more attractive and appealing material than traditional 'medical' approaches to health promotion. Aaro also suggests that the process of behaviour change needs to be viewed in several ways.

> It is important to point out that behavioural outcomes are not the only criteria of success in mass media campaigns promoting fitness. The change of health-related behaviour can be regarded as a process in which change in the actual behaviour itself is an end product of a number of less visible (perhaps invisible) intermediate changes. Sometimes . . . a series of campaigns with no effect on behaviour produces a substantial change in behaviour when the results are summed. (Aaro, 1991, p. 199)

Training Exercise Leaders

It is unlikely that in this century Europeans will have access to an exercise leader in the same way as to a medical doctor, a health visitor or a social worker. If one accepts this premise, the only way to personalise the physical activity message to the community is through nonspecialist health professionals. This may enhance the attitude change process and encourage an actual change in behaviour. In Somerset, for example, one of us (Smith) has been involved in the establishment of a training module for primary health care nurses. The objective of this has been to empower such people to promote physical activity with their client groups. The training course has focused on behavioural change strategies rather than teaching a repertoire of physical movement skills. In short, the health visitors will go back into their communities and promote physical activity rather than simply teach exercise classes. By the nature of their role, health visitors will come into contact with the sedentary 'core' of our community. They deal with young mothers, older adults and single-parent families. These groups, who would not normally come into contact with an exercise leader, can be advised through their existing relationship with a health professional. We hope that this 'back door approach' will be extended to medical doctors. According to Fishbein and Ajzen's theory, such doctors tend to elicit a high 'motivation to comply' from their patients, but may not always give the 'normative belief' we would desire!

Promoting Physical Activity in the Workplace

The workplace has been identified as a location for health promotion for two reasons. Firstly, it is an environment in which a sedentary population can be located and targeted. Secondly, the 'gatekeepers' (i.e., the management), are often willing to grant access. Health professionals in the United States would appear to have been more successful than their European counterparts in exploiting this favourable environment for both health promotion projects and research investigations. European workplace initiatives have tended to focus on safety rather than preventative medicine, as seen in the UK's 1974 Health and Safety at Work Act.

To understand this cultural difference, and the key to a successful workplace health promotion initiative, it is necessary to have a detailed understanding of the motivation of the corporation, factory or office involved in the project. Often it can simply be a case of economic self-interest. This motivation accounts for the rapid growth of fitness campaigns in American corporations. The huge financial costs of private health insurance for American companies provides a powerful motivator for such initiatives. In the UK, the system of National Insurance Contributions and the National Health Service has removed the urgency to address such issues in the workplace.

Lack of economic self-interest is not the only reason for the scarcity of health promotion initiatives by European corporations, it also determines the techniques that exercise psychologists might use. The traditional workplace fitness campaign reported in the literature contains one, if not all, of the following elements:

- Fitness testing
- Exercise prescription
- The provision of exercise facilities
- The employment of exercise leaders
- Behavioural change strategies (e.g., goal-setting, identification of barriers).

Two themes can be detected in such programmes. The first is the strong influence of the American College of Sports Medicine and the concept of a formalised exercise prescription based on frequency, intensity and duration. The potential problems with such an approach were highlighted by Dishman in 1988:

The appropriate volume of exercise for promoting adherence and health outcomes remains to be identified. Not only may rigid fitness prescriptions be too behaviourally challenging for some, they may not be biologically necessary. (Dishman, 1988, p. 53)

Such concerns are supported by empirical research that demonstrates the lack of adherence to workplace fitness programmes (Shephard, 1986). In light of this evidence it may be prudent for European workplace projects to focus on habitual physical activity rather than structured and formalised exercise. A good example of this is the work of Oja et al. (1991) in Finland where the use of physical activity for commuting to the workplace has been studied. A programme was initiated in a paper manufacturing company in Tampere, Finland, over a 6-month period. 'The programme was targeted to increase the awareness and knowledge of possibilities to use walking and cycling as forms of transportation to and from work and to stimulate the participation in safe walking and cycling during work commuting' (Oja et al., 1991, p. 237). The promotion campaign was found to have a positive effect in terms of greater awareness, increased participation in physical activity as a means of commuting to work and an increase in physical activity in leisure time. However, problems associated with pedestrian and road safety were noted and highlight the importance of environmental changes to physical activity promotion.

The second theme that can be identified within the American literature on physical activity in the workplace is an uncritical acceptance by fitness promoters of the agenda set by management. Economic self-interest may not be equated directly with profit maximisation but it is certainly not conducive to a radical rethinking and restructuring of the workplace. To date, workplace fitness programmes have tackled the consequences of twentieth-century work practices rather than the causes of ill health. One of the effects of this is a 'victim blaming' approach in workplace programmes—a focus on individual responsibility and individual action. The individual is asked to be more active, drink less and take relaxation classes. The question must be asked, given the scale of control over our lifestyle, should not management take some of the responsibility? Shift work, deadlines, design of jobs, factory conditions, even canteen menus are often controlled by management, and all affect our ability to achieve a satisfactory level of wellness.

If this somewhat radical analysis is accepted, where does it leave fitness programmes based on fitness testing and exercise prescription? On the one hand they appear rather naive attempts to tackle a problem that is far more complex than is sometimes acknowledged. On the other hand, they represent a foundation on which to build. The way forward in Europe may be a combined approach. As well as providing fitness testing for companies, exercise leaders need to consult with management on working practices. There is little point, for example, in providing back care programmes if the company runs a production line that is not ergometrically sound for posture and low back health. Similarly, there is little point in having relaxation classes if the dominant management style within the company is confrontational.

Exercise psychologists who become involved in workplace fitness promotion must bring many skills with them. These include not only the traditional tools of fitness promotion, such as goal-setting, but also a wider comprehension of the corporate culture and its effects on the lifestyle of individual employees. The exercise psychologist must also have a sense of realism. It seems to us that when one mentions workplace health promotion many colleagues have visions of office complexes and 'hi-tech' business parks. This often blinds us to the reality of the workplace for many Europeans. Our counterparts in some areas of Europe will experience a very different environment as they bring the health-related fitness message to their own locations. We look forward to the accounts of their work and experiences to help balance the American literature.

Promoting Physical Activity in Schools

The school is seen as a vital place in which to establish and develop behavioural patterns appropriate for health and well-being, including physical activity. Children are often identified as an important target group in health promotion, and recently physical education has taken a much more prominent role in such matters, even though 'health' has featured in school physical education curricula for many years. Williams (1988), for example, claims that the emphasis in British physical education has changed from a narrow medical rationale to one based on a more holistic approach stressing lifetime participation, enjoyment and motivation. This is probably true, although an ideology centred on the disease-prevention medical model is still dominant today (Armstrong, 1990). Devis and Peiro (1992) have found that the medical model ('body as machine' metaphor) has been used in Spain. They argue, however, that two other perspectives require consideration. First, a psychological and educational approach should allow students the opportunity to make informed decisions about future participation based on experiential physical education that informs them of the benefits of participation and the practical strategies required for involvement. This parallels Fox and Whitehead's (1987) call for a fundamental change in British physical education curricula.

Second, Devis and Piero highlight the need to consider a 'critical' model of health within physical education whereby pupils are made aware of the social inequalities in health, the incompleteness of the approach that stresses individualism above all else and the need to consider 'emancipatory health education'. Sparkes (1989, 1991) has made similar points in his critiques of the approaches used in Britain to promote health-related exercise and fitness. Davis and Piero conclude that all three of the models they describe have value and require consideration, although it is fair to say that the first two have dominated (see Sparkes, 1991).

The 1980s saw a huge increase in the UK in the interest of teachers in health-related fitness and exercise (HRE) programmes in schools (see Armstrong & Biddle, 1992; Biddle, 1987). Unfortunately no consensus on the way such material should be delivered has developed, lending confusion to the situation (see Biddle & Mutrie, 1991). Indeed, at a time when teachers are placing health and fitness high on their list of curricular objectives (Physical Education Association, 1987), the new National Curriculum in England and Wales (Department of Education and Science/Welsh Office, 1991) could be accused of marginalising such work in the physical education curriculum. This could have stemmed from the mistaken belief, often promoted by prominent physical educators, that HRE is simply a matter of getting children to be more active. Such mechanistic beliefs take no account of the sociocultural and behavioural factors influencing children's participation in HRE and other forms of physical activity. Many others have believed HRE in schools to be theory lessons on the biological consequences of physical exercise. Clearly such an approach will have limited impact on behaviour. This section of the chapter, therefore, will focus on the issues of exercise and physical activity promotion in schools from the point of view of psychological and social-psychological factors. Sadly, these are usually ignored or, at best, only implicitly recognised.

Do Childhood Habits Transfer to Adulthood?

One justification for teaching HRE in school physical education is that habits formed in childhood will carry over to adult life. Although this assumption seems reasonable, evidence to substantiate it is weak or inconsistent (Powell & Dysinger, 1987). Many factors in the transition from school to adult life are likely to affect the levels and patterns of physical activity. Changes in the adult life cycle itself will affect the extent that adults are active (Mihalik, O'Leary, McGuire, & Dottavio, 1989). Nevertheless, evidence from the Allied Dunbar National Fitness Survey (ADNFS) in England (ADNFS, 1992) does support the view that early participation is associated with a greater likelihood of involvement later in life.

An extensive survey of 10 European countries and over 39,000 schoolchildren shows the importance of peers and family members in the promotion of children's physical activity (Wold & Anderssen, 1992). Results showed that children whose parents, best friends and siblings take part in sport and physical activity are much more likely to take part themselves. Participation of their best friend was the strongest predictor, while among family members same-gender individuals had the strongest influence.

Many have questioned the relevance of current physical education curricula to the development of active lifestyles in adulthood. For example, Coakley and White (1992), in a qualitative study with British adolescents, found that participation in community sport programmes was influenced by past experiences in school physical education classes, as discussed in chapter 1. In particular, such memories guided future expectations of sport and exercise. Negative memories centred on boredom and lack of choice, feeling stupid and incompetent, and receiving negative evaluation from peers. Such reflections, found through in-depth semi-structured interviews, parallel theoretical developments in sport and exercise psychology concerning intrinsic motivation, enjoyment, achievement goal orientations and motivational climate (see Roberts, 1992). For example, the reactions reported by Coakley and White are consistent with the need to promote intrinsic motivation and high perceptions of autonomy and competence by allowing participants to make choices and have some involvement in decision-making procedures, and allowing for individual interpretations of success for the maximisation of enjoyment (see Roberts, 1992). In addition, the class climate may need reappraisal so that all pupils are valued for their own efforts. This might help reduce negative peer evaluation and increase intrinsic motivation (Goudas & Biddle, 1994).

Researchers in Belgium have also questioned the relevance of physical education curricula to the promotion of active leisure time. Bollaert, De Knop, and Theeboom (1992) found that traditional team sports still dominate the Belgian school curriculum yet trends indicate that students prefer individual pursuits. This argument finds support in the 'lifetime sports' movement in the USA where some physical educators have argued that children should be better prepared for adult life by teaching them activities relevant to adults (Corbin & Lindsey, 1988). Certainly, this provides a strong rationale for teaching fitness activities to adolescents, such as weight training and aerobics.

In Germany, Franke (1991) has suggested that physical education needs to cover a wider variety of activities.

It is only when physical education in school develops ways of including these liberal aspects of fun and choice into the thrust of its pedagogic programme with equal importance, next to the prevailing principle of achievement, that there will be a chance for those pupils to be reached who would otherwise continue to be sceptical, full of refusal, or even full of rejection. (Franke, 1991, p. 470)

In summary, it would appear wholly logical for experiences in childhood physical education to affect behaviour later in life. However, the evidence is not currently available to support or refute this. As we have stated elsewhere, 'the notion of an "activity habit" is not well supported, although Engstrom (1986) suggests that the perceptions children hold about physical activity might be a more fruitful line of enquiry, particularly when put alongside the influence of the environment' (Biddle, 1992a, p. 171). Indeed, the assumption that physical education will influence adult participation patterns is too simplistic, and adult physical activity should be viewed in the wider context of other leisure choices (Glyptis, 1992).

Fitness Testing

The increased interest shown in teaching HRE in schools has also led to the greater use of fitness tests. We have argued for many years that the primary aim of using such activities in the school curriculum is not to see how fit the pupils are, but to assist in the development of pupils' understanding of fitness concepts (Fox & Biddle, 1986, 1987, 1988). That is to say, fitness tests should have an educational aim.

One could argue that the fitness test will have a powerful psychological influence on the child. Indeed, many teachers claim that they use fitness tests to motivate their classes. However, research on this is sparse and only now starting to emerge. For example, Whitehead and Corbin (1991) found that intrinsic motivation after fitness testing was related to the normative feedback given after the test. Pupils who were told that they were in the lowest 20% declined in intrinsic motivation, but those in the highest 20% increased in intrinsic motivation. Analyses showed that such changes were mediated by perceptions of competence. From this study alone, therefore, we can conclude that fitness tests are motivating—but only if you do well!

A recent study (Goudas, Biddle, & Fox, 1994) also showed that psychological influences in fitness testing can be strong. Over 200 children were assessed on ego and task achievement goal orientations (see Duda, 1993 and chapters 10 and 12) prior to the completion of a 20m progressive shuttle run. This test of endurance requires the participant to run between two lines 20m apart at a pace dictated by a tone emitted from a tape recorder. The time interval between tones becomes progressively shorter, giving the runner less time to reach the line. Runners drop out of the test when they can no longer reach the line in the required time. This usually is after 10 to 15 min of running. It takes considerable effort at the end to maintain the required pace.

On conclusion of the run, the children rated their perception of success on the test, and they then completed the Intrinsic Motivation Inventory (Ryan, 1982; Ryan, Mims, & Koestner, 1983) modified for the activity. We found the highest levels of intrinsic motivation towards running among those who were high in task orientation but low in ego orientation. This was particularly true of children in the lower half of the group when split by run performance. For those in this lower half who are low in task orientation and high in ego orientation, the fitness testing environment appears to be motivationally threatening.

Finally, we have recently concluded a number of studies investigating a measure of self-motivation in children (Biddle et al., in press). This is a modified version of an adult scale developed by Dishman and colleagues in the USA (Dishman & Ickes, 1981; Dishman, Ickes, & Morgan, 1980). We found that the modified self-motivation inventory (SMI-C) was correlated with endurance running performance in a small group of boys ($r = 0.70$, $p < 0.01$; $n = 24$) and a larger group of boys ($n = 128$) and girls ($n = 129$) ($r = 0.33$; $p < 0.01$). Another study of 69 pupils found a correlation between the SMI-C and performance on a sprint agility run ($r = -0.26$) and a significant correlation was even found between SMI-C and flexibility test performance under two different conditions ($r = 0.42$ and 0.49, both $p < 0.05$). These results confirm the widely held belief that performance in field tests of fitness are often influenced by the motivation of the participant.

Fitness tests, therefore, are not automatically beneficial for the promotion of exercise and physical activity. The psychological influence of tests appears to be related to a number of self-perception variables. Whether the suggested educational use of fitness tests provides more positive experiences for all children has yet to be investigated, although it appears to be a better route to follow. It is unfortunate, therefore, that the best-known European initiative in this area—the 'Eurofit' project—ignores the behavioural issues associated with fitness tests, yet at the same time assumes that fitness testing children will have beneficial psychological effects.

The Eurofit project (Council of Europe, 1988) was initiated in 1977 with the aims of establishing a common test battery in Europe, of assisting teachers in the assessment of school pupils' physical fitness, and of assessing the health-related fitness of the population. The tests include a mix of what are usually referred to as health-related and skill (motor)-related components of physical fitness. We are less concerned here with the type of tests used and more interested in the psychological issues associated with Eurofit. For example, the handbook (Council of Europe, 1988) states that the Eurofit tests,

> can help to develop a positive attitude to the body; can enable him or her to achieve a self-awareness of his or her physical state and *thus become better motivated to maintain or improve his or her fitness.* (p. 9; our emphasis)

Recent research studies have shown how simplistic such statements are. The Eurofit handbook reflects a physiological and measurement approach to fitness testing (this is also evident in the composition of the committee advising the project), and seems to assume that simply measuring fitness will automatically have beneficial psychological effects. The handbook is in need of additional material suggesting how such tests can be used to change behaviour and what factors might mediate such effects.

Daily Physical Education

One strategy that has been used in an effort to increase the involvement in physical activities is the introduction of daily lessons of physical education. Although this would appear, superficially at least, to be a positive thing, a number of factors raise doubts that daily physical education will actually promote physical activity in the long term. The main danger is that daily physical education may become more associated with 'drill' and 'training' than education. Related to this is our belief that teachers are likely to find daily lessons difficult to vary and thus to keep the interest of students. Finally, the evidence that daily physical education actually works is weak or inconclusive.

A study on daily physical education was undertaken in Scotland by Pollatschek and O'Hagan (1989). They compared over 200 children experiencing daily physical education with a group participating in 'normal' physical education for one lesson each week. They assessed the children on physical, academic and attitudinal measures before and after the programme. The study showed that the daily physical education intervention had no effect on academic or attitudinal measures, other than through anecdotal reports from teachers. It was not clear whether such results were due to a response bias (halo effect) among the teachers or the actual intervention. Similarly, research in Finland (Sarlin, 1992) showed no effects on perceived physical competence as a result of a daily physical education programme. There is certainly a need for further research in Europe on the psychological effects of increasing physical education contact time for children.

Conclusion

It is our belief that applying psychological principles to the promotion of physical activity and exercise will be a major endeavour in the near future in European initiatives in health promotion. The significant political and economic changes in

East and Central Europe, for example, may well lead to much greater research and promotion efforts in physical activity and health.

Despite this optimism, there is still a long way to go in convincing influential groups and organisations, such as the medical profession or research funding agencies, of the importance of behavioural issues alongside the traditional study and promotion of physical health outcomes per se. A shift from the product of physical activity to a greater understanding of the process, or processes, involved in the promotion of physical activity should serve us well in the important period ahead of us in a changing Europe.

References

Aaro, L.E. (1991). Fitness promotion programs in mass media: Norwegian experiences. In P. Oja & R. Telama (Eds.), *Sport for all* (pp. 193-200). Amsterdam: Elsevier.

Ajzen, I. (1985). From intentions to actions: A theory of planned behaviour. In J. Kuhl & J. Beckman (Eds.), *Action control: From cognition to behaviour* (pp. 11-39). Berlin: Springer-Verlag.

Ajzen, I., & Fishbein, M. (1980). *Understanding attitudes and predicting social behaviour.* Englewood Cliffs, NJ: Prentice Hall.

Allied Dunbar National Fitness Survey. (1992). *Main findings.* London: Sports Council and Health Education Authority.

Armstrong, N. (1990). Children's physical activity patterns: The implications for physical education. In N. Armstrong (Ed.), *New directions in physical education* (Vol. I, pp. 1-15). Champaign, IL: Human Kinetics.

Armstrong, N., & Biddle, S.J.H. (1992). Health-related physical activity in the national curriculum. In N. Armstrong (Ed.), *New directions in physical education: Vol. II. Towards a national curriculum* (pp. 71-110). Champaign, IL: Human Kinetics.

Bandura, A. (1977). Self-efficacy: A unifying theory of behavioural change. *Psychological Review*, **84**, 191-215.

Bandura, A. (1986). *Social foundations of thought and action: A social-cognitive theory.* Englewood Cliffs, NJ: Prentice Hall.

Becker, M.L., Haefner, D.P., Kasl, S.V., Kirscht, J.P., Maiman, L.A., & Rosenstock, I.M. (1977). Selected psychosocial models and correlates of individual health-related behaviours. *Medical Care*, **15**(Suppl. 5), 27-46.

Biddle, S.J.H. (Ed.) (1987). *Foundations of health-related fitness in physical education.* London: Ling.

Biddle, S.J.H. (1992a). Adherence to physical activity and exercise. In N. Norgan (Ed.), *Physical activity and health* (pp. 170-189). Cambridge, England: Cambridge University Press.

Biddle, S.J.H. (1992b). Exercise psychology. *Sport Science Review*, **1**(2), 79-92.

Biddle, S.J.H., Akande, D., Armstrong, N., Ashcroft, M., Brooke, R., & Goudas, M. (in press). The Self-Motivation Inventory modified for children: Evidence on psychometric properties and its use in physical exercise. *International Journal of Sport Psychology*.

Biddle, S.J.H., & Mutrie, N. (1991). *Psychology of physical activity and exercise: A health-related perspective.* London: Springer-Verlag.

Biddle, S.J.H., & Smith, R.A. (1991). Motivating adults for physical activity: Towards a healthier present. *Journal of Physical Education, Recreation and Dance*, **62**(7), 39-43.

Bollaert, L., De Knop, P., & Theeboom, M. (1992, July). *The leisure relevance of a physical education curriculum.* Paper presented at the Olympic Scientific Congress, Benalmadena, Málaga, Spain.

Bouchard, C., Shephard, R.J., Stephens, T., Sutton, J.R., & McPherson, B.D. (Eds.) (1990). *Exercise, fitness, and health: A consensus of current knowledge.* Champaign, IL: Human Kinetics.

Carron, A.V., Widmeyer, W.N., & Brawley, L.R. (1988). Group cohesion and individual adherence to physical activity. *Journal of Sport and Exercise Psychology*, **10**, 127-138.

Coakley, J., & White, A. (1992). Making decisions: Gender and sport participation among British adolescents. *Sociology of Sport Journal*, **9**, 20-35.

Corbin, C.B. (1984). Self-confidence of females in sports and physical activity. *Clinics in Sports Medicine*, **3**, 895-908.

Corbin, C.B., & Lindsey, R. (1988). *Concepts of physical fitness.* Dubuque, IA: Brown.

Council of Europe. (1988). *Eurofit: Handbook for the Eurofit tests of physical fitness.* Rome: Author.

Department of Education and Science/Welsh Office. (1991). *Physical education for ages 5 to 16.* London: Author.

Devis, D., & Peiro, V.C. (1992, July). *Physical education and health: An educational foundation.* Paper presented at the Olympic Scientific Congress, Benalmadena, Málaga, Spain.

Dishman, R.K. (1988). Behavioural barriers to health-related physical fitness. In L.K. Hall & G.C. Meyer (Eds.), *Epidemiology, behaviour change, and intervention in chronic disease* (pp. 49-83). Champaign, IL: Life Enhancement.

Dishman, R.K. (1990). Determinants of participation in physical activity. In C. Bouchard, R.J. Shephard, T. Stephens, J.R. Sutton, & B.D. McPherson (Eds.), *Exercise, fitness, and health: A consensus of current knowledge* (pp. 75-101). Champaign, IL: Human Kinetics.

Dishman, R., & Gettman, L.R. (1980). Psychobiologic influences in exercise adherence. *Journal of Sport Psychology*, **2**, 295-310.

Dishman, R.K., & Ickes, W. (1981). Self-motivation and adherence to therapeutic exercise. *Journal of Behavioral Medicine*, **4**, 421-438.

Dishman, R.K., Ickes, W., & Morgan, W.P. (1980). Self-motivation and adherence to habitual physical activity. *Journal of Applied Social Psychology*, **10**, 115-132.

Dishman, R.K., Sallis, J.F., & Orenstein, D. (1985). The determinants of physical activity and exercise. *Public Health Reports*, **100**, 158-171.

Duda, J.L. (1993). Goals: A social-cognitive approach to the study of achievement motivation in sport. In R.N. Singer, M. Murphey, & L.K. Tennant (Eds.), *Handbook of research on sport psychology* (pp. 421-436). New York: Macmillan.

Dzewaltowski, D.A. (1989). Toward a model of exercise motivation. *Journal of Sport and Exercise Psychology*, **11**, 251-269.

Engstrom, L.M. (1986). The process of socialisation into keep-fit activities. *Scandinavian Journal of Sport Sciences*, **8**, 89-97.

Fishbein, M., & Ajzen, I. (1975). *Belief, attitude, intention and behaviour: An introduction to theory and research.* Reading, MA: Addison-Wesley.

Fox, K.R. (1991). Motivating children for physical activity: Towards a healthier future. *Journal of Physical Education, Recreation and Dance*, **62**(7), 34-38.

Fox, K.R. (1992). A clinical approach to exercise in the markedly obese. In T.A. Wadden & T.B. Van Itallie (Eds.), *Treatment of the seriously obese patient* (pp. 354-382). New York: Guilford.

Fox, K.R., & Biddle, S.J.H. (1986). Health-related fitness testing in schools: I. Introduction and problems of interpretation. *Bulletin of Physical Education*, **22**, 54-64.

Fox, K.R., & Biddle, S.J.H. (1987). Health-related fitness testing in schools: II. Philosophical and psychological implications. *Bulletin of Physical Education*, **23**, 28-39.

Fox, K.R., & Biddle, S.J.H. (1988). The use of fitness tests: Educational and psychological considerations. *Journal of Physical Education, Recreation and Dance*, **59**(2), 47-53.

Fox, K.R., & Whitehead, J.R. (1987). Student-centered physical education. In S.J.H. Biddle (Ed.), *Foundations of health-related fitness in physical education* (pp. 94-102). London: Ling.

Franke, E. (1991). School physical education as a promoter of sport for all among the population. In P. Oja & R. Telama (Eds.), *Sport for all* (pp. 465-471). Amsterdam: Elsevier.

Glyptis, S. (1992). Leisure lifestyles: Present and future. In N. Norgan (Ed.), *Physical activity and health* (pp. 230-245). Cambridge, England: Cambridge University Press.

Godin, G., & Shephard, R.J. (1986). Psychosocial factors influencing intentions to exercise of young students from grades 7 to 9. *Research Quarterly for Exercise and Sport*, **57**, 41-52.

Godin, G., & Shephard, R.J. (1990). Use of attitude-behavior models in exercise promotion. *Sports Medicine*, **10**, 103-121.

Goudas, M., & Biddle, S.J.H. (1994). Perceived motivational climate and intrinsic motivation in school physical education classes. *European Journal of Psychology of Education* **9**, 241-250.

Goudas, M., Biddle, S.J.H., & Fox, K.R. (1994). Achievement goal orientations and intrinsic motivation in physical fitness testing in children. *Pediatric Exercise Science*, **6**, 159-167.

Ingjer, F., & Dahl, H.A. (1979). Dropouts from an endurance training programme: Some histochemical and physiological aspects. *Scandinavian Journal of Sport Sciences*, **1**, 20-22.

Kendzierski, D. (1990). Decision making versus decision implementation: An action control approach to exercise adoption and adherence. *Journal of Applied Social Psychology*, **20**, 27-45.

Kendzierski, D., & LaMastro, V.D. (1988). Reconsidering the role of attitudes in exercise behaviour: A decision theoretic approach. *Journal of Applied Social Psychology*, **18**, 737-759.

Knapp, D. (1988). Behavioural management techniques and exercise promotion. In R.K. Dishman (Ed.), *Exercise adherence: Its impact on public health* (pp. 203-235). Champaign, IL: Human Kinetics.

Lee, C., & Owen, N. (1986). Exercise persistence: Contributions of psychology to the promotion of regular physical activity. *Australian Psychologist*, **21**, 427-466.

Locke, L., & Latham, G. (1990). *A theory of goal-setting and task performance*. Englewood Cliffs, NJ: Prentice Hall.

Macleod, D., Maughan, R., Nimmo, M., Reilly, T., & Williams, C. (Eds.) (1987). *Exercise: Benefits, limits and adaptations*. London: Spon.

Marlatt, G.A. (1985). Relapse prevention: Theoretical rationale and overview of the model. In G.A. Marlatt & J.R. Gordon (Eds.), *Relapse prevention: Maintenance strategies in the treatment of addictive behaviours* (pp. 3-70). New York: Guilford Press.

Martinsen, E.W. (1989). *Physical fitness training in the treatment of patients with nonpsychotic mental disorders*. Forde, Norway: Department of Psychiatry, Central Hospital.

Mihalik, B.J., O'Leary, J.T., McGuire, F.A., & Dottavio, F.D. (1989). Sports involvement across the life span: Expansion and contraction of sports activities. *Research Quarterly for Exercise and Sport*, **60**, 396-398.

Morgan, W.P., & Goldston, S.E. (Eds.) (1987). *Exercise and mental health*. Washington, DC: Hemisphere.

Norgan, N. (Ed.) (1992). *Physical activity and health*. Cambridge, England: Cambridge University Press.

Normand, C.E.M., & Vaughan, J.P. (Eds.) (1993). *Europe without frontiers: The implications for health*. Chichester, England: Wiley.

Oja, P., Paronen, O., Manttari, A., Kukkonen-Harjula, K., Laukkanen, R., Vuori, I., & Pasanen, M. (1991). Occurrence, effects and promotion of walking and cycling as forms of transportation during work commuting: A Finnish experience. In P. Oja & R. Telama (Eds.), *Sport for all* (pp. 233-238). Amsterdam: Elsevier.

Oldridge, N.B., & Jones, N.L. (1983). Improving patient compliance in cardiac rehabilitation: Effects of written agreement and self-monitoring. *Journal of Cardiac Rehabilitation*, **3**, 257-262.

Owen, N., & Lee, C. (1986). Issues in changing behaviour to promote health. *Behaviour Change*, **3**, 150-157.

Physical Education Association. (1987). *Physical education in schools: Report of a commission of enquiry*. London: Author.

Pollatschek, J.L., & O'Hagan, F.J. (1989). An investigation of the psycho-physical influences of a quality daily physical education programme. *Health Education Research: Theory and Practice*, **4**, 341-350.

Powell, K.E., & Dysinger, W. (1987). Childhood participation in organized school sports and physical education as precursors of adult physical activity. *American Journal of Preventive Medicine*, **3**, 276-281.

Prochaska, J.O., & DiClemente, C.C. (1986). Towards a comprehensive model of change. In W. Miller & N. Heather (Eds.), *Treating addictive behaviours: Processes of change* (pp. 3-27). New York: Wiley.

Rejeski, W.J., & Kenney, E.A. (1988). *Fitness motivation*. Champaign, IL: Life Enhancement.

Roberts, G.C. (Ed.) (1992). *Motivation in sport and exercise*. Champaign, IL: Human Kinetics.

Ryan, R.M. (1982). Control and information in the intrapersonal sphere: An extension of cognitive evaluation theory. *Journal of Personality and Social Psychology*, **43**, 450-461.

Ryan, R.M., Mims, V., & Koestner, R. (1983). Relation of reward contingency and interpersonal context to intrinsic motivation: A review and test using cognitive evaluation theory. *Journal of Personality and Social Psychology*, **45**, 736-750.

Sallis, J.F., & Hovell, M.F. (1990). Determinants of exercise behaviour. *Exercise and Sport Sciences Reviews*, **18**, 307-330.

Sarlin, E.L. (1992, July). *Effects of daily physical education on perceived competence and correlations between perceived competence and measured motor fitness, ball-handling and gymnastic skills*. Paper presented at the Olympic Scientific Congress, Benalmadena, Málaga, Spain.

Shephard, R.J. (1986). *Economic benefits of enhanced fitness*. Champaign, IL: Human Kinetics.

Smith, R.A., & Biddle, S.J.H. (1992). Attitudes and health-related exercise: Review and critique. In T. Williams, L. Almond, & A.C. Sparkes (Eds.), *Sport and physical activity* (pp. 347-352). London: Spon.

Sparkes, A.C. (1989). Health-related fitness: An example of innovation without change. *British Journal of Physical Education*, **20**(2), 60-63.

Sparkes, A.C. (1991). Alternative visions of health-related fitness: An exploration of problem-setting and its consequences. In N. Armstrong & A.C. Sparkes (Eds.), *Issues in physical education* (pp. 204-227). London: Cassell.

Steptoe, A., & Bolton, J. (1988). The short-term influence of high and low intensity physical exercise on mood. *Psychology and Health*, **2**, 91-106.

Steptoe, A., & Cox, S. (1988). Acute effects of aerobic exercise on mood. *Health Psychology*, **7**, 329-340.

Vanden Auweelle, Y., Rzewnicki, R., & Van Mele, V. (1993). *Reasons for not exercising and exercise intentions: A study of middle-aged sedentary adults.* Unpublished manuscript, Catholic University of Leuven, Belgium.

Wankel, L. (1984). Decision-making and social support strategies for increasing exercise involvement. *Journal of Cardiac Rehabilitation*, **4**, 124-135.

Wankel, L. (1985). Personal and situational factors affecting exercise involvement: The importance of enjoyment. *Research Quarterly for Exercise and Sport*, **56**, 275-282.

Wankel, L., Yardley, J.K., & Graham, J. (1985). The effects of motivational interventions upon the exercise adherence of high and low self-motivated adults. *Canadian Journal of Applied Sport Sciences*, **10**, 147-156.

Whitehead, J.R., & Corbin, C.B. (1991). Youth fitness testing: Effects of percentile-based evaluative feedback on intrinsic motivation. *Research Quarterly for Exercise and Sport*, **62**, 225-231.

Williams, A. (1988). The historiography of health and fitness in physical education. *British Journal of Physical Education Research Supplement*, **3**, 1-4.

Wold, B., & Anderssen, N. (1992). Health promotion aspects of family and peer influences on sport participation. *International Journal of Sport Psychology*, **23**, 343-359.

II
PART

PSYCHOLOGY OF
SPORT PERFORMANCE

There has been a recognisable growth during the latter part of the 1980s and into the 1990s in the area of enhancing performance in sport through psychological means. Practical 'applied' services have been in great demand and, while this has brought its problems in terms of quality control, it has also been associated with an increase in valuable and important research concerning sport performance.

This part of the book attempts to provide a flavour of such research currently underway in Europe. For example, in chapter 6, Erwin Apitzsch proposes that we rethink the issue of personality in sport by adopting a psychodynamic approach. He provides evidence of how this might be beneficial in sport by drawing on his own research findings on soccer. Clearly this is a controversial chapter if one adopts the traditional perspectives on personality in sport. However, it illustrates the need to adopt a broader perspective and be aware of different approaches looking at the same problem.

Graham Jones' chapter on competitive anxiety (chapter 7) is a good example of how a researcher has challenged and extended the commonly held assumptions of the dominant themes in the research literature. His overview provides some excellent ideas and evidence that have impact on both theory and practice, such as the need to study cognitive intrusions, and the measurement of frequency and direction as well as intensity of anxiety.

This is also true in the area of psychophysiology where the results presented in David Collins' chapter (chapter 8) have clear implications for the type of mental training adopted in sport for certain tasks. Whilst this research requires sophisticated and expensive equipment, and as such could be interpreted as being less relevant to the real world, it provides good insights into how the mind functions during, or just prior to, performance. It would be a mistake, therefore, to think that it is not applicable to sports practice. Finally, Guido Schilling and Hanspeter Gubelmann provide a short commentary on mental training and provide data showing the benefits of mental training on performance (see chapter 9).

Applied delivery of sport psychology for performance enhancement requires further understanding of the underlying mechanisms of such changes in behaviour. The research considered here helps to provide this.

6
CHAPTER

Psychodynamic Theory of Personality and Sport Performance

Erwin Apitzsch

SWEDEN

Bakker, Whiting, and van der Brug (1990) have argued recently that despite tremendous attention to personality research in sport psychology, the findings are not particularly impressive. Similarly, Fisher (1984), who has indicated that well over 1,000 studies of the relationship between personality and sport performance have been carried out, suggests that very limited knowledge has been gained. Fisher also reported that personality studies relating to sport performance declined markedly in number between the late 1970s and the early 1980s. According to LeUnes, Wolf, Ripper, and Anding (1990), this trend is still continuing. Despite this, many researchers (e.g., Gill, 1986) still regard personality as a highly worthwhile topic of study, because they feel that individual differences may well play a crucial role in sport performance.

Three major directions in personality research are trait theory, social learning theory and psychodynamic theory. Of these, trait theory and social learning theory have received the most attention in the area of sport, whereas psychodynamic theory has played almost no role.

Currently there is no commonly accepted definition of the personality concept. However, the common core in all investigations of personality is to study the individual's unique and relatively stable personal or behavioural tendencies.

Personality Theories

Trait theories are based on the assumption that personality can be described in terms of basic traits that individuals possess. Such traits, considered to be stable, enduring and consistent, can, it is suggested, predict an individual's behaviour in a variety of situations. Thus, an ice hockey player considered to be aggressive could be expected to behave aggressively not only when playing ice hockey, but in other situations as well. Trait theories have generated vast research and many familiar personality tests. However, general personality traits have tended to be poor predictors of behaviour in sport. Fisher (1984) maintains, in fact, that personality traits explain no more than 10% of the behavioural variability in any given sport situation.

In recent years interest in a trait approach to research on sport psychology appears to have declined in favour of social learning theory. This theory frequently adopts an interactionist approach, which considers a combination of personality and situational factors to be major determinants of performance (Gill, 1986). In addition, factors associated with learning, such as reinforcement, vicarious experience and punishment, are thought to be important determinants of personality and behaviour. Accordingly, an aggressive ice hockey player would be expected to display aggressive behaviour only in certain situations, such as when it might be rewarded with a goal or towards the end of a close match, whereas much less aggressive behaviour might be expected throughout a match against weak opposition or with no clear overt reward. Bowers (1973) claims that the interaction between person and environment accounts for about 20% of the variance in performance; Kane (1977) increases the level to some 30% to 50%.

Psychodynamic theories are based on the idea that subconscious processes affect behaviour. For example, it is assumed that in stressful situations intrapsychic defensive processes are initiated in order to reduce an intensely unpleasant emotional state. These defensive mechanisms operate in such a way as to distort the perception of a situation and make it less threatening. Although interventions based on psychodynamic theory have been made by some sport psychologists, according to Silva (1984) this theory has contributed little to an understanding of the relationship between personality and sport. Silva maintains that despite its impact in other areas of psychology, psychodynamic theory has been considered to have little to offer in the area of sport performance.

Contradictory findings with regard to relationships between personality and sport performance (e.g., Bakker et al., 1990; Singer, 1986), methodological shortcomings (e.g., Silva, 1984; Singer, 1986) and relatively low ability to explain behavioural variability in any given situation (Fisher, 1984) have contributed to a general decline in research on personality and sport. The inability of trait theories to predict behaviour has resulted in two different viewpoints. The more sceptical view is that personality traits are of little value in explaining differences between athletes and nonathletes, between athletes of different levels of ability and between athletes in one type of sport versus another. The more credulous view maintains that tests of personality traits provide useful means of studying the relationship between personality and sport behaviour. Singer (1986) calls for personality research within a societal context and renounces more global approaches. He claims that it is futile to assess personality in terms of broad traits when looking for a specific type of sport performance in a special type of situation.

In summary, it seems as if the pure trait theory has been largely abandoned as the primary approach to research on personality within the area of sport. By and large the social learning and interactionist approaches seem to be favoured currently, whereas few studies based on psychodynamic theory have been reported.

In general, psychodynamic approaches to personality and sport have not appealed to researchers in sport psychology. Silva (1984) states that specific and testable hypotheses relevant to sport have not been generated or investigated from this point of view. Furthermore, psychodynamic theories are critised for their inability to predict behaviour and the difficulty of measuring cause and effect relations between psychic processes and overt behaviour. Gill (1986) is also clear in her viewpoint, completely dismissing the impact of psychodynamic aspects of the individual on sport performance:

> Psychodynamic theory is mainly an after-the-fact explanation based on infor-
> mal observations and clinical intuition; psychoanalytical approaches focus on
> psychopathology and offer few testable predictions, especially about healthy
> personalities. (p. 26)

However, in my opinion sport psychology researchers from North America are, by and large, ignorant of the existence of scientific studies on psychodynamic theory reported in languages other than English and, therefore, too hastily jump to conclusions concerning the usefulness of this theory.

The Psychodynamic Approach

This chapter will be devoted to broadening perspectives on psychodynamic theory and pointing to the potential contribution of this theory to understanding behaviour in sport. However, this is not done with the aim of dismissing other theories, or of claiming the superiority of psychodynamic theory over other personality theories.

Why does a skilful athlete not always perform optimally? It is an indisputable fact that two equally skilful athletes may perform quite differently under the same objective conditions. For example, in a closely fought match it may be noted that some players perform up to their usual standard, whereas others play well below their standard. One reason for this may be different abilities in coping with stress. One player may experience the 'make-or-break' situation of a tight cup match as a challenge, but another player may be so overwhelmed by nervousness that he or she wants most of all that the match should finish as soon as possible. This difference in perception makes it obvious that psychological factors play an important role in this type of athletic performance.

To understand how a team achieves optimal performance, it is necessary to know why one player can rise to the demands of competition while another player suffers a whole or partial breakdown in performance. During a match, time for an efficient evaluation of a situation is often limited and this frequently produces stress. Both the adequacy of the assessment of the situation and the subsequent decision may be negatively affected by stress. Top-level athletes of all kinds frequently perform in an environment which by its very nature generates a great deal of pressure (Jones & Hardy, 1990). Decisions under extreme time pressure add further to stress. It is assumed that stress affects psychologically labile athletes in such a way that the decisions they have to make under the pressure of limited time might well be different if more time were available (Bezak & Macak, 1976).

The way in which people tend to perceive situations as stressful is generally considered to be a function of personality. In stress and anxiety research it is commonly accepted that a distinction can be made between anxiety as a relatively stable personality trait (trait anxiety) and anxiety as a transitory emotional state (state anxiety; Spielberger, 1989). Individuals with a high level of trait anxiety tend to show high levels of state anxiety in stressful situations. High levels of state anxiety are experienced as unpleasant, and in such a situation individuals will take steps, either consciously or subconsciously, to protect themselves against any disruption or disorganization of function that might otherwise ensue. The primary way in which this adaptation takes place is by the initiation of intrapsychic defensive processes in order to reduce the intensely unpleasant emotional state. These defensive mechanisms operate in such a way as to distort the perception of a situation, making it less threatening. This is done at the expense of a large amount of psychic energy devoted to reducing state anxiety while the actual source of the perceived danger remains unchanged (Spielberger, 1989). Thus the chain of events, according to psychodynamic theory, may begin with external threat, a situation considered to be threatening to most people (e.g., to mark a world-class soccer player in a match), that elicits anxiety. Anxiety can also be elicited by internally perceived threat—a situation considered to be threatening to a specific person—for example, to mark a soccer player in an opposing team whom the individual has failed to mark success-fully in the past. To get rid of the extremely unpleasant feeling of anxiety, defence mechanisms are used, resulting in reduction of anxiety. According to Apitzsch and Berggren (1993), the resulting distortion of reality can be adaptive (favouring the sport performance) or maladaptive (unfavourable to performance).

The Defence Mechanism Test

One way of assessing personality in terms of defence mechanisms is by using the projective test The Defence Mechanism Test (DMT). Projective methods àre based on the assumption that the individual's perception of the external world is not objective but is influenced by subjective interpretations emanating from needs and past experience. The DMT purports to reveal the defence mechanisms used by subjects exposed to some kind of threat or pressure.

The basic apparatus used in the DMT procedure is a tachistoscope with a shutter which accurately regulates the time of exposure of the stimulus material. The range of exposure time varies from a minimum of 10 ms to a maximum time of 2 s. Each subject is exposed to the same stimulus picture 20 times, the exposure time of each successive stimulus being gradually increased. If the subject reaches the level of correct recognition and can describe the picture accurately before the twentieth exposure the test is discontinued. In the test manual, Kragh (1969) refers to Freud (1949) and writes that the mechanisms of defence work roughly in the sequence of: threat or danger → anxiety → defence against the anxiety. When Kragh constructed the DMT his aim was to replicate this sequence in the test situation. Thus, the corresponding sequence in the DMT is: subliminal threat → subliminal anxiety → perceptual defence. Distortions, additions and exclusions to which the stimulus pictures are subjected on the way to a correct perception are interpreted as signs of the effect of defence mechanisms. After a number of trials with various pictures taken from the Thematic Apperception Test (Murray, 1938), two drawn pictures were chosen, each portraying a threatening scene designed to activate Oedipal conflict and superego threat. In the center of the picture there is a neutral looking young person, the Hero, with whom the subject supposedly identifies. Beside the Hero, there is a hideously ugly looking person, threatening the Hero from a position diagonally behind him.

This threatening scene, presented to the subject initially at a subliminal level, arouses anxiety that is followed by defensive psychological action. The short period of exposure allows, or 'forces', the subject to respond by giving subjective interpretations of what has been seen. Thus as the time of exposure increases the degree of subjectivity of the report would be expected to decrease. After each exposure the subject is requested to give a verbal description of what has been seen, and this is recorded verbatim by the tester. Furthermore, the subject is also requested to draw as accurately as possible on paper what has been seen in the tachistoscope.

The purpose of the DMT is to elicit the defensive activity that the subject habitually uses when confronted with a threatening situation. In addition, according to the underlying theory that the perceptual process can be broken down into micro-processes which temporally replicate the ontogenesis of perceptual development, the theory also predicts that the activated defences revealed by the DMT follow a sequential pattern corresponding to the defence development that evolved and was established during childhood. Since 1970, the use of the DMT by the Swedish Air Force Selection Board has been cited as a major factor in the reduced incidence of airplane crashes previously considered to be associated with the presence of maladaptive psychological defence mechanisms (Sandahl, 1988).

The starting point for Kragh when originally constructing the test was that there is no clear difference between the normal person's use of perceptual defence and that of individuals considered to be disturbed (Kragh & Smith, 1970). Thus the DMT can be used on normal groups as well as on clinical groups. All people use defensive mechanisms in order to handle the pressure of everyday life. The defence mechanisms can be viewed as the mental equivalent to white blood cells. The white blood cells are necessary for the survival of the individual because, for example, they increase in number during times of infection. Their task is to defend the body by attacking and destroying alien objects. However, there are instances when they cause a breakdown of the body. For example, an overproduction of white blood cells, as is the case in leukaemia, may cause death. In the same way, the positive function of the defence mechanisms can change to something detrimental to the individual if they are used in a maladaptive way. For example, a compulsive behaviour may become so dominant as to cause severe restrictions in everyday life.

As mentioned above, defence mechanisms are used to protect the individual from excessive threat. However, there are some difficulties with this. One question that may be raised is when is a defensive action adaptive and when is it maladaptive? Recently, Cramer (1991) has discussed the dual functions of defence mechanisms and has written:

> If the defence is used for healthy adaptation, in the service of maturation, growth and mastery of the drives, then it serves a normal function. On the other hand, if the defence is used primarily to ward off anxiety, strong instinctual demands and unconscious conflict, then it serves an abnormal function. (p. 10)

Recent views suggest that whether or not defence mechanisms may be considered adaptive or maladaptive actually depends on the individual's ego strength, the intensity of the threat and on previous experiences of that specific threat.

Ozolins (1989) outlined the rationale underlying the possibility of revealing the defence mechanisms that is the basis of Kragh's paradigm. The main points of the underlying rationale are based on findings showing that there are a number of similarities between signs of defence, as revealed in tests using percept-genetic techniques, and manifestations of defence mechanisms in clinical groups (Kragh, 1969; Kragh & Smith, 1970; Sharma, 1977).

There are, however, a number of questions regarding the validity of the test. Cooper (1988, p. 381) writes 'there really is little hard evidence showing that the test measures defence mechanisms, rather than, for example, traits of neuroticism or psychoticism', and Kline (1987, 1988) claims that visual distortions need not necessarily reflect defence mechanisms alone. Some distortions might represent other processes, which he does not specify, and he says 'the threatening figure will trigger off anxiety only in those subjects for whom the scowling face is indeed a threat' (Kline, 1988, p. 385).

If this is really the case, the explanation may be that the subject's main psychological conflicts lie outside the Oedipal sphere, which is the specific psychological area the stimulus picture addresses in the DMT. If the aim is to elicit defences associated with other developmental stages it is necessary to use a stimulus which addresses those other levels of development (Nilsson, Andersson, Lavillat, & Nilner, 1986; Nilsson, Haglund, & Lofstedt, 1986).

As the development of the DMT technique and theory is beyond the scope of this chapter, I will adhere to the point of view taken by Nilsson (1983) that the perceptual defences revealed in the DMT are parallel phenomena or have close affinity to the psychodynamic defences used by the tested subject and that 'the deviations (from the picture content) have the same function as the mechanisms of defence in the psychoanalytical theory' (Sundbom, Armelius, & Fransson, 1987, p. 8). Further comments on the validity of the DMT have been made, among others, by Kragh and Smith (1970), Neuman (1978), Ozolins (1989), Sharma (1977), Smith and Westerlundh (1980) and Westerlundh (1976). On the reliability of the DMT, see Kragh (1969), Kragh and Smith (1970), Neuman (1967), Ozolins (1989) and Westerlundh (1976).

How Defence Mechanisms Are Used in Sport

I shall now describe the classical defence mechanisms and how they may be manifested in sport, using soccer as an example. The following account is based on a study by Apitzsch and Berggren (1993), which is the only study known by this author that uses the DMT in a sport context. The descriptions given are restricted to those used in the DMT manual (Kragh, 1969), and each is followed by suggestions for an adaptive and a maladaptive endpoint along the dimension of each defence mechanism, in an attempt to describe the possible consequences for overt behaviour of using the different defence mechanisms. The essence of the descriptions is taken from Fenichel (1945).

The defence mechanisms are unconscious and divided into 10 main categories. Within each category, there are a number of different sign variants. Because the defence mechanisms by definition are unconscious, no attempt is made to compare them with other conceptual approaches to the same phenomenon. Furthermore, because the mechanisms are illustrated with male soccer players, the male perspective is used in the remainder of this paper. Finally, because some readers may not be totally familiar with the terminology of the psychodynamic theory, concepts specific to this theory are explained.

Repression

The perceived threat is repressed into the unconscious part of the mental apparatus. This defence mechanism is primarily directed against inner instinctual drives that may be perceived as threats or impulses and is considered to be one of the most basic neurotic defences. The thought that was connected to the impulse is repressed to the unconscious, and the process is perceived as forgetfulness by the outside observer.

Adaptive Endpoint: Energetic. The athlete acts instantaneously without any hesitation. He uses his motor skills energetically, has a flexible mind and has a capacity to work on many tracks simultaneously. The player meets the demands of the situation vigorously, doing things fast when in possession of the ball and running for free areas when not in possession of the ball.

Maladaptive Endpoint: 'Frozen Play' (Play Stiffness). The athlete is 'paralyzed' or 'frozen' on the spot where he is standing. He suddenly 'forgets' what he is occupied with at the moment and becomes absent-minded. The player may be in the right position but fails to do what the situation demands or may stand 'frozen' in a wrong position, unaware of what his action should be.

Isolation

Emotion and cognition are separated from each other, that is, a fantasy can become conscious, but the usually painful feeling associated with the fantasy remains unconscious. According to Kragh (1969), isolation has an affinity to compulsion neurosis. The compulsive personality has the habit of separating the emotional content of an incident from its cognitive content (Fenichel, 1945). This keeps the representation of the incident conscious, but weakened and isolated (Freud, 1955). When the ideational content and the affect of an experience are separated, the subject puts up a 'mental wall' to keep the affect out of consciousness. This is an endless task that must be continually and rigidly repeated. Thus, the isolater strives for a clear mind and tries to keep the emotional storms out of his consciousness by distancing them.

Adaptive Endpoint: Stability.   The athlete does what he is expected to do and does it reliably. He does so even if the task requires him to change his activity or his thinking in a new direction. The player plays up to his standards irrespective of the importance of the game or the skill of his immediate opponent. He can also change strategy during a match.

Maladaptive Endpoint: Inflexibility.   The athlete is unchangeable in his general habits, opinions and feelings. He ruminates on trivialities, has difficulties in starting new tasks and meeting new challenges. The athlete cannot change strategy, tactics or renew his play. He makes the same turns and movements, and has the same thoughts about the game incessantly. The player cannot change his play according to situational demands.

Denial

Threats against the mental equilibrium are denied. Denial is regarded as a primitive defence. Denial is described as a semi-conscious defence and as such, it only functions successfully in people with major or minor disturbances in their reality testing (Fenichel, 1945). Reality testing, according to psychoanalytic theory, occurs when the individual is aware of the demands of the surroundings and is able to adapt to them. Sjoback (1977, p. 259) calls denial 'the last line of defence' and there is general agreement that denial is directed against upsetting perceptions of the external world (Fenichel, 1945; Freud, A. 1946; Freud, S. 1949).

Adaptive Endpoint: Ignorance of Adversity.   This athlete does not reduce his performance level whatever work, activity or life situation he faces, even if the chance of a positive outcome would be regarded as very small by most other people. As the player does not perceive any dangers at all, he is not aware of the danger of losing the match, even if the team is trailing 0 to 3 with 5 min left to play.

Maladaptive Endpoint: Ignorance of Reality.   The real dangers of the external world are not comprehended. Therefore, the player misjudges his own behaviour in relation to the events in the external world. For example, playing against a much higher-ranked opponent requires a great deal of effort, but the player may totally underestimate the strength of an opponent, thus failing to put enough effort into his play.

Reaction Formation

Emotions are reversed to the opposite. Feelings of hatred, for example, may become unconscious through over-emphasis on the opposite feeling, love, which is a much more socially acceptable feeling. The original feeling of hatred remains unconscious. Fenichel (1945, p. 273) says this defence 'is a constant finding in compulsion neurotics,' and in this respect is similar to isolation. Reaction formation is further associated with occurrence of aggression, inhibition and psychosomatic symptoms such as stomach ulcers (Kragh, 1969). Any reaction elicited from a subject who utilises the defence of reaction formation, and whose goal is to conceal the original impulse, may be both exaggerated and ambiguous. Examples include showing your teeth when you are smiling or cleaning up unnecessarily, perhaps with the aim of getting a chance to be in contact with dirt under acceptable moral conditions.

Adaptive Endpoint: Benign Interpersonal Relationships.   The athlete almost always disguises his aggressive impulses. Thus he gives the impression of being a kind, social person 'overtly caring for someone else when he wishes to be cared for himself' (Vaillant, 1971, p. 117). The player maintains a good positive relationship with his team-mates, never criticising them for mistakes.

Maladaptive Endpoint: Ambiguous Interpersonal Relationships and Behaviour.   The athlete cannot communicate in a straightforward way and misjudges other peoples' emotional signals or attempts to establish contact. The player does not exert all his efforts in man-to-man duels and may even make passes that favour the opponent. Under severe stress, this player may mix up opponents with team-mates. As one player during the research interview answered the question about whether he had ever made a 'fatal mistake' in a match: 'I got the ball, looked up, and saw an opponent and passed the ball to him'.

Identification With the Aggressor

A person who is exposed to aggressiveness in childhood will be aggressive as an adult. This way of functioning may be established during childhood, especially if the child grows up under conditions in which being aggressive is seen as a good strategy for survival in an aggressive environment. The child reduces the anxiety evoked by hostile persons by assimilating the other's behaviour into his own play and later into his social contacts.

Adaptive Endpoint: Assertiveness. This is the ability to perform powerfully and be determined. The player does not hesitate to take on tough infighting and acts resolutely in any situation.

Maladaptive Endpoint: Aggressiveness. The inability to control aggressiveness, manifesting itself in brutality beyond the rules of the game. The player is likely to be penalised by being booked or sent off, to the detriment of his team.

Introaggression

Aggressive impulses are directed against the self. The underlying assumption here is that an outwardly directed aggressive impulse is turned back against the self and that this renders the subject vulnerable to depressed or passive moods. According to Sjoback (1977), this defence might explain why some people are self-destructive and have feelings of inferiority. Fenichel (1945) points out a connection to masochism.

Adaptive Endpoint: Ability to Withstand Pain. The player shows mental and physical tolerance for pain giving him the ability to work hard for long periods regardless of the strain and pressure in various situations. An example is a goalkeeper who can withstand dives on hard surfaces and who does not mind constantly being subjected to hard shots against the body.

Maladaptive Endpoint: Pain Seeking. The player seeks active involvement in and exposure to painful situations with a detrimental outcome for the player and the team. The player is likely to get injured. There is also a risk of bad passes resulting in goals for the opposition, or even own goals.

Introjection: Identification With the Opposite Sex

The implications of this defence are that the subject supposedly has conflicts over his sexual identity. The process of this defence is an internalisation of the subject's representations of the external mother-woman into his own psychological sphere. In other words, through the process of identification, the male subject internalises features typically associated with female subjects. If the introjected figure is eventually assimilated and becomes a part of the subject's identity, it may manifest itself as homosexuality (Fenichel, 1945).

Adaptive Endpoint: Immediate Adaptiveness. The player adapts quickly to new situations and has the capacity to change according to the demands of the new situation. If the opponent changes his moves on the pitch or tactics in the game, the player can easily adapt to this and change his own play accordingly.

Maladaptive Endpoint: Softness. The athlete does not behave like a man, according to cultural expectations, when manful behaviour is appropriate. The player does not use his physical capacity when the situation calls for it (e.g., he fails to tackle when that would be appropriate).

Polymorphous Introjection

Self-representations are built on several other internalised objects. In the case of this defence, not only a significant female may be introjected, but there might also be several other 'omnipotent' persons who can satisfy the subject's need for a helping ego (Fenichel, 1945; Kragh, 1969).

Adaptive Endpoint: Ability to Thrive on Others. The athlete's primary aim is to gain the approval of others. This makes him a loyal team member, performing to full capacity when he perceives support from team-mates. In a match, this player may perform to the extent of his capacity when encouraged by a colleague.

Maladaptive Endpoint: Dependency. The player is 'adhesive', searching for approval from his coach and team-mates in a demanding way, continually struggling against depressive moods. This player cannot make his own decisions and is thus totally dependent on other players' initiative.

Projection

The internal threatening impulse is placed outside the subject. The subject may project his feelings and impulses towards objects around him and thus avoid threats from the inside. The threat is replaced with an external object that can be dealt with in a more convenient way (Fenichel, 1945). It is often hostile feelings that are cast out but also loving and erotic impulses can be projected. In general, subjects who use projection are observant people who are alert in psychological terms and are physiologically aroused.

Adaptive Endpoint: Sensitivity. The athlete has the ability to feel, recognise and anticipate what is going on in the minds of team-mates and opponents. The sensitive player can read the reactions of his team-mates and opponents. Therefore, he can intervene in a beneficial way, such as intercepting a pass.

Maladaptive Endpoint: Suspiciousness. The athlete has his 'guard up', not trusting anyone. Thereby he may be a source of low morale for the team. If a player does not receive any passes for a while, he may wonder whether there is a conspiracy against him.

Regression

The objective real world falls apart. Regression means 'going back' and in this context it indicates a return to a previous, more primitive level of mental functioning (Fenichel, 1945). Ozolins (1989) writes that the ego is not active in eliciting this particular defence, as is the case with the other defences.

Adaptive Endpoint: Creativity. The player has the capacity to find new and better solutions to old problems. He never reverts to old routines and, therefore, he is regarded as unpredictable by opponents. The player constantly changes his movements and tricks, playing in varying ways throughout the matches, thereby disturbing his opponents.

Maladaptive Endpoint: Fragmentation.   There is a temporary breakdown of the athlete's mental apparatus, resulting in loss of reality-testing. The player disappears mentally from the game for periods, not participating in the action.

Case Studies From Soccer

The following case studies are presented to illustrate ways in which the defence mechanisms may operate concretely in soccer players in different playing positions. In order not to reveal the identity of the players appearing in these case studies, some facts have been omitted.

Case 1—Goalkeeper: 25 Years Old

This player has been a substitute in a Swedish first division team but has only played a few matches at that level. He has been with the current team for a couple of years. He seems to have mixed feelings towards playing soccer. Currently, he is studying as well as working in a firm, which he is eventually likely to manage. His leisure time is filled with a variety of activities which need regular and extensive attention. He thinks that the time available to associate with his wife is too scarce, but his wife supports him wholeheartedly in his soccer involvement.

With regard to soccer, he complains about the training sessions, which he considers to be too frequent. He admits that he finds it less enjoyable to play soccer than it used to be. His soccer ambitions do not include first division play any longer. Before matches he feels very nervous. This feeling manifests itself in having trouble sleeping the night before a match. He does not like the team talks about the matches and is very sensitive to critical remarks in the newspapers; these increase his tension. The feeling of being nervous causes him to cough and is accompanied by a feeling of wanting to vomit. During the warm-up before matches he has a feeling of not having enough air, which causes him to pull the collar of his training shirt. He states that he is not mentally strong, although he thinks that he should be one of the two in the squad who should assume a leadership role.

In a hypothetical match situation with 10 minutes left to play and his team trailing by two goals, he expressed the following feelings: 'I have always had problems with this. I feel the match is already lost. My head hangs down when the opposing team scores. I have tried to work on this but without success. The goalkeeper has such a great responsibility. The pressure is enormous. It takes me about 45 minutes to overcome such a mistake. It is hard to put the thoughts away'.

It takes him a day or so to overcome an unnecessary defeat: 'I feel like quitting soccer. Then I forget it. I don't know exactly'. His self-confidence is above average on a self-rating scale. If there is a penalty kick against his team, he is not confident about saving it. His strategy is to make the penalty kicker shoot by pretending not to be ready, but he is always going in the same direction himself regardless of what the shooter does. If a penalty kick is given to his team, he is not confident that it will result in a goal. He says that he sometimes gets the feeling that the penalty kicker will fail. He feels nervous and does not always watch the penalty, either closing his eyes or turning his back.

This player displays social tendencies, seeking the support of others and being a loyal team member (polymorphous introjection). His loyalty is perhaps best expressed by the fact that he turns up for every team training session, although he has a long distance to travel and soccer is no longer as important as it used to be (reaction formation). A big asset, and perhaps a necessary prerequisite for being a successful goalkeeper, is his tolerance for pain (introaggression). It is obvious that a goalkeeper will receive many hard shots to his body and must be prepared to make dives on frozen as well as muddy grounds. Furthermore, he seems to have the ability to act according to the demands of the situation (introjection) and to play energetically (repression). On the other hand, if the pressure is too great, he has a tendency to 'freeze', resulting in rigid behaviour, such as always going in the same direction for penalty kicks. His psychological makeup may be detrimental to the team for two reasons. Firstly, it affects his self-confidence. He has trouble seeing himself in a winning position, such as saving a penalty kick. Secondly, unconsciously he acts weakly and may let in goals to seek pleasure from the scolding of his teammates and the spectators, when playing at home (introaggression). He needs the support of others (polymorphous introjection), enabling him to assume the leadership role in the team he feels he should take.

Case 2—Backline Player: 25 Years Old

This is a player who was purchased by the team before the start of the season for the purpose of being the 'lock' in the backline. He has played in another team at the same level for several years. He settled into the new environment fairly quickly and was satisfied with his new team-mates. He considered that he and two other players were the psychologically strongest members of the team. However, on one occasion, in his former club, he reported a psychological block in a decisive match. He rated himself very high on self-confidence. Before the season, the other players considered him to have good psychological strength and expected him to assume a leadership role on the pitch. He therefore had expectations to live up to.

This player is a central defender and thus has a key role in the team. His psychological profile revealed by the DMT indicated that, in times of no subjectively experienced threat, he is an energetic player (repression), a social person (reaction formation), has the ability to change his play according to actual demands (introjection) and can withstand substantial pain (introaggression). However, when the pressure is high he is an obvious risk for his team. The presence of introaggression and the absence of isolation, which could help him to keep his mind clear in critical situations, make him a potentially dangerous player. The risk for bad passes to the goalkeeper or even own goals is clear. He actually made a very dangerous backpass to the goalkeeper, almost resulting in a goal for the opposing team in the third match of the season. He was then injured (possibly due to his introaggression) and was unable to play for a considerable number of matches. He returned to the team with five matches of the season left and with the team near the bottom of the division. In one of the three last decisive matches he scored an own goal and the team lost that match by one goal. The team was subsequently relegated to a lower division.

It seems as if this player does not have the mental skills needed at this level. He meets the demands of playing in the second division under normal conditions due to his soccer skills, which conceal his psychological weaknesses. However, when the pressure is on, he does not seem to be able to cope. A follow-up questionnaire after the end of the season revealed that nobody in the squad considered him to have executed the leadership role on the pitch and the high performance that was expected of him before the start of the season. He was released to his former club after the season was completed.

Case 3—Midfield Player: 30 Years Old

This player has been with the team for more than 10 years. The coach claims that he is one of the most talented players in the whole country. As a junior player he played for the national team, but has not represented Sweden as an adult. He is pleased with his job, in particular the freedom to structure it according to his personal needs. He claims to have improved his psychological strength and rates himself very high in self-confidence. A few years ago he was very susceptible to remarks from spectators. Due to experience he is now in a better position to handle this.

He plays primarily in midfield but has a very free role. 'I prefer to play in a position where I often get in touch with the ball'. He identifies very much with the team and claims that team spirit is very important. He emphasises that soccer is a team sport: 'It is easier to keep a high performance level if the others are encouraging me. To succeed you are dependent on the other players in the team'. This player is identified by his team-mates as the one who first gives up in times of setbacks. He reports no psychological problems. His anxiety level increases before matches, and this may be manifested in an upset stomach. In his words: 'you should be nervous before a match'.

On the positive side this player can be expected to display a lot of energy (repression) and to produce stable performances (isolation). Furthermore, he is likely to socialise with others (reaction formation) and to be a loyal team member (polymorphous introjection). This latter aspect is well documented in the above mentioned description of this player's opinion about team cohesion.

The existence of repression in this player's psychological profile is likely to elicit high energy outbursts on wrong occasions, thus wasting his energy. The use of isolation in threatening situations makes this player inflexible; he relies on the same moves and skills instead of playing more flexibly against his opponents. The apparent lack of assertiveness makes it difficult for this player to make constructive plans. Finally, his dependency on his team-mates (i.e., to sacrifice his own goals and wishes if they diverge from those of the team-members) is not consistent with high self-confidence. As stated above, this player does not have a good record with regard to self-confidence. The fact that he rates himself very high in self-confidence is probably a result of 'unrealistic optimism.' Available research data suggest that a bias towards viewing one's own chances positively as compared to others' is prevalent among human beings (Weinstein, 1980).

Conclusion

Psychodynamic theory has generally been dismissed as having little to offer the study of sport performance. Usually tests such as the TAT and Rorschach are referred to in this context. The existence of the DMT seems to be largely unknown in the English language sport psychology literature. In this chapter, an attempt has been made to show the potential use of the DMT in top-level sport, using mainly examples from soccer. Based on the assumption that top-level sport performers generate anxiety, defence mechanisms, as revealed by the DMT, were identified as being adaptive or maladaptive. If we know which defence mechanisms are in operation in individual athletes, we can predict under what circumstances their performances will be promoted or impeded.

Thus by using psychological profiles the individual player's characteristics can be better utilised in team sports. If the players agree to have their DMT results shown to the coach, he would have access to systematic information on the position in which each player is expected to contribute optimally to the success of the team. Equipped with this knowledge, the coach would be better prepared to adapt the team composition with regard to substitute players, the current score in the matches, whether the match is played at home or away and the importance of the match.

References

Apitzsch, E., & Berggren, B. (1993). *The personality of the elite soccer player*. Lund, Sweden: Studentlitteratur.

Bakker, F.C., Whiting, H.T.A., & van der Brug, H. (1990). *Sport psychology: Concepts and applications*. Chichester, England: Wiley.

Bezak, J., & Macak, I. (1976). Versuch zur Bewertung der Fahigkeiten von Fussballern nach der Methode der Tachistoskopie [Efforts for evaluating the abilities of soccer players with the use of tachistoscope methods]. In P. Kunath (Ed.), *Psychologie im Sport* (pp. 49-69). Berlin: Sportverlag.

Bowers, K. (1973). Situationism in psychology: An analysis and critique. *Psychological Review*, **90**, 307-336.

Cooper, C. (1988). The scientific status of the Defence Mechanism Test: A reply to Kline. *British Journal of Medical Psychology*, **61**, 381-384.

Cramer, P. (1991). *The development of defence mechanisms*. New York: Springer-Verlag.

Fenichel, O. (1945). *The psychoanalytic theory of neuroses*. London: Routledge & Kegan.

Fisher, A.C. (1984). New directions in sport personality research. In J.M. Silva & R.S. Weinberg (Eds.), *Psychological foundations of sport* (pp. 70-80). Champaign, IL: Human Kinetics.

Freud, A. (1946). *The ego and the mechanisms of defence*. London: Hogart Press.

Freud, S. (1949). *Inhibitions, symptoms and anxiety*. London: Hogart Press.

Freud, S. (1955). *Studies on hysteria* (Standard ed. II). London: Hogart Press.

Gill, D.L. (1986). *Psychological dynamics of sport*. Champaign, IL: Human Kinetics.

Jones, J.G., & Hardy, L. (Eds.) (1990). *Stress and performance in sport*. Chichester, England: Wiley.

Kane, J.E. (1977, October). *Personality research: The current controversy and implications for sports studies*. Paper presented at the IV International Society of Sport Psychology Congress, Praha Czechoslovakia.

Kline, P. (1987). The scientific status of the Defence Mechanism Test. *British Journal of Medical Psychology*, **60**, 53-59.

Kline, P. (1988). The scientific status of the Defence Mechanism Test: A response to Cooper. *British Journal of Medical Psychology*, **61**, 385-386.

Kragh, U. (1969). *Manual till DMT: Defense Mechanism Test*. Stockholm, Sweden: Skandinaviska Testforlaget.

Kragh, U., & Smith, G.J.W. (Eds.) (1970). *Percept-genetic analysis*. Lund, Sweden: Gleerup.

LeUnes, A., Wolf, P., Ripper, N., & Anding, K. (1990). Classic references in Journal of Sport Psychology, 1979-1987. *Journal of Sport and Exercise Psychology*, **12**, 74-81.

Murray, H.A. (1938). *Explorations in personality*. New York: Oxford University Press.

Neuman, T. (1967). Personlighet och anpassning till militar flygning, forsvarsmekanismer som stabila personlighetsstrukturer. Tva studier over DMT-seriers reliabilitet [Personality and adaptation to military aeronautics, defence mechanisms as stable personality structures. Two studies of the reliability of the DMT-series]. *MPI Rapport*, **52**, Stockholm, Sweden: Forsvarets Forskningsanstalt.

Neuman, T. (1978). *Dimensionering och validering av perceptgenesens forsvarsmekanismer. En hierarkisk analys mot pilotens stressbeteende* [Dimensioning and validation of the percept-genetic defence mechanisms. A hierarchical analysis of behaviour of pilots under stress] (FOA Rapport C 55020-H6). Stockholm, Sweden: Forsvarets Forskningsanstalt.

Nilsson, A. (1983). *The mechanisms of defence within a developmental frame of reference*. Lund, Sweden: Gleerup.

Nilsson, A., Andersson, I., Lavillat, C., & Nilner, K. (1986). Affective and defensive characteristics of patients with so called "oral galvanism" or diffuse complaints connected with the oral cavity: A percept-genetic study. *Psychological Research Bulletin*, **26**, 3-4.

Nilsson, A., Haglund, N., & Lofstedt, M. (1986). Affective and defensive behaviour in patients with ulcerative colitis: A percept-genetic study. *Psychological Research Bulletin*, **26**, 5-6.

Ozolins, A. (1989). *Defence patterns and noncommunicative body movements*. Stockholm, Sweden: Almqvist & Wiksell International.

Sandahl, F. (1988). *The Defense Mechanism Test, DMT, as a selection instrument when testing applicants for training as military pilots*. Sartryck ur Kungliga Krigsvetenskapsakademins handlingar: Tidskrift **4**, 132-154.

Sharma, V.P.S. (1977). *Application of a percept-genetic test in a clinical setting*. Unpublished doctoral dissertation, Lund University, Lund, Sweden.

Silva, J.M. (1984). Personality and sport performance: Controversy and challenge. In J.M. Silva & R.S. Weinberg (Eds.), *Psychological foundations of sport* (pp. 59-69). Champaign, IL: Human Kinetics.

Singer, R. (1986). Sport und Personlichkeit [Sport and personality]. In H. Gabler, J.R. Nitsch & R.N. Singer (Eds.), *Einfuhrung in die Sportpsychologie* (pp. 145-187). Schorndorf, Germany: Verlag Karl Hofmann.

Sjoback, H. (1977). *Psykoanalysen som livslognsteori* [Psychoanalysis as a theory of lifelong deception]. Lund, Sweden: Cavefors.

Smith, G.J.W., & Westerlundh, B. (1980). Perceptgenesis: A process perspective on perception-personality. *Review of Personality and Social Psychology, 1*, 94-124.

Spielberger, C.D. (1989). Stress and anxiety in sports. In D. Hackfort & C.D. Spielberger (Eds.), *Anxiety in sports: An international perspective*. London: Hemisphere.

Sundbom, E., Armelius, B-A., & Fransson, P. (1987). *Personality organization defined by a subliminal perceptual test (DMT) and the structural interview* (Report No. 17). Umea, Sweden: Umea University, Department of Applied Psychology.

Vaillant, G.E. (1971). Theoretical hierarchy of adaptive ego mechanisms. *Archives of General Psychiatry, 24*, 107-118.

Weinstein, N.D. (1980). Unrealistic optimism about future life events. *Journal of Personality and Social Psychology, 39*, 806-820.

Westerlundh, B. (1976). *Aggression, anxiety and defence*. Lund, Sweden: Gleerup.

7
CHAPTER

Competitive Anxiety in Sport

Graham Jones
GREAT BRITAIN

It is widely acknowledged that the competitive sport environment provides an ideal situation in which to study human behaviour. This 'natural laboratory' has been employed to investigate a wide range of cognitions and emotions underlying behaviour, especialy in the area of stress and anxiety. The considerable amount of interest and research attention devoted to this area of enquiry is reflected in the recent publication of specialised texts on anxiety (Hackfort & Spielberger, 1989; Martens, Vealey, & Burton, 1990) and stress (Jones & Hardy, 1990a) in sport.

Modern day sport, particularly at a more elite level, is often characterised by the intense pressure under which the participants are expected to perform to high levels. This is largely a function of the highly visible and competitive nature of the situation and also the substantial material rewards often available. Patmore (1986), in an intuitive analysis of the psychological factors influential in sports performance, has referred to the 'Sport Experiment'. In this experiment, involving elite performers, the skill level of the subjects is essentially controlled since there is very little difference in the physical ability of each subject. Consequently, the factor distinguishing the winner from the loser in this experiment is psychological in nature, specifically the subjects' ability to cope with the stress of competition. Many performers appear to cope very well under these circumstances, and some even thrive in them (see Jones & Hardy, 1990b). For some others, however, it can be a rather traumatic experience, characterised by anxiety and likely under-achievement. Indeed, in my work as an applied sport psychologist, many of the sports performers who have approached me for help and advice have done so because they have had problems coping with the pressure of competition, experiencing intense anxiety symptoms before or during competitive performance (or both) (for example, see Jones, 1993).

The study of anxiety and stress in sport can serve two very important functions: first, to increase knowledge of a complex phenomenon that has proved somewhat elusive to examine in some other situational contexts, and second, to aid the applied sport psychologist in providing a quality service to sports performers suffering from debilitating anxiety. Until recently, competitive anxiety research emanating from North America tended to dominate the sport psychology literature. Rainer Martens and colleagues, in particular, have played a very influential role in determining the direction of this research. However, recently there has been an increased contribution from European researchers to knowledge of competitive anxiety and its relationship with performance. Indeed many of the recent theories and findings of these European researchers are now gaining prominence in the sport psychology literature. The purpose of this chapter, therefore, is to focus on some of this work, although work outside Europe will be referred to where appropriate.

The chapter comprises three major sections. The first is concerned with the specific nature of the competitive anxiety response in terms of: unidimensional versus multidimensional conceptualisations, measurement, antecedents and precompetition temporal patterning. The second section considers the notions of 'cognitive intrusions' and also 'debilitating versus facilitating competitive anxiety' as a means of extending knowledge of the precise nature of competitive anxiety. The third section examines the various approaches to the relationship between competitive anxiety and performance. This comprises discussion of arousal-based explanations, zone of optimal functioning, reversal theory, multidimensional anxiety theory and, finally, catastrophe theory.

What Do We Know About Competitive Anxiety?

Considering the relative infancy of sport psychology as an academic discipline, it is not surprising that researchers have tended to follow the trends laid down in other, more established, areas of psychology. This has been particularly evident in competitive anxiety research. One of the early developments was to adopt Spielberger's (1966) state-trait approach and also his State-Trait Anxiety Inventory (STAI; Spielberger, Gorsuch, & Lushene, 1970) to examine anxiety in sport. Spielberger (1989) argued that this research has provided evidence that the state version of the STAI (i.e., SAI) is a sensitive index of the changes in anxiety levels produced by practice versus competition (Klavora, 1974), physical activity (Rhodes, 1980), by perceived or experienced success or failure (Martens & Gill, 1976), and by level of competition (Tenenbaum & Milgram, 1978). However, findings using the trait version (i.e., TAI) are less conclusive (Spielberger, 1989).

Although the research evidence suggests that the SAI may have some utility in sport settings, it remains a general anxiety scale. Evidence from other disciplines in psychology has suggested that anxiety is situation-specific and that anxiety measures should be sensitive to the unique characteristics of different situations. Mandler and Sarason (1952), for example, devised the Test Anxiety Scale, which predicted anxiety effects in academic achievement situations better than general anxiety scales. Situation-specific anxiety scales have since been developed to measure audience anxiety (Paivio & Lambert, 1959), social anxiety (Watson & Friend, 1969) and fear of snakes, height and darkness (Mellstrom, Cicala, & Zuckerman, 1976).

Based on the proposition that a sport-specific trait anxiety scale would likely be a better predictor of state anxiety in competitive situations than a general anxiety scale, Martens (1977) developed the Sport Competition Anxiety Test (SCAT). This scale demonstrated impressive psychometric properties in both laboratory and field settings and has been used extensively in subsequent research. Martens, Vealey, and Burton (1990) cited 88 published empirical studies that have used the SCAT, and Sonstroem (1984) claimed that '. . . in its short history SCAT has uniquely advanced an understanding of anxiety' (p. 113). It subsequently became apparent that a sport-specific state anxiety scale was also required. Consequently, Martens, Burton, Rivkin, and Simon (1980) developed the Competitive State Anxiety Inventory (CSAI), and subsequent research verified that this was a more sensitive scale than the SAI. Whilst the use of the CSAI has not been as extensive as that of the SCAT, a number of studies have provided evidence of the significant relationship between competitive trait and state anxiety in competitive situations (e.g., Cooley, 1987; Scanlan & Lewthwaite, 1984).

Although the developments traced above helped to advance knowledge of the area, they failed to take into account advances in educational and clinical psychology that provided even greater conceptual clarity. The work of Liebert and Morris (1967) and Davidson and Schwartz (1976) demonstrated that anxiety could be conceptualised as multidimensional, comprising cognitive and somatic components. Subsequent evidence (e.g., Barrett, 1972; Morris, Davis, & Hutchings, 1981; Morris, Harris, & Rovins, 1981; Morris & Liebert, 1973; Schwartz, Davidson, & Goleman, 1978) supported this distinction, and multidimensional scales were developed to measure state anxiety (e.g., Worry-Emotionality Inventory; Morris, Davis, & Hutchings, 1981) and trait anxiety (e.g., Cognitive Somatic Anxiety Questionnaire; Schwartz et al., 1978).

Researchers in sport psychology finally took a lead from this work, the move towards a multidimensional conceptualisation of competitive state anxiety being largely stimulated by the work of Martens, Burton, Vealey, Bump, and Smith (1990)[1]. They developed a multidimensional measure of competitive state anxiety, the Competitive State Anxiety Inventory-2 (CSAI-2), which was originally designed to measure cognitive and somatic components. However, during the extensive validation work on this scale, a third dimension emerged which was later identified as self-confidence. The CSAI-2 has been the major measuring instrument in competitive state anxiety research since the mid-1980s and will receive considerable attention

---

[1]Although this work was not formally published until 1990, the scale described has been employed widely since the early 1980s.

in the following sections. There has also been recent work on developing a trait measure of multidimensional competitive anxiety. This has culminated in the Sport Anxiety Scale (SAS) (Smith, Smoll, & Schutz, 1990) which measures the tendency to experience worry, somatic reactions and disrupted concentration in competitive situations. There is as yet little published research employing this scale. However, because of the psychometric properties of the SAS, it is likely to figure prominently in future research on competitive anxiety.

In summary, competitive anxiety is now viewed as multidimensional in nature, both as a state and a trait. This development has advanced knowledge of the competitive anxiety response and its relationship with performance. The following sections discuss some of the issues concerned.

Antecedents of Competitive Anxiety

As stated earlier, a large number of sports performers who seek the help and guidance of a sport psychologist do so because they experience problems coping with the intense pressure of competition. The likely action of the sport psychologist in such circumstances will be to implement and educate the performer in some form of stress management technique designed to alleviate the symptoms of anxiety. However, in many cases it would be more appropriate and logical to adopt some preventative strategy that would preclude the onset of the symptoms in the first place. However, the literature tends to be rather unhelpful in this area since relatively little research attention has been devoted to identifying the factors associated with such symptoms.

Early research in this area can be traced back to the late 1960s and early 1970s (e.g., Hanson, 1967; Lowe & McGrath, 1971). This research gathered pace towards the end of the 1970s with Scanlan and Passer's (1978, 1979) work on the sources of stress in young athletes. Further research on young athletes followed from Pierce and Stratton (1981), Gould, Horn, and Spreeman (1983) and Scanlan and Lewthwaite (1984). More recently, interview techniques have been used to examine sources of stress and anxiety in elite athletes in Britain (Jones & Hardy, 1990b) and the USA (Scanlan, Stein, & Ravizza, 1991).

The studies which sought to measure anxiety by questionnaire employed a unidimensional conceptualisation of anxiety. Recent research from the multidimensional anxiety perspective gives a more detailed view since it seeks to identify the antecedents of specific types of anxiety symptoms. Using a theoretical perspective and drawing on findings from the test anxiety literature, Martens, Burton et al. (1990) hypothesised that the antecedents of cognitive anxiety and self-confidence are those factors in the environment which are related to the athlete's expectations of success, including perception of one's own and opponents' ability. Alternatively, cues which elicit elevated somatic anxiety are thought to be nonevaluative, of shorter duration and consist mainly of conditioned responses to stimuli, such as changing room preparation and precompetition warm-up routines (Gould, Petlichkoff, & Weinberg, 1984; Martens et al., 1990).

Few published empirical studies have employed the CSAI-2 in this context, but they have provided some interesting findings. Gould et al. (1984) examined intercollegiate wrestlers and found that the number of years experience in the sport was negatively related to cognitive anxiety, and perceived ability was positively related to self-confidence. The only predictor of somatic anxiety was SCAT score. McAuley (1985) found that golfers' performance was a significant predictor of postcompetitive cognitive anxiety and self-confidence, but not somatic anxiety, although this study did not consider antecedents of precompetition anxiety. More recently, our own research (Jones, Swain, & Cale, 1990) examined antecedents of precompetition anxiety and self-confidence in a sample of elite British intercollegiate middle-distance runners. Perceived readiness and attitude towards previous performance were found to be negative predictors of cognitive anxiety. A factor concerned with goal-setting also contributed to the prediction, cognitive anxiety being positively related to the difficulty of the goals set in relation to the runners' finishing positions and negatively related to their perceptions of whether they could achieve the goals. Perceived readiness, as well as perceptions of the external environment (i.e., weather and track conditions) contributed to the prediction of self-confidence.

The antecedents of anxiety and confidence also appear to be a function of gender. In a sample of male and female team sport performers we found that in females predictors of cognitive anxiety and self-confidence tended to be associated with personal goals and standards, whilst predictors of these variables in males were associated with interpersonal comparison and winning (Jones, Swain, & Cale, 1991). The reliability of these findings requires further examination but they do point to the need for more research into other individual differences in anxiety antecedents.

The findings just described demonstrate that cognitive anxiety and self-confidence have some common antecedents but that there are also factors unique to each. The findings concerning somatic anxiety are rather inconsistent, but research to date shows that cognitive anxiety and somatic anxiety are predicted by different antecedents. Further detailed study of this area is likely to aid understanding at a theoretical level as well as providing knowledge of more practical significance that would enhance the mental preparation of sports performers.

Competition Temporal Patterning

The temporal patterning of anxiety in the period leading up to and during competition has attracted research interest. Fenz and Epstein (1967); Mahoney and Avener (1977); Meyers, Cooke, Cullen, and Liles (1979); and Highlen and Bennett (1979) are frequently cited studies that have examined the potential of the temporal patterning of anxiety as a means of distinguishing between successful and less successful performers, and between experienced and less experienced ones. These studies used a variety of means of monitoring anxiety, including heart rate, questionnaires and interviews, and have generally shown that experienced and elite performers show a different patterning from less experienced and less successful performers. Specifically, less experienced and less successful participants show a steady increase in anxiety right up to and even during performance; experienced and elite performers, in contrast, experience a similar pre-event increase, but then a reduction just prior to and during performance.

Utilising the multidimensional approach, later investigators examined the precompetition temporal patterning of cognitive and somatic anxiety components and also self-confidence. Martens, Burton et al. (1990), in validation work on the CSAI-2, found that cognitive anxiety and self-confidence generally remained stable during the precompetition period, but somatic anxiety increased just prior to competition. The findings on cognitive and somatic anxiety have been substantiated by researchers (e.g., Gould et al., 1984; Jones & Cale, 1989a; Parfitt & Hardy, 1987; Ussher & Hardy, 1986), although the findings concerning self-confidence appear to be less consistent.

Recent research has, however, found individual differences in the patterning of the multidimensional competitive state anxiety components. Krane and Williams (1987), for example, found that the patterning differed according to the nature of the sport. Jones and Cale (1989b) demonstrated that males and females respond differently during the precompetition period. Specifically, males conformed to theoretical predictions for all CSAI-2 subcomponents; females, in contrast, showed a progressive increase in cognitive anxiety, an earlier increase in somatic anxiety than the males and a reduction in self-confidence as the competition neared. The differential patterning of cognitive anxiety and self-confidence was supported in a follow-up study by Jones et al., 1991. Even more recent findings suggest that the precompetition temporal patterning of the CSAI-2 subcomponents is mediated by the individual difference variables of gender role (Swain & Jones, 1991) and competitiveness (Swain & Jones, 1992). These findings appear to imply that both the nature and the specific timing of any intervention strategy during the precompetition period should be considered at an individual level. This clearly has implications for the sport psychologist acting as consultant to, say, a large squad or team.

Finally, the dissociation of cognitive and somatic anxiety as the event approaches supports the notion of the independence of the two anxiety components. However, the majority of studies have shown moderate intercorrelations (Martens, Burton et al., 1990). Some research has investigated this relationship as a function of the proximity of competition. These studies have generally found the intercorrelations to be moderate throughout the precompetition period (Gould et al., 1984; Karteroliotis & Gill, 1987). However, we found the relationship between cognitive and somatic anxiety to be low and nonsignificant one week before competition but becoming progressively greater as the competition approached (Swain, Jones, & Cale, 1990).

Advances in the Understanding of Competitive Anxiety

Recent research on competitive anxiety has resulted in some encouraging conceptual and methodological advances. Knowledge of the antecedents, temporal patterning and nature of competitive state anxiety, in particular, has been enhanced by the available research findings. The important role played by the CSAI-2 in this development is undeniable. However, it is important to recognise that the CSAI-2, like the majority of other anxiety measures, is based on a somewhat limited view of the competitive anxiety response, only measuring its *intensity*. Recently, some research-ers (Burton, 1990; Jones, 1991, in press; Parfitt, Jones, & Hardy, 1990) have argued that an even greater understanding of competitive anxiety can be gained by examining additional dimensions of the response. It is proposed that two factors, in particular, are worthy of careful research attention; these are 'frequency of cognitive intrusions' and 'direction'.

Frequency of Cognitive Intrusions

The notion of cognitive intrusions has been proposed by Parfitt et al. (1990) and Jones (1991, in press) and is particularly relevant when viewed in the context of the time-to-event paradigm in which repeated measurements of subjects are taken during the period leading up to competition. This paradigm has been employed regularly in competitive anxiety research, particularly since the development of the CSAI-2. This research has generally supported theoretical predictions that pre-competition cognitive anxiety and self-confidence remain stable and that somatic anxiety becomes elevated just prior to competition, although individual differences play a key role in this patterning.

The limited nature of these predictions and findings is illustrated when considering the case of cognitive anxiety, which, to re-emphasise, is hypothesised to remain unchanged during the pre-competition period. Items comprising the cognitive anxiety subscale of the CSAI-2 include statements such as 'I am concerned about this competition' and 'I'm worried about performing poorly', with responses ranging from 'not at all' to 'very much so'. The possible responses to such items essentially represent the intensity of the cognitive anxiety symptoms, but another factor not considered is the frequency with which the symptoms are experienced at any particu-lar time. The same score for cognitive anxiety on two or more occasions may represent the same intensity of the response, but does it actually represent the same cognitive state on those occasions? It is argued that cognitions regarding the upcoming competition may well be of the same level of intensity but less frequent, say, 1 week before than 2 hr before. Consequently, even if cognitive anxiety intensity scores are the same on both occasions, the frequency of 'cognitive intrusions' (the amount of time that cognitions about a specific competition occupy an individual's thoughts) is likely to be much greater 2 hr before the competition than 1 week before.

Two studies (Swain & Jones, 1990) support these proposals. In the first, we measured precompetition anxiety and self-confidence levels in a sample of 60 male track and field athletes during the week preceding a competition. The CSAI-2 and a single 'percentage thinking time' item were administered to the athletes 1 week, 2 days, 1 day, 2 hr and 30 min prior to the start of their respective events. The percentage thinking time item asked the athletes to rate 'What percentage of the time are thoughts about the event occupying your mind at this stage?', with a response scale ranging from 0 to 100% and with gradations at every 5%. The findings for cognitive anxiety and percentage thinking time are presented in Figure 7.1 and show that cognitive anxiety remained unchanged from 1 week to 2 hours before competition, but increased significantly 30 minutes prior to competition.

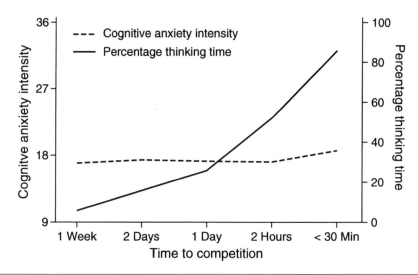

Figure 7.1   Precompetition patterning of cognitive anxiety intensity and percentage thinking time.

Somatic anxiety displayed the predicted patterning; it did not increase until on the day of competition, and self-confidence decreased on the day of competition. There was a progressive increase of percentage thinking time during the whole precompetition period, with mean scores rising from 5.7% one week before to 15.3%, 26.1%, 59.6% and finally to 82.4% at the respective stages. Eleven postcompetition interviews conducted with a representative cross-section of the sample provided corroborating evidence for these data. In summary, the intensity of cognitive anxiety remained unchanged from 1 week to 2 hr before the competition, but competition-related cognitive intrusions increased from 6 to 60% during this period.

In a second study, we examined the frequency of cognitive intrusions in more detail (Swain & Jones, 1990). Track and field athletes ($n = 49$) responded to a modified version of the CSAI-2 2 days, 1 day, 2 hr and 30 min prior to competition. The questionnaire included the existing CSAI-2 intensity scale as well as a specially developed frequency scale for each of the 27 items. The frequency scale asked the athlete to rate 'How frequently are you experiencing this thought/feeling at this stage?'. The response scale ranged from 1 ('not at all') to 7 ('all of the time') so that possible frequency scores on each of the subscales ranged from 9 to 63. The findings for cognitive anxiety are presented in Figure 7.2 and again show that cognitive anxiety intensity increased only at the 30 min stage. Somatic anxiety again showed the predicted increase on the day of competition, whilst self-confidence remained unchanged during the whole pre-competition period. The frequency of cognitive anxiety increased from 25.49 2 days before competition to 28.37, 34.90 and 40.13 at the respective stages. These data support those from our first study in that although cognitive anxiety remained stable until 30 min before the event, the frequency with which the symptoms were experienced increased substantially.

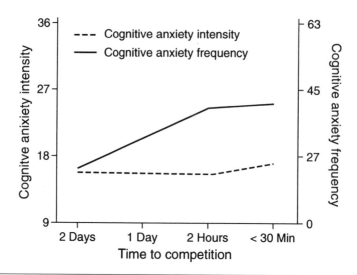

Figure 7.2   Precompetition patterning of the intensity and frequency of cognitive anxiety symptoms.

Again, follow-up interviews with eight of the sample corroborated these quantitative findings.

Both these investigations showed that although cognitive anxiety was at the same level of intensity for most of the precompetition period, the frequency with which the symptoms were experienced increased as the competition approached. Thus, cognitive anxiety 1 week before and 2 hr before a competition may be at the same level of intensity on the two occasions, but the cognitive states are likely to be very different. A cognitive state in which worries about the upcoming event are only intruding for 5% of the time is very different from one in which they are occurring 60% of the time. These findings have gained further support in a more recent study reported by Swain and Jones (1993). Thus the approach focusing only on intensity, which characterises the anxiety literature, provides a limited picture.

Direction of Cognitive Intrusions

A further factor concerns the 'direction' of the cognitive intrusions. In this context, direction refers to the nature of the competition-related cognitions—are they positively or negatively oriented? For example, one individual's cognitive intrusions might be positively oriented in the form of, say, anticipatory excitement, but another's cognitive intrusions might be negatively oriented in the form of images of failure. In yet another individual, the intrusions might change from positive to negative, or vice-versa, as the competition approaches.

Neiss (1988) emphasised that the '. . . recurrent conceptual problem (of examining anxiety) has been caused by the tendency to face important challenges . . . in mixed states' (p. 357). Neiss was referring to the different emotions that individuals experience in challenging situations, a number of which are not necessarily debilitating. However, investigators have commonly labelled the entire range of emotional responses to evaluation as 'anxiety' and have not distinguished between facilitative and debilitative states. Consequently, the word anxiety has been employed to describe what Sarbin (1968) and Sarason (1978) viewed as an extremely broad continuum of states, ranging from 'virtual immobilization in the face of potential criticism to exhilaration at the prospect of receiving accolades' (Sarason, 1978; p.193). The labelling of internal states in such situations has been regarded as crucially important in predicting behaviour (Geen, 1980). As Schachter (1964) commented, 'it could be anticipated that precisely the same state of physiological arousal could be labelled 'joy' or 'fury' or any of a great diversity of emotional labels, depending upon the cognitive aspects of the situation' (p. 53). The work of Thayer (1967, 1978), Mackay, Cox, Burrows, and Lazzerini, (1978), and Hardy and Whitehead (1984) in this area is also important because it demonstrates that positive (activation) and negative (anxiety) components of the stress response need to be differentiated.

The test anxiety literature is relevant to this issue. Wine (1980) proposed a bidirectional model of test anxiety which supports the notion of positive and negative dimensions and argues for even greater specificity of the state anxiety response. As far back as 1960, Alpert and Haber proposed that an anxiety scale should measure the presence and intensity of both kinds of anxiety response; those that interfere with performance and those that facilitate it. They found that a scale measuring the debilitating facilitating effects of anxiety (i.e., the Achievement Anxiety Test) provided a significantly stronger predictor of academic performance scores than a conventional debilitating anxiety scale. Moormann and van der Knoop (1987) adopted a similar scale, developed by Hermans (1967) in the context of ice dancing performance, but found it had low predictive value. This is perhaps not surprising since, as they emphasised, the scale was constructed primarily for intellectual activities. Wine (1980) has argued for further measurement devices directed at the specific concomitants of test anxiety and not based on the assumption that anxiety is debilitating for all respondents.

This issue is highly relevant to the adequacy of the CSAI-2, because of its popularity in competitive anxiety research. The inventory essentially measures certain cognitive and perceived physiological symptoms that have been deemed to reflect anxiety. But consider the first item on the CSAI-2: 'I am concerned about this competition'. One performer might be extremely concerned about the competition, to the extent that he or she is worried and in a near-panic state. On the other hand, another performer who is 'very concerned' about the competition might view this as very necessary since it is a sign that it is an important event and that he or she is highly motivated for it. These two hypothetical individuals, who would have the same score for this item, are likely to label their cognitive symptoms in very different ways. For the first individual, the cognitive state being experienced is likely to be anxiety, but, for the second one, it is probably something more akin to excitement. The same argument applies to both somatic anxiety and self-confidence.

The direction (i.e., positive or facilitating versus negative or debilitating) of the competitive anxiety and self-confidence symptoms measured via the CSAI-2 has been examined in three recent studies (Jones & Swain, 1992; Jones, Swain, & Hardy, 1993; Swain, 1992)[2]. Jones and Swain (1992) divided 69 subjects into high and low competitive groups based on their responses on the Sport Orientation Questionnaire (Gill & Deeter, 1988). All subjects completed a modified version of the CSAI-2 30 min prior to competition. This inventory included the original intensity scale plus a direction scale in which subjects rated the degree to which the experienced intensity of each symptom was either facilitative or debilitative to subsequent performance. The response scale ranged from −3 ('very debilitative') to +3 ('very facilitative') so that possible direction scores on each subscale ranged from −27 to +27. There were no significant group differences in intensity of cognitive anxiety or of somatic anxiety, or in direction of somatic anxiety. However, the highly competitive group reported their cognitive anxiety to be more facilitative and less debilitative than the low competitive group. This supports the notion that measuring intensity alone can be misleading since in the case of cognitive anxiety, the two groups did not differ on intensity, but they did differ on how they perceived the intensity of the symptoms for the purpose of their impending performance.

In a second study, we examined relationships between intensity and direction dimensions of competitive state anxiety and also relationships with beam performance in a sample of female gymnasts (Jones et al., 1993). The 48 gymnasts, whose ages ranged from 14 to 16 years, were divided into poor performance and good performance groups based on the median score in a beam competition. All subjects completed the modified version of the CSAI-2 10 minutes prior to performance. Analyses showed no significant group differences on any of the CSAI-2 subcomponent intensity scores or on somatic anxiety and self-confidence direction scores. However, the good performance group reported their cognitive anxiety intensity to be more facilitating and less debilitating to performance than the poor performance group. Further analyses showed that the only significant predictor of beam performance was self-confidence intensity. This study again supports the importance of direction, indicating that elevated cognitive anxiety is not necessarily detrimental to performance and, in fact, may even serve to enhance motivation and facilitate an appropriate attentional focus for some athletes. The finding that self-confidence intensity was the best predictor of performance emphasises the importance of this key construct. It is also interesting to note that the findings from this study demonstrated that self-confidence intensity was significantly and positively correlated with both cognitive anxiety direction and somatic anxiety direction scores. No causal inferences are possible but future researchers examining the interaction between the CSAI-2 subscale intensity and direction dimensions may wish to employ this approach as a means of specifically addressing the causality debate among self-efficacy theorists (e.g., Bandura, 1977) and anxiety reductionists (e.g., Borkovec, 1976).

---

[2]Further research findings in this area have been published since the completion of this chapter. See Jones (in press) for an update.

Finally, Swain (1992) has reported an in-depth investigation of intensity and direction dimensions in a longitudinal study of individual players in a varsity basketball team. In addition to administering the modified version of the CSAI-2, he conducted detailed interviews with the players after each of six league and cup matches. The findings showed that different players with the same intensity scores on the CSAI-2 could experience very different emotions and cognitive states, thus supporting the findings reported above. Interestingly, it was also found that although a player could have the same score on somatic anxiety, for example, before two different games, his affective experience could be very positive on one occasion but negative on the other. The complexity of this type of finding was partially explained by data acquired by administration of Thayer's (1978) Activation-Deactivation Checklist. This showed that a positive perception was associated with high arousal and low stress, whilst a negative perception of the same anxiety intensity was associated with lower arousal and higher stress.

In addition to the theoretical implications of this work, the practical implications for precompetition mental preparation strategies are also significant. Firstly, sport psychologists should recognise that relatively high levels of anxiety are not necessarily debilitating and can actually be facilitating in some cases. Secondly, for sports performers who are experiencing debilitating levels of anxiety, a cognitive restructuring technique, involving a relabelling of anxiety symptoms as positive and facilitating (see Apter, 1982; Kerr, 1990), may be just as effective as attempting to reduce the intensity of the symptoms through various relaxation strategies.

Competitive Anxiety and Performance

This section examines various approaches to the relationship between competitive anxiety and performance. This comprises discussion of arousal-based explanations, zone of optimal functioning, reversal theory, multidimensional anxiety theory and, finally, catastrophe theory.

Arousal-Based Explanations

Until quite recently, arousal-based explanations have represented the most simple and common interpretations of the relationship between anxiety and performance. These explanations focus on the assumption that performance changes associated with anxiety are due to changes in a single underlying dimension of arousal. Many researchers have debated the merits of Drive Theory and the Inverted-U Hypothesis in this context (e.g., Martens, 1974; Weinberg, 1979).

Drive Theory, originally proposed by Hull (1943) and later modified by Spence and Spence (1966), hypothesises that increases in drive (often used synonymously with arousal and anxiety) are associated with a linear increase or decrease in performance, depending upon the dominant response. Drive Theory was adopted by social facilitation theorists (e.g., Zajonc, 1965) to explain audience effects, but it has been criticised on a number of grounds, including the following:

- Failure to find consistent support for the theory (Martens, 1971, 1974)
- Failure of the theory to accommodate the effects of complex tasks (Martens, 1971; Tobias, 1980; Weinberg, 1979), making it too simple to explain motor or sport performance (Fisher, 1976)
- Difficulty in determining habit hierarchies of correct and incorrect responses in most motor skills (Martens, 1974; Neiss, 1988)

Drive Theory has largely been superseded by the Inverted-U Hypothesis, which has its origins in the work of Yerkes and Dodson (1908). This predicts that performance improves as arousal increases to a moderate, optimum level, after which further increases result in performance decrements. Until very recently, the Inverted-U Hypothesis was the focal point of discussions on anxiety and performance in virtually every sport psychology textbook. Recent developments in this area, particularly in Europe, seriously questioning the validity of this hypothesis, have been aptly traced by Gould and Krane (1992):

> In recent years, however, a number of European sport psychologists (Hardy & Fazey, 1987; Jones & Hardy, 1989; Kerr, 1985, 1987) have questioned both its conceptual and practical utility. These same criticisms have also begun to emerge in the North American sport psychology literature (Martens, 1987; Neiss, 1988; Weinberg, 1990). (p. 120)

Indeed, the criticisms of the Inverted-U Hypothesis have been numerous, the major ones including the following:

1. The failure to explain why performance is impaired at arousal levels above and below the optimum (Eysenck, 1984; Landers, 1980).
2. The lack of clear empirical support (Hockey, Coles, & Gaillard, 1986; Naatanen, 1973; Neiss, 1988). Although laboratory-based studies do not generally support an inverted-U relationship, support has emerged from field studies of arousal and motor behaviour (e.g., Klavora, 1978; Martens & Landers, 1970), although these too produced inconsistent findings.
3. It only relates to general effects on global performance rather than specific effects upon information processing efficiency (Eysenck, 1984) and is therefore incapable of explaining the complexity of the relationship between arousal and subcomponents of performance (Hockey & Hamilton, 1983).
4. The face validity of the shape of the curve has been questioned on the grounds that it is unrealistic to assume that once performers become overaroused and performance declines, then a reduction in arousal to previous levels will restore optimum performance (Fazey & Hardy, 1988; Hardy, 1990; Hardy & Fazey, 1987; see 'Catastrophe Theory').
5. Recent approaches to the arousal-performance relationship express a general dissatisfaction with the use of arousal as a unitary concept (Hockey et al., 1986) due to its inability to account for the highly differentiated pattern of arousal accompanying the primary emotions (Posner & Rothbart, 1986). Indeed, there is convincing evidence to demonstrate that arousal is multidimensional and not unidimensional (see Jones, 1990; Lacey, 1967).

A further problem with both Drive Theory and the Inverted-U Hypothesis is that they have been adopted to explain arousal, activation, anxiety *and* stress effects on performance. The use of such constructs, without clearly differentiating between them, has tended to preclude significant developments in the area. However, recent theorists have moved away from general arousal-based explanations, and these approaches are considered in the following sections.

Zone of Optimal Functioning

This approach is derived from Hanin's (1980, 1989) social psychological perspective on the anxiety-performance relationship. Adopting a person-environment interaction model and employing a Russian adaptation of Spielberger et al.'s (1970) STAI (Hanin & Spielberger, 1983), Hanin has assessed three aspects of state anxiety that are considered to influence performance. These are: interpersonal state anxiety (S-Aint), referring to the performer's involvement with a particular partner; intragroup state anxiety (S-Agr), referring to the performer's involvement as a member of a group or team; and performance anxiety. Hanin also referred to optimal state anxiety (S-Aopt) as the level of performance state anxiety associated with optimal performance.

Two approaches have been employed in the examination of S-Aopt: first, through multiple observations of individuals' performance levels and associated precompetition and performance state anxiety levels; and, second, through a retrospective approach in which performers assess their feelings prior to their most successful performances. Hanin proposed that a 'zone of optimal functioning' (ZOF) can be identified whereby the zone is defined as a performer's mean precompetition state anxiety score plus or minus four points. Some empirical support for ZOF has been forthcoming. Hanin (1980) reported a study with weight lifters in which those lifters whose state anxiety levels were outside their ZOF 3 days prior to competing produced inferior performance compared with those who remained within their optimal zones. Further, Gould and Krane (1992) have identified studies using the Body Awareness Scale (a measure of self-reported somatic activation), as opposed to the STAI, which support the existence of ZOFs for distance runners (e.g., Morgan, O'Connor, Ellickson, & Bradley, 1988).

The ZOF notion has the advantage of being intuitively appealing and making relatively precise predictions concerning which state anxiety levels are likely to produce optimum performance (Gould & Krane, 1992). At this level, therefore, it provides a useful practical tool for the athlete and applied sport psychologist. However, several criticisms can be levelled at the ZOF approach: first, it offers no underlying explanation; second, the central measuring instrument (i.e., the STAI) is not sport-specific; and, third, it is based upon a unidimensional conceptualisation of anxiety. A further criticism relates to the findings of Swain (1992) reported earlier. He found that the same two levels of anxiety intensity in an individual on two different occasions were not necessarily associated with the same level of performance on both occasions since the performer interpreted the facilitating/debilitating consequences for performance in different ways. Thus, the ZOF, as currently operationalised, is limited in that it does not allow for directional perceptions of anxiety symptoms. Nevertheless, it does provide an interesting approach that has aided understanding of the anxiety-performance relationship.

Reversal Theory

The application of Reversal Theory (Apter, 1982) to the sport environment (Kerr, 1987, 1989, 1990, 1993) provides a further perspective from which to view the anxiety-performance relationship. According to Reversal Theory, 'metamotivational states' are postulated to exist together in opposite pairs and are subject to sometimes quite rapid changes or reversals in one of two directions. The 'telic-paratelic' pair has been the focus of much of the work on Reversal Theory and is particularly interesting in the context of how sports performers perceive their arousal levels. The distinction between telic and paratelic states is as follows: '. . . in the paratelic state, behaviour tends to be spontaneous, playful and present-oriented, with a preference for high arousal . . . in the telic state, behaviour tends to be serious and planning-oriented, with a preference for low arousal' (Kerr, 1990, p. 108).

Kerr postulated that the experience of felt arousal and hedonic tone (i.e., interpretation of affect as pleasant or unpleasant) are particularly relevant to sports performance. Specifically, it is proposed that levels of arousal in particular metamotivational states may be interpreted in four different ways; low arousal can be experienced as relaxation (pleasant) or boredom (unpleasant), and high arousal can be experienced as excitement (pleasant) or anxiety (unpleasant). In the telic state, in which low arousal is preferred, low arousal will be experienced as relaxation and high arousal as anxiety. In the paratelic state, on the other hand, in which high arousal is preferred, low arousal will be experienced as boredom and high arousal as excitement. A reversal occurs when there is a change from telic to paratelic and vice-versa.

Apter and Svebak (1990) have identified two types of stress in Reversal Theory. In the context of arousal, 'tension-stress' occurs when there is a discrepancy between preferred and actual level of arousal. This would occur when high arousal is experienced whilst in a telic state, resulting in anxiety, or low arousal is experienced in a paratelic state, leading to boredom. The second form of stress is 'effort-stress', which occurs as a consequence of attempting to reduce tension-stress. In the telic state, effort-stress is experienced when attempting to reduce high arousal, and in the paratelic state it occurs when attempting to increase arousal. However, the intervention options are not merely concerned with increasing or decreasing arousal levels. Another option includes inducing reversals from, on the one hand, paratelic to telic in the case of tension-stress caused by low arousal and, on the other hand, from telic to paratelic when tension-stress is caused by high arousal. Kerr (1987) has suggested that it is possible for sports performers, after the required training, to induce the necessary reversals via a cognitive restructuring or imagery strategy. However, no research has been carried out to date to examine these proposals.

A distinction is also made in Reversal Theory between metamotivational 'dominance' and 'state'. Metamotivational dominance, measured via the Telic Dominance Scale (TDS) (Murgatroyd, Rushton, Apter, & Ray, 1978), acknowledges individuals' preferences for one metamotivational state over another. A state version of the TDS, the Telic State Measure, has also been developed. Some preliminary research has been carried out to examine the role of these factors in sport (Kerr & Cox, 1990), but a comprehensive programme of sports-specific research is required to test the principles of Reversal Theory (Kerr, 1990).

Reversal Theory is an interesting approach and certainly has encouraging potential for furthering understanding of the anxiety-performance relationship. However, one important limitation is that it is difficult to test, which accounts for the scant amount of empirical support currently available. A conceptual limitation is that it is based upon unidimensional conceptualisations of arousal and anxiety, which, as indicated in previous sections, is a rather outdated approach. Finally, its practical significance is limited by the lack of clarity and precision concerning how reversals can be brought about.

Multidimensional Approach

The adoption of the multidimensional approach to anxiety has been an encouraging and important step forward in the empirical examination of the anxiety-performance relationship in sport psychology (see Parfitt et al., 1990 for a review) because it has encouraged the adoption of more precise definitions and terminology. This has led, in turn, to an increasing number of studies attempting to examine the relationship between performance and the specific components of the competitive state anxiety response. For example, using this approach, Burton (1988) carried out a study on swimmers and found the following results:

1. Cognitive anxiety was related to performance in the form of a negative linear trend, with performance deteriorating with increases in cognitive anxiety.
2. There was an inverted-U relationship between somatic anxiety and perfor-mance, supporting Gould, Petlichkoff, Simons, and Vevera's (1987) finding and suggesting that an inverted-U curve may exist but certainly not in terms of a general, undifferentiated arousal system.
3. There was a positive linear relationship between self-confidence and per-formance.

Other studies, however, have generally failed to find strong relationships between the variables concerned (e.g., Caruso, Dzewaltowski, Gill, & McElroy, 1990; Karter-oliotis & Gill, 1987; Krane & Williams, 1987; Maynard & Howe, 1987), although this may be partly due to the fact that they have not employed the same intra-individual approach as Burton (1988) and Gould et al. (1987).

Some other recent work has moved away from examining global sports perfor-mance such as swimming and has adopted Hockey and Hamilton's (1983) approach of examining anxiety effects on components of performance. For example, we examined discrimination reaction time in a sample of cricket batsmen just before they went out to bat in a cricket match (Jones, Cale, & Kerwin, 1988). We found that greater errors in discrimination were associated with an increase in somatic anxiety and a reduction in self-confidence just before batting. Impaired performance is perhaps not surprising since the batsmen were unlikely to be concerned about performing well on a reaction time task just before batting. This probably reduced both attention and effort they devoted to the task compared to similar tests at other times. However, studies by Parfitt and Hardy (1987) and Jones and Cale (1989a) have shown that elevated cognitive anxiety and somatic anxiety had positive effects on performance in tasks when the capacity of the tasks to predict subsequent sports performance had been emphasised to the subjects. The Parfitt and Hardy study showed that, in a sample of basketball players, improvements in working memory performance were associated with elevated cognitive anxiety, and our study showed a positive relationship between perceptuo-motor speed and somatic anxiety in hockey players (Jones & Cale, 1989a). It has become increasingly clear from this line of research that competitive state anxiety does not necessarily impair performance and can, in some circumstances, enhance it. Measurement of the direction (i.e., facilitating versus debilitating) dimension of anxiety symptoms, as advocated earlier, is likely to prove particularly useful in explaining such findings.

Catastrophe Theory

A recent approach that has attracted research interest has been the application to sports performance of Catastrophe Theory (Fazey & Hardy, 1988; Hardy, 1990; Hardy & Fazey, 1987; Hardy & Parfitt, 1991). Catastrophe Theory has been proposed as an alternative to the Inverted-U Hypothesis as a result of Fazey and Hardy's (1988) concerns over the face validity of the inverted-U curve once arousal level increases above the optimum. According to the Inverted-U Hypothesis, as arousal increases above the optimum level, performance declines in a symmetrical, curvilinear fashion. However, Catastrophe Theory, when applied to sports performance, hypothesises that once a certain level of arousal is reached beyond the optimum level, performance will drop off in a sudden and dramatic manner onto a lower performance curve.

Catastrophe Theory was developed by Thom (1975) as a mathematical model for describing discontinuities that occur in the physical world. Zeeman (1976) later demonstrated that the model could be applied to a wide range of social science phenomena. Several catastrophe models have been developed, but the most commonly applied and easily understood is the cusp catastrophe model (Hardy, 1990). This is a three-dimensional model that consists of a normal factor, a splitting factor and a dependent variable (Zeeman, 1976). The normal factor is the variable in which increases are associated with increases in the dependent variable. The splitting factor determines the effect of the normal factor on the dependent variable; thus an interaction occurs between the normal and splitting variables. The bifurcation set represents an area in which two values of the dependent variable are possible, depending on whether the normal factor variable is increasing or decreasing.

In applying Catastrophe Theory to sports performance, Fazey and Hardy (1988) adopted the multidimensional anxiety perspective discussed earlier. Interestingly, they preferred to employ an objective operationalisation of 'physiological arousal' as opposed to the perception of physiological arousal referred to as somatic anxiety; physiological arousal represents the normal factor in the cusp catastrophe model.

Cognitive anxiety represents the splitting factor and is hypothesised to mediate the effects of physiological arousal on the dependent variable, performance. The predictions of this three-dimensional model are complex and can only really be adequately understood when represented graphically (see Figure 7.3).

As the splitting factor, the level of cognitive anxiety determines whether the effect of physiological arousal upon performance will be minimal, catastrophic or somewhere in between. A number of predictions are implicit within the model as depicted in Figure 7.3:

1. When cognitive anxiety is low, there will be a gentle inverted-U relationship between physiological arousal and performance (see back face of Figure 7.3).
2. When cognitive anxiety is very high, performance will improve as physiological arousal increases to a critical threshold, after which further increases in physiological arousal will result in a catastrophic drop from the upper to the lower performance curve (see front face of Figure 7.3). The performance curves representing the upper and lower performance surfaces are opposing curves, the upper one representing performance as physiological arousal increases and the lower one representing performance as physiological arousal decreases. This situation is referred to as 'hysteresis', and the result is a 'bifurcation set' where the same level of physiological arousal is associated

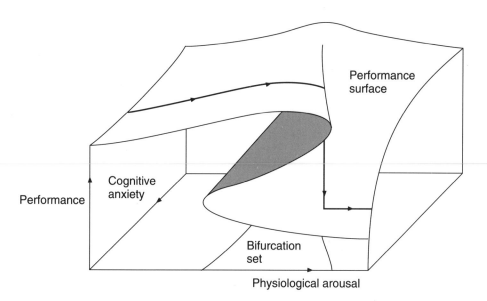

Figure 7.3 Hardy and Fazey's (1987) catastrophe model of the relationship between cognitive anxiety, physiological arousal and performance.
Note. From 'The Inverted-U Hypothesis: A Catastrophe for Sport Psychology' by J. Fazey and L. Hardy. In *Bass Monograph No. 1* (p. 25), 1988, Leeds, U.K.: British Association of Sports Sciences and National Coaching Foundation. Adapted by permission.

with two different levels of performance, depending on whether physiological arousal is increasing or decreasing.

3. When physiological arousal is high, a negative correlation is predicted between cognitive anxiety and performance (see right face of Figure 7.3).
4. When physiological arousal is low, a positive correlation is predicted between cognitive anxiety and performance (see left face of Figure 7.3).

The second prediction has been supported by studies on basketball (Hardy & Parfitt, 1991) and bowls players (Hardy, Parfitt, & Pates, 1994). In both studies, when cognitive anxiety was high, performance showed a different patterning when physiological arousal was increasing as opposed to decreasing, thus supporting the hysteresis prediction. On the other hand, when cognitive anxiety was low, performance did not differ as a function of increasing versus decreasing physiological arousal. Furthermore, both studies showed that

> the highest levels of performance achieved in the high cognitive anxiety condition were significantly higher than the highest levels of performance achieved in the low cognitive anxiety condition. Conversely, the lowest levels of performance achieved in the high cognitive anxiety condition were significantly lower than the lowest levels of performance achieved in the low cognitive anxiety condition. These results were interpreted as indicating the potential gains and catastrophic drops which can occur in performance in conditions of high cognitive anxiety. (Hardy, 1990; pp. 93-94)

These findings, therefore, offer encouraging support for the predictions of the cusp catastrophe model.

This approach to the anxiety-performance relationship is innovative in that it examines the combined influence of cognitive anxiety and physiological arousal on performance, as opposed to their separate effects. It also helps to explain some of the previously referred to inconsistent findings in this area. Furthermore, Hardy (1990) has speculated about the role of self-confidence and task difficulty in more complex versions of Catastrophe Theory. These are beyond the scope of this discussion, but offer a fertile area for future research. Drawbacks of this approach include the complex nature of the model and difficulties in testing some of its predictions. However, complexity in research is inevitable, considering the complexity of the anxiety-performance relationship itself.

Conclusion

This chapter has attempted to trace the development of early research in competitive anxiety and then to focus on the most recent developments and issues. Sport psychology researchers interested in anxiety have, quite understandably, tended to follow the trends laid down by anxiety researchers and theorists in other, more established, areas of psychology. However, recent research within sport psychology, much of it emanating from Europe, has resulted in some encouraging conceptual and methodological advances in the specific area of 'competitive anxiety'. Consequently, much more is now known and understood about the experiences of sport performers in the specific and unique environment of sport competition.

However, much remains to be learned about this complex phenomenon and how it interacts with performance (Jones, in press). Current issues include the following:

* Identification of the antecedents of anxiety within specific sports, and also comparisons across different sports and as a function of individual differences, such as gender
* The measurement of direction of anxiety symptoms and examination of relationships with performance
* The influence of self-confidence on the direction of anxiety symptoms; comparison of the efficacy of different theoretical models in the prediction of performance
* Identification of the precise nature of the complex interaction between cognitive anxiety and physiological arousal in the context of Catastrophe Theory

Issues of a more methodological nature include the following:

* The adoption of both quantitative and qualitative research methodologies in order to provide a more detailed and clearer perspective on the experience of competitive anxiety and its effects upon performance
* Improved performance measures
* The development of means of measuring competitive anxiety during performance

As these are only a few of the issues that need to be addressed, researchers in competitive anxiety will be kept busy for many years to come.

References

Alpert, R., & Haber, R.N. (1960). Anxiety in academic achievement situations. *Journal of Abnormal and Social Psychology*, **61**, 207-215.

Apter, M.J. (1982). *The experience of motivation: The theory of psychological reversals.* London: Academic Press.

Apter, M.J., & Svebak, S. (1990). Stress from the reversal theory perspective. In C.D. Spielberger & J. Strelau (Eds.), *Stress and anxiety* (Vol. 12). New York: Hemisphere/McGraw-Hill.

Bandura, A. (1977). Self-efficacy: Toward a unifying theory of behavioral change. *Psychological Review*, **84**, 191-215.

Barrett, E.S. (1972). Anxiety and impulsiveness: Toward a neuro-psychological model. In C.D. Spielberger (Ed.), *Anxiety: Current trends in theory and research* (Vol. 1, pp. 195-222). New York: Academic Press.

Borkovec, T.D. (1976). Physiological and cognitive processes in the regulation of anxiety. In G.E. Schwartz & D. Shapiro (Eds.), *Consciousness and self-regulation: Advances in research* (pp. 261-312). New York: Plenum.

Burton, D. (1988). Do anxious swimmers swim slower? Reexamining the elusive anxiety-performance relationship. *Journal of Sport and Exercise Psychology*, **10**, 45-61.

Burton, D. (1990). Multi-modal stress management in sport: Current status and future directions. In G. Jones & L. Hardy (Eds.), *Stress and performance in sport* (pp. 171-201). Chichester, England: Wiley.

Caruso, C.M., Dzewaltowski, D.A., Gill, D.L., & McElroy, M.A. (1990). Psychological and physiological changes in competitive state anxiety during noncompetition and competitive success and failure. *Journal of Sport and Exercise Psychology*, **12**, 6-20.

Cooley, E.J. (1987). Situational and trait determinants of competitive state anxiety. *Perceptual and Motor Skills*, **64**, 767-773.

Davidson, R.J., & Schwartz, G.E. (1976). The psychobiology of relaxation and related states: A multiprocess theory. In D.I. Mostofsky (Ed.), *Behavioral control and modification of physiological activity* (pp. 399-442). Englewood Cliffs, NJ: Prentice Hall.

Eysenck, M.W. (1984). *A handbook of cognitive psychology*. London: Erlbaum.

Fazey, J.A., & Hardy, L. (1988). The inverted-U hypothesis: A catastrophe for sport psychology. *British Association of Sports Sciences Monograph 1*. Leeds, England: The National Coaching Foundation.

Fenz, W.D., & Epstein, S. (1967). Gradients of physiological arousal in parachutists as a function of an approaching jump. *Psychosomatic Medicine*, **29**, 33-51.

Fisher, A.C. (Ed.) (1976). *Psychology of sport*. Palo Alto, CA: Mayfield.

Gauron, E.F. (1984). *Mental training for peak performance*. Lansing, NY: Sports Science Associates.

Geen, R.G. (1980). Test anxiety and cue utilization. In I.G. Sarason (Ed.), *Test anxiety: Theory, research and applications* (pp. 43-61). Hillsdale, NJ: Erlbaum.

Gill, D.L., & Deeter, T.E. (1988). Development of the Sport Orientation Questionnaire. *Research Quarterly for Exercise and Sport*, **59**, 191-202.

Gould, D., Horn, T., & Spreeman, J. (1983). Sources of stress in junior elite wrestlers. *Journal of Sport Psychology*, **5**, 159-171.

Gould, D., & Krane, V. (1992). The arousal-athletic performance relationship: Current status and future directions. In T. Horn (Ed.), *Advances in sport psychology* (pp. 119-141). Champaign, IL: Human Kinetics.

Gould, D., Petlichkoff, L., Simons, J., & Vevera, M. (1987). Relationship between Competitive State Anxiety Inventory-2 subscale scores and pistol shooting performance. *Journal of Sport Psychology*, **9**, 33-42.

Gould, D., Petlichkoff, L., & Weinberg, R.S. (1984). Antecedents of temporal changes in and relationships between CSAI-2 components. *Journal of Sport Psychology*, **6**, 289-304.

Hackfort, D., & Spielberger, C.D. (1989). Sport-related anxiety: Current trends in theory and research. In D. Hackfort & C.D. Spielberger (Eds.), *Anxiety in sports: An international perspective* (pp. 261-267). New York: Hemisphere.

Hanin, Y.L. (1980). A study of anxiety in sports. In W.F. Straub (Ed.), *Sport psychology: An analysis of athlete behavior* (pp. 236-249). Ithaca, NY: Mouvement.

Hanin, Y.L. (1989). Interpersonal and intragroup anxiety in sports. In D. Hackfort & C.D. Spielberger (Eds.), *Anxiety in sports: An international perspective* (pp. 19-28). New York: Hemisphere.

Hanin, Y.L., & Spielberger, C.D. (1983). The development and validation of the Russian Form of the State-Trait Anxiety Inventory. In C.D. Spielberger & R. Diaz-Guerrero (Eds.), *Cross-cultural anxiety* (Vol. 12). New York: Hemisphere.

Hanson, D.L. (1967). Cardiac response to participation in Little League baseball competition as determined by telemetry. *Research Quarterly*, **38**, 384-388.

Hardy, L. (1990). A catastrophe model of performance in sport. In G. Jones & L. Hardy (Eds.), *Stress and performance in sport* (pp. 81-106). Chichester, England: Wiley.

Hardy, L., & Fazey, J.F. (1987, June). *The inverted-U hypothesis: A catastrophe for sport psychology*. Paper presented at the Annual Conference of the North American Society for Psychology of Sport and Physical Activity, Vancouver, BC.

Hardy, L., & Parfitt, G. (1991). A catastrophe model of anxiety and performance. *British Journal of Psychology*, **82**, 163-178.

Hardy, L., Parfitt, G., & Pates, J. (1994). Performance catastrophes in sport: A test of the hysteresis hypothesis. *Journal of Sports Sciences*, **12**, 327-334.

Hardy, L., & Whitehead, R. (1984). Specific modes of anxiety and arousal. *Current Psychological Research and Reviews*, **3**, 14-24.

Hermans, H.J.M. (1967). *Motivatie en prestatie*. Amsterdam: Swets & Zeitlinger.

Highlen, P.S., & Bennett, B.B. (1979). Psychological characteristics of successful and unsuccessful elite wrestlers: An exploratory study. *Journal of Sport Psychology*, **1**, 123-137.

Hockey, G.R.J., Coles, M.G.H., & Gaillard, A.W.K. (1986). Energetical issues in research on human information processing. In G.R.J. Hockey, M.G.H. Coles, & A.W.K. Gaillard (Eds.), *Energetics and human information processing* (pp. 3-21). Dordrecht, The Netherlands: Martinus Nijhoff.

Hockey, G.R.J., & Hamilton, P. (1983). The cognitive patterning of stress states. In G.R.J. Hockey (Ed.), *Stress and fatigue in human performance* (pp. 331-362). Chichester, England: Wiley.

Hull, C.L. (1943). *Principles of behavior*. New York: Appleton-Century.

Jones, G. (1990). A cognitive perspective on the processes underlying the relationship between stress and performance in sport. In G. Jones & L. Hardy (Eds.), *Stress and performance in sport* (pp. 17-42). Chichester, England: Wiley.

Jones, G. (1991). Recent developments and current issues in competitive state anxiety research. *Psychologist*, **4**, 152-155.

Jones, G. (1993). The role of performance profiling in cognitive-behavioural interventions in sport. *The Sport Psychologist*, **7**, 160-172.

Jones, G. (in press). More than just a game: Research developments and issues in competitive anxiety in sport. *British Journal of Psychology*.

Jones, G., & Cale, A. (1989a). Precompetition temporal patterning of anxiety and self-confidence in males and females. *Journal of Sport Behavior*, **12**, 183-195.

Jones, G., & Cale, A. (1989b). Relationships between multidimensional competitive state anxiety and cognitive and motor subcomponents of performance. *Journal of Sports Sciences*, **7**, 229-240.

Jones, G., Cale, A., & Kerwin, D. (1988). Multidimensional competitive state anxiety and psychomotor performance. *Australian Journal of Science and Medicine in Sport*, **4**, 3-7.

Jones, G., & Hardy, L. (1989). Stress and cognitive functioning in sport. *Journal of Sport Sciences*, **7**, 41-63.

Jones, G., & Hardy, L. (Eds.) (1990a). *Stress and performance in sport*. Chichester, England: Wiley.

Jones, G., & Hardy, L. (1990b). Stress in sport: Experiences of some elite performers. In G. Jones & L. Hardy (Eds.), *Stress and performance in sport* (pp. 247-277). Chichester, England: Wiley.

Jones, G., & Swain, A.B.J. (1992). Intensity and direction dimensions of competitive state anxiety and relationships with competitiveness. *Perceptual and Motor Skills*, **74**, 467-472.

Jones, G., Swain, A.B.J., & Cale, A. (1990). Antecedents of multidimensional competitive state anxiety and self-confidence in elite intercollegiate middle-distance runners. *Sport Psychologist*, **4**, 107-118.

Jones, G., Swain, A.B.J., & Cale, A. (1991). Gender differences in precompetition temporal patterning and antecedents of anxiety and self-confidence. *Journal of Sport and Exercise Psychology*, **13**, 1-15.

Jones, G., Swain, A.B.J., & Hardy, L. (1993). Intensity and direction dimensions of competitive state anxiety and relationships with performance. *Journal of Sports Sciences*, **11**, 525-532.

Karteroliotis, C., & Gill, D.L. (1987). Temporal changes in psychological and physiological components of state anxiety. *Journal of Sport Psychology*, **9**, 261-274.

Kerr, J.H. (1985). The experience of arousal: A new basis for studying arousal effects in sport. *Journal of Sports Sciences*, **3**, 169-179.

Kerr, J.H. (1987). Structural phenomenology, arousal and performance. *Journal of Human Movement Studies*, **13**, 211-229.

Kerr, J.H. (1989). Anxiety, arousal and sport performance: An application of reversal theory. In D. Hackfort & C.D. Spielberger (Eds.), *Anxiety in sports: An international perspective* (pp. 137-151). New York: Hemisphere.

Kerr, J.H. (1990). Stress and sport: Reversal theory. In G. Jones & L. Hardy (Eds.), *Stress and performance in sport* (pp. 107-131). Chichester, England: Wiley.

Kerr, J.H. (1993). An eclectic approach to psychological interventions in sport. *The Sport Psychologist*, **7**, 400-418.

Kerr, J.H., & Cox, T. (1990). Cognition and mood in relation to the performance of a squash task. *Acta Psychologica*, **73**, 103-114.

Klavora, P. (1974). *State anxiety and athletic competition*. Unpublished doctoral dissertation, University of Alberta-Edmonton, Canada.

Klavora, P. (1978). An attempt to derive inverted-U curves based on the relationship between anxiety and athletic performance. In D.M. Landers & R.W. Christina (Eds.), *Psychology of motor behavior and sport* (pp. 369-377). Champaign, IL: Human Kinetics.

Krane, V., & Williams, J.M. (1987). Performance and somatic anxiety, cognitive anxiety, and confidence changes prior to competition. *Journal of Sport Behavior*, **10**, 47-56.

Lacey, J.I. (1967). Somatic response patterning of stress: Some revisions of activation theory. In M. Appley & R. Trumbell (Eds.), *Psychological stress* (pp. 14-44). New York: Appleton.

Landers, D.M. (1980). The arousal/performance relationship revisited. *Research Quarterly for Exercise and Sport*, **51**, 77-90.

Liebert, R.M., & Morris, L.W. (1967). Cognitive and emotional components of test anxiety: A distinction and some initial data. *Psychological Reports*, **20**, 975-978.

Lowe, R., & McGrath, J.E. (1971). *Stress, arousal and performance: Some findings calling for a new theory* (Proj. Rep. No. AF 1161-67). AFOSR.

Mackay, C.J., Cox, T., Burrows, G.C., & Lazzerini, A.J. (1978). An inventory for the measurement of self-reported stress and arousal. *Journal of Social and Clinical Psychology*, **17**, 283-284.

Mahoney, M.J., & Avener, M. (1977). Psychology of the elite athlete: An exploratory study. *Cognitive Therapy and Research*, **1**, 135-141.

Mandler, G., & Sarason, S.B. (1952). A study of anxiety and learning. *Journal of Abnormal and Social Psychology*, **47**, 166-173.

Martens, R. (1971). Internal-external control and social reinforcement effects on motor performance. *Research Quarterly*, **42**, 107-113.

Martens, R. (1974). Arousal and motor performance. *Exercise and Sport Sciences Reviews*, **2**, 155-188.

Martens, R. (1977). *Sport Competition Anxiety Test*. Champaign, IL: Human Kinetics.

Martens, R. (1987). *Coaches guide to sport psychology*. Champaign, IL: Human Kinetics.

Martens, R., Burton, D., Rivkin, F., & Simon, J. (1980). Reliability and validity of the Competitive State Anxiety Inventory (CSAI). In C.H. Nadeau, W.C. Halliwell, K.M. Newell, & G.C. Roberts (Eds.), *Psychology of motor behavior and sport: 1979* (pp. 91-99). Champaign, IL: Human Kinetics.

Martens, R., Burton, D., Vealey, R.S., Bump, L.A., & Smith, D.E. (1990). Development and validation of the Competitive State Anxiety Inventory-2 (CSAI-2). In R. Martens, R.S. Vealey, & D. Burton (Eds.), *Competitive anxiety in sport* (pp. 117-190). Champaign, IL: Human Kinetics.

Martens, R., & Gill, D.L. (1976). State anxiety among successful and unsuccessful competitors who differ in competitive trait anxiety. *Research Quarterly*, **47**, 698-708.

Martens, R., & Landers, D.M. (1970). Motor performance under stress: A test of the inverted-U hypothesis. *Journal of Personality and Social Psychology*, **16**, 29-37.

Martens, R., Vealey, R.S., & Burton, D. (Eds.) (1990). *Competitive anxiety in sport*. Champaign, IL: Human Kinetics.

Martin, J.J., & Gill, D.L. (1991). The relationships among competitive orientation, sport confidence, self-efficacy, anxiety and performance. *Journal of Sport and Exercise Psychology*, **13**, 149-159.

Maynard, I.W., & Howe, B.L. (1987). Interrelations of trait and state anxiety with game performance of rugby players. *Perceptual and Motor Skills*, **64**, 599-602.

McAuley, E. (1985). State anxiety: Antecedent or result of sport performance? *Journal of Sport Behavior*, **8**, 71-77.

Mellstrom, M., Cicala, G.A., & Zuckerman, M. (1976). General versus specific trait anxiety measures in the prediction of fear of snakes, heights, and darkness. *Journal of Consulting and Clinical Psychology*, **44**, 83-91.

Meyers, A.W., Cooke, C.J., Cullen, J., & Liles, L. (1979). Psychological aspects of athletic competitors: A replication across sports. *Cognitive Therapy and Research*, **3**, 361-366.

Moormann, P.P., & van der Knoop, A. (1987). Effects of physical and psychological responses to stress on motor performance in competitive sport. In *Proceedings of the 7th Congress of the European Federation of Sports Psychology* (Vol. 3, pp. 910-923). Bad Blankenberg, Germany: FEPSAC.

Morgan, W.P., O'Connor, P.J.O., Ellickson, K.A., & Bradley, P.W. (1988). Personality structure, mood states, and performance in elite male distance runners. *International Journal of Sport Psychology*, **19**, 247-263.

Morris, L.W., Davis, M.A., & Hutchings, C.H. (1981). Cognitive and emotional components of anxiety: Literature review and a revised Worry-Emotionality Scale. *Journal of Educational Psychology*, **73**, 541-555.

Morris, L.W., Harris, E.W., & Rovins, D.S. (1981). Interactive effects of generalized and situational expectancies on cognitive and emotional components of social anxiety. *Journal of Research in Personality*, **15**, 302-311.

Morris, L.W., & Liebert, R.M. (1973). Effects of negative feedback, threat of shock and trait anxiety on the arousal of two components of anxiety. *Journal of Counseling Psychology*, **20**, 321-326.

Murgatroyd, S., Rushton, C., Apter, M.J., & Ray, C. (1978). The development of the Telic Dominance Scale. *Journal of Personality Assessment*, **42**, 519-528.

Naatanen, R. (1973). The inverted-U relationship between activation and performance: A critical review. In S. Kornblum (Ed.), *Attention and performance* (Vol. IV, pp. 155-174). New York: Academic Press.

Neiss, R. (1988). Reconceptualizing arousal: Psychobiological states in motor performance. *Psychological Bulletin*, **103**, 345-366.

Paivio, A., & Lambert, W.E. (1959). Measures and correlates of audience anxiety. *Journal of Personality*, **27**, 1-17.

Parfitt, C.G., & Hardy, L. (1987). Further evidence for the differential effect of competitive anxiety upon a number of cognitive and motor sub-systems. *Journal of Sports Sciences*, **5**, 62-63. (Abstract)

Parfitt, C.G., Jones, G., & Hardy, L. (1990). Multidimensional anxiety and performance. In G. Jones & L. Hardy (Eds.), *Stress and performance in sport* (pp. 43-80). Chichester, England: Wiley.

Patmore, A. (1986). *Sportmen under stress*. London: Stanley Paul.

Pierce, W.J., & Stratton, R.K. (1981). Perceived sources of stress in youth sports participants. In G.C. Roberts & D.M. Landers (Eds.), *Psychology of motor behavior and sport: 1980* (p. 116). Champaign, IL: Human Kinetics.

Posner, M.I., & Rothbart, M.K. (1986). The concept of energy in psychological theory. In G.R.J. Hockey, M.G.H. Coles, & A.W.K. Gaillard (Eds.), *Energetics and human information processing* (pp. 23-40). Dordrecht, The Netherlands: Martinus Nijhoff.

Rhodes, D.L. (1980). Mens sana, corpore sano: A study of the effect of jogging on depression, anxiety and self-concept (Doctoral dissertation, Duke University, 1980). *Dissertation Abstracts International*, **41**, 1500A.

Sarason, I.G. (1978). The Test Anxiety Scale: Concept and research. In C.D. Spielberger & I.G. Sarason (Eds.), *Stress and anxiety* (Vol. 5, pp. 193-216). Washington, DC: Hemisphere.

Sarbin, T.R. (1968). Ontology recapitulates philology: The mythic nature of anxiety. *American Psychologist*, **23**, 411-418.

Scanlan, T.K., & Lewthwaite, R. (1984). Social psychological aspects of competition for male youth sport participants: 1. Predictors of competitive stress. *Journal of Sport Psychology*, **6**, 208-226.

Scanlan, T.K., & Passer, M.W. (1978). Factors related to competitive stress among male youth sport participants. *Medicine and Science in Sport*, **10**, 103-108.

Scanlan, T.K., & Passer, M.W. (1979). Sources of competitive stress in young female athletes. *Journal of Sport Psychology*, **1**, 151-159.

Scanlan, T.K., Stein, G.L., & Ravizza, K. (1991). An in-depth study of former elite figure skaters: 3. Sources of stress. *Journal of Sport and Exercise Psychology*, **13**, 103-120.

Schachter, S. (1964). The interaction of cognitive and physiological determinants of emotional state. In L. Berkowitz (Ed.), *Advances in experimental social psychology* (Vol. 1). New York: Academic Press.

Schwartz, G.E., Davidson, R.J., & Goleman, D.J. (1978). Patterning of cognitive and somatic processes in the self-regulation of anxiety: Effects of meditation versus exercise. *Psychosomatic Medicine*, **40**, 321-328.

Smith, R.E., Smoll, F.L., & Schutz, R.W. (1990). Measurement and correlates of sport-specific cognitive and somatic trait anxiety: The Sport Anxiety Scale. *Anxiety Research*, **2**, 263-280.

Sonstroem, R.J. (1984). An overview of anxiety in sport. In J.M. Silva & R.S. Weinberg (Eds.), *Psychological foundations of sport* (pp. 104-117). Champaign, IL: Human Kinetics.

Spence, J.T., & Spence, K.W. (1966). The motivational components of manifest anxiety drive and drive stimuli. In C.D. Spielberger (Ed.), *Anxiety and behavior* (pp. 291-360). New York: Academic Press.

Spielberger, C.D. (1966). Theory and research on anxiety. In C.D. Spielberger (Ed.), *Anxiety and behavior* (pp. 3-20). New York: Academic Press.

Spielberger, C.D. (1989). Stress and anxiety in sports. In D. Hackfort and C.D. Spielberger (Eds.), *Anxiety in sports: An international perspective* (pp. 3-17). New York: Hemisphere.

Spielberger, C.D., Gorsuch, R.L., & Lushene, R.L. (1970). *Manual for the State-Trait Anxiety Inventory*. Palo Alto, CA: Consulting Psychologists.

Swain, A.B.J. (1992). *Competitive state anxiety: Towards a clearer understanding*. Unpublished doctoral dissertation, Loughborough University, England.

Swain, A.B.J., & Jones, G. (1990). Intensity, frequency and direction dimensions of competitive state anxiety and self-confidence. *Journal of Sports Sciences*, **8**, 302-303. (Abstract)

Swain, A.B.J., & Jones, G. (1991). Gender role endorsement and competitive anxiety. *International Journal of Sport Psychology*, **22**, 50-65.

Swain, A.B.J., & Jones, G. (1992). Relationships between sport achievement orientation and competitive state anxiety. *Sport Psychologist*, **6**, 42-54.

Swain, A.B.J., & Jones, G. (1993). Intensity and frequency dimensions of competitive state anxiety. *Journal of Sports Sciences,* **11**, 533-542.

Swain, A.B.J., Jones, G., & Cale, A. (1990). Interrelationships among multidimensional competitive state anxiety components as a function of the proximity of competition. *Perceptual and Motor Skills*, **71**, 1111-1114.

Tenenbaum, G., & Milgram, R.M. (1978). Trait and state anxiety in Israeli student athletes. *Journal of Clinical Psychology*, **34**, 691-693.

Thayer, R.E. (1967). Measurement of activation through self-report. *Psychological Reports*, **20**, 663-678.

Thayer, R.E. (1978). Toward a psychological theory of multidimensional activation (arousal). *Motivation and Emotion*, **2**, 1-34.

Thom, R. (1975). *Structural stability and morphogenesis*. New York: Benjamin-Addison-Wesley.

Tobias, R. (1980). Individual differences and the response to evaluative situations. In I.G. Sarason (Ed.), *Test anxiety: Theory, research and applications* (pp. 266-291). Hillsdale, NJ: Erlbaum.

Ussher, M.H., & Hardy, L. (1986). The effect of competitive anxiety on a number of cognitive and motor subsystems. *Journal of Sports Sciences*, **4**, 232-233. (Abstract)

Watson, D., & Friend, R. (1969). Measurement of social-evaluative anxiety. *Journal of Consulting and Clinical Psychology*, **33**, 448-457.

Weinberg, R.S. (1979). Anxiety and motor performance: Drive theory versus cognitive theory. *International Journal of Sport Psychology*, **10**, 112-121.

Weinberg, R.S. (1990). Anxiety and motor performance: Where to go from here? *Anxiety Research*, **2**, 227-242.

Wine, J.D. (1980). Cognitive-attentional theory of test anxiety. In I.G. Sarason (Ed.), *Test anxiety: Theory, research and applications* (pp. 349-385). Hillsdale, NJ: Erlbaum.

Yerkes, R.M., & Dodson, J.D. (1908). The relation of strength of stimulus to rapidity of habit formation. *Journal of Comparative Neurology and Psychology*, **18**, 459-482.

Zajonc, R.B. (1965). Social facilitation. *Science*, **149**, 269-274.

Zeeman, E.C. (1976). Catastrophe theory. *Scientific American*, **234**, 65-82.

8

CHAPTER

Psychophysiology and Sport Performance

David Collins

GREAT BRITAIN

The classic paper by Hatfield and Landers (1983)—'Psychophysiology: A New Direction for Sport Psychology'—was a recognition of the great potential offered by this subdiscipline of psychology. Psychophysiology, defined as 'the scientific study of cognitive, emotional and behavioural phenomena as related to and revealed through physiological principles and events' (Cacioppo & Tassinary, 1990, p. ix), can provide an objective and relatively noninvasive method of examining the complex processes involved in sport performance as they take place. The attraction of such an ecologically valid technique over the more usual self-report approach is obvious, and more recent reviews (e.g., Smith & Collins, 1991) identify sport psychophysiology as an important and current research thrust. However, the interpretation of the physiological signals mentioned in the definition is the crucial consideration here. Accurate and meaningful conclusions require a rigorous appreciation and application of the theories underpinning the techniques used. All too often studies fall into the trap of searching for correlation rather than causation (Donchin & Coles, 1988; Zani & Rossi, 1991a). Correct application of psychophysiology requires that the physiological events recorded be interpreted by reference to their underlying causes and not just identified as a convenient concomitant of an assumed mental set or behaviour. Sadly, this has not always been the case in sport-related studies. Also, although studies in mainstream psychophysiology address topics relevant to sport, they may appear too esoteric and academic for those more interested in application.

Even worse, but also apparent, are the oversimplified generalisations made from such studies. However, even with all these problems of interpretation and hardware requirements, psychophysiology has made, and should continue to make, a substantial contribution to sport psychology.

The main aim of this chapter is to demonstrate that contribution by reference to a range of sport-related or sport-pertinent studies. Although not exhaustive nor comprehensive, it is hoped that the chapter will interest the reader and increase future attention to, or even involvement in, this area. Also, a cursory review of the recent literature suggests that, with certain notable exceptions, most sport-related research in this field appears to have taken place in North America. There are, however, a number of excellent European investigations, both in sport and other fields, which have perhaps received less attention in terms of replication or extension. An implicit aim of this chapter is to highlight key European research and, perhaps, contribute to the continued development of cooperation and discourse between Europe and elsewhere, including North America.

Methodological Considerations for Psychophysiological Investigations

Although this is not a training manual, no critical discussion of psychophysiological investigations can be attempted without some basic knowledge of the technical and procedural considerations which, for the novice at least, make the area appear such a minefield.

The range of measures available to the aspirant researcher is both large and confusing. Peripheral indices, which are usually used to reflect changes in the autonomic nervous system (ANS), include heart rate (HR) and more complex examinations of the complete waveform (Electrocardiography—ECG), skin conductance or resistance (variously termed as Galvanic Skin Response—GSR, Skin Conductance Level/Response—SCL/SCR, or Electrodermal Activity—EDA), eye movements (Electro-occulography—EOG), and levels of muscle activity (Electromyography—EMG). Respiration, blood pressure (BP) and skin temperature are other less commonly applied measures. The interested reader is referred to Cacioppo and Tassinary (1990) for a detailed review of the technical and theoretical considerations pertaining to the use of the measures referred to here.

Central processes can be extrapolated from peripheral changes but by far the most effective procedure is to access them directly by means of the electroencephalogram (EEG) or its various 'offshoots', most of which are discussed later in the chapter. Once again consultation of a specific reference such as Binnie, Rowan, and Gutter (1982), should provide a more critical and effective understanding of the techniques involved.

In most cases, psychophysiological investigations are based on the analogue waveform generated by the activity or, more usually, on numerical data that provide a more quantitative assessment of some aspect of the activity. Such numbers can represent amplitude or power (the 'size' of the signal), the frequency or rate, change from baseline (typically labeled delta) and may be expressed in standard units (e.g., beats per minute, microvolts) or arbitrary ones. Two key considerations in most studies are the amplification or filtering applied to the raw signal and to the 'sampling rate'.

Psychophysiological signals can be very small and are liable to contamination by a wide variety of 'artefacts' (often measures themselves but not relevant to that particular study). Digitisation (changing the analogue waveform signal into numbers suitable for display or manipulation), requires an Analogue (waveform) to Digital (number), or 'A to D', converter to take a series of 'pictures' or samples of the waveform over a finite time period. Faster sampling (usually expressed in number of samples per second or hertz—Hz) is usually better because it generates a more accurate picture. The idea is somewhat akin to increasing sample size in a standard research paradigm. If the sampling rate is too slow, artefactual signals can be generated that can almost nullify conclusions drawn from the resulting data. Any reputable study should provide information about these factors (the signal conditioning performed). An electronics technician with programming skills is a vital ally in making sense of these requirements and several innovative institutions in Europe offer training courses for such technicians alongside conventional sports science courses.

Regarding experimental design, the utilisation of a measure should be justified in terms of past research and theoretical considerations. Given the multidimensional nature of the measures and their interrelationship with other psychological constructs, such a justification should form a part of any good research study. Especially in cases when several such measures are used, the emphasis must be on the individual and his or her reactions in meaningful (i.e., usually field) situations. Group predictive power of psychophysiological measures is questionable as a number of studies have shown (e.g., Fahrenberg, Foerster, Schneider, & Muller, 1986). Repeated measures designs are therefore usually the best option.

Two other statistical considerations are necessary. Firstly, the nature of psychophysiological data is such that it frequently violates certain important assumptions of the typically employed univariate analysis of variance (ANOVA). One such assumption, termed sphericity or circularity, is complex, and in general the best solution may be the routine use of multivariate techniques (Vasey & Thayer, 1987) which, though less powerful statistically, are robust to violation of such assumptions. Finally, given the multiple comparisons and plethora of data common in psychophysiological investigations, inflation of Type I error is highly likely and many studies have employed adjustments, such as the Greenhouse-Geisser or Bonferroni techniques, to guard against this. Unfortunately, routine application of this procedure may be overly conservative and potential workers in the field should consider the nature and aims of their investigation before selecting a procedure. Wilcox (1987) has shown that, in a hypothesis testing mode, when contrasts are specified a priori, alternative approaches are desirable. In the particular case of multiple comparisons (another common occurrence with psychophysiological data), Seaman, Levin, and Serlin (1991) have ably demonstrated the more powerful options available.

Preperformance and Performance Concomitants

Until the late 1980s, this topic was probably the primary area of sport psychophysiological interest. This interest took three major forms: the assessment of activation associated with optimum performance, the identification of attentional capacity and allocation, and the identification of central processing (plus related peripheral changes) associated with good performance. A major facet of all this work, very much the vogue in the 1970s and early 1980s, was the modification of these factors through the medium of biofeedback. Integral to much of the work on the third topic was the concept of hemispheric specialisation—the idea that since the various parts of the cerebrum are 'allocated' to different jobs, the differential engagement of these areas, as revealed by EEG, would reveal the nature of cognition associated with elite performance. This was an application of enormous potential, and despite the fact that many of the underlying tenets of the construct have now been questioned, it is still so popular in sport psychology (or at least the 'pop' version) that it receives special attention in a later section of this chapter.

Historically, the sport applications of psychophysiology have largely changed emphasis from the first to the second topic (i.e., from activation to attention). Methodologically, HR emerges as the clear favourite, with EEG closing rapidly as the technical knowledge and equipment necessary for its use become more widespread. Recent investigations have used both, and other techniques are also apparent, so this review will be accomplished chronologically on each of the two topics, finishing with a brief review of biofeedback, the major practical sport application of psychophysiology to date.

Arousal and Activation

The classic and much quoted HR study by Fenz and Epstein (1967) on sport parachutists is a good starting point. The differential pattern of prejump HR between novices and experts was discovered at a time when personality research was the vogue, and hence the data were viewed in trait terms. It is interesting to note that, 8 years later when Fenz described the 'notch' effect of sharp HR deceleration observed in experts as they mounted the aircraft (Fenz, 1975), the underlying explanation given for this effect was in terms of an acquired cognitive-attentional framework.

Early use of the full spectrum of psychophysiological measures was based (erroneously in hindsight) on what was later termed the unidimensional theory of activation (Duffy, 1962). The basic idea was that, under conditions of increased activation, all the indices would display the same trend and thus were relatively interchangeable. In opposition to this, Lacey's multidimensional theory (Lacey, 1967), an important contribution to the literature, suggested that different measures would covary (i.e., under increased arousal some would go up while others would decrease). This was, in fact, shown to be the most likely scenario. For example, as far as EMG is concerned, anxiety is associated with bursts of activity rather than with general increases in tone (Fridlund, Hatfield, Cottam, & Fowler, 1986). Furthermore, researchers have identified relatively stable gender differences in stress responses indicated by the various measures (e.g., Martinez-Selva, Gomez-Amor, Olmos, Navaro, & Roman, 1987). Indeed, such differences between individuals are seen by many as representative of psychometrically-derived hereditary traits (e.g., Rodger & Jamieson, 1988). An excellent review of the personality aspects of psychophysiological individuality is provided by Fahrenberg (1986). These response patterns have also been applied to sport-pertinent trait constructs, including locus of control (Gale & Edwards, 1984) and sensation seeking (Zuckerman, Buchsbaum, & Murphy, 1980).

A similar pattern of changing emphasis can be discerned in sport research. Early studies used a variety of these measures to evaluate general arousal. For example, Bethune (1980) used HR and SCL as measures of general stress associated with high-risk sports. Similarly, Hoffman (1983) used HR as an indicator of what he termed 'physical impetus', an acute, exercise-induced increase in activation, in an assessment of its effect on strength performance. More recently, these same measures have been used to identify specific trait-related differences or states related to differences in performance. In a rather ingenious study (given the prohibitive regulations and importance and magnitude of the competition), Schmid and Peper (1987) used finger temperature to assess arousal states of rhythmic gymnasts in the 1984 Olympics. Higher temperatures immediately prior to performance were associated with worse performance. Helin, Sihvonen, and Hanninen (1987) showed that elite marksmen possessed the ability to execute shots consistently in the inter-beat interval (IBI) when physiological disturbance was at its lowest. Psychophysiological techniques have also been used to examine practice-performance tension differences in ballet dancers (Helin, 1988) and suggested as an important data source for the planning of performance-related interventions (Davis, 1991). A review by Turner (1989) provides a good introduction to aspects of the necessary methodology and design for such studies, at least with regard to HR.

The more recent trend towards relating activation levels and attentional processes is evidenced by Schrode, Larbig, Heitkamp, and Wurster (1986) who used EEG, HR, BP and a variety of endocrine measures to examine coping strategies during and after marathon and ultramarathon running. These data, in association with the self-report and performance measures taken, furnished empirical evidence for some of the speculation then current on association and disassociation in marathoners. Trait differences in anxiety and defensiveness were examined by Tremayne and Barry (1988) who used HR responses associated with laboratory-type stimuli to extrapolate attentional strategies under competitive stress. Although the thrust of the investigation was activation level, attention was the construct employed to explain the observed effects on HR level and variability.

Although from the perspective of these studies attention is seen as the root cause of the observed relationships, alternative or related explanations are tenable. Recent studies utilising regional cerebral blood flow (rCBF) paradigms have suggested that effects of anxiety on the central cortex are the mediating factors in the arousal-performance relationship (e.g., Gur et al., 1988). The extent to which this fits within more recent conceptualisations, such as catastrophe theory (Fazey & Hardy, 1988), reversal theory (Apter, 1976), or zone of optimal functioning (Hanin, 1980), is another fruitful direction for investigations of the interaction between anxiety and attentional processes (see chapter 7). Finally, given the multidimensional nature of stress responses and the differential effects of various stressors, both implicit factors within these more recent theories, stress research may benefit from psychophysiological techniques pioneered in Europe and designed for industrial and business settings (e.g., Boucsein, 1990).

Attention

Early studies in psychophysiology outside the sport domain demonstrated the interaction of activation with attention which sport researchers took a little time to take up. The intake-rejection hypothesis (Lacey & Lacey, 1964) is the underlying construct most commonly used, and its validity has been examined in a wide variety of settings. Essentially, the hypothesis distinguishes between tasks requiring outer-directed attention (intake tasks), which are associated with decreased activation, and rejection tasks (an inward orientation), which result in general increases in arousal measures. Thus, the tennis player, waiting to receive a service, is performing an intake task and, according to the hypothesis, would demonstrate a lowering of arousal level. In contrast, the server, having decided where to place the ball, is concentrating internally on focussing power and technique to produce an ace. Such an inward focus, characteristic of a rejection task, should, according to the theory, result in an arousal increase. Such changes in arousal can be conceptualised as reflecting an orienting response or reflex.

In the late 1970s, the effects of such tasks and the predictions of the hypothesis received a great deal of critical attention. Studies utilised HR (e.g., Kjellberg & Magnusson, 1979) and a variety of other measures (e.g., Blakeslee, 1979). It is interesting to note that even then, those in the forefront of research (e.g., Carroll & Anastasiades, 1978), were suggesting that HR changes must be considered in association with other superordinate variables since the predictions of the hypothesis were often unsupported to an almost fatal extent. This process was immediately implemented in studies which emanated largely from Europe (e.g., Weinrich, 1979).

Links between activation and attention in sports settings first became apparent when Tretilova and Rodimski (1979) reported the tonic increases in HR associated with an elite Soviet shooter's performance. This was supported in a later investigation by Landers, Daniels, Hatfield, and Wilkinson (1982) and explained by both groups in terms of Lacey and Lacey's (1970) visceral afferent feedback hypothesis. According to this, peripheral increases in activation serve to inhibit the sensorimotor capacity of the cerebral cortex (by gaining and keeping the attention of its sensorimotor systems) and thereby decrease the effect of external distractions. The most tenable and commonly applied alternative, the cardiac coupling hypothesis (Obrist et al., 1974), suggests HR deceleration and sees it as a concomitant to motor quietening—a seemingly inevitable requirement for facilitation of stimulus detection. Preperformance HR deceleration, presumed to be indicative of increased attention, has been shown to be typical of better performers and better performance in archery (Wang &

Landers, 1987) and golf putting (Boutcher & Zinsser, 1990), although such an effect was notably absent in a later archery study (Salazar et al., 1990). It should be noted that in the golf study, there was a positive correlation between the magnitude of deceleration and performance, a finding with important implications for feedback-based interventions. Older athletes may also care to remember that the heart rate patterning associated with concentration may vary with age (HR acceleration rather than deceleration; Molander & Backman, 1989). This is an important consideration since the older (and richer) performer may be the best market for such high-tech feedback interventions!

This central-peripheral relationship outlined at the start of this section was pursued for several years by Landers and his colleagues (based on directions described in Landers, 1981), resulting in a new direction in sport psychology, namely the use of background EEG. The EEG examination of elite marksmen by Hatfield, Landers, and Ray (1984) was a milestone development in sport psychophysiological research, the potential for such investigations having been suggested independently by Zaich-kowsky (1984) in the same year. The paper by Hatfield et al. is examined in more depth in the next section. It should be noted here that HR and EEG protocols have been used to examine psychophysiology before and during performance in a variety of closed skill sports including shooting (Bird, 1987), archery (Salazar et al., 1990), golf (Crews, 1991) and non-competitive weight lifting (Gannon, 1991). In most of these studies, better performance and performers were exemplified by preperfor-mance decreases in HR, lower overall activation and a different hemispheric pattern of EEG activity, most apparent in the alpha wavebands. These findings were mostly explained as indicators of heightened attention to relevant cues. This explanation signals a move away from the visceral-afferent explanation employed in earlier studies. A similar pattern of EEG in marksmen was later termed 'concentrative meditation' by Losel (1991).

Two other central psychophysiological measures have also recently received attention in the sports literature. These are the variety of slow wave potentials (SP) and event-related potentials (EP) apparent in the brain. Some explanation of both the genesis and interpretation of these waves is necessary. EPs and SPs can be distinguished from background EEG, one major difference being the way they are recorded. Background, ongoing EEG is made up of many different electrical signals or potentials, only some (mostly one) of which are associated with a particular event. With this notable exception, however, the rest of the activity can be considered random because it will tend to cancel itself out over a number of trials. It is this process of averaging, the superimposing of many records, that enables the emergence of the single electrical signal or potential evoked by the particular stimulus or task. This process is shown in Figure 8.1. To do this effectively, the signals must be time-locked by some stimulus so that the averaging process can be performed accurately. The resulting waveform, produced only by processes associated with preparation for, or performance of, the stimulus or task, will typically consist of positive or negative (P or N) spikes which are referred to by the average latency (time after) the stimulus in ms, e.g., the P300.

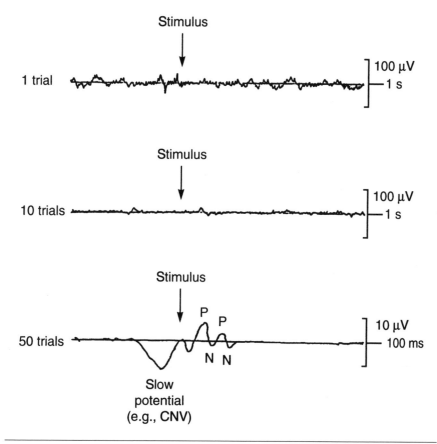

Figure 8.1 A diagrammatic representation of the derivation and presentation of slow wave evoked potentials. (NB. Waveforms are totally hypothetical.)

Slow wave potentials (SPs) will also emerge as slowly changing but definite trends in the waveform. These are frequently indicative of the subject's attention. The association of these two potentials with vigilance and motor preparation has commended them to sport researchers. Early studies outside sport tended to confound the stimulus anticipation and motor preparation aspects of a particular SP, the contingent negative variation (CNV). This situation was clarified by Brunia and Damen (1987; Damen & Brunia, 1987a) who distinguished between the stimulus preceding negativity (SPN), which was also associated with HR deceleration, and the readiness potential (RP), which was ascribed to preparation for movement. Differences in SPs associated with preparation (the Bereitschaftpotential—BP), execution (motor cortex potential—MCP) and evaluation (skilled performance positivity—SPP) were also discernible between adults and children and between success and failure on a skilled perceptual task (Chiarenza, Vasile, & Villa, 1990). Though jargon abounds in this area, with different terms often representative of extremely subtle differences in the same basic construct, these measures can be employed to good effect in sport psychophysiology.

The use of EPs in sport research was proposed by Rossi and Zani (1988). In 1990 they completed an examination of skeet and trap shooters that suggested the existence of skill-relevant differences in attentional style between the sports. A further study also demonstrated differences in decision-making style (Zani & Rossi, 1991a). Such evidence for event-related differences in information processing can now be used as the basis for the more objective and empirically-based design of performance enhancement strategies. Another important potential development, suggested by Zani and Rossi in an informative introduction and review of the topic (1991a; see also 1991b), is to utilise this methodology to examine sport practice-related modifications in information processing and other cognitive factors. Although these directions are both important and exciting it is important to record the caution expressed by other authors (e.g., Tinsit-Berthier, 1991) that such measures be applied in a rigorous and critical manner. If such a rigorous approach is maintained the use of EP and SP measures offers a rich potential for the future. Developing just such a scientific and demonstrably efficacious approach is an important aim for the discipline of sport psychology.

Using a different, more performance-related approach, Konttinen and Lyytinen (1992) employed HR, respiration and SP measures, averaged across more than 300 trials, to compare and contrast the preshot physiology of elite and novice marksmen. They found that better shots were associated with greater HR deceleration (peaking at trigger pull), slowed respiration with steady exhalation prior to the shot and a symmetric negative shift most marked at central sites. A particular feature of this shift, however, was that attenuation of the shift in the elite group was associated with better shots. No consistent pattern or result differences occurred in the novice group. The lower negativity preceding good shots was interpreted in terms of lower general arousal (which led to a good shot) or ascribed to competing positive shifts from another source, representative of motor inhibition (i.e., holding the muscles tense and still). In contrast, Crews, Martin, Hart, and Piparo (1991) found better performance on a golf putting task to be associated with asymmetric negative SP.

Further investigation of SPs preceding performance is important, both because of the potentially wide sports applications and to clarify the nature of SP changes associated with success. It is worth noting that in cognitive tasks (which would probably require greater processing than the well-learned sports tasks), success is associated with greater negativity in the BP (Freude, Ullsperger, Kruger, & Pietschmann, 1989). Perhaps this difference is due to the automated nature of skilled motor control, so essential for sport, which manifests itself as apparently lower attention to preparation.

One other study, worthy of special mention because of its novel use of telemetry to provide 'in game' data, is that conducted on tennis players by Schrode and Gabler (1987). This investigation found significant changes in attention, indexed by occipital EEG measures, related to task difficulty (repeated volleying) and physical stress. The authors also furnished examples of how knowledge gleaned by this method could be applied to the design of concentration training programmes. Telemetric and ambulatory measures have been rarely utilised in sport studies. Since the importance of assessment and systematic development of cognitive factors, such as attention and processing capacity, is increasingly stressed in the context of improving performance (Konzag, 1991), the potential of these and more orthodox psychophysiological techniques needs to be more fully exploited.

Biofeedback

Early sport applications of biofeedback were designed to modify the athlete's arousal state (e.g., Zaichkowsky, 1983). Under the assumption that lower arousal was equated with better performance, biofeedback was employed almost exclusively as a means of learning to relax. In a typical study, Blais and Vallerand (1986) used EMG frontalis biofeedback (together with HR this was the most commonly used index in this context) to modify the response to competition of highly trait-anxious boys. However, although this application is still valid and evident (Hosek & Man, 1989), the uses of biofeedback have been extended.

As research started to identify psychophysiological conditions associated with better performance, the emphasis changed and to date, closed skill sports, particularly target sports, have offered the best avenue for such applications. Modification of the HR and eye blink of rifle marksmen has been achieved by several researchers (e.g., Hosek, Dvoracek, & Cech, 1985). Recent application of EEG biofeedback to target sports has also been effective. Crews et al. (1991) used biofeedback of slow potentials to improve golf putting performance. In view of the somewhat contradictory results associated with biofeedback in the literature it is interesting to note that, in the study by Crews et al., it was more effective in improving performance than a more traditional imagery intervention, and an intervention based on relaxation training actually lowered performance.

Landers et al. (1991) found that EEG biofeedback based on temporal activity patterns, shown previously to be associated with better performance, was effective in archery. The inclusion of an incorrect feedback group (a quasi-double disassociation paradigm), was a particularly strong feature of this investigation; this group exhibited decrements in performance whilst a no-feedback control group remained unchanged. This study illustrates two important considerations for biofeedback studies. First, there is an a priori requirement to show that the activity encouraged by the feedback process is associated with, or preferably causative of, the desired improvement in performance (Salazar et al., 1990). Second, claims that the feedback is truly causing the improvement can only be totally substantiated if incorrect feedback (i.e., that which decreases the incidence of the performance concomitant) lowers performance. Catering for these two conditions, as the study by Landers et al. (1991) did, will ensure that biofeedback interventions are really effective.

It should be noted that biofeedback has also received a new lease of 'sporting life' via its increasing application to technical matters in sport. An excellent example of this is reported by Krueger, Ruehl, Scheel, and Franz (1988) who used EMG biofeedback to optimise technique with the new 'wing' Kayak paddle. Such multidisciplinary projects, which draw substantially from both motor learning and biomechanics, signal an exciting new direction for research. Further study into the most efficacious protocols for the biofeedback intervention is highly desirable. More comprehensive training packages, which utilised immediate performance feedback from video (Edge & Fazey, 1986), EMG and other mediums described earlier to address attentional factors, could offer very rapid and high quality learning indeed! Such 'high-tech' solutions must, however, be practical. The intervention based on brain imaging (magnetic resonance imaging—MRI) suggested by Powers (1983) may be slightly outside the price range of most sports governing bodies! With this caveat in mind, biofeedback programmes can be made more user-friendly and are potentially very powerful.

Central Cerebral Processes and Hemisphericity

The idea of the EEG providing 'a window on the mind' originated with Berger (1929) and is intuitively appealing to many workers in the field of sport psychology. Psychological investigations outside sport provide examples of the wide ranging potential for this measure. EEG has been used to provide a picture of ongoing activity in complex visual-motor tasks, such as flying (Schummer, 1987), rhythmic movement (Pogelt & Roth, 1982) and target tracking (Cooper, McCallum, & Cornthwaite, 1989). It has also been suggested as an index of memory retrieval speed (Klimesch, Schmike, Ladurner, & Pfurtscheller, 1990) and trace strength (Bentin & Moscovitch, 1990). The potential of EEG is such that Coles (1989) terms its application 'modern mind-brain reading'. In sport, documented applications are apparent in the examination of visual-motor behaviour (Ripoll, 1987), prediction of performance under stress (Bagrova, Korobov, & Gromov, 1984) and most commonly in the work of Landers and his colleagues on cerebral activity before and during performance.

Hatfield et al. (1984) used an EEG protocol to examine the preshot cerebral activity of rifle marksmen. The observed pattern of increased temporal alpha activity (8-13 Hz) in the left hemisphere immediately prior to trigger pull was hypothesised as being indicative of the most effective mental set. Based on the premise that greater alpha is associated with less processing, (an erroneous assumption as later studies have shown, e.g., Petsche, Pockberger, & Rappelsberger, 1988), Hatfield et al. suggested that the greater involvement of the right hemisphere was associated with better performance because this region of the brain was best suited to the requirements of the shooting task. This finding was reiterated in a second examination of marksmen (Hatfield, Landers, & Ray, 1987) and supported in studies of archery (Salazar et al., 1990), although it should be noted that in the later studies observed changes were ascribed to attentional processes rather than to hemispheric specialisation. Also worthy of mention are studies that have linked post exercise increases in alpha to affect. Boutcher and Landers (1988), for example, suggest that changes in this and other physiological measures may be indicative of the well-documented anxiety reduction and 'feel better' states associated with aerobic exercise.

In studies using externally-paced tasks (i.e., tasks in which responses are made to command or under external control or both), a slightly different pattern has been found. A series of studies we conducted using karate, soccer and cricket tasks has demonstrated increased alpha band activity in both hemispheres (Collins, Powell, & Davies, 1990, 1991a, 1991b). The magnitude of the response was also associated with result; increases in temporal and central alpha power preceded success, and failure was associated with decreased activity.

Typical result from these studies are presented in Figures 8.2 and 8.3. Figure 8.2 displays the differences in quantity or power of activity in the alpha waveband (8-13 Hz) associated with success or failure at a low-effort, high-accuracy kicking task. Figure 8.3 reveals a similar pattern of activity in the series of readings (epochs) taken prior to a cricket task, namely hitting the wicket with a throw over 22 yd (23.8m). Identification of such patterns has obvious applicability in sport psychology.

As the initial correlation versus causation arguments earlier in the chapter have shown, however, there is also a need for the underlying causes to be discussed. Our studies (Collins et al., 1990, 1991a, 1991b), hypothesised that the effects are caused by the mu rhythm (whose frequency of 9-12 Hz falls within the alpha waveband), which is associated with imposed stillness. This conscious inhibition of movement (see Konttinen & Lyytinen, 1992) was a precursor of effective applied effort or attention, a finding that seems to fit in with the cardiac coupling hypothesis of Obrist et al. (1974) cited earlier. Symmetric patterns were also reported in earlier non-sport, but movement-related, studies (Ford, Goethe, & Dekker, 1986; Pfurtscheller & Aranibar, 1980). It is essential for the future of sport psychophysiology that the factors causing the observed effects be explored or at least proposed.

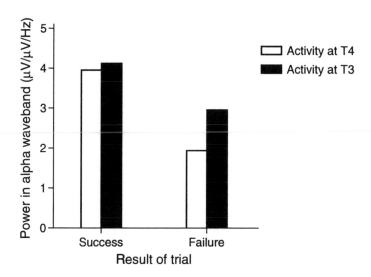

Figure 8.2   Temporal site power (quantity of activity) in the alpha waveband immediately preceding successful and unsuccessful performance on a soccer kicking task.
Note. From 'Cerebral Activity Prior to Motion Task Performance: An Electroencephalographic Study' by D.J. Collins, G.E. Powell, & I. Davies, 1991, *Journal of Sports Sciences*, **9**, pp. 313-324. Copyright 1991 by E. & F.N. Spon. Reprinted by permission.

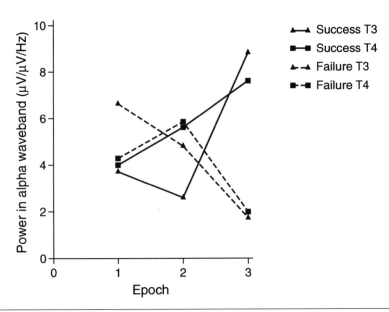

Figure 8.3 Temporal site power in seconds preceding successful and unsuccessful performance of cricket throwing task.

Note. From 'Cerebral Activity Prior to Motion Task Performance: An Electroencephalographic Study' by D.J. Collins, G.E. Powell, & I. Davies, 1991, *Journal of Sports Sciences*, **9**, pp. 313-324. Copyright 1991 by E. & F.N. Spon. Reprinted by permission.

Differences in the American and European findings must be considered in light of the technical and design characteristics of the studies. Such a detailed discussion is beyond the scope of this chapter. All the studies on both sides of the Atlantic, however, do at least show that preperformance states can be reliably and effectively examined by psychophysiological techniques and, furthermore, that result-related differences are detectable.

One major problem is also apparent. A significant number of sport psychologists have extrapolated from hemispheric effects in psychophysiological studies and produced substantial body of literature on the right-left brain dichotomy. What Goleman (1977) described as 'the fad of the year' (p. 89) has mushroomed! Given the contradictions in this literature, such a preoccupation must be questioned and re-examined in the light of all the available research. Some of the studies already cited illustrate that hemisphericity is far from a certainty. Lateralisation of SPs also demonstrates the complex nature of hemisphericity. SPs associated with ipsilateral movements may frequently appear at sites on both sides of the head where only contralateral effects may be expected. Lateral dominance (e.g., handedness) may also co-vary with this effect (Damen & Brunia, 1987b).

That some functions, notably language, are lateralised is not in question. However, it should be noted that, often due both to methodological inadequacies and to the complex nature of cerebral innervation, 'lateral activation does not necessarily measure hemispheric specialisation for the process which the experimenter seeks to investigate' (Butler & Glass, 1985, p. 386). Recorded patterns of asymmetry are highly individual and variable (Heister, Landis, Regard, & Schroeder-Heister, 1989). Furthermore, notable authorities in the field have even questioned the existence of such a construct: 'it would seem prudent to abandon the notion of hemisphericity, *at least in so far as it claims to make any reference to the lateral function of the cerebral hemispheres*' (my emphasis; Beaumont, Young, & McManus, 1984, p. 206).

The effects observed in many of the studies cited are, of course, still valid. The vast majority of the studies are academically and technically rigorous and provide excellent insights into the sport preparation process. It is the blanket application (and misinterpretation?) of such findings that must be viewed with extreme caution, especially when sweeping generalisations are made. Authors have related right brain advantages to stress reduction (Scelba, 1985), the runner's high (Sachs, 1984), which way a gymnast twists (Kassel, 1985), general sports performance (Hall & Hardy, 1982), athletic ability (Griffin, 1985; Rossi & Zani, 1986), and the effectiveness of different coaching and mental training strategies (Madden & McGown, 1989; Syer & Connolly, 1984). It may be rather provocative, but should nevertheless be noted, that the majority of these studies are of North American origin. Personally, I can only see a large proportion of this burgeoning literature as somewhat speculative, but the reader is advised to read more widely in this area before accepting either standpoint. Future investigations in this area should proceed from a sound conceptual framework (Ulrich, 1990), and given the contradictory findings apparent in the literature, a series of studies and replications should be encouraged.

Performance-Related Mental Training: Imagery

Given the central role of imagery in applied sport psychology (McCaffrey & Orlick, 1989), a greater understanding of how it works (and thus how it may be more effectively applied), is important for the discipline. Psychophysiological techniques can be used to good effect in this. Early studies, building on the original findings of Jacobson (1930), emphasised the relationship between the use of imagery and EMG-detected covert muscular activity (e.g., Suinn, 1984). The strong relationship between imagery and autonomic processes has also been examined (Pickenhain 1976), furnishing evidence of the temporal organisation of mental simulation of movement (MSM), which is crucial to its effective application (Suinn, 1976). Finally, examination of the link between imagery content and autonomic arousal has shown that assessment of the efficacy of imagery-inducing scripts and the vividness of the image itself are accessible through peripheral measures such as EMG, HR and SCL (Lang, 1984). However, burgeoning support for the symbolic learning hypothesis as the construct that best accounts for the imagery-performance relationship (Feltz & Landers, 1983) may have led to the increasing emphasis on central processes and the way in which they are involved in actual and imaged performance. In an excellent and important paper by Decety and Ingvar (1990), MSM has been associated with both visual and movement 'design' or programming structures. Implications for the use of imagery scripts (Hale, 1982; Lang, 1979) and other cues such as video or audio tape (Ainscoe & Hardy, 1987) are substantial.

Language has been identified by several authors (e.g., Annett, 1988) as an important bridge between actual and MS movement. Annett points to the ways in which video examination of covert movement whilst imaging (not strictly a psychophysiological measure, of course) reveals this link. This finding applies directly to the preparation of imagery scripts and the ways in which subjects may perceive and control their images. The evidence linking imagery and perceptual processes has mostly utilised evoked potential (EP) techniques. In a typical study, Peronnet, Farah, and Gonon (1988) found that imagery did engage the visual system in a similar way as in actual perception. Arguments against this assertion and neuropsychological evidence refuting them were summarised by Farah (1988).

The most recent trend in this area has been to search for the engagement of central processes by both MSM and actual movement. Improved techniques and technology resulted in such evidence from conventional EEG research (Petsche et al., 1988). The seminal paper by Decety and Ingvar (1990), which reviews past psychophysiological investigations and itself reports on the employment of rCBF protocols, also shows that certain components of motor programmes are activated by MSM. A variety of studies showed that MSM resulted in significant increases in activity, most particularly in the supplementary motor area and prefrontal cortex. Similar changes were also apparent with actual movement. Based on this evidence, Decety and Ingvar suggest that imagery involves a 'virtual simulation of motor behaviour' (p. 26). The study has substantial implications for the direction of future research in the area.

The application of 'chaos theory' to EEG (e.g., Lutzenberger, Elbert, Birbaumer, Ray, & Wells, 1992, an excellent example of international co-operation), has also led to the identification of differences in cerebral activity associated with different images and between imagery and perceptual processing. These findings, which have far-reaching implications for both general and sport-related research, are attributed by the authors to the greater sensitivity of this protocol compared with more traditional techniques.

Finally, in another paper that may have considerable ramifications within this field, Birbaumer et al. (1988) investigated the assertion that imagery ability is related to an individual's ability to control certain aspects of cortical activity, notably slow potentials (SP). Although the link between these two factors was lower than hoped for (but still significant), the more accurate and comprehensive assessment of central concomitants of imagery, together with the fact that SPs can be developed through training (Rockstroh, Elbert, Birbaumer, & Lutzenberger, 1990), may provide a new direction for the development and assessment of imagery ability. This ability is apparently an important factor in sport performance.

Performance-Related Traits

Since the time when personality research was the vogue in sport psychology, there have been frequent attempts to identify inherited or developed trait characteristics of the individual that may influence or be related to performance. Psychophysiologi-cally, the existence and relevance of such constructs can also be discerned. The quality of visceral perception, the individual's ability to discriminate certain physio-logical changes or states, is one such construct. This appears to be important for two reasons. First, this ability may relate autonomic changes to self-reported emotion (Schachter & Singer, 1962), which may, in turn, mediate the stress response. Second, it may mediate the efficacy of biofeedback techniques (Brener, 1977).

In sport psychology, identification of psychophysiological 'types' and their rele-vance for sports seems to have been a particularly European concern. In the mid 1980s, several researchers from Eastern Europe employed psychophysiological tech-niques in this way. In Russia, Tolotchek (1984) and Chebykin and Abolin (1984) related the characteristic patterning of wrestlers' physiological responses to the types of tactics they employed and their typical wrestling style. The latter study also made recommendations for the kinds of regulatory skills that would best suit each type of wrestler. A similar idea was proposed by Biro (1987) who identified four different types, and four related stress and social reaction patterns, in a sample of team games players. Meanwhile, in an unrelated project, Biondi and Venturi (1985) highlighted the importance of matching mental training to personality and fear response traits. A common theme in these investigations is that reactions to stress, and hence coping behaviours, are highly individual. As a consequence, training to cope must also be personalised if it is to be effective—a suggestion recently demonstrated empirically by Bull (1991).

More recently, Braathen and Svebak (1990) have identified differences in task-induced EMG responses between athletes in explosive and endurance sports. These differences were also, they claimed, indicative of differences in metamotivational state. These data fit well with previous investigations relating sports participation to personality variables such as impulsivity (Svebak & Kerr, 1989) and may also provide an important step towards the integration of psychophysiological variables with Reversal Theory in sport, as suggested earlier in the chapter. Yet another important potential direction may be the extension of these and other studies to identify exactly what sort of changes in central processes, and specifically informa-tion processing changes, are associated with, or induced by, long-term practice of sports skills (see Zani & Rossi, 1991a).

Exercise Effects on Stress Response

With regard to physical activity, one other relevant factor is the differences in response patterns associated with, or induced by, exercise. Exercise has increasingly been promoted as a therapy for psychological disorders and as an effective coping mechanism in its own right (see chapters 3 and 4). The link between psychophysio-logical measures and the stress response has received extensive attention (for an excellent introduction to coping with non-physical stressors see Steptoe, 1989), and although this chapter focuses on sports performance, the popularity of the topic in the current literature requires a brief discussion of exercise.

The literature is generally supportive to the role of exercise in mediating stress responses. Exercise has been shown to have both an acute effect on stress responses (Otto, 1990) and a chronic effect (Norris, Carroll, & Cochrane, 1990; Subhan, White, & Kane, 1987). Furthermore, this effect seems to hold for real-life, genuine stressors as well as for laboratory tasks. Brooke and Long (1987) found aerobic fitness level to be associated with the coping efficiency of novice abseilers ('rappeling'). There are, however, contradictory findings. Steptoe, Moses, Mathews, and Edwards (1990), and de Geus, Van Doornen, de Visser, and Orlebeke (1990), found no changes in stress responsivity following fitness training programmes. Van Doornen, de Geus, and Orlebeke (1988) had earlier attributed such inconsistencies to problems with exact terminology for constructs such as aerobic fitness, training or activity level. Given these contradictions, the need for a causal rather than associative model is apparent.

In a meta-analysis, Crews and Landers (1987), although supporting the association of fitness with decreased stress reactivity, expressed the commonly held view that decreased sympathetic influence of cardiovascular responses may be the likely explanation for the effects observed. The application of various measures to examine this assertion, an increasing feature of European research, may provide the answer to this problem. Parasympathetic HR control can be accessed by measurement of the respiratory sinus arrhythmia (RSA), and this was used in a typical study by Grossman and Svebak (1987) to examine parasympathetic control during active coping. Examination of the ECG waveform by autoregressive spectral analysis (Pagani et al., 1986) may hold even more promise because, under certain circumstances, it can provide information about both sympathetic and parasympathetic influences apparent in HR control. Changes in this balance associated with increased fitness or genetic factors may be at the root of the observed relationships, and current research should provide a new impetus for work in this area.

Conclusion

It is hoped that the sample of studies reviewed has served to secure interest in the topic of psychophysiology in sport. The limitations of the present review must also be recognised. For example, hardly any mention has been made of psycho-endocrinological measures (e.g., Grossman et al., 1984). Readers are referred to a more exercise-oriented review by Hatfield and Landers (1987).

Finally, for applied sport-based investigations, it is essential to recognise the large differences that may exist between laboratory and field measures. This was demonstrated by Marstaller and Meischner (1990) who carried out a psychophysical examination of emotional states associated with mental and autogenic training in gymnasts. Psychophysiology is increasingly recognising the strengths inherent in the use of field settings and data assessed by ambulatory techniques, especially for the examination of clinical problems. Given the discipline's applied orientation, sport psychology has an inherent advantage that must not be cast aside in the interests of the greater academic respectability perceived to be afforded by laboratory designs.

In summary, the chapter has attempted to provide an overview of the physiological measures most commonly used and to highlight the theoretical bases by which they are interpreted and applied. As a general rule it could be said that our understanding and application of peripheral measures are more precise than they are of central indices. Even in the case of the former, however, contradictions abound, and the area of psychophysiology, with all the potential it offers, is still comparatively untapped.

References

Ainscoe, M., & Hardy, L. (1987). Cognitive warm-up in a cyclical gymnastics skill. *International Journal of Sport Psychology*, **18**, 269-275.

Annett, J. (1988). Imagery and skill acquisition. In M. Denis, J. Engelkamp, & J.T.E. Richardson (Eds.), *Cognitive and neuropsychological approaches to mental imagery* (pp. 259-268). Amsterdam: Martinus Nijhoff.

Apter, M.J. (1976). Reversal theory and personality: A review. *Journal of Research in Personality*, **18**, 265-288.

Bagrova, N.D., Korobov, R.N., & Gromov, Y.M. (1984). Informativeness of EEG data in prediction of working capacity of operators. *Human Physiology*, **10**, 18-23.

Beaumont, J.G., Young, A.W., & McManus, I.C. (1984). Hemisphericity: A critical review. *Cognitive Neuropsychology*, **1**, 191-212.

Bentin, S., & Moscovitch, M. (1990). Psychophysiological indices of implicit memory performance. *Bulletin of the Psychonomic Society*, **28**, 346-352.

Berger, H. (1929). Uber das Elektroenkephalogramm des Menschen. *Arciva fur Psychiatrik*, **87**, 527-570.

Bethune, P. (1980). Psychophysiological response to high risk sports: The interplay of stress and performance in dangerous activities. In *Proceedings of the 17th Annual Scientific Conference: The hazards of outdoor sports and recreation* (pp. 113-116). Hobart: Australian Sports Medicine Federation.

Binnie, C.D., Rowan, A.J., & Gutter, T.H. (1982). *A manual of electro-encephalographic technology*. Cambridge, England: Cambridge University Press.

Biondi, M., & Venturi, P. (1985). Psicofisiologia della paura nello sport. *Movimento*, **1**, 15-18.

Birbaumer, N., Lang, P.J., Cook, E., Elbert, T., Lutzenberger, W., & Rockstroh, B. (1988). Slow brain potentials, imagery and hemispheric differences. *International Journal of Neuroscience*, **39**, 101-116.

Bird, E.I. (1987). Psychophysiological processes during rifle shooting. *International Journal of Sport Psychology*, **18**, 9-18.

Biro, V. (1987). Factor analysis of psychophysiological functions. *Studia Psychologica*, **29**, 97-111.

Blais, M.R., & Vallerand, R.J. (1986). Multimodal effects of electromyographic biofeedback: Looking at children's ability to control precompetitive anxiety. *Journal of Sport Psychology*, **8**, 283-303.

Blakeslee, P. (1979). Attention and vigilance: Performance and skin conductance response changes. *Psychophysiology*, **16**, 413-419.

Boucsein, W. (1990, June). *The use of psychophysiological methods in stress-strain research*. Paper presented at the 19th annual meeting of the German Psychophysiology Society (DGPA), University of Giessen.

Boutcher, S.H., & Landers, D.M. (1988). The effects of vigorous exercise on anxiety, heart rate, and alpha activity of runners and nonrunners. *Psychophysiology*, **25**, 696-702.

Boutcher, S.H., & Zinsser, N.W. (1990). Cardiac deceleration of elite and beginning golfers during putting. *Journal of Sport and Exercise Psychology*, **12**, 37-47.

Braathen, E.T., & Svebak, S. (1990). Task-induced tonic and phasic EMG response patterns and psychological predictors in elite performers of endurance and explosive sports. *International Journal of Psychophysiology*, **9**, 21-30.

Brener, J. (1977). Sensory and perceptual determinants of voluntary visceral control. In G.E. Schwartz & J. Beatty (Eds.), *Biofeedback: Theory and research* (pp. 29-66). New York: Academic Press.

Brooke, S.T., & Long, B.C. (1987). Efficiency of coping with a real life stressor: A multimodal comparison of aerobic fitness. *Psychophysiology*, **24**, 173-179.

Brunia, C.H.M., & Damen, E.J.P. (1987). Distribution of slow brain potentials related to motor preparation and stimulus anticipation in a time estimation task. *Electroencephalography and Clinical Neurophysiology*, **69**, 234-243.

Bull, S.J. (1991). Personal and situational influences on adherence to mental skills training. *Journal of Sport and Exercise Psychology*, **13**, 121-132.

Butler, S., & Glass, A. (1985). The validity of EEG alpha asymmetry as an index of the lateralisation of human cerebral function. In D. Papakostopoulos (Ed.), *Clinical and experimental neurophysiology* (pp. 370-393). London: Croom Helm.

Cacioppo, J.Y., & Tassinary, L.G. (Eds.) (1990). *Principles of psychophysiology: Physical, social and inferential elements*. Cambridge, England: Cambridge University Press.

Carroll, D., & Anastasiades, P. (1978). The behavioural significance of heart rate: The Lacey's hypothesis. *Biological Psychology*, **7**, 249-275.

Chebykin, A-Y., & Abolin, L.M. (1984). A study of emotional stability and psychological means of its formation. *Psikologicheskii-Zhurnal*, **5**, 83-89.

Chiarenza, G.A., Vasile, G., & Villa, M. (1990). Goal or near miss! Movement potential differences between adults and children in skilled performance. *International Journal of Psychophysiology*, **10**, 105-115.

Coles, M.G. (1989). Modern mind-brain reading: Psychophysiology, physiology and cognition. *Psychophysiology*, **26**, 251-269.

Collins, D.J., Powell, G.E., & Davies, I. (1990). An electroencephalographic study of hemispheric processing patterns during karate performance. *Journal of Sport and Exercise Psychology*, **12**, 223-234.

Collins, D.J., Powell, G.E., & Davies, I. (1991a). Cerebral activity prior to motion task performance: An electroencephalographic study. *Journal of Sports Sciences*, **9**, 313-324.

Collins, D.J., Powell, G.E., & Davies, I. (1991b, September). *Further electroencephalographic examination of the pre-performance mental set*. Paper presented at the annual meeting of the British Psychophysiology Society, Birkbeck College, London.

Cooper, R., McCallum, W.C., & Cornthwaite, S.P. (1989). Slow potential changes related to the velocity of target movement in a tracking task. *Electroencephalography and Clinical Neurophysiology*, **12**, 14-23.

Crews, D.J., & Landers, D.M. (1987). A meta-analytic review of aerobic fitness and reactivity to psychosocial stressors. *Medicine and Science in Sports and Exercise*, **19** (Suppl. 5), S114-S120.

Crews, D.J., Martin, J.J., Hart, E.A., & Piparo, A.J. (1991, June). *The effectiveness of EEG biofeedback, relaxation and imagery training on golf putting performance*. Paper presented at the North American Society for the Psychology of Sport and Physical Activity (NASPSPA) Annual Conference, Asilomar, CA.

Crews, D.L. (1991). *The influence of attentive states on golf putting as indicated by cardiac and electrocortical activity.* Eugene, OR: Microform.

Damen, E.J.P., & Brunia, C.H.M. (1987a). Changes in heart rate and slow brain potentials related to motor preparation and stimulus anticipation in a time estimation task. *Psychophysiology*, **24**, 700-713.

Damen, E.J.P., & Brunia, C.H.M. (1987b). Precentral potential shifts related to motor preparation and stimulus anticipation: A replication. In R. Johnson, J.W. Rohrbaugh, & R. Parasuraman (Eds.), *Current Trends in Event-Related Potential Research*, (EEG, Suppl. 40), 13-16. Amsterdam: Elsevier.

Davis, H. (1991). Passive arousal and optimal recovery in ice hockey. *Perceptual and Motor Skills*, **72**, 513-514.

Decety, J., & Ingvar, D.H. (1990). Brain structures participating in mental simulation of motor behavior: A neuropsychological interpretation. *Acta Psychologica*, **73**, 13-34.

de Geus, E.J., Van Doornen, L.J., de Visser, D.C., & Orlebeke, J.F. (1990). Existing and training induced differences in aerobic fitness: Their relationship to physiological response patterns during different types of stress. *Psychophysiology*, **27**, 457-478.

Donchin, E., & Coles, M.G.H. (1988). On the conceptual foundations of cognitive psychophysiology. *Behavioral and Brain Sciences*, **11**, 408-419.

Duffy, E. (1962). *Activation and behavior.* New York: Wiley.

Edge, A., & Fazey, J. (1986). *The development and evaluation of a delayed feedback video recording system for use in sport coaching situations.* Leeds, England: National Coaching Foundation.

Fahrenberg, J. (1986). Psychophysiological individuality: A pattern analytic approach to personality research and psychosomatic medicine. *Advances in Behavioural Research and Therapy*, **8**, 43-100.

Fahrenberg, J., Foerster, F., Schneider, H-J., & Muller, W. (1986). Predictability of individual differences in activation processes in a field setting based on laboratory measures. *Psychophysiology*, **23**, 323-333.

Farah, M.J. (1988). Is visual imagery really visual? Overlooked evidence from neuropsychology. *Psychological Review*, **95**, 307-317.

Fazey, J., & Hardy, L. (1988). *The inverted-U hypothesis: A catastrophe for sport psychology?* (British Association of Sports Sciences Monograph No. 1). Leeds, England: British Association of Sports Sciences & National Coaching Foundation.

Feltz, D.L., & Landers, D.M. (1983). The effects of mental practice on motor skill learning and performance: A meta-analysis. *Journal of Sport Psychology*, **5**, 25-57.

Fenz, W.D. (1975). Coping mechanisms and performance under stress. In D.M. Landers (Ed.), *Psychology of sport and motor behavior* (Vol. II, pp. 3-24). University Park: Pennsylvania State University.

Fenz, W.D., & Epstein, S. (1967). Gradients of physiological arousal of experienced and novice parachutists as a function of an approaching jump. *Psychosomatic Medicine*, **29**, 33-51.

Ford, M.R., Goethe, J.W., & Dekker, D.K. (1986). EEG coherence and power changes during a continuous movement task. *International Journal of Psychophysiology*, **4**, 99-110.

Freude, G., Ullsperger, P., Kruger, H., & Pietschmann, M. (1989). Bereitschaftspotential and the efficiency of mental task performance. *Journal of Psychophysiology*, **3**, 377-385.

Fridlund, A.J., Hatfield, M.E., Cottam, G.L., & Fowler, S.C. (1986). Anxiety and striate-muscle activation: Evidence from electromyographic pattern analysis. *Journal of Abnormal Psychology*, **95**, 228-236.

Gale, A., & Edwards, J. (1984). Individual differences. In M.G.H. Coles, E. Donchin, & S.W. Porges (Eds.), *Psychophysiology: Systems, processes and applications* (pp. 523-541). New York: Guilford.

Gannon, T.L. (1991). *An analysis of temporal EEG patterning prior to initiation of the arm curl.* Eugene, OR: Microform.

Goleman, D. (1977). Split-brain psychology: Fad of the year. *Psychology Today,* **11**, 88-90, 149-150.

Griffin, J. (1985). *Hemisphericity in athletes and dancers.* Eugene, OR: Microform.

Grossman, A., Bouloux, P., Price, P., Drury, P.L., Lam, K.S.L., Turner, T., Thomas, J., Besser, G.M., & Sutton, J. (1984). The role of opioid peptides in the hormonal responses to acute exercise in man. *Clinical Sciences,* **67**, 231-232.

Grossman, P., & Svebak, S. (1987). Respiratory sinus arrhythmia as an index of parasympathetic cardiac control during active coping. *Psychophysiology,* **24**, 228-237.

Gur, R.C., Gur, R.E., Skolnick, B.E., Resnick, S.M., Silver, F.L., Chawluk, J., Muenz, L., Obrist, W.D., & Reivich, M. (1988). Effects of task difficulty on regional cerebral blood flow: Relationships with anxiety and performance. *Psychophysiology,* **25**, 392-399.

Hale, B.D. (1982). The effects of internal and external imagery on muscular and ocular concomitants. *Journal of Sport Psychology,* **4**, 379-387.

Hall, E.G., & Hardy, C.J. (1982). Using the "right" brain in sport. In J.H. Salmela, J.T. Partington, & T. Orlick (Eds.), *New paths of sport learning and excellence* (pp. 104-108). Ottawa, ON: Sport in Perspectives.

Hanin, Y.L. (1980). A study of anxiety in sports. In W.F. Straub (Ed.), *Sport psychology: An analysis of athlete behavior* (pp. 236-249). Ithaca, NY: Mouvement.

Hatfield, B.D., & Landers, D.M. (1983). Psychophysiology: A new direction for sport psychology. *Journal of Sport Psychology,* **5**, 243-259.

Hatfield, B.D., & Landers, D.M. (1987). Psychophysiology in exercise and sport: An overview. *Exercise and Sport Sciences Reviews,* **15**, 351-387.

Hatfield, B.D., Landers, D.M., & Ray, W.J. (1984). Cognitive processes during self-paced motor performance: An electro-encephalographic profile of skilled marksmen. *Journal of Sport Psychology,* **6**, 42-59.

Hatfield, B.D., Landers, D.M., & Ray, W.J. (1987). Cardiovascular-CNS interactions during a self-paced, intentional attentive state: Elite marksmanship performance. *Psychophysiology,* **24**, 542-549.

Heister, G., Landis, T., Regard, M., & Schroeder-Heister, P. (1989). Shift of functional cerebral asymmetry during the menstrual cycle. *Neuropsychologica,* **27**, 871-880.

Helin, P. (1988). Activation in professional ballet dancers. *Physiology and Behavior,* **43**, 783-787.

Helin, P., Sihvonen, T., & Hanninen, O. (1987). Timing of the triggering action of shooting in relation to the cardiac cycle. *British Journal of Sports Medicine,* **21**, 33-36.

Hoffman, A.J. (1983). An analysis of the relationship between "physical impetus" and physiology among competitive athletes. *International Journal of Sport Psychology,* **14**, 270-281.

Hosek, V., Dvoracek, V., & Cech, J. (1985). Regulation of shooter's activity by means of biofeedback. In G. Schilling & K. Herren (Eds.), *Angst, Freude und Leistung im sport* (pp. 313-314). Magglingen, Switzerland: Fédération Européene de Psychologie des Sports et des Activités Corporelles.

Hosek, V., & Man, F. (1989). Training to reduce anxiety and fear in top athletes. In D. Hackfort & C.D. Spielberger (Eds.), *Anxiety in sports: An international perspective* (pp. 247-260). New York: Hemisphere.

Jacobson, E. (1930). Electrical measurements of neuromuscular states during mental activities: I. Imagination of movement involving skeletal muscle. *American Journal of Physiology*, **91**, 567-608.

Kassel, J. (1985). Which way do you twist? A study of twisting as related to brain hemisphere dominance. *International Gymnast*, **27**, 46-47.

Kjellberg, A., & Magnusson, E. (1979). Physiological response patterns during intake and rejection tasks. *Biological Psychology*, **9**, 63-76.

Klimesch, W., Schmike, H., Ladurner, G., & Pfurtscheller, G. (1990). Alpha frequency and memory performance. *Journal of Psychophysiology*, **4**, 381-390.

Konttinen, N., & Lyytinen, H. (1992). Physiology of preparation: Brain slow waves, heart rate and respiration preceding triggering in rifle shooting. *International Journal of Sport Psychology*, **23**, 110-127.

Konzag, G. (1991). Conoscere e giocare. *Scuola dello Sport: Rivista di Cultura Sportiva*, **21**, 57-62.

Krueger, K.M., Ruehl, M., Scheel, D., & Franz, U. (1988). Die Anwendbarkeit von EMG Biofeedback zur optimierung sportlicher techniken im motorischen lerprozess von ausdauersportarten am beispiel des kanurennsports. *Theorie und Praxis Leistungssport (Leipzig)*, **26**, 128-142.

Lacey, J.I. (1967). Somatic response patterning and stress: Some revisions of activation theory. In M.H. Appley & R. Trumbull (Eds.), *Psychological stress* (pp. 312-355). New York: Century Crofts.

Lacey, J.I., & Lacey, B.C. (1964, October). *Cardiac deceleration and simple visual reaction time in a fixed foreperiod experiment.* Paper presented at the meeting of the Society for Psychophysiological Research, Denver.

Lacey, J.I., & Lacey, B.C. (1970). Some autonomic-central nervous system interrelationship. In P. Black (Ed.), *Physiological correlates of emotion* (pp. 118-139). New York: Academic Press.

Landers, D.M. (1981). Arousal, attention and skilled performance: Further considerations. *Quest*, **33**, 271-283.

Landers, D.M., Daniels, F.S., Hatfield, B.D., & Wilkinson, M.O. (1982). Respiration, shot, heart. *Journal of the International Shooting Union*, **46**, 22-26.

Landers, D.M., Petruzzello, S.J., Salazar, W., Crews, D.L., Kubitz, K.A., Gannon, T.L., & Han, M. (1991). The influence of electrocortical biofeedback on performance in pre-elite archers. *Medicine and Science in Sports and Exercise*, **23**, 123-129.

Lang, P.J. (1979). A bio-informational theory of emotional imagery. *Psychophysiology*, **16**, 495-521.

Lang, P.J. (1984). Cognition in emotion: Concept and action. In C. Izard, J. Kagan, & R. Zajonc (Eds.), *Emotions, cognition and behavior* (pp. 192-226). New York: Cambridge University Press.

Losel, H. (1991). Gehirnstromkurven als kriterium konzentrativer versenkung waehrend des ziel-undabzugsvorganges im schiesssport. *U.I.T. Journal (Munich)*, **22**, 8-15.

Lutzenberger, W., Elbert, T., Birbaumer, N., Ray, W.J., & Wells, R. (1992). The scalp distribution of the fractal dimension of the EEG and its variation with mental tasks. *Brain Topography*, **5**(1), 27-34.

Madden, G., & McGown, C. (1989). The effect of the inner game method versus the progressive method on learning motor skills. *Journal of Teaching in Physical Education*, **9**, 39-48.

Marstaller, H., & Meischner, K. (1990, June). *The predictability of psychophysical states (laboratory-field comparison).* Paper presented at the 19th annual meeting of the German Psychophysiology Society (DGPA), University of Giessen.

Martinez-Selva, J.M., Gomez-Amor, J., Olmos, E., Navaro, N., & Roman, F. (1987). Sex and menstrual cycle differences in the habituation and spontaneous recovery of the electrodermal orienting reaction. *Personality and Individual Differences*, **8**, 211-217.

McCaffrey, N., & Orlick, T. (1989). Mental factors related to excellence among top professional golfers. *International Journal of Sports Psychology*, **20**, 256-278.

Molander, B., & Backman, L. (1989). Age differences in heart rate patterns during concentration in a precision sport: Implications for attentional functioning. *Journal of Gerontology*, **44**, 80-87.

Norris, R., Carroll, D., & Cochrane, R. (1990). The effects of aerobic and anaerobic training on fitness, blood pressure and psychological stress and well-being. *Journal of Psychosomatic Research*, **34**, 367-375.

Obrist, P.A., Howard, J.L., Lawler, J.E., Galosy, R.A., Meyers, K.A., & Gaeelein, C.J. (1974). The cardiac-somatic interaction. In P.A. Obrist, A.H. Black, & L.V. DiCara (Eds.), *Cardiovascular psychophysiology* (pp. 212-236). Chicago: Alsine.

Otto, J. (1990). The effects of physical exercise on psychophysiological reactions under stress. *Cognition and Emotion*, **4**, 341-357.

Pagani, M., Lombardi, F., Guzzetti, S., Rimoldi, O., Furlan, R., Pizzinelli, P., Sandrone, G., Malfatto, G., Dell'Orto, S., Piccaluga, E., Turiel, M., Baselli, G., Cerutti, S., & Malliani, A. (1986). Power spectral analysis of heart rate and arterial pressure variabilities as a marker of sympatho-vagal interaction in man and in conscious dog. *Circulatory Research*, **59**, 178-193.

Peronnet, F., Farah, M.J., & Gonon, M-A. (1988). Evidence for shared structures between imagery and perception. In M. Denis, J. Engelkamp, & J.T.E. Richardson (Eds.), *Cognitive and neuropsychological approaches to mental imagery* (pp. 357-362). Amsterdam: Martinus Nijhoff.

Petsche, H., Pockberger, H., & Rappelsberger, P. (1988). EEG topography and mental performance. In F.H. Duffy (Ed.), *Topographic mapping of brain electrical activity* (pp. 63-98). London: Butterworths.

Pfurtscheller, G., & Aranibar, A. (1980). Changes in central EEG activity in relation to voluntary movement: I. Normal subjects. *Progress in Brain Research*, **54**, 225-231.

Pickenhain, L. (1976). *Die Bedeutung innerer Ruckkoppelungskreise fur den Lernvorgang*. Leipzig, Germany: Zeitschrift fur Psychologie.

Pogelt, B., & Roth, N. (1982). Frequency and phase relationship between the EEG and rhythmic automated movements. *Acta Neurobiologica Experimenti*, **42**, 163-173.

Powers, C. (1983). *Neuropsychology of achievement and self-confidence and brain imaging workshops*. ON: Ministry of Tourism and Recreation.

Ripoll, H. (1987). Strategies oculo-motrices impliquees dans l'execution des habiletes sportives de precision. In H. Ripoll & G. Azemar (Eds.), *Neurosciences du sport: Traitement des informations visuelles, prises de decision et realisation de l'action en sport* (pp. 301-325). Paris: Institut National du Sport et de l'Education Physique.

Rockstroh, B., Elbert, T., Birbaumer, N., & Lutzenberger, W. (1990). Biofeedback-produced hemispheric asymmetry of slow cortical potentials and its behavioural effects. *International Journal of Psychophysiology*, **9**, 151-165.

Rodger, D., & Jamieson, J. (1988). Individual differences in delayed heart rate recovery following stress: The role of extraversion, neuroticism and emotional control. *Personality and Individual Differences*, **9**, 721-726.

Rossi, B., & Zani, A. (1986). Differences in hemispheric functional asymmetry between athletes and nonathletes: Evidence from a unilateral tactile matching task. *Perceptual and Motor Skills*, **62**, 295-300.

Rossi, B., & Zani, A. (1988). Informazione e sport. I processi di elabarazione dell informazione nello sport: Utilizzo di metodologie neuro-psicofisiologiche di studio fondate sulla registrazione. *Scuola dello Sport: Rivista di Cultura Sportiva*, **7**, 50-56.

Sachs, M.L. (1984). The runner's high. In M.L. Sachs & G.W. Buffone (Eds.), *Running as therapy: An integrated approach* (pp. 97-112). Lincoln: University of Nebraska Press.

Salazar, W., Landers, D.M., Petruzzello, S.J., Han, M., Crews, D.L., & Kubitz, K.A. (1990). Hemispheric asymmetry, cardiac response and performance in elite archers. *Research Quarterly for Exercise and Sport*, **61**, 351-359.

Scelba, A. (1985). *Exercise for stress reduction: A right brain function.* Eugene, OR: Microform.

Schachter, S., & Singer, J.E. (1962). Cognitive, social and physiological determinants of emotional state. *Psychological Review*, **69**, 379-399.

Schmid, A.B., & Peper, E. (1987). Psychological readiness states of the top 1984 rhythmic gymnasts. In J.H. Salmela, B. Petoit, & T.B. Hoshizaki (Eds.), *Psychological nurturing and guidance of gymnastic talent* (pp. 128-139). Montreal, PQ: Sport Psyche Editions.

Schrode, M., & Gabler, H. (1987). Aufmerksamkeitsveraenderungen beim Tennisspiel. Eine elektroenzephalographische studie mit telemetrischer messwerterfassung. *Leistungssport*, **17**, 25-30.

Schrode, M., Larbig, W., Heitkamp, H.C., & Wurster, K.G. (1986). Veraenderung psychophysiologischer parameter beim marathonlauf. *Sportwissenschaft*, **16**, 303-315.

Schummer, G.J. (1987). Electroencephalographic correlates of performance during a sustained visual-motor task. (Doctoral dissertation, California School of Professional Psychology, Los Angeles, 1987). *Dissertation Abstracts International*, **49**, 1986B.

Seaman, M.A., Levin, J.R., & Serlin, R.C. (1991). New developments in pairwise multiple comparisons: Some powerful and practicable procedures. *Psychophysiology Bulletin*, **110**, 577-585.

Smith, N.J., & Collins, D.J. (1991, September). *The role of psychophysiology as a research and intervention tool in sport psychology.* Paper presented at the annual meeting of the British Psychophysiology Society, Birkbeck College, London.

Steptoe, A. (1989). Coping and psychophysical reactions. *Advances in Behavioural Research and Therapy*, **11**, 259-270.

Steptoe, A., Moses, J., Mathews, A., & Edwards, S. (1990). Aerobic fitness, physical activity and psychophysiological reactions to mental tasks. *Psychophysiology*, **27**, 264-274.

Subhan, S., White, J.A., & Kane, J. (1987). The influence of exercise on stress states using psychophysiological indices. *Journal of Sports Medicine and Physical Fitness*, **27**, 223-229.

Suinn, R.M. (1976). Body thinking: Psychology for Olympic champs. *Psychology Today*, **10**, 38-43.

Suinn, R.M. (1984). Imagery and sports. In W.F. Straub & J.M. Williams (Eds.), *Cognitive sport psychology* (pp. 253-271). Lansing, NY: Sport Science Associates.

Svebak, S., & Kerr, J. (1989). The role of impulsivity in preference for sports. *Personality and Individual Differences*, **10**, 51-58.

Syer, J., & Connolly, C. (1984). *Sporting body, sporting mind.* Cambridge, England: Cambridge University Press.

Tinsit-Berthier, M. (1991). Toward a dynamic and integrative approach in sport psychology. *International Journal of Sport Psychology*, **22**, 399-401.

Tolotchek, V.A. (1984). Structure and form of individual style in sports. *Voprosy Psikhologii*, **5**, 137-141.

Tremayne, P., & Barry, R.J. (1988). An application of psychophysiology in sports psychology: Heart rate responses to relevant and irrelevant stimuli as a function of anxiety and defensiveness in elite gymnasts. *International Journal of Psychophysiology*, **6**, 1-8.

Tretilova, T.A., & Rodimski, E.M. (1979). Investigation of the emotional state of rifle shooters. *International Sport Sciences*, **1**, 745.

Turner, J.R. (1989). Individual differences in heart rate response during behavioral challenge. *Psychophysiology*, **26**, 497-504.

Ulrich, G. (1990). Oculomotor activity and the alpha rhythm. *Perceptual and Motor Skills*, **70**, 1099-1104.

Van Doornen, L., de Geus, E.J., & Orlebeke, J.F. (1988). Aerobic fitness and the physiological stress response: A critical evaluation. *Social Science and Medicine*, **26**, 303-307.

Vasey, M.W., & Thayer, J.F. (1987). The continuing problem of false positives in repeated measures ANOVA in psychophysiology: A multivariate solution. *Psychophysiology*, **24**, 479-486.

Wang, M.Q., & Landers, D.M. (1987). *Cardiac responses and hemispheric differentiation during archery performance: A psychophysiological investigation of attention.* Unpublished manuscript, Arizona State University, Tempe.

Weinrich, L. (1979). Psychophysiological studies on selected attention in humans. *Zeitschrift fur Psychologie*, **187**, 28-66.

Wilcox, R.R. (1987). New designs in analysis of variance. *Annual Review of Psychology*, **38**, 29-60.

Zaichkowsky, L.D. (1983). The use of biofeedback for self-regulation of performance states. In L-E. Unestahl (Ed.), *The mental aspects of gymnastics* (pp. 95-105). Orebro, Sweden: Veje Foerlag.

Zaichkowsky, L.D. (1984). Attentional styles. In W.F. Straub & J.W. Williams (Eds.), *Cognitive sport psychology* (pp. 140-150). Lansing, NY: Sport Science Associates.

Zani, A., & Rossi, B. (1991a). Cognitive psychophysiology as an interface between cognitive and sport psychology. *International Journal of Sport Psychology*, **22**, 376-398.

Zani, A., & Rossi, B. (1991b). Psychophysiology, psychological theory, and the study of skilled psycho-motor performance. *International Journal of Sport Psychology*, **22**, 402-406.

Zuckerman, M., Buchsbaum, M.S., & Murphy, D.L. (1980). Sensation seeking and its biological correlates. *Psychological Bulletin*, **88**, 605-632.

9

CHAPTER

Enhancing Performance
With Mental Training

Guido Schilling
Hanspeter Gubelmann

SWITZERLAND

Those involved in sport today, whether they be athletes, coaches, sport scientists, officials or spectators, are becoming increasingly aware of the importance of mental aspects of performance. For example, a lack of 'mental toughness' is a common reason cited for unsuccessful performance. Indeed, one of the goals of applied sport psychology is to build mental toughness in an effort to stabilise and enhance performance (Seiler, 1992).

'Mental training', especially in the English language literature of sport psychology, refers to

> the formal, structured application of psychological techniques to enhance sport performance. Other terms such as psychological preparation or mental preparation are also used, but mental training appears to be the most popular. This is perhaps because it implies processes and objectives similar to those with which sports performers are very familiar through their use of the term physical training. (Morris & Bull, 1991, p. 4)

The study of preperformance strategies in sport has a long tradition. Feltz and Landers (1983) conducted a meta-analytic review of 60 studies and found that mental practice had a significantly larger effect on cognitive tasks than on motor or strength tasks. However, the literature at the same time suggested that 'psych-up' strategies were particularly effective for strength tasks (see Weinberg, 1984). Biddle (1985) attempted to resolve the apparent contradiction by distinguishing between mental practice and mental preparation (also see Murphy & Jowdy, 1992; Suinn, 1993). Mental practice was seen to be akin to mental imagery and the visualisation of skills and thus supporting the symbolic learning theory of mental imagery (Murphy & Jowdy, 1992; Suinn, 1993). Mental preparation, on the other hand, could apply to a variety of preperformance strategies aimed at enhancing performance. These may include psych-up strategies, such as preparatory arousal, or other strategies like relaxation and self-statements (see Biddle, 1985; Shelton & Mahoney, 1979).

In the 1960s and 1970s, in the German language literature the term *mental training* ('Mentales Training') was restricted to the mental rehearsal of motor skills: The athlete thinks about a skill and rehearses the movement through visualisation, looking at a mental image or picture in the mind. There appear to be at least three ways of imagining a skill. The person can remain in the body looking out (internal perspective) or can watch the self from outside as if on film (external perspective). A third way of imagining a skill is to watch somebody else performing an ideal prototype movement.

In sport psychology and coaching, mental training is an often-used expression in both the restricted (narrow) and broader (wider) perspectives. In the last few years many articles and books have been published on mental training, but, as we know from investigations in Germany (Gabler, Janssen & Nitsch, 1990) and Switzerland (Keller & Steiger, 1992), athletes and coaches know about it, but its integration into daily training programmes is inconsistent.

An Integrated Model of Sport Performance

Athletic performance in elite sport is not only the result of action during the competition itself. The performance is built up over a long training period. High-level performance in sport demands that both physiological and psychological components combine—body and mind must form a unit (see Schilling, 1993).

The conditioning of physical factors like strength, endurance with aerobic and anaerobic capacities, power and flexibility is now well known and described in books on coaching theory. However, athletes often appear 'overeducated' on physical factors and 'undereducated' on mental factors. Too many athletes and coaches still try to develop the human capacity for sport performance only through physical conditioning. However, some have now started to enrich their training programmes with relaxation methods such as autogenic training (Schultz, 1976) or progressive muscle relaxation (Jacobson, 1934). It is assumed that there is a direct line of causation from the muscular system to the inner emotional state. Athletes who undertake relaxation training do so in order to find the optimum arousal and activation for performance. Various forms of Eastern-oriented meditation methods (Chinmoy &

Heer, 1990) are also used for relaxation, as well as for preparation for imagery or goal-setting techniques.

There is evidence (see Biddle, 1986; Seiler, 1992) that an athlete can use cognitive elements to good effect in sport. Human beings can make their body and mind partners ('The Sporting Bodymind', Syer & Connolly, 1987). 'The Sporting Body-mind' can be seen as a system tending towards a 'floating homeostasis', or equilib-rium. We can look at it as a tube system with two ends filled with liquid (see Figure 9.1). For optimal sports performance the level of performance of body and mind should be the same. If there is a discrepancy, the athlete will not be able to perform optimally. In top-level sport, it seems that very often the mental side (function) is not trained well enough and so the performance level decreases (see Figure 9.2) because of this deficit. If the whole system adjusts to the lower level, the athlete feels 'psyched-out' and performs badly. If athletes can adjust the system to their higher level, they will feel 'psyched-up' and able to produce a peak performance.

Peak Performance

Athletes, artists and other performers report that during times of great personal achievement they experience total calmness and attention, total relaxation and con-centration, total freedom and body-mind unification. Unestahl (1986) describes the 'Ideal Performing State' (IPS) through the words of an athlete:

> Suddenly everything worked. I did not wonder any longer what to do or how to do it—everything was automatic. I just looked on. Nothing could have disturbed me in that moment. I was completely involved with what was

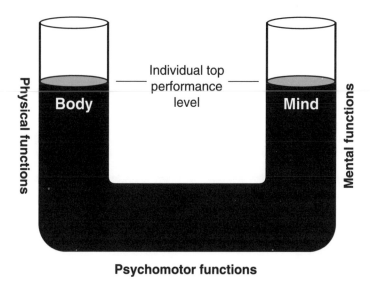

Figure 9.1   The unit of body and mind for the production of top-level performance.

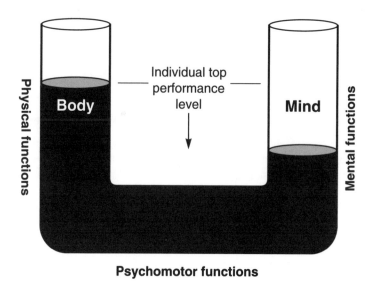

Figure 9.2   The unit of body and mind: individual performance decrease.

happening. I had no thoughts of doing it correctly, no thoughts of failure, no thoughts of fatigue. I felt an inner security and confidence that was tremendous. It was completely natural that I would succeed. I watched my accomplishment and enjoyed it while at the same time I was as one with it. It was a trance-like state, which I would like to experience every time, but which I probably won't experience again for a long time. (p. 22)

Athletes of different levels—not only top performers—can experience the IPS. They feel a balance between skill and capability, and the challenge they face. Csikszentmihalyi (1990) describes this optimal experience as 'flow'. Many participants in sporting activities—mountain climbing or marathon running, for example—report this flow experience. They feel happy to exercise or to run in a race, and doing this they experience and develop their human capacities and potential. It seems that the length of a performance or of a training workout, or the rhythm in long-distance running, might be prerequisites to the experience of flow, although this has yet to be demonstrated with certainty. This feeling of a balance between body and mind gives human beings great satisfaction and happiness. If the ratio between challenge and capability is out of balance, either boredom or anxiety will result (Csikszentmihalyi, 1975).

Mental Training

The aim of the training process in top-level sport is to bring the athlete to peak performance for the most important competition. In physical and mental training the athlete and coach have to define the abilities and capacities they want to work for before the season, during competition and after the season. For most athletes, daily training is scheduled for the physical aspects of performance. Many authors (see Seiler, 1992) propose that mental training should also be incorporated into the normal training programme at least for a complete training season and for important championships over a period of several years. 'Trouble shooting' interventions on a short-term basis are, in fact, a very common way to introduce psychology into sport, but they are mostly ineffective and often cause more problems than they solve.

In the last 10 years, mainly in Europe and North America, several articles and manuals on mental training have been published (e.g., Eberspacher, 1990; Loehr, 1988; Porter & Foster, 1986; Railo, 1986; Sonnenschein, 1989; Suinn, 1989; Terry, 1989; Unestahl, 1986; Venzl & Schori, 1993). These instructional programmes explain the theory and the methods of enhancing sport performance through mental training. Mental training for coaches and athletes was also a topic at the Fifth World Congress for Sport Psychology in Ottawa, Canada in 1981 (Orlick, Partington, & Salmela, 1982), at the Eighth European Congress in 1991 in Cologne, Germany, and at the Eighth World Congress in 1993 in Lisbon, Portugal. Some sports governing bodies and training centres are also trying to integrate mental training into their normal training programmes (Straub, 1992).

In the former GDR, mental training (Mathesius, 1992) and 'psychoregulation' had a long tradition with elite athletes (Kunath & Schellenberger, 1991). Only recently have the details of the methods and techniques used with East German top-level athletes been published. According to Kratzer (1991), psychological training in the GDR was structured and applied to regulate the psychic state in four dimensions:

1. Cognitive training, including perception training, concentration training and mental training (imagery)
2. Sensory motor training, including reaction training, co-ordination training and rhythm training
3. Motivation training, including goal-setting, goal programming and actual motivation
4. Psychoregulation training, including a so-called 'unit for psychoregulation', activation and autogenic training

For the cognitive and sensory motor training, special apparatus was installed in a laboratory. In the psychoregulation training a special 'unit for psychoregulation' (Psychoregulative Einheit) was used (Kratzer 1991). It had three important points: relaxation, self-instruction and imagery. Through breath control and the breathing rhythm the athlete calms down and is able to learn arousal regulation. Self-instruction or self-talk can be useful for affirmations to develop self-confidence. Imagery is used to recall the exact and optimal realisation of a sporting skill.

Human Potential Training

At the Department for Physical Education Teachers at the Swiss Federal Institute of Technology in Zürich, we have developed a mental training programme for athletes. This has been called 'Human Potential Training' (HPT). Introductory training courses are offered to athletes and sport governing bodies or clubs. The training has to be given by members of the Swiss Working Group for Sport Psychology (SASP). The HPT introduction course (Parts 1 and 2) take two days, and after 1-2 months a feedback meeting, including Part 3, takes place. Venzl and Schori (1993) presented the programme at the FEPSAC Congress in Cologne.

The HPT programme was developed in response to requests from athletes and coaches. The course provides an introduction to the training of mental skills as they are needed in athletic competitions. Relaxation training and stress management are discussed in all three parts of the programme, together with the following main topics: Part 1: goal-setting and motivation; Part 2: psych-up strategies for self-confidence and self-talk; Part 3: cognitive techniques for concentration and imagery.

Relaxation Training and Stress Management

In many mental training programmes, relaxation procedures and stress management are used as core or basic skills. Everybody has their own experience with their own failure or success in handling stressful situations. As Orlick (1980) states, loss of relaxation often prevents top performances. An athlete may not achieve the desired result because of excessive nervousness, anxiety and tension. This may result in the failure of the athlete to activate the correct muscles efficiently. It is vital, therefore, to be able to achieve mental relaxation in the quest for top performance and to achieve a balanced activation level. An optimum level of arousal is necessary for this. Morris and Bull (1991) define arousal as

> a general physiological state relating to levels of activation. High arousal may be associated with pleasant or unpleasant experiences such as excitement or fright, and low arousal with relaxation, calmness or lethargy. (p. 7)

Coaches and athletes must try to manipulate and regulate the level of arousal in order to reach the optimum for a particular situation. Relaxation procedures can have a considerable effect on anxiety, which can be described as a mixture of feelings of tension, worry and apprehension. It is important to note that relaxation procedures can have an effect on anxiety reduction before, during and after sport competition.

Goal-Setting and Motivation

To realise a goal in sport or in daily life motivation has to be directed towards this goal. Coaches and athletes are interested in learning how goal-setting or motivating can be achieved and made operational.

Motivation is the link between the drive and the goal. Goal-setting consists of identifying the drive and linking it to the goal. It is a mechanism for motivation;

it is identifying your motivation and the goals you are trying to accomplish. Goal-setting creates a focus of attention and action. Through this our actions have a purpose. Persistence and effort are influenced by goal-setting since varying goals require varying amounts of effort and persistence, depending on the requirements of the task. 'In short, goal-setting provides the structure for motivation which . . . is directing effort over a period of time' (Harris & Harris 1984, p. 133). A high level of motivation can also be a source of satisfaction for the coach. Equally, the coach can be frustrated when the talented athlete shows low effort or motivation.

Most books and articles on mental training, especially on goal-setting, are concerned with individual sports. Syer's (1986) book *Team Spirit: The Exclusive Experience* is a welcome exception to this.

Strategies for Psyching-Up

Many coaches, particularly in team sports, use the pregame 'pep talk' (Klavora, 1979) or the mid-game motivational talk to 'psych-up' the players. We know that powerful talking can influence or even alter human beings. Prayer, magical evocation, chants and various healing rituals throughout the world are evidence of the effect of language.

Although pep talks should not be the only mental technique a coach uses, they can complement self-talk and thus be an additional resource to enhance performance, especially in team sports.

Cognitive Techniques

Handling the cognitive aspects of sport performance is one of the challenges in sport today. Physical practice is often the only component of a training programme and it can be difficult to convince some coaches and athletes that every performance, and especially every top performance, 'starts in the head'. Some athletes use naive techniques of imagery or concentration techniques, but, according to Orlick (1980), very few practice them systematically.

Mental imagery is a way of dealing mentally with the situation before it occurs in practice. By confronting possible problems, practising means of coping with them and overcoming them in mental imagery, the athlete should be better able to cope in the reality of the sports competition.

However, athletes need advice and experience in using cognitive techniques, as Nideffer (1979) has stated. For example, everyone knows that concentration is important for peak performance. However, athletes should not be told to concentrate, but *how* to concentrate. The athlete must be taught what to concentrate on, when to concentrate and how to maintain concentration at critical periods.

Mental Skill Training

Here we shall use 'mental training' in the restricted sense of mental rehearsal, mental skill training or mental practice of movement. In this kind of mental training, the athletes look at themselves replaying or preplaying an optimal skill performance. They should experience all sensory perceptions by mentally performing a movement or an action. Cratty (1989) refers to the Carpenter Effect, postulating that any idea in our mind finds its way into the muscles. Various investigations have shown the positive effects of this kind of training. Recently, Schlicht (1992) showed that mental skill training has a positive effect on learning and improving athletic skills. Bakker, Whiting, and van den Brug (1992) have reported a survey of over 60 experiments in which mental skill training improved sport performances. Grouios (1992) also reported that mental practice improved diving performance.

Mental Practice Training With School Children

In the 1970s, the Institute for Applied Psychology at the University of Zurich started a series of investigations of mental skill training of children. More recently, Gubelmann, Venetz, and Dieth (1990) and Doninelli and Tami (1991) have reported similar work.

Our research (e.g., Gubelmann, 1993) studied children aged 15 years who completed a series of tests and were requested to run a standardised obstacle course ('parcour') on a volleyball court (see Figures 9.3, a and b). All children in both the experimental group and the control group had to run the course twice, with a week between the two trials. Between trials the experimental group attended a mental training session twice a day and so completed altogether ten training sessions. No treatment was given to the control group.

Our results were similar to those of Mader, Ospelt, and Schutz (1974). Children with regular mental training made significantly better progress than those without. There were no significant gender differences in improvement (see Figure 9.4).

Inner Training

How mental training works is not yet fully explained by cognitive psychology, or by information theory. What happens with the information brought into the human system as input? How does the brain process the input? What role has our memory in processing? These questions can only be partly answered. In many respects the processes that occur between perceptions and actions are a kind of 'black box'. In a simple model of the person acting in the environment we can identify three main components: stimulus perception, processing of the stimulus and reaction to the stimulus (see Figure 9.5).

In mental training—in the sense of mental imagery and in a general sense—neither a stimulus from the environment nor an action can be observed if we ignore the minireaction of the Carpenter Effect. Mental training takes place in the 'inside' (Gallwey & Kriegel, 1977), and is therefore called 'inner training' by some authors (see Figure 9.6). We know that human beings are able to process and experience

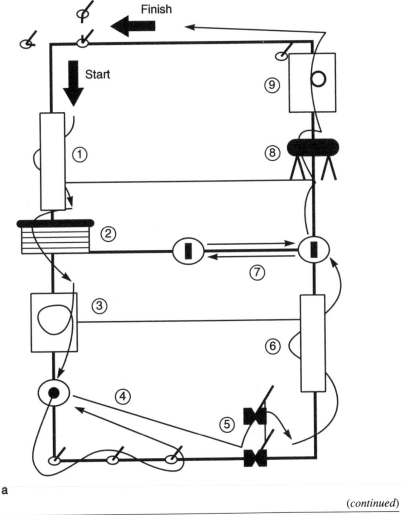

Finish

Start

a

(continued)

Figure 9.3 (a) Standardised obstacle course (b) explanation of parcour course.

Parcour set up on a volleyball court:

1. Crawl under bench.

2. Go over "Swedish vault box" (height 1.1 m).

3. Roll backward on mat.

4. Slalom with medicine ball (weight 2 kg).

5. Jump over rubberband (height 1.0 m).

6. Crawl under bench.

7. Shuttle run with baton.

8. Jump over vault.

9. Forward roll on mat.

b

Figure 9.3 (*continued*)

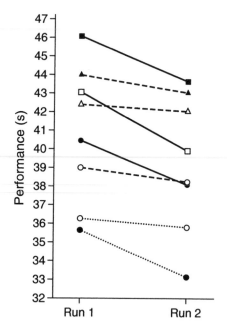

■—■ Experimental group girls 1991 (67)

▲--▲ Control group girls 1991 (14)

□—□ Experimental group girls 1989 (75)

△--△ Control group girls 1989 (57)

●—● Experimental group boys 1991 (56)

○-○ Control group boys 1991 (10)

●···● Experimental group boys 1989 (48)

○···○ Control group boys 1989 (48)

Figure 9.4 Mental training experimental group versus no training control group results comparing the results of Gubelmann.
Note. Data from Gubelmann (1993, p. 76).

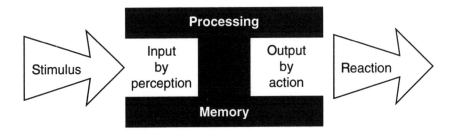

Figure 9.5   Human Perception-Action Model.

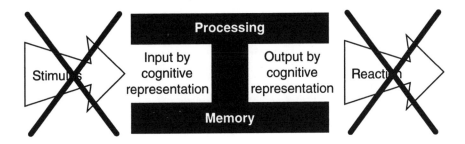

Figure 9.6   Inner Training Model.

a sports performance by cognitive representation alone. We can do a 400 m hurdle race mentally—in our heads—and feel the physical effects as if we had run a real race.

Inner Performing

According to our model, it must also be possible to run the obstacle course mentally without any practical experience or physical training. In 1991-92 we discussed this question with students in our physical education department. In two groups (first semester = first year and sixth semester = third year), we instructed the students in the classroom by use of a slide illustrating the layout of the obstacle course. Without any physical training, but after a short mental training session, we asked the students to run through the course in their heads and to give a hand signal when they passed the finishing line. We noted the time for each student. We were surprised by the results. Without any stimuli from outside and without reacting to the outside—except the signal for having finished—the average time of both student groups (first and sixth semester) was almost identical to the average time realised by the different groups of children actually running through the course (see Table 9.1).

Conclusion

In conclusion, we believe that contemporary sport and the sport sciences have a chance to become more humanistic and interdisciplinary, developing the awareness

Table 9.1 Mental Performance Versus Real Performance

	N	Time (means)	Standard deviation
Mental performance (Physical education students 1st semester '92)	57	36.45	8.1
Mental performance (Physical education students 6th semester '91)	14	36.91	4.4
Real performance (Secondary school children, 16 years old, boys and girls)	116	37.05	5.2

of 'The Sporting Bodymind' (Syer & Connolly, 1987). The unit of 'bodymind' is important in the pursuit of excellence by top athletes and also for well-being in our daily lives. Consequently, sport psychologists will play an important role in developing mental training, not only in sport but probably also in 'wellness' education.

References

Bakker, F.C., Whiting, H.T.A., & van den Brug, H. (1992). *Sportpsychologie: Grundlagen und Anwendungen*. Bern, Switzerland: Huber.

Biddle, S.J.H. (1985). Mental preparation, mental practice and strength tasks: A need for clarification. *Journal of Sports Sciences*, **3**, 67-74.

Biddle, S.J.H. (1986). Personal beliefs and mental preparation in strength and muscular endurance tasks: A review. *Physical Education Review*, **8**, 90-103.

Chinmoy, S., & Heer, H. (1990). *Sport and meditation*. Zurich, Switzerland: Sri Chinmoy Verlag.

Cratty, B.J. (1989). *Psychology in contemporary sport* (3rd ed.). Englewood Cliffs, NJ: Prentice Hall.

Csikszentmihalyi, M. (1975). *Beyond boredom and anxiety*. San Francisco: Jossey-Bass.

Csikszentmihalyi, M. (1990). *Flow: The psychology of optimal experience*. New York: Harper & Row.

Doninelli, A., & Tami, R. (1991). *Applicazione dell'allenamento mentale nello sport scolastico*. Unpublished manuscript. Zurich, Switzerland: Swiss Federal Institute of Technology, Division of P.E.

Eberspacher, H. (1990). *Mentale Trainingsformen in der Praxis*. Oberhaching, Germany: Sportinform Verlag.

Feltz, D.L., & Landers, D.M. (1983). The effects of mental practice on motor skill learning and performance: A meta-analysis. *Journal of Sport Psychology*, **5**, 25-57.

Gabler, H., Janssen, J.P., & Nitsch, J.R. (1990). *Gutachten "Psychologisches Training" in der Praxis des Leistungssports*. Koln, Germany: Sport und Buch Strauss.

Gallwey, T., & Kriegel, B. (1977). *Inner skiing*. New York: Random House.

Grouios, G. (1992). The effect of mental practise on diving performance. *International Journal of Sport Psychology*, **23**, 60-69.

Gubelmann, H.-P. (1993). *Mentales Training im Schulsport*. Unpublished thesis, University of Zurich, Division of Applied Psychology, Zurich, Switzerland.

Gubelmann, H.-P., & Osterwalder, R. (1989). *Kopfchen im Schulsport*. Unpublished manuscript. Zurich, Switzerland: Swiss Federal Institute of Technology, Division of Physical Education.

Gubelmann, H.-P., Venetz, M., & Dieth, M. (1990). *Intelligenz als Voraussetzung fur die erfolgreiche Anwendung des Mentalen Trainings im Schulsport?* Unpublished research paper. Zurich, Switzerland: University of Zurich, Division of Applied Psychology.

Harris, D.V., & Harris, B.L. (1984). *The athlete's guide to sports psychology: Mental skills for physical people*. Champaign, IL: Leisure Press.

Jacobson, E. (1934). *You must relax*. New York: Bantam.

Keller, B., & Steiger, J. (1992). *Psychologisches Training in Sportspielmannschaften: Eine Erkundunggsstudie in der Praxis des Leistungssports*. Unpublished thesis. Zurich, Switzerland: University of Zurich, Division of Applied Psychology.

Klavora, P. (1979). Customary arousal for peak athletic performance. In P. Klavora & J.V. Daniel (Eds.), *Coach, athlete and the sport psychologist* (pp. 155-163). Toronto, ON: University of Toronto Press.

Kratzer, H. (1991). Psychische Belastungswirkungen und ihre Berucksichtigung im Trainingsprozess. In P. Kunath & H. Schellenberger (Eds.), *Tatigkeitsorientierte Sportpsychologie* (pp. 262-264). Frankfurt, Germany: Verlag Harri Deutsch.

Kunath, P., & Schellenberger, H. (Eds.) (1991). *Tatigkeitsorientierte Sportpsychologie*. Frankfurt, Germany: Verlag Harri Deutsch.

Loehr, J.E. (1988). *Personliche Bestform durch Mentaltraining fur Sport, Beruf und Ausbildung*. Munchen, Germany: BLV.

Mader, F., Ospelt, R., & Schutz, B. (1974). *Intelligenz-Struktur und Erfolg im Mentalen Training*. Unpublished research paper. Zurich, Switzerland: University of Zurich, Division of Applied Psychology.

Mathesius, R. (1992). Sportpsychologie am ehemaligen FKS in Leipzig. *Sportpsychologie*, **3**, 25-32.

Morris, T., & Bull, S.J. (1991). *Mental training in sport: An overview* (BASS Monograph No. 3). Leeds, England: White Line Press.

Murphy, S.M., & Jowdy, D.P. (1992). Imagery and mental practice. In T.S. Horn (Ed.), *Advances in sport psychology* (pp. 221-250). Champaign, IL: Human Kinetics.

Nideffer, R.M. (1979). The role of attention in optimal athletic performance. In P. Klavora & J.V. Daniel (Eds.), *Coach, athlete and the sport psychologist* (pp. 99-112). Toronto, ON: University of Toronto Press.

Orlick, T. (1980). *In pursuit of excellence*. Champaign, IL: Human Kinetics.

Orlick, T., Partington, J.T., & Salmela, J.H. (1982). *Mental training for coaches and athletes*. Champaign, IL: Human Kinetics.

Porter, K., & Foster, J. (1986). *The mental athlete: Inner training for peak performance*. Dubuque, IA: Brown.

Porter, K., & Foster, J. (1987). *Mentales Training: Der moderne Weg zur sportlichen Leistung*. Munchen, Germany: BLV.

Railo, W. (1986). *Besser sein wenn's zahlt: Wege zum Erfolg in Sport und Beruf*. Friedberg, Germany: Pagina GmbH.

Schilling, G. (1993). Mental training. In *Proceedings of the 8th World Congress of Sport Psychology*. Lisboa, Portugal: Universidade Tecnica, Faculdade de Motrocidade Humana.

Schlicht, W. (1992). Mentales Training: Lern- und Leistungsgewinne durch Imagination? *Sportpsychologie*, **2**, 24-29.

Schori, B. (1989). Mentale Starke ist trainierbar. *Sportpsychologie*, **3**(4), 5-10.

Schultz, J.H. (1976). *Das Autogene Training: Konzentrative Selbstentspannung. Versuch einer klinisch-praktischen Darstellung*. Stuttgart, Germany.

Seiler, R. (1992). Performance enhancement: A psychological approach. *Sport Science Review*, **1**(2), 29-45.

Shelton, T.O., & Mahoney, M.J. (1979). The content and effect of 'psyching-up' strategies in weightlifters. *Cognitive Therapy and Research*, **2**, 275-284.

Sonnenschein, I. (1989). *Das Kolner Psychoregulationstraining: Ein Handbuch fur Trainingsleiter* (3 Aufl.). Koln, Germany: bps.

Straub, S. (1992). Mentale Trainingsprogramme am Olympiastutzpunkt Freiburg-Schwarzwald. *Sportpsychologie*, **1**, 17-20.

Suinn, R.M. (1989). *Seven steps to peak performance*. Toronto, ON: Huber.

Suinn, R.M. (1993). Imagery. In R.N. Singer, M. Murphey, & L.K. Tennant (Eds.), *Handbook of research on sport psychology* (pp. 492-510). New York: Macmillan.

Syer, J. (1986). *Team spirit: The exclusive experience*. London: Kingswood Press.

Syer, J., & Connolly, C. (1987). *Psychotraining fur Sportler*. Hamburg, Germany: Rowohlt.

Terry, P. (1989). *Mental zum Sieg. Aengste erkennen. Motivation steuern, Leistung steigern*. Munchen, Germany: BLV.

Unestahl, L.-E. (1986). The ideal performance. In L.-E. Unestahl (Ed.), *Sportpsychology in theory and practise* (pp. 20-37). Orebro, Sweden: VEJE.

Venzl, R., & Schori, B. (1993). Psychoregulation und Selbstmanagement im Schweizer Sport: Das Human Potential Training (HPT). In Jurgen R. Nitsch & Roland Seilen, *Proceedings of the 8th European Congress of Sport Psychology*, Koln, Germany: Academia Sankt Augustin.

Weinberg, R.S. (1984). Mental preparation strategies. In J.M. Silva & R.S. Weinberg (Eds.), *Psychological foundations of sport* (pp. 145-156). Champaign, IL: Human Kinetics.

III
PART

MOTIVATION AND SOCIAL PSYCHOLOGY IN SPORT AND PHYSICAL EDUCATION

The social cognitive perspective has become increasingly popular in psychology and has recently been adopted in sport psychology. Theoretical trends in this field include those associated with intrinsic motivation, achievement goal orientations and attributions. These three themes are addressed in this section. Edgar Thill and Philippe Brunel summarise their research in France in integrating perspectives from intrinsic motivation, and in particular cognitive evaluation theory, and goal perspectives (chapter 10). As such, this complements the detailed exploration of situational and dispositional goal orientations provided by Athanasios Papaioannou (see chapter 12). This chapter focusses on school physical education and is a welcome addition to the literature on children that usually deals with youngsters in volunteer sport contexts. There is little high-quality research on psychological aspects of school physical education. This is surprising given the importance of studying children and the fact that physical education is the only time when physical activity is guaranteed to be provided to all individuals, often with qualified professional leadership. The results from research on physical education using the constructs of achievement goal orientations and class climate should have a significant impact on teaching strategies and practices.

The chapter by Klaus Willimczik and Sabine Rethorst on 'Cognitions and Emotions in Sport Achievement Situations' adopts a strong attributional perspective in discussing the likely connections between thoughts about achievement in sport and subsequent emotional feelings. This chapter also complements Papaioannou's chapter by clearly demonstrating the link between achievement goals, attributions and emotions. These chapters demonstrate the need for integrated approaches to the study of motivation. Many of the theoretical perspectives have commonalities that need to be exploited if we are to fully understand human motivation in physical activity. All three chapters draw on a wealth of personal research experience, in France, Greece and Germany, and yet they all develop and extend research perspectives well known in North America.

Finally, the area of group psychology is tackled, but this time from the more unusual perspective of the sports spectator rather than the sports participant. Given the importance of spectators in sport it is surprising how little we know about the psychology of crowds. Much of the research has centred on crowd 'trouble', such as hooliganism, and often the research has adopted a sociological stance. Pavel Slepicka's chapter provides a summary of his social psychological research on sports spectators in the Czech Republic (see chapter 13). This is one of the areas that most clearly illustrate cultural differences between countries. Spectator behaviour appears to be quite different for different sports and the cultures of different countries.

10
CHAPTER

Cognitive Theories of Motivation in Sport

Edgar E. Thill
Philippe Brunel

FRANCE

The motivational precursors and regulating factors of sport and physical activity are complex. To help our understanding and explanation of the reasons for millions of people turning to sport, it is important to analyse the relationships between intrinsic and extrinsic motivation.

Sport enables some to earn money, to travel, to acquire new sports clothes or even gain in social standing. Clearly, these forms of extrinsic motivation are important elements of commitment and persistence in sport. However, if sport participation relies on such sources of motivation, they can become not means to an end, but the end itself. When these incentives are missing, athletes may forget the initial reasons for their commitment to sport. For instance, recently the skiing champions from many countries threatened to withdraw from the races at Val d'Isére in France because the prize money of $11,000 compared poorly with that offered in Park City, USA ($22,000). The intrinsic motivation of the athletes appeared to have shifted to a more extrinsic form.

To understand the mechanisms and analyse the consequences of these shifts in motivation, we first present two theories of motivation that have had important applications in sport and exercise settings: Deci and Ryan's Cognitive Evaluation Theory (CET) (1980, 1985a) and Nicholls's Social Cognitive Theory (SCT) (1984).

As they emphasise different aspects of the antecedents of intrinsic motivational states, as well as their consequences, we shall use the Control Theory of Carver and Scheier (1981, 1982) as an integrative framework to show both convergence and specificity of the approaches. Secondly, as the Nicholls's theory considers goals to be the main precursors of achievement behaviours, we shall analyse different studies conducted in this perspective in sport settings, by taking into account several variables, such as age, gender and social differences. Third, referring to Deci and Ryan's theory, we shall analyse different meanings of extrinsic events (e.g., rewards) and consequences for the motivational state of participants in sport settings. In particular, we shall see that these differences affect the meaning that participants attach to extrinsic events (Deci & Ryan) or lead them to analyse, in a special way, their success or failure (Nicholls). From these analyses, we shall try to draw general implications for action.

Goals, Feedback and Motivation

In the goal-setting literature (e.g., Locke, Shaw, Saari, & Latham, 1981), goals are generally considered as immediate precursors of behaviours. Goals can be objectives or states against which selected aspects of the perceived environment are compared. According to Control Theory (Carver & Scheier, 1981, 1982; Hyland, 1988; Lord & Hanges, 1987), not only are goals organised into hierarchical systems, but also the differences between goals and the feedback about behaviour in relation to the goals, generate a signal called 'detected error'. The detected error arising in a cognitive comparator initiates and energises, in turn, a particular behaviour designed to elimi-nate that difference. A central argument in Control Theory is that current theories of motivation focus on different aspects of the processes involved in the negative control loop (Hyland, 1988; Klein, 1989; Thill, 1991).

The social cognitive approach to achievement presented by Nicholls (1984) assumes that two major goals lead to specific attribution patterns; intrinsic interest and behav-iours. In contrast, Deci and Ryan's (1980, 1985a) Cognitive Evaluation Theory analysed the meaning and effects of specific aspects of individual environments (i.e., sensed feedback), in order to predict states of motivation which, in turn, induce various consequences. It is also assumed, however, that the meaning of external events—antecedent to error sensitivity—is affected by individual differences.

Since Control Theory stresses the need to provide both goals and feedback in order to increase performance, we can consider Cognitive Evaluation Theory and Nicholls's theory as focusing on different components of an underlying mechanism described by this 'meta-theory' and highlight their usefulness for application to specific motivational concerns.

Cognitive Evaluation Theory

In the first study designed to assess the effects of monetary rewards on intrinsic motivation, Deci (1971) reported greater decreases in the amount of time spent by rewarded subjects on an intrinsically motivating activity during a free-choice period than by subjects not rewarded. It was shown that some kinds of rewards would have detrimental effects on intrinsic motivation, and using previous work of de Charms and Muir (1968), Deci sought to explain this specific phenomenon by 'Cognitive Evaluation Theory'.

According to this theory (Deci, 1975; Deci & Ryan, 1980, 1985a), inputs relevant to the initiation and regulation of behaviour can have several functional meanings. External events, such as the promise of rewards, feedback, supervision, appraisals or deadlines that are associated with an external locus of causality can put pressure on individuals because of their 'controlling' aspects. This can lead to a reduction in perceived autonomy and a consequent decrease in intrinsic motivation. Conversely, external events (or interpersonal contexts) promoting self-determination are associated with a more internal locus of causality which enhances intrinsic motivation. Within this context of self-determination, such inputs could also promote greater perceived competence and enhance intrinsic motivation, or reduce perceived ability and undermine intrinsic motivation.

Monetary rewards or feedback, therefore, do not convey similar information to all individuals. Their functional significance of being either supportive of autonomy or controlling is related to the quality of the individual's previous experience and actual behaviour (Deci & Ryan, 1985a, 1987). When intrinsic and extrinsic motivation have been defined operationally in line with Cognitive Evaluation Theory, considerable empirical evidence confirms the theory's predictions in various settings (for a review of findings in sport contexts see Ryan, Vallerand, & Deci, 1984; Thill, 1989; Vallerand, Deci, & Ryan, 1987).

However, not only do varied social-contextual factors have different functional significance, but also dispositional factors characterise people as either autonomy-supportive or controlling (Ryan, 1982) and orient them towards situations that are either autonomy-supportive or controlling (Deci & Ryan, 1987). Consequently, it appears important to consider that the controlling and informational aspects that promote an external or internal locus of causality are not synonymous with whether the events occur outside or inside the person. For instance, a thought such as 'I have to train hard in order to avoid criticism from my coach' pressures an athlete to behave in a specific way, but internal events ensure that the behaviour will be initiated and regulated autonomously. Since Ryan's (1982) study, these internal events have been equated with ego versus task orientations, that is, individual differences in goal orientations. Such conceptual links with Nicholls's theory of achievement motivation are interesting to consider in terms of Control Theory. According to Control Theory, internal controlling rather than informational events are antecedents of error sensitivity (i.e., a way of representing the salience of goals), while the need for self-determination appears to be a superordinate goal leading to lower-level goals against which external events are compared.

Social Cognitive Theory

The concept of ego involvement has a long history, but it has been Nicholls (1984) who studied this concept in a developmental perspective and analysed some cognitive consequences of goals, such as competence attributions and effort ascriptions, as well as affective and behavioural consequences. According to Nicholls, when individuals seek to exhibit competence in an achievement setting, they can set themselves two kinds of goals. When individuals set ego-involving goals, they seek to assess what they can master and whether this results from higher capacity than others possess. In such cases, the mastery tends to be experienced as a means to an end, that is, a means to surpassing others or current norms in a socially-referenced perspective. Dweck and her colleagues (Dweck & Elliott, 1983; Dweck & Leggett, 1988) have used the term 'performance goal' for such situations in which individuals seek social judgement of their competence, and they have linked this to vulnerability to the helpless pattern under some conditions.

Alternatively, individuals can simply try to improve their own performance or master the various components of the task, without considering others' performances. The expression 'task involvement' is used to characterise achievement behaviours in which goals are self-referenced and where subjects seek to improve their ability, want to discover new insights into a task or, more simply, master the task itself. According to Dweck and her colleagues (e.g., Dweck & Elliott, 1983; Dweck & Leggett, 1988), if such individuals are concerned with increasing their performance rather than demonstrating their competence, they are pursuing 'learning goals' which lead to a mastery documented behaviour pattern.

In this chapter we shall only use the terms 'ego' and 'task' involvement in order to distinguish clearly between the two kinds of achievement goals. Situations involving direct or indirect competition, social comparison or normative evaluation are more likely to induce a state of ego involvement and threats to self-esteem (de Charms, 1968). Conversely, social surroundings promoting learning mastery as an end in itself tend to induce a state of task involvement. Since it is assumed that individuals differ in their dispositional goal orientations (task and ego), goal perspectives in particular settings appear to be a function of both situational or induced state factors and individual factors (Ames & Archer, 1988; Maehr & Braskamp, 1986; Nicholls, 1989; see also chapter 10).

These goal perspectives have disparate consequences for self-perception and performance in school settings. For instance, compared to ego-involved subjects, task-involved learners report stronger attributions to high ability when they expend high effort (Nicholls, 1984), feel more pride in success resulting from effort (Jagacinski & Nicholls, 1984), express greater enjoyment (Duda, Chi, & Newton, 1990), or seem more interested in the task and in their resulting performance (Butler, 1987). Moreover, being interested in learning for its own sake rather than considering learning as a means of outperforming others, results not only in more generalised effort, but leads to deeper information processing (Graham & Golan, 1991; Nolen, 1988; Thill & Brunel, in press).

In sum, Nicholls and his colleagues (e.g., Duda & Nicholls, 1989, 1992; Nicholls, 1984, 1989; Nicholls & Miller, 1984), consider goal perspectives as the immediate precursors of varied consequences, while Deci and Ryan (e.g., 1980, 1985a; Ryan et al., 1984; Vallerand et al., 1987) propose that intrinsic motivation and its consequences are a function of both immediate environment and people's differences in their need for self-determination and competence. Emphazising sport contexts, we shall now show that surroundings that facilitate ego involvement or promote an external locus of causality can be detrimental to intrinsic motivation, but procedures that minimise such threats to self-esteem have more positive effects on self perceptions and attitudes, as well as on performance.

Goals as Immediate Determinants of Action

Sport settings are conceived, like classical achievement contexts, as environments wherein individuals strive to achieve goals or standards of excellence (Roberts, 1984a). As in academic contexts (Maehr & Braskamp, 1986; Maehr & Nicholls, 1980), research in sport has provided empirical support for the relevance of the distinction between two major goal perspectives (for a review see Duda, 1992, 1993). Goals associated with an ego orientation are related to objective success, that is, linked to extrinsic motivation because people try to be better than others. Individuals who are ego oriented tend to withhold effort when success appears not to be within reach, choose tasks that are too easy or too difficult and quit after failure. Roberts (1984a, 1984b) argues that ego-oriented individuals do not persist in sport as soon as their ability is doubted. On the other hand, the goals of task orientation are consistent with optimal performance and subjective success and are linked to intrinsic motivation because people are focused on the activity for its own sake. Individuals tend to exert more effort, choose moderately difficult tasks and persist more, even in failure conditions.

The literature on goal perspectives indicates that being ego or task involved is dependent on gender, on social group and on age differences (Duda, 1987).

Influence of Goal Orientation on Behaviour

In sport, the feeling of competence seems to be an important determinant of the construing of achievement behaviors (Bukowski & Moore, 1980; Diener & Dweck, 1978; Roberts, 1984a, 1984b), and seems to affect not only participation (Burton & Martens, 1986; Feltz, Gould, Horn, & Petlichkoff, 1982), but also persistence (Duda, 1989b). Individuals assess their demonstrated competence in terms of success and failure, which are not necessarily synonymous with winning or losing. For instance, if you play against a superior opponent in tennis, you can feel successful even if you lose the match, by gaining a set or several games.

In their conceptualisation of achievement motivation, Maehr and Nicholls (1980) have considered success and failure as psychological states rather than reflecting objective levels of performance. Studies of the ascriptions of success and failure in sport have indicated that perceptions of competence underlie the perceptions of success and failure (Kimiecik, Allison, & Duda, 1986). For some athletes, game outcome and subjective assessment of performance are not linked (Roberts & Duda, 1984). It depends on whether an individual interprets the outcome objectively or subjectively (Biddle & Hill, 1992; McAuley, 1985; Spink & Roberts, 1980).

Studies using factor analysis have confirmed that not all adolescents and college students define success as winning, basing their definition on other-referenced factors using external standards; some of them use self-referenced, private standards (Ewing, 1981; Gill, 1986).

Recently, Duda and Nicholls (1992) replicated classroom-based research by Nicholls and his colleagues (Nicholls, Cheung, Lauer, & Patashnick, 1989; Nicholls, Patashnick, & Nolen, 1985) by studying students' beliefs about success in sport. Factor analysis revealed that students attribute their outcomes to four major factors: effort (try hard), ability (beat others), deception (unsportsmanlike) and external factors (luck). Task orientation was found to be positively correlated with effort attributions and ego orientation was found to be positively linked with beliefs that ability was important in sport success. Such findings have now been replicated in Europe (Duda, Fox, Biddle, & Armstrong, 1992).

Following these investigations, Duda, Olson, and Templin (1991) studied the relationship between goal perspectives, sportsmanlike attitudes and legitimacy of intentional injurious acts among 123 white interscholastic basketball players in the USA. Subjects had to indicate their degree of approval of three kinds of behaviours: unsportsmanlike play and cheating (e.g., breaking the rules), strategic (e.g., drawing a high scorer into making a foul), and sportsmanlike behaviours (e.g., respect for one's opponent). Results indicated that low-task orientation and high ego orientation were related to unsportsmanlike behaviours. Concerning the legitimacy of injurious acts, six written scenarios were presented depicting aggressive acts. Individuals had to answer the question 'Is this OK (legitimate) to do if it was necessary in order to win the game?' (Duda et al., 1991, p. 81). High ego orientation correlated with the legitimation of aggressive behaviours.

These results suggest that the athlete's goal orientation is a superordinate and relatively concrete goal that determines how to perform. When individuals wish to demonstrate their superior ability (i.e., they are ego oriented), they select several kinds of play induced by the chosen goal (e.g., product focused, cheat, etc.). Furthermore, goal orientations could be considered to be the subordinate goal of the implicit theory held by individuals about their conception of ability; the implicit theory is itself superordinate and an abstract goal.

Gender and Social Group Differences in Goal Perspectives

Sport research emphasises the role played by gender differences in goal perspectives. It has been assumed that males are more likely to be ego involved than females (Duda, 1986a, 1986b, 1988; Duda et al., 1992; Ewing, 1981; Gill, 1986). In a study of 321 American varsity interscholastic athletes, Duda (1989a) reported males to be higher in ego orientation than females, whereas females were higher in task orientation. Moreover, mastery or co-operation was the major purpose of sport for females. Males, in contrast, emphasised competitiveness and social status. Thus it seems that males and females may construe their level of competence differently and define success and failure in different ways.

Concerning cross-cultural analyses, many investigations in sport have assumed that there are race or ethnic differences in motor skill performance (see Duda & Allison, 1990). In general, these studies indicate that African Americans perform better in basketball (Eitzen & Yetman, 1977), in baseball slugging (Christiano, 1986), and in track and field sprint events, but Caucasian athletes perform better in long-distance running (Samson & Yerles, 1988). These findings are relevant to the fact that the meaning of an activity may vary across cultural and racial groups.

In her cross-cultural analysis of achievement goals, Duda confirms that people's goal perspective varies as a function of race and culture (Duda, 1985, 1986a, 1986b; Duda & Allison, 1989). A study of 80 male and female Navajo and Anglo high school athletes (Duda, 1986a) showed differences in goal orientations across groups. Navajos defined success or failure subjectively, whereas Anglo participants defined success or failure more objectively in terms of performance outcomes. Furthermore, Anglo athletes, especially males, tended to be higher in ego involvement than Navajos, who showed a tendency towards higher task involvement. These results are all the more interesting because Hispanic minorities or Indian ethnic groups may be, in part, influenced by the American way of life. As far as possible, it would be useful to complete these investigations by comparing groups in their own and adopted countries, or people from different cultural and sociological ways of life (e.g., European people living in Europe and Americans in the USA).

Age Differences in Goal Perspectives

Weiner (1986), in his attribution theory of achievement motivation, indicates that individuals often explain outcomes in terms of effort, ability, task difficulty and luck, as well as other factors. This implies that these attributions can be clearly differentiated one from another. In contrast with adults, children find these terms difficult to differentiate. Nicholls (1990; Nicholls & Miller, 1984) has studied the relationships between competence and effort from a developmental perspective and has established that subjects' differentiation of competence from effort is a function of age.

Considering the less differentiated conception of ability, it is assumed that the subjective level of task difficulty is related to perceived mastery, understanding and knowledge. Furthermore, greater effort may lead to a high perception of competence. Nicholls (1984, 1990; Nicholls & Miller, 1984) indicates that children under 10 years old are more likely to use the less differentiated conception of ability. In other words, children are task-involved and use a covariation schema (Kun, 1977). This means that they report more exerted effort when ability is perceived as high, and vice versa (Jagacinski & Nicholls, 1984).

It is only after 12 years of age that effort and competence are completely differentiated, enabling the use of the more differentiated conception of ability. According to Nicholls (1984, 1990; Nicholls & Miller, 1984) when children are ego involved, and use compensation schema (Kun, 1977) that lead them to perceive their ability as high, they report less exerted effort (Jagacinski & Nicholls, 1984).

In sport settings, Ewing, Roberts, and Pemberton (1983), in agreement with Nicholls' developmental perspective, found 9- to 11-year olds to be task involved, whereas 12- to 14-year olds were ego involved. Beyond this finding which indicates people establish different goals for themselves at different ages, it seems interesting to show that people mobilise different conceptions of ability when manipulating goal perspectives.

We have conducted two studies of young soccer players, replicating the method of one of our previous studies with adults (Brunel & Thill, 1993; Study I). One study was with 32 children aged 6 to 10 years and one with 32 adolescents aged 11 to 15 years. Subjects had to kick 10 penalty shots from a point located 11 m away from the goal, which itself was divided at each extremity by two metallic frames made of six boxes 0.75m × 0.60m. According to the difficulty of location in the frame, different points were allocated to each box (e.g., 10 points to the upper right or left). In each study, 16 individuals were given task-involved instructions (e.g., 'It's not a competition so try to improve your penalty kicks'), and 16 were given ego-involved instructions (e.g., 'You have to score as many points as possible in order to outperform the others'). In each condition, and following every third trial, eight of the children received positive verbal feedback related to competence while eight received negative verbal feedback. In order to assess level of exerted effort, subjects were asked to place a vertical mark on a 10cm line ranging from 'not at all' to 'very high'.

A 2 × 2 analysis of variance (ANOVA) on the data from the 6- to 10-year olds revealed a main effect for feedback (see Figure 10.1). Children who received positive

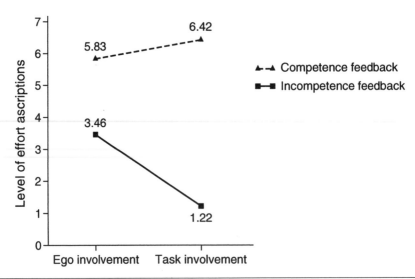

Figure 10.1   Level of effort ascriptions in relation to task versus ego involvement and competence versus incompetence feedback in child soccer players.

Note. From 'La motivation en contexte sportif: Les effets des buts sur les cognitions et les conduites' by P. Brunel and E. Thill, *Science et Motricité*, **19**, p. 47. Reprinted by permission of *Science et Motricité*.

feedback on their competence reported higher effort than those who received negative feedback in both task and ego conditions.

These results indicate that in sport settings children from 6 to 10 years of age use the less differentiated conception of ability in both task- and ego-involving conditions.

Concerning the adolescents, a 2×2 ANOVA showed a significant interaction between the kind of induced involvement (ego vs. task) and the kind of competence feedback (high vs. low) (see Figure 10.2). As we predicted, in ego-involving conditions, positive competence feedback led to attributions of significantly weaker effort than negative competence feedback, which itself induced the ascription of high effort. Concerning the task-involving condition, we observed the contrary trend. Youth who received positive competence feedback reported greater exerted effort than those who received negative ability feedback. Furthermore, negative competence feedback led to higher effort attributions in the ego-involving than in the task-involving context. There was, however, no difference when positive ability feedback was given in ego- and task-involving conditions.

These results, therefore, show that young people between 11 and 15 years of age tend to use the differentiated conception of ability more when they are ego involved. These two studies are thus in agreement with the developmental perspective of Nicholls. Near 12 years of age, individuals can use the differentiated conception of ability. Thus adolescents or adults can be either task involved or ego involved but not dependent on the real level of sport competence. Indeed, ego- or task-involved

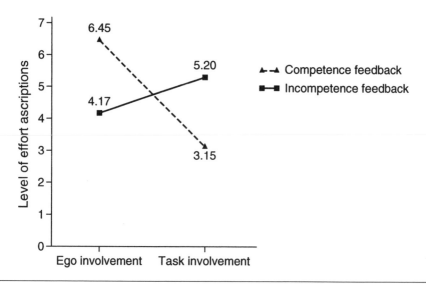

Figure 10.2 Interaction between the kind of involvement and competence feedback on effort attributions among adolescent soccer players.

Note. From 'La motivation en contexte sportif: Les effets des buts sur les cognitions et les conduites' by P. Brunel and E. Thill, *Science et Motricité*, **19**, p. 47. Reprinted by permission of *Science et Motricité*.

professional soccer players use respectively the more or less differentiated conception of ability as well as ego- or task-oriented varsity soccer players (Thill & Brunel, in press). When adolescents or adults, but not children, receive negative verbal feedback of competence, they seem to reduce their intended effort to protect their self-esteem and to cope with possible failure (Pyszczynski & Greenberg, 1983). Subjects explain that they don't use this kind of strategy for themselves, but that the others are more disposed to do it (Jagacinski & Nicholls, 1990). It seems that individuals tend to use self-handicapping strategies in order to either protect or enhance their self-esteem in public image-threatening situations (Berglas & Jones, 1978; Covington & Omelich, 1979; Snyder, 1990; Tice, 1991).

The Influence of External Events: Feedback and Rewards

Although Nicholls and his associates discuss the implications or consequences of personal goals, Deci and Ryan (1987) have argued that specific environmental events and interpersonal or social contexts play a central role in the initiation and regulation of behaviours. Concerning the effects of specific environmental events, numerous studies have shown that rewards or feedback can have a functional significance for perceptions of control, although under certain circumstances they can also promote autonomy. It appears that when being autonomy supportive (i.e., encouraging people to make their own choices), reward or feedback maintains or enhances intrinsic motivation whereas reward or feedback experienced as controlling (i.e., pressuring people to behave in a particular way) undermines intrinsic motivation. In this section, therefore, we present some studies conducted in sport that have explored the specific effects of rewards and feedback having different functional meanings.

Rewards Affect Intrinsic Motivation

Operationalisation and manipulation of extrinsic rewards plays an important role in the validation of Cognitive Evaluation Theory. In sport or exercise contexts, laboratory or field studies have shown that, on average, monetary payments (Ryan, 1977, 1980) and trophies or symbolic tokens (Halliwell, 1978; Orlick & Mosher, 1978) undermine intrinsic motivation when participants are given rewards for actually completing an intrinsically interesting task.

In a field study (Thill & Mailhot, 1993), we selected 88 high school students to take part in a (European) handball penalty shooting task that they judged interesting. These students were selected after they had completed the General Causality Orientations Scale (Deci & Ryan, 1985b) and a questionnaire assessing their imagery capacities. Half the 88 students were told that they would receive a portable stereo ('walkman') holster for completing penalty shoots, while no mention of tangible rewards was made for the other students.

Mayo's (1977) Task Reaction Questionnaire (TRQ) served as a measure of intrinsic motivation, and results revealed significant effects on a posttest measure of motivation. Although no differences were found between the groups in the first phase of the study—conducted in order to provide baseline measures—rewarded subjects reported lesser intrinsic motivation than the non-rewarded subjects after completing the task twice and only when high imagery capacities increased the salience of the expected task-contingent reward. Such results could be interpreted in line with CET, considering that the reward tended to lead the subjects to experience the task as being controlled by these external events. Because participation became a means to an end, and because the meaning associated with the reward resulted in loss in self-determination, subjects were led to be less intrinsically motivated in comparison to non-rewarded subjects.

Performance-Contingent Feedback Affects Intrinsic Motivation

The above study confirmed that intrinsic motivation for a sport task can be undermined if rewards are task contingent (for the classification of contextual factors and results see Deci & Ryan, 1985a). Such effects appear neither when rewards (or feedback) are given for a specified level of performance so that they convey feelings of competence (performance-contingent rewards), nor when external events enhance feelings of self-determination. For instance, in a study involving participation in a fitness programme, Thompson and Wankel (1980) showed that when participants had the possibility of choosing exercises, their subsequent attendance during a 6-week period was significantly higher than that of the subjects who believed that the programme had been imposed. More recently, Vallerand and Brawley (1984) confirmed that a combination of choices—choice of what activity to do and choice of how to do an assigned activity—enhances intrinsic motivation.

In order to compare specific predictions of Deci and Ryan's (1980, 1985a) motivational approach and Bandura's (1986) social cognitive theory, Thill and Mouanda (1990, Study II) assessed the short-term and differing effects of choice possibilities, efficacy expectations and verbal feedback on intrinsic motivation. Because establishment of a valid intrinsically motivating task seems crucial (Rummel & Feinberg, 1988), 72 French national handball league players displaying the highest intrinsic motivation were selected from 95 after they had answered Mayo's (1977) TRQ. On the basis of their expectations of the efficacy of collective exercises in handball, players were divided into two groups of 32, one with high efficacy expectations and one with lower expectations. Then the players were randomly assigned either choice exercises or no-choice exercises, and each of these subgroups was given positive or negative performance-contingent feedback. Thus eight groups were created in all. The analysis of intrinsic motivation level involved a $2 \times 2 \times 2$ design (high vs. low efficacy expectations × choice vs. no-choice × positive vs. negative performance-contingent feedback), with repeated measures across three time phases.

When differences between pretest and the first posttest 1 week later were considered, all main effects and interactional effects were significant. Choice possibilities, efficacy expectations and performance-contingent feedback each accounted for about the same proportion of total variance. It is also of interest to note that, as predicted by the CET, subjects were more sensitive to collective verbal feedback (e.g., 'you're doing really well; your movements and passes are well performed') when they worked at the exercises with collective choice. Furthermore, the greatest increases in intrinsic motivation (+38, 33) occurred in the conditions in which they believed they were sufficiently competent to execute the requisite behaviour (Bandura, 1977). Low competence expectations combined with negative competence collective feedback in no-choice conditions induced the greatest decrease in intrinsic motivation (−6, 33). In sum, increases in intrinsic motivation appeared not only when players felt a greater personal causality because they expected that intentional outcomes would be closely related to variations of their behaviours (see Bandura, 1977, 1986), but also when an experience of choice highlighted the perceived internal locus of causality (see Deci & Ryan's [1985a] organismic approach).

Interestingly, the difference between the pretest and the second posttest measures of intrinsic motivation 3 weeks later showed a quite different pattern. Although other main and interactional effects remained significant, neither the main effect of efficacy expectations, nor the interaction between efficacy expectations and the other factors reached significance. Because efficacy expectations were probably altered by previous feedback two weeks earlier (Weinberg, Gould, Yukelson, & Jackson, 1981), only actual performance-contingent feedback provided in a context of self-determination led to an increase in intrinsic motivation. Thus the locus of causality probably remained internal over time, and when initially encouraged to make their own choice, players later displayed greater increases in intrinsic motivation in line with competence information provided. Moreover, whatever the period considered, collective performance-contingent feedback had the same effects as individual performance-contingent feedback.

Effects of Private and Public Performance-Contingent Conditions

As in school settings, it has been shown in sport contexts that positive verbal feedback and negative verbal feedback respectively increase and decrease intrinsic motivation compared to no feedback (Vallerand, 1983, Weinberg, & Jackson, 1979; Whitehead & Corbin, 1991), and that these changes in motivation are mediated by alteration in perceived competence (Vallerand & Reid, 1984; Whitehead & Corbin, 1991). Competence information can also be conveyed, however, through reward structures (Ryan, Mims, & Koestner, 1983). When rewards are performance contingent, their effects on intrinsic motivation depend on whether informational or controlling aspects are more salient. It would appear that both feedback and rewards have additive effects that enhance or undermine intrinsic motivation depending on the way they are administered.

After their selection from 118 subjects, we asked 72 African handball players from the national Congo league to shoot from behind a screen so that it was possible to manipulate their competence perceptions (Thill & Mouanda, 1990, Study I). The subjects displaying the highest intrinsic motivation were randomly assigned to different treatment conditions.

Subjects given positive standardised verbal feedback, with an individual performance-contingent monetary reward, displayed the greatest subsequent increase in intrinsic motivation; subjects who neither expected nor received competence feedback or performance-contingent monetary reward displayed the greatest decrease in intrinsic motivation. Both individual and collective performance-contingent reward resulted in a greater increase in intrinsic motivation compared with the absence of reward. Although differences did not reach statistical significance, individual performance rewarded subjects displayed higher increases in motivation than collective performance rewarded subjects. This tendency could be interpreted by considering that attainment of rewards is perceived as more controlled by other players' accomplishments in the collective performance-contingent conditions, and individual performance-contingent conditions encourage belief in personal causality and competence.

Because these information or controlling effects could be amplified by private versus public administration of tangible rewards, we (Thill & Mouanda, 1992) conducted the following study. A reward is not likely to have the same motivational impact when it is public and known to all participants as when it is given privately. Therefore it seems interesting to simulate this practice in sport in order to test its motivational importance. Our experiment involved 80 handball players from the French national league, who were asked to attempt a series of 10 angled shots at a goal from a fixed wing zone. The goal was divided into six parts by elastic bands, and points were awarded according to the part the ball went into. The 50 players with the highest scores on a measure of intrinsic motivation were assigned 3 weeks later to the following conditions. The experimenter informed each player either alone (individual private reward) or conspicuously in front of the team members (public individual reward) that he would get a reward if he scored well. In the same way, players were either privately (collective private reward) or publicly (collective public reward) informed that they would be rewarded if their group scored well. The reward was in all cases a fast-food voucher worth 55 FF (about 10 U.S. dollars). No reward was either promised or given to any subject in a control group. Before and after these experimental conditions, we also recorded intrinsic motivation using Mayo's questionnaire, competence perceptions and interest expressed. Because the pattern of results proved to be the same whatever the variables considered, we shall only consider here differences between pretest and posttest scores in performance shots.

It was verified that the different groups were equivalent in performance before they were assigned to experimental conditions. A main effect for the mode of reward allocation (private vs. public) and a strong interaction effect between the mode of allocation and the kind of contingency (individual vs. collective) were observed. As shown in Figure 10.3, when differences between posttest and pretest measures of performance were considered, a reward promised in private was associated with reduced performance (−2.4), whether these rewards were individual or collective. Conversely, performance improved when the reward was publicly announced, either individually or collectively (+2.35). In a situation of social visibility, a reward for good performance provides feedback relative to the merits of the participant— positive credit in a situation that elicits potential social accreditation. The task in such a case can be described as activating the 'public facet' of the self, and the

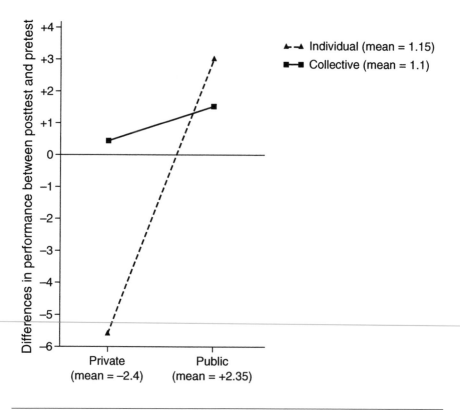

Figure 10.3   Level of performance differences between posttest and pretest measures following individual or collective performance-contingent rewards administered privately or
publicly.
Note. From 'La signification fonctionnelle des récompense: Leurs effets motivationnels en cas d'administration privée ou publique' by E. Thill and J. Mouanda, 1992, *Nouvelles de la Science et des
Technologies (Belgique)*, **10**(1-2), p. 86. Reprinted by permission of *Nouvelles de la Science et des
Technologies*.

goal is to gain the approval of others (Breckler & Greenwald, 1986). Moreover,
observation of the interaction effect shows that performance improves mostly with
the individual's accomplishments in a situation of potential accreditation (i.e., in
public), while performance decreases dramatically if these same individual accomplishments are rewarded when only an inner audience is available (i.e., in private).
Thus, the greatest improvements in performance (and also in perceptions of competence, interest and intrinsic motivation) appeared in a public and individual performance-contingent reward context—when rewards established the person's self-worth
in a significant social evaluation context. Comparatively, the collective performance-
contingent rewards did not generate differences in performance whatever the mode
of reward allocation (public vs. private). When partially 'controlled' by the accomplishment of others in the collective performance-contingent rewarded condition,
the performances reach an intermediate level of improvement. Finally, it appeared,

as expected, that it was the *meaning* of the reward, and not the reward itself (voucher), that induced such variations in performance.

Individual Differences in Intrinsic Motivation

As the studies reviewed so far have shown, the contextual factors can promote either an external or an internal perceived locus of causality and have effects on intrinsic motivation. This supports Ryan's (1982) suggestion that internal events, like feelings or thoughts, could also be either controlling or informational. For instance, the thought that 'I do not have to cheat or attempt to hurt an opponent' is a form of internal control quite similar to being asked by coaches to avoid unsportsmanlike behaviours. According to Ryan, such an internally controlling event corresponds to a state of ego involvement—a state making the subject's self-esteem contingent upon sportsmanship. On the other hand, when the motivation to perform an activity is linked to its intrinsic properties, rather than threat of self-esteem, such events are consistent with a state of task involvement.

Because ego involvement is a state induced by external circumstances, or because ego orientation corresponds to a personal causality orientation (i.e., a form of internal motivation that is controlling), Ryan says that such a state undermines intrinsic motivation and interest. Results of his investigations support this hypothesis (Plant & Ryan, 1985; Ryan, 1982). Similarly, Nicholls (1984) reported several studies showing that when ego involved, subjects chose either very easy or very difficult tasks in order to protect the public image of their self, rather than engage in activities for the sake of learning itself. The purpose of another investigation we conducted with handball players was to test such predictions in a sport context, particularly when personal causality orientations interact with external incentives.

In this study (Thill & Mailhot, 1993) measures of individual differences were first focused on the degree to which 182 high school students were to some extent oriented to select or interpret internal or external events as informational (i.e., the autonomy orientation), or tended to select or interpret such initiating or regulatory events as controlling (i.e., the controlling orientation). For that purpose, we used the General Causality Orientation Scale developed by Deci and Ryan (1985b). The questionnaire has been translated into French and validated by Vallerand, Blais, Lacouture, and Deci (1987). Furthermore, because it has been shown that the salience of an anticipated reward influences the duration of performance of target activities (Newman & Layton, 1984; Ross, 1975), we also assessed the individual imagery abilities of players. It was hypothesised that high vividness and high control of visual imagery may improve the salience of expected rewards when individuals are asked to think about them as long as they like. More specifically, it was predicted that individuals with high imagery ability are likely to highlight the controlling effect of rewards offered for performing an interesting activity. Imagery ability was checked with an instrument specially devised in order to tap the subjects' ability to imagine the relevant situation. Consequently, 88 subjects, averaging just over 16 years of age, were selected and assigned to four independent groups on the basis of both their General Causality Orientations (Autonomy vs. Control) and their imagery abilities (high vs. weak).

As reported earlier, half of these 88 students were told that they would receive a stereo ('walkman') holster for completing standardised penalty shots, and tangible rewards were neither promised nor given to the remaining students. Before and after these experimental conditions, performances of the subjects were recorded, as were their level of intrinsic motivation, competence perceptions and interest expressed. There were no differences between the groups on these measures, but strong effects appeared, as predicted, according to the individual differences and the conditions of reward manipulation.

If we consider differences between posttest and pretest measures of intrinsic motivation in Figure 10.4, not only did autonomy-oriented players display significantly more intrinsic motivation than control-oriented players, but also high imagery capacities resulted in greater intrinsic motivation than weak imagery capacities. It seems therefore, as predicted, that autonomy-oriented individuals experienced the same situation as providing more sense of competence and autonomy than did their control-oriented counterparts.

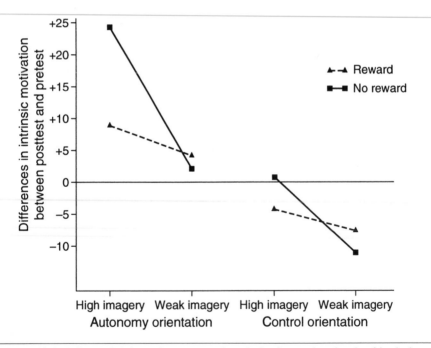

Figure 10.4   Effects of task-contingent rewards or lack of reward on levels of intrinsic motivation among autonomy- versus control-oriented subjects showing high or weak imagery capacities.

Note. From *On the Relationships Between Task-Contingent Rewards, Individual Differences in Causality Orientations and Imagery Abilities to Intrinsic Motivation and Performance* by E. Thill and L. Mailhot, 1993, manuscript submitted for publication.

We also found that, irrespective of their causality orientation, subjects whose high imagery capacities increased the salience of expected task-contingent rewards reported significantly less intrinsic motivation than did those whose imagery capacities were low. Individual differences in imagery capacities may thus enhance the controlling aspects of expected rewards. Furthermore, the functional meaning of rewards seemed to be related to individual differences in both causality orientation and imagery capacities. In particular, as shown in Figure 10.4, lack of reward resulted in a higher state of intrinsic motivation among autonomy-oriented subjects displaying high imagery capacities than among control-oriented subjects with high imagery capacity. Also, task-contingent reward led to higher intrinsic motivation among autonomy-oriented subjects with high imagery capacities than among control-oriented subjects with high imagery capacities. Finally, when the behaviour was attributed to a cause unlikely to be internal (control-oriented subjects), and, hence, not changed by the alternative salient external causes (weak imagery), task-contingent reward merely compensated for the loss of motivation incurred because of a lack of incentives (Newman & Layton, 1984).

In summary, the detrimental effects of an extrinsic reward on intrinsic motivation, and subsequently on performance, depend upon the meaning of the information carried by the reward. When people receive a reward for working on an intrinsically interesting activity, they tend to display less intrinsic motivation than do people who work on the target activity without receiving a reward. Also, the more strongly the incentive is imagined (greater salience), the stronger the undermining effects. However, because people differ in the extent to which they are oriented to interpret events as informational or controlling (and to some extent also as 'amotivating'), they form and refine a kind of internal structure resulting from an interaction between individual differences and contextual factors.

Conclusion

Concordant results show that reward or feedback can stimulate the level of participants' motivation, particularly if they yield information on competence. Conversely, when the situation is seen as controlling, motivation is weakened. If the informational aspects of the situation overrule the controlling aspects, competence feedback improves performance.

The effects of feedback or rewards, however, also depend on other contextual factors and individual motivational orientations. When participants focus on competitive or performance outcomes, many become ego involved, with negative consequences on cognitions, affect, learning and performance, especially if their perceived competence is low. When ego oriented or ego involved, subjects consider applying greater effort when receiving negative verbal feedback. Various results suggest, however, that subjects threatened by the possibility of appearing incompetent in a valued activity reduce their effort in order to protect their perceived ability and self-esteem (e.g., Jones & Berglas, 1978; Frankel & Snyder, 1978; Thill, 1993). Because sport sometimes becomes a means to superior performance rather than an end in itself, individuals with high perceived ability may expend just enough effort to outperform others (Nolen, 1988; Thill & Brunel, in press).

In contrast, task orientation involves a commitment to learning for its own sake, and task-involved sport participants tend to use deeper processing strategies, such as trying to compare actual feedback with previous attempts. In sum, contemporary approaches to instruction, stimulated by cognitive views of learning (e.g., Graham & Golan, 1991; Grolnick & Ryan, 1987; Nolen, 1988), indicate that task involvement or task orientations are favourable for some kinds of learning and may increase effort.

Consequently, although the two theoretical points of view presented here are not contradictory (see Ryan & Deci, 1989), they have different focuses and different practical implications. As middle-range theories, Deci and Ryan's CET and Nicholls's SCT are useful for application to specific motivational problems, whereas the Control Theory Model provides a general framework for the better understanding of components of theories. Moreover, this meta-theory has specific and additive implications for sport and exercise settings (Lord & Hanges, 1987), especially in relation to standards and feedback.

References

Ames, C., & Archer, J. (1988). Achievement goals in the classroom: Students' learning strategies and motivation processes. *Journal of Educational Psychology*, **80**, 260-267.

Bandura, A. (1977). Self-efficacy: Toward a unifying theory of behavioral change. *Psychological Review*, **84**, 191-215.

Bandura, A. (1986). *Social foundations of thought and action*. Englewood Cliffs, NJ: Prentice Hall.

Berglas, S., & Jones, E.E. (1978). Drug choice as self-handicapping in response to noncontingent success. *Journal of Personality and Social Psychology*, **36**, 405-417.

Biddle, S.J.H., & Hill, A.B. (1992). Attributions for objective outcome and subjective appraisal of performance: Their relationship with emotional reactions in sport. *British Journal of Social Psychology*, **31**, 215-226.

Breckler, S., & Greenwald, A. (1986). Motivational facets of the self. In R.M. Sorrentino & E.T. Higgins (Eds.), *Motivation and cognition* (pp. 145-164). New York: Guilford Press.

Brunel, P., & Thill, E. (1993). La motivation en contexte sportif: Les effets des buts sur les cognitions et les conduites. *Science et Motricité*, **19**, 43-52.

Bukowski, W.M., & Moore, D. (1980). Winners' and losers' attributions for success and failure in a series of athletic events. *Journal of Sport Psychology*, **2**, 195-210.

Burton, D., & Martens, R. (1986). Pinned by their own goals: An exploratory investigation into why kids drop out of wrestling. *Journal of Sport Psychology*, **8**, 183-197.

Butler, R. (1987). Task-involving and ego-involving properties of evaluation: The effects of different feedback conditions on motivational perceptions, interest and performance. *Journal of Educational Psychology*, **79**, 474-482.

Carver, C.S., & Scheier, M.F. (1981). *Attention and self-regulation: A control theory approach to human behavior*. New York: Springer-Verlag.

Carver, C.S., & Scheier, M.F. (1982). Control theory: A useful conceptual framework for personality, social, clinical, and health psychology. *Psychological Bulletin*, **9**, 111-135.

Christiano, K. (1986). Salary discrimination in major league baseball: The effect of race. *Sociology of Sport Journal*, **2**, 323-333.

Covington, M., & Omelich, C.L. (1979). Effort: The double-edged sword in school achievement. *Journal of Personality and Social Psychology*, **71**, 169-182.

DeCharms, R. (1968). *Personal causation: The internal affective determinants of behavior.* New York: Academic Press.

DeCharms, R., & Muir, M. (1968). Motivation: Social approaches. *Annual Review of Psychology*, **29**, 91-113.

Deci, E.L. (1971). Effects of externally mediated rewards and intrinsic motivation. *Journal of Personality and Social Psychology*, **18**, 105-115.

Deci, E.L. (1975). *Intrinsic motivation.* New York: Plenum Press.

Deci, E.L., & Ryan, R.M. (1980). Self-determination theory: When mind mediates behavior. *Journal of Mind and Behavior*, **1**, 3-43.

Deci, E.L., & Ryan, R.M. (1985a). *Intrinsic motivation and self-determination in human behavior.* New York: Plenum Press.

Deci, E.L., & Ryan, R.M. (1985b). The "General Causality Orientation Scale": Self-determination in personality. *Journal of Research in Personality*, **19**, 109-134.

Deci, E.L., & Ryan, R.M. (1987). The support of autonomy and the control of behavior. *Journal of Personality and Social Psychology*, **53**, 1024-1037.

Diener, C., & Dweck, C.S. (1978). An analysis of learned helplessness: Continuous changes in performance, strategy and achievement cognitions following failure. *Journal of Personality and Social Psychology*, **36**, 451-462.

Duda, J.L. (1985). Goals and achievement orientations of Anglo and Mexican-American adolescents in sport and the classroom. *International Journal of Intercultural Relations*, **9**, 131-155.

Duda, J.L. (1986a). A cross-cultural analysis of achievement motivation in sport and the classroom. In L. Vander Velden & J. Humphrey (Eds.), *Current selected research in the psychology and sociology of sport* (pp. 115-132). New York: AMS Press.

Duda, J.L. (1986b). Perceptions of sport success and failure among white, black, and hispanic adolescents. In J. Watkins, T. Reilly, & L. Burwitz (Eds.), *Sport science* (pp. 214-222). London: Spon.

Duda, J.L. (1987). Toward a developmental theory of achievement motivation in sport. *Journal of Sport Psychology*, **9**, 130-145.

Duda, J.L. (1988). The relationship between goal perspectives and persistence and intensity among recreational sport participants. *Leisure Sciences*, **10**, 95-106.

Duda, J.L. (1989a). Goal perspectives and behavior in sport and exercise settings. In C. Ames & M. Maehr (Eds.), *Advances in motivation and achievement* (Vol. VI, pp. 81-115). Greenwich, CT: JAI Press.

Duda, J.L. (1989b). Goal perspectives, participation and persistence in sport. *International Journal of Sport Psychology*, **20**, 42-56.

Duda, J.L. (1992). Motivation in sport settings: A goal perspective approach. In G.C. Roberts (Ed.), *Motivation in sport and exercise* (pp. 57-91). Champaign, IL: Human Kinetics.

Duda, J.L. (1993). Goals: A social-cognitive approach to the study of achievement motivation in sport. In R.N. Singer, M. Murphey, & L.K. Tennant (Eds.), *Handbook of research on sport psychology* (pp. 421-436). New York: Macmillan.

Duda, J.L., & Allison, M.T. (1989). The attributional theory of achievement motivation: Cross-cultural considerations. *International Journal of Intercultural Relations*, **9**, 131-155.

Duda, J.L., & Allison, M.T. (1990). Cross-cultural analysis in exercise and sport psychology: A void in the field. *Journal of Sport and Exercise Psychology*, **12**, 114-131.

Duda, J.L., Chi, L., & Newton, M. (1990, May). *Psychometric characteristics of the TEOSQ*. Paper presented at the annual meeting of the North American Society for the Psychology of Sport and Physical Activity, Houston, TX.

Duda, J.L., Fox, K.R., Biddle, S.J.H., & Armstrong, N. (1992). Children's achievement goals and beliefs about success in sport. *British Journal of Educational Psychology*, **62**, 313-323.

Duda, J.L., & Nicholls, J.G. (1989). *The Task and Ego Orientation in Sport Questionnaire: Psychometric properties*. Unpublished manuscript, Purdue University, West Lafayette, IN.

Duda, J.L., & Nicholls, J. (1992). Dimensions of achievement motivation in schoolwork and sport. *Journal of Educational Psychology*, **84**, 290-299.

Duda, J.L., Olson, L.K., & Templin, T. (1991). The relationship of task and ego orientation to sportsmanship attitudes and the perceived legitimacy of injurious acts. *Research Quarterly for Exercise and Sport*, **62**, 79-87.

Dweck, C.S., & Elliott, E.S. (1983). Achievement motivation. In E.M. Hetherington (Ed.), *Handbook of child psychology: Vol. IV. Socialisation, personality and social development* (pp. 643-691). New York: Wiley.

Dweck, C.S., & Leggett, E.L. (1988). A social cognitive approach to motivation and personality. *Psychological Review*, **95**, 256-273.

Eitzen, D.S., & Yetman, N.R. (1977). Immune from races? *Civil Rights Digest*, **7**, 3-13.

Ewing, M.E. (1981). *Achievement orientations and sport behavior of males and females*. Unpublished doctoral dissertation, University of Illinois at Urbana-Champaign.

Ewing, M.E., Roberts, G.C., & Pemberton, C.L. (1983, May). *A developmental look at children's goals for participating in sport*. Paper presented at the annual meeting of the North American Society for the Psychology of Sport and Physical Activity, East Lansing, MI.

Feltz, D.L., Gould, D., Horn, T.S., & Petlichkoff, L. (1982). *Perceived competence among youth sport participants and dropouts*. Paper presented at the annual meeting of the North American Society for the Pychology of Sport and Physical Activity, College Park, MD.

Frankel, A., & Snyder, M.L. (1978). Poor performance following unsolvable problems: Learned helplessness or egotism? *Journal of Personality and Social Psychology*, **36**, 1415-1423.

Gill, D.L. (1986). Competitiveness among females and males in physical activity classes. *Sex Roles*, **15**, 233-247.

Graham, S., & Golan, S. (1991). Motivational influences on cognition: Task involvement, ego involvement, and depth of information processing. *Journal of Educational Psychology*, **83**, 187-194.

Grolnick, W.S., & Ryan, R.M. (1987). Autonomy in children's learning: An experimental and individual difference investigation. *Journal of Personality and Social Psychology*, **32**, 890-898.

Halliwell, W.R. (1978). The effect of cognitive development on children's perceptions of intrinsically and extrinsically motivated behavior. In D.M. Landers & R. Christina (Eds.), *Psychology of motor behavior and sport* (pp. 403-418). Champaign, IL: Human Kinetics.

Hyland, M.E. (1988). Motivational control theory: An integrative framework. *Journal of Personality and Social Psychology*, **55**, 642-651.

Jagacinski, C.M., & Nicholls, J.G. (1984). Conceptions of ability and related affects in task involvement and ego involvement. *Journal of Educational Psychology*, **76**, 909-919.

Jagacinski, C.M., & Nicholls, J.G. (1990). Reducing effort to protect perceived ability: "They'd do it but I wouldn't." *Journal of Educational Psychology*, **82**, 15-21.

Jones, E.E., & Berglas, S. (1978). Control of attributions about the self through self-handicapping strategies: The appeal of alcohol and the role of underachievement. *Personality and Social Psychology Bulletin*, **4**, 200-206.

Kimiecik, J.C., Allison, M.T., & Duda, J.L. (1986). Performance satisfaction, perceived competence, and game outcome: The competitive experience of Boys' Club youth. *International Journal of Sport Psychology*, **17**, 255-268.

Klein, H.T. (1989). An integrated control theory model of work motivation. *Academy of Management Review*, **14**, 150-172.

Kun, A. (1977). Development of the magnitude-covariation and compensation schemata in ability and effort attributions of performance. *Child Development*, **48**, 862-873.

Locke, E.A., Shaw, K.N., Saari, L.M., & Latham, G.P. (1981). Goal-setting and task performance: 1969-1980. *Psychological Bulletin*, **90**, 125-152.

Lord, R.G., & Hanges, P.J. (1987). A control system model of organisational motivation: Theoretical development and applied implications. *Behavioral Science*, **32**, 161-178.

Maehr, M.L., & Braskamp, L. (1986). *The motivation factor: A theory of personal investment.* Lexington, MA: Heath.

Maehr, M.L., & Nicholls, J.G. (1980). Culture and achievement motivation: A second look. In N. Warren (Ed.), *Studies in cross-cultural psychology* (Vol. II, pp. 221-267). New York: Academic Press.

Mayo, R.J. (1977). The development and construct validation of a measure of intrinsic motivation. *Dissertation Abstracts International*, **37**, 5417B.

McAuley, E. (1985). Success and causality in sport: The influence of perception. *Journal of Sport Psychology*, **7**, 13-22.

Newman, J., & Layton, B.D. (1984). Overjustification: A self-perception perspective. *Personality and Social Psychology Bulletin*, **10**, 419-425.

Nicholls, J.G. (1984). Achievement motivation: Conceptions of ability, subjective experience, task choice, and performance. *Psychological Review*, **91**, 328-346.

Nicholls, J.G. (1989). *The competitive ethos and democratic education.* Cambridge, MA: Harvard University Press.

Nicholls, J.G. (1990). What is ability and why are we mindful of it? A developmental perspective. In R.J. Sternberg & J. Kolligian (Eds.), *Competence considered* (pp. 11-40). New Haven, CT: Yale University Press.

Nicholls, J.G., Cheung, P.C., Lauer, J., & Patashnick, M. (1989). Individual differences in academic motivation: Perceived ability, goals, beliefs, and values. *Learning and Individual Differences*, **1**, 63-84.

Nicholls, J.G., & Miller, A. (1984). Development and its discontents: The differentiation of the concept of ability. In J.G. Nicholls (Ed.), *Advances in motivation and achievement: The development of achievement motivation* (pp. 185-218). Greenwich, CT: JAI Press.

Nicholls, J.G., Patashnick, M., & Nolen, S.B. (1985). Adolescents' theories of education. *Journal of Educational Psychology*, **77**, 683-692.

Nolen, S.B. (1988). Reasons for studying: Motivational orientations and study strategies. *Cognition and Instruction*, **5**, 269-287.

Orlick, T.D., & Mosher, R. (1978). Extrinsic awards and participant motivation in a sport related task. *International Journal of Sport Psychology*, **9**, 27-39.

Plant, R.W., & Ryan, R.M. (1985). Self-consciousness, self-awareness, ego-involvement, and intrinsic motivation: An investigation of internally controlling styles. *Journal of Personality*, **39**, 377-389.

Pyszczynski, T., & Greenberg, J. (1983). Determinants of reduction of intented effort as a strategy for coping with anticipated failure. *Journal of Research in Personality*, **17**, 412-422.

Roberts, G.C. (1984a). Achievement motivation in children's sport. In J.G. Nicholls (Ed.), *Advances in motivation and achievement: The development of achievement motivation* (pp. 251-281). Greenwich, CT: JAI Press.

Roberts, G.C. (1984b). Toward a new theory of motivation in sport: The role of perceived ability. In J. Silva & R.S. Weinberg (Eds.), *Psychological foundation of sport* (pp. 214-228). Champaign, IL: Human Kinetics.

Roberts, G.C., & Duda, J.L. (1984). Motivation in sport: The mediating role of perceived ability. *Journal of Sport Psychology*, **6**, 312-324.

Ross, M. (1975). Salience of reward and intrinsic motivation. *Journal of Personality and Social Psychology*, **33**, 245-254.

Rummel, A., & Feinberg, R. (1988). Cognitive evaluation theory: A meta-analytic review of the literature. *Social Behavior and Personality*, **16**, 147-164.

Ryan, E.D. (1977). Attribution, intrinsic motivation and athletics. In L. Gedvilas & M. Kneer (Eds.), *Proceedings of the National College Physical Education Association for Men/ National Association for Physical Education of College Women National Conference* (pp. 346-353). Chicago: University of Illinois at Chicago Circle, Office of Publications Service.

Ryan, E.D. (1980). Attribution, intrinsic motivation and athletics. In C. Nadeau, W. Halliwell, K. Newell, & G.C. Roberts (Eds.), *Psychology of motor behavior and sport—1979* (pp. 19-26). Champaign, IL: Human Kinetics.

Ryan, R.M. (1982). Control and information in the intrapersonal sphere: An extension of cognitive evaluation theory. *Journal of Personality and Social Psychology*, **43**, 450-461.

Ryan, R.M., & Deci, E.L. (1989). Bridging the research traditions of task/ego involvement and intrinsic/extrinsic motivation: Comment on Butler (1987). *Journal of Educational Psychology*, **81**, 265-268.

Ryan, R.M., Mims, V., & Koestner, R. (1983). The relationships of reward contingency and interpersonal context to intrinsic motivation: A review and test using cognitive evaluation theory. *Journal of Personality and Social Psychology*, **45**, 736-750.

Ryan, R.M., Vallerand, R.J., & Deci, E.L. (1984). Intrinsic motivation in sport: A cognitive evaluation theory interpretation. In W.F. Straub & J. Williams (Eds.), *Cognitive sport psychology* (pp. 231-242). Lansing, NY: Sport Science Associates.

Samson, J., & Yerles, M. (1988). Racial differences in sports performance. *Canadian Journal of Sport Sciences*, **13**, 109-116.

Snyder, C.R. (1990). Self-handicapping processes and sequelae: On the taking of the psychological dice. In R.L. Higgins, C.R. Snyder, & S.C. Berglas (Eds.), *Self-handicapping: The paradox that isn't* (pp. 107-145). New York: Plenum Press.

Spink, K., & Roberts, G.C. (1980). Ambiguity of outcome and causal attributions. *Journal of Sport Psychology*, **2**, 237-244.

Thill, E. (1989). *Motivation et stratégies de motivation en milieu sportif*. Paris: Presses Universitaire de France.

Thill, E. (1991). Autonomie ou contrôle dans les organisations: Une analyse intégrative de théories de la motivation. *Le Travail Humain*, **54**, 129-149.

Thill, E. (1993). Conceptions differenciees et non differenciées de la compétence et de l'effort en fonction de l'âge: Consequences sur les affects et sur les stratégies d'auto-handicap. *Journal International de Psychologie*, **28**(6), 845-859.

Thill, E., & Brunel, P. (in press). Ego-involvement versus task-involvement: Related conceptions of ability and learning strategies among soccer players. *International Journal of
Sport Psychology.*

Thill, E., & Mailhot, L. (1993). *On the relationships between task-contingent rewards,
individual differences in causality orientations and imagery abilities to intrinsic motivation and performance.* Manuscript submitted for publication.

Thill, E., & Mouanda, J. (1990). Autonomie ou contrôle en contexte sportif: Validité de la
théorie de l'évaluation cognitive. *International Journal of Sport Psychology*, **21**, 1-20.

Thill, E., & Mouanda, J. (1992). La signification fonctionnelle des récompense: Leurs effets
motivationnels en cas d'administration privée ou publique. *Nouvelles de la Science et
des Technologies (Belgique)*, **10**(1-2), 83-87.

Thompson, C.E., & Wankel, L.M. (1980). The effect of perceived choice upon frequency of
exercise behavior. *Journal of Applied Social Psychology*, **10**, 436-443.

Tice, D.M. (1991). Esteem protection or enhancement? Self-handicapping motives and attributions differ by trait self-esteem. *Journal of Personality and Social Psychology*, **60**,
711-725.

Vallerand, R.J. (1983). Effects of differential amounts of positive feedback on the intrinsic
motivation of male hockey players. *Journal of Sport Psychology*, **5**, 100-107.

Vallerand, R.J., Blais, M.R., Lacouture, Y., & Deci, E.L. (1987). L'échelle des orientations
générales a la causalite: Validation Canadienne Francaise du General Causality Orientation Scale. *Canadian Journal of Behavioral Sciences*, **19**, 1-15.

Vallerand, R.J., & Brawley, L.R. (1984). *Self-determination and intrinsic motivation: A look
at outcome and processes.* Unpublished manuscript, University of Quebec at Montreal.

Vallerand, R.J., Deci, E.L., & Ryan, R.M. (1987). Intrinsic motivation in sport. *Exercise and
Sport Sciences Reviews*, **16**, 389-425.

Vallerand, R.J., & Reid, G. (1984). On the causal effects of perceived competence on intrinsic
motivation: A test of cognitive evaluation theory. *Journal of Sport Psychology*, **6**,
94-102.

Weinberg, R.S., Gould, D., Yukelson, D., & Jackson, A. (1981). The effects of self- and
manipulated-efficacy on a competitive muscular endurance task. *Journal of Sport
Psychology*, **4**, 345-354.

Weinberg, R.S., & Jackson, A. (1979). Competition and extrinsic rewards: Effect on intrinsic
motivation and attribution. *Research Quarterly*, **50**, 492-502.

Weiner, B. (1986). *An attributional theory of motivation and emotion.* New York: Springer-Verlag.

Whitehead, J.R., & Corbin, C.B. (1991). Youth fitness testing: The effect of percentile-based
evaluative feedback on intrinsic motivation. *Research Quarterly for Exercise and Sport*,
62, 225-231.

11

Cognitions and Emotions in Sport Achievement Situations

Klaus Willimczik
Sabine Rethorst

GERMANY

Participation in sport produces several distinct emotions. After a win one feels happy; one is probably proud of a performance. The counterpart to the winner's joy is the loser's disappointment, annoyance or even anger. It may also be that one merely feels surprised at the outcome of a match.

Sport activities also involve cognitive thought processes; participants are 'naive psychologists' who analyse sport situations, calculate their actions, make prognoses for the outcome of actions, seek out reasons for success or failure and draw conclusions for their further actions.

This chapter gives an overview of some concepts and investigations of cognitions and emotions in achievement situations in sport, based on a cognitive approach. This approach asserts that a number of emotions depend on participants' cognitions, especially their causal attributions, which are influenced by their perceptions of their own and others' ability.

The chapter starts with a characterisation of achievement situations in general and in sport, because these constitute the base for the occurrence of the special cognitions and emotions under consideration. This will be followed by a critical discussion of the research methods used in this field. This seems necessary because the validity of our knowledge is restricted by the methods on which the results are based. Some results of investigations of concepts of ability, attributions and emotions, and their interrelationships, are then discussed.

Achievement Situations in Sport

Achievement situations in sport possess certain specific characteristics. Most authors agree that achievement and competition are essential to the definition of sport (e.g., Carl, Kayser, Mechling, & Preising, 1984; Hägele, 1982; Hutzlar, 1981; Loy, 1968, 1978; Meier, 1981; Willimczik, 1991). For these authors the term 'achievement situation in sport' is redundant. Here the use of this term has two functions. First, the addition 'achievement situation' is intended to stress the specific aspect of sport that is the focus of this chapter. The second function is to clarify that although the chapter refers to a wide range of sport activities (not exclusively to high-level sport), it does not necessarily cover those fashionable varieties of sport (for example, 'never-never-games' that are considered to be non-competitive recreation (e.g., Heinemann, 1989) or expressive sport involving nonutilitarian activity ('not as play' e.g., Loy, 1978). These latter forms of sport exclude the aspect of social comparison and competition.

In sport and sport science the term achievement has a variety of meanings. The psychological perspective of achievement situations has been treated by Heckhausen, who has dealt with achievement-related situations, with the principles of achievement and achievement motivation and their relevance for cognitions and emotions (see Heckhausen, 1974). He referred to Murray (1938) and McClelland, Atkinson, Clark, and Lowell (1953). According to Heckhausen five conditions have to be fulfilled so that one can speak of achievements:

1. There has to be an objectifiable result of an action that fulfils task character-istics.
2. It must be possible to measure the effort necessary for a successful perfor-mance on a scale of difficulty or effort.
3. Actions must result in either success or failure.
4. The scale for the difficulty or the required effort has to be recognised by the participant as a standard of excellence.
5. The result has to be caused by the acting person.

Above all, however, it has to be recognised that achievement situations are constituted by the individual perception of the acting person (see e.g., Furnham & Argyle, 1981) and do not exist independently.

Sport fits the five conditions for achievement situations mentioned by Heckhausen. The outcomes of soccer games, tennis matches, track and field events or swimming competitions are objective and measurable (condition 1). The same is true of the distance run by a health-oriented jogger or the successful descent of a skier, who engages in this sport only once a year during holidays, or for the hitting of a golf ball. All these outcomes have the characteristics of a task that demands minimising time or mistakes, maximising distances or goals (Göhner, 1979).

In order to perform tasks in sport the athlete must be able to calculate the necessary motor and cognitive efforts (condition 2). The longer the person participates in that sport the better he or she will know the requirements of that particular kind of sport and be able to judge the degree of effort necessary to perform the task.

The standards prevailing in sport which have to be accepted by the acting person can be social, individual or objective ones, depending on whether the athlete competes with others, whether he or she compares his or her performance with earlier ones of his or her own or whether the athlete is just interested in achieving a certain aim like climbing a mountain (condition 4).

Finally, achievement in sport depends to a high degree on the personality of the athlete (condition 5). This is the special point in which it differs from situations in which the outcome is determined solely by chance (Caillois, 1960).

The fact that achievement is involved is the basis for the occurrence of certain cognitions and emotions in sport. In terms of cognitive achievement motivation theory (see Weiner, 1985, 1986), which this chapter is based on, the connections between cognitions and emotions in sport can be outlined in the following way:

- Expectancies concerning the outcome of an action can be regarded as a function of the demands of a task and the individual's perception of competence. Expectancies may be higher the lower the difficulty of the task is rated and the higher one rates one's own ability. The larger the discrepancy between the expectancy and the actual result the greater the surprise will be.
- Pride occurs only if success can be attributed to one's own abilities or effort.

Research Methods Used to Investigate Cognitions and Emotions

The terms cognition and emotion describe a great number of different phenomena. Cognition is a collective term for all processes of perception, thought, recognition, imagining and recollection. Cognitions involve the gain of information and are contrasted with emotions, which are experienced as subjective moods. Emotions are connected with evaluations of one's personal situation, processes of physiological arousal and activity impulses towards behaviour (Gabler, 1986). Cognitions and emotions are to a great extent interdependent. This is obvious from the definition of emotions which contains a cognitive aspect in the evaluation of one's situation. This evaluation centres on causal attributions for the outcomes of actions in achievement situations and the concept of ability.

Emotion also describes a wide range of feelings. It includes anxiety as well as annoyance, joy, hate, boredom, envy, pride, sadness and anger. Anxiety in sport will not be discussed here because it has been studied extensively and is covered by Graham Jones in chapter 7.

The interdependence of cognitions and emotions has prompted sport psychologists to analyse their relation more closely. Accordingly, cognition-emotion relationships will be the focus of this chapter.

Scientific findings do not produce an absolute truth; their validity is restricted by the methods used to establish them. It seems necessary, therefore, to summarise recent discussions of the research methods used in investigating cognitions and emotions in sport before presenting any results (see also Biddle, 1988).

Four methodological problems are to be considered:

1. Hypothetical versus 'real-life' events: what degree of validity for sport do findings from experiments or findings based on hypothetical situations have? To what extent do the two kinds of findings have external or ecological validity?
2. Individual perceptions versus objective characteristics: what consequences should be drawn from the view that individual perception is the crucial element for a psychological analysis of achievement situations?
3. Respondent versus projective questioning: in which way are the answers of subjects influenced if they have to rate cognitions and emotions from a given set and do not have the possibility of choosing cognitions and emotions by themselves?
4. Generality versus specificity: is it justified to use methods from other fields of psychology for research on sport or is it necessary to develop sport-specific methods?

Hypothetical Versus 'Real-Life' Events

In many fields of psychology, research is often carried out on the basis of hypothetical situations. Subjects are asked to imagine an event and identify with the actor and then state their cognitions and emotions or give their ratings of the intensity of certain cognitions and emotions based on a given set presented to them. This method offers the advantage of a systematic variation of different research conditions and increases internal validity.

By contrast, in psychology in applied sport science the number of field experiments or surveys using 'real-life' events has been relatively high. Its advantage of being closer to the practical field of sport is matched by the disadvantage that a validation of the obtained effects, i.e., a proof of their internal validity, is often difficult and problematic (see also Biddle, 1988; Gotlib & Olson, 1983; Russell & McAuley, 1986).

Research comparing the use of hypothetical and 'real-life' events in investigating attributions and emotions in sport is rare. We interviewed 30 sport students from a rowing class before and after practice (Willimczik & Rethorst, 1988b). In both cases the questionnaire used contained descriptions of hypothetical situations. The students were asked for their perceived rowing ability, their fear of social consequences of poor performance and their attributions of causality after success and failure. The correlation between the before- and after-practice perceptions of ability was 0.75.

Between the two measures of the fear of social consequences it was 0.86. Both correlations were significant ($p < .01$ for both cases). The differences in the two variables before and after experience were also very small and not significant. Therefore it seems justified to use hypothetical situations for investigating the perception of ability and the fear of social consequences. However, the influence of experience seems to be significantly higher on causal attributions. There was a strong and significant change in the attribution pattern among the sport students after success as well as after failure. After practical experience the importance of the internal and variable factor of effort increased (see Figure 11.1). This result implies increased motivation, which is the aim of attribution training (see Försterling, 1985).

In investigations using hypothetical situations, it is usually easier to find support for the underlying hypotheses than in 'real-life' situations. This is especially true for attribution-emotion links (Gotlib & Olson, 1983). It follows that for hypothetical situations there could be an overrating of relations, or that there could be an underrating in 'real-life' situations.

The differences between the results obtained before and after an actual experience in the study mentioned previously are quite plausible and can be explained by theory. They can be traced to the following contrasts between hypothetical and 'real-life' situations:

- Different amounts of information are available to the person interviewed in hypothetical and 'real-life' situations. These different amounts of information influence the attribution process, as comparative studies on the attributions of

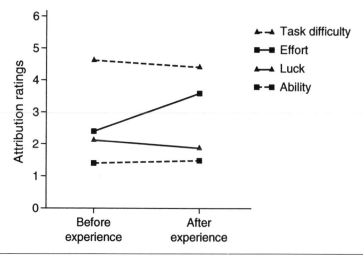

Figure 11.1   Causal attributions for failure before and after practical experience (rowing class).
Note. From 'Sportpsychologische Forschungsmethoden im Spannungsfeld von Grundlagen—und Anwendungsforschung—ein empirischer Methodenvergleich' by K. Willimczik and S. Rethorst. In *Sportpsychologische Diagnostik, Intervention und Verantwortung* (pp. 215-231) by P. Schwenkmezger (Ed.), 1988, Köln, Germany: bps. Copyright 1988 by bps-Verlag. Reprinted by permission.

actors and observers show. It can be assumed that the use of hypothetical situations will produce an underrating of internal and variable attributions, particularly effort.

- In hypothetical situations the trait component is more affected whereas results obtained from interviews carried out immediately after sports events are to a greater extent influenced by state factors.

Subjective Perceptions Versus Objective Characteristics

For cognitions and emotions the demand for subjectivity, in the sense of an individual's analysis of achievement situations, has two aspects. First, the appearance of cognitions and emotions is not necessarily linked with the objective results (outcome) but with a subjective evaluation of these results. Second, the dimensions (locus, stability, controllability) of the causes have to be determined by the subject, not the researcher.

Attribution theorists have pointed out many times that attributions do not refer to objective results but are made on the basis of evaluations of these results (Biddle, 1988; Vallerand, 1987; Weiner, 1986). Concerning sport, this means that there should not be a reference to losing or winning but to the subjective evaluations of the outcome, that is perceived success or failure. The decision in favour of a subjective approach towards attributions has far-reaching consequences. The subject's evaluation of the result as more or less successful reflects the fact that the world of sport is not neatly divided into winning and losing. It is rather characterised by a continuum within which success and failure can appear in different degrees and intensities. This assumption counteracts those unfounded views in sport and social theory according to which the outcome of actions occurs only in the form of the extremes of (positive) success and (negative) failure. It is easily overlooked that in sport we already have to differentiate concerning the objective outcome. In individual sports the outcome is not identified as either a win or loss but is measured in interval scales (time and distance) and rank scales (position in a run). And for many games a possible result apart from win and loss is a draw. These facts are more or less neglected in scientific analyses of cognitions and emotions although they may actually be of great interest.

Only a small number of methodological investigations have been carried out on the relation between objective outcomes in sport and their evaluations as successes or failures (McAuley, 1985; Rethorst, 1991b; Spink & Roberts, 1980). In McAuley's investigation with female gymnasts, the correlations between the scores and the individual evaluations of their performances in each of the four Olympic events ranged from $r = .59$ to $r = .74$. Rethorst found a correlation of 0.53 between the objective results of a track and field competition and the evaluations by the participants (students in physical education classes). Spink and Roberts showed that perceived and absolute results are not isomorphic and that perceptions are important antecedents of subsequent cognitions and emotions.

Research findings obtained on the basis not of evaluations but of outcomes alone can be summarised as follows. Using objective results leads to an underrating of the effects because a neglect of the evaluation factor increases the error variance. This makes a significant verification of effects more difficult.

For causal attributions, the demand for an individual analysis of achievement situations requires that the categorisation of attributions into dimensions should not be done by the researcher but must be carried out by the subject (see Russell, 1982). On the question of whether an a priori dimensional categorisation is justified, or will produce false results, only a few studies exist. On the basis of hypothetical situations Rethorst (1992) found in three studies with three different samples (high school and sport students) that there is a close correspondence between a priori and subjective dimensions. This is especially true for the locus dimension. Small differences occurred between the a priori and subjective dimensions on the stability and controllability dimensions.

Very similar findings were obtained by Si (1992) for three different samples in China. There appear to be no culture-specific differences in dimensions of causes although the concrete cause of a result may be quite different depending on the cultural background (e.g., Schuster, Försterling, & Weiner, 1986).

The methodological comparison shows that investigations on the basis of a priori dimensions produce only a small error rate, which may lead to underrating effects rather than to overrating. However, a priori classifications may increase the error variance and in consequence the difficulty of verifying dimension effects.

Nevertheless, the scales developed by Russell (1982; Causal Dimension Scale [CDS]) and Rethorst (1991a; Kausaldimensionsskala [KDS]) should be applied because they avoid the above-mentioned problem of predefining sport-specific causes. If the CDS is used it is not the researcher who predetermines the causes but the subject.

Respondent Versus Projective Questioning

One of the main criticisms of cognitive motivation theory (and theories of causal attribution and emotions) is that many findings are due to methodological artefacts. In everyday life subjects may not be seeking for causes, at least not in the majority of cases, and they may not be experiencing the emotions given in the questionnaire but are merely rating them because they are presented to them (see Ryan, 1980; Weiner, Russell & Lerman, 1978). In order to avoid these artefacts a projective procedure, which allows a free choice of answers, is suggested as an alternative. But this procedure is also controversial. Weiner, Russell, and Lerman (1978), for example, consider the vocabulary of subjects to be too restricted for this approach and therefore argue for a list of emotions for subjects to choose from.

Concerning sport-specific emotions, it can be concluded that those emotions which form the basis of research do actually appear. Rethorst (1992) was able to verify this in two studies in which she employed free answers instead of a given set. The subjects did mention those emotions which theorists consider in their lists. Nevertheless, it seems necessary before carrying out an investigation that employs a questionnaire to ensure that the given emotions are relevant for the field of interest and the subjects concerned.

Generality Versus Specificity

It is not at all surprising that methodological development in sport psychology usually stays one step behind that in its parent science of psychology. Because psychology supplies already widely validated research methods there is the danger that these may be used in the field of sport without their appropriateness having been tested.

For cognitive motivation psychology, sport-specific scales have been developed and tested in relation to the perceptions of ability and achievement motivation (see, among others, Gabler, 1972; Willimczik & Rethorst, 1988b). As regards emotions, it can be shown that in studies requiring a rating of given emotions, not only those emotions should be considered that are proposed by psychologists. It is, moreover, necessary to use those emotions which are relevant for special situations in sport. As far as the attributions are concerned, the generality-specificity controversy does not have to be considered when the CDS is applied because the main reason is always linked to a specific outcome and is therefore, by definition, a specific cause. The dimensions of the causes are general properties of reasons. These properties make up the crucial relation between cognitions and emotions in the process suggested by Weiner (1985, 1986).

In summary, examination of all four methodological problems shows that the development of research methods in this field is linked to the development of cognitive motivation psychology. Therefore, when weighing research findings (especially earlier ones), it is necessary to consider whether the studies can withstand criticism of their methods. Misinterpretation of earlier studies can arise in two ways: first, findings may be accepted although they were obtained by an inadequate scientific method. Second, although earlier findings may be rejected because they may have been the result of an inadequate scientific method, they may nevertheless be accurate. For example, it does not seem justified to reject all results obtained on attributions in sport that have been found on the basis of a priori dimensions, even though we would now prefer methods that take the subjective aspect into consideration.

Self-Perceptions of Ability

Perception of one's own ability is an important aspect of achievement situations, and it is a part of more global self-perceptions (see Bandura, 1977; Covington & Omelich, 1979; Deci, 1975; Kukla, 1972; Meyer, 1973, 1976; Mischel, 1979). According to Meyer, interest in the perceived ability derives from the fact that ability is of immense importance in our society. Additionally, it has gained this importance because the assessment of one's own abilities influences the way we perceive the environment and behave, and influences the way we act. People's perceptions of their ability influence many aspects of achievement motivation and are highly correlated with hope for success (Halisch, 1985), indicating that persons with high perceived ability usually have a strong hope for success. Attributions of causality are also influenced by the perception of ability. Persons with high perceived ability tend to attribute success to internal causes, whereas persons with low perceived ability tend to attribute it to external causes. Those with high perceived ability are therefore likely to show greater pride in success than those with low perceived ability.

The psychological relevance of this construct results from the finding that the individual's perceived ability sometimes does not correspond with actual ability. Many problems are associated with an unrealistically low perception of ability (Meyer, 1981, 1983, 1984).

General and Situation-Specific Perceptions of Ability

An explanation of the structure of the perception of ability is important in understanding its influence on motivation and behaviour in sport. It is clear that, in addition to a general perception of ability, people have situation-specific perceptions. Thus people may have a perception of their ability for mathematics, music and languages, and also for sport. Until now, however, it has not been shown whether it is necessary to differentiate between specific perceptions of ability for different kinds of sports such as skiing, gymnastics, volleyball, although this does seem likely. Three models are discussed for an understanding of the structure of the perception of ability:

1. Shavelson, Hubner, and Stanton (1976) postulate that the different aspects of the perceived ability are hierarchically structured. The bases of the hierarchy consists of situation-specific self-perceptions; at the top is general self-esteem.
2. The "taxonomic model" (Soares & Soares, 1983, cited in Byrne, 1984) assumes that apart from situation-specific perceptions of ability (i.e., for sport, music, languages), which are relatively independent from each other, a general perception of ability exists.
3. Winne and Marx (1981, cited in Byrne, 1984) propose a compensatory model. In contrast to the hierarchic and taxonomic models, the two authors suppose that there is a compensation among situation-specific perceptions of ability in such a way that people with low perceived ability in one domain compensate for this with a high perception in another.

As yet there has been no sound empirical validation of these models. It is generally regarded as certain, however, that situation-specific perceptions of ability are relatively independent. For example, Marsh and Richards (1988), as well as Willimczik and Zastrow (1988), have found results that lend support to the hierarchical model. But above all Marsh and Richards's findings suggest that for certain areas there is an intermediate level. First of all, their results suggest that there exists one perception of ability for mathematics and natural sciences and one for languages. Art, music, sport and home economics do not seem to have a place in this intermediate level. Secondly the results suggest that there is a tendency to compensate, that is a lower perceived ability for languages, for example, is compensated for by a higher one for mathematics.

Studies now suggest that the sport-specific perception of ability is hierarchically structured (see Fox & Corbin, 1989). An intermediate level can be assumed here, too. One may suppose that there are independent perceptions of ability for those types of sport in which condition or technique play a central role.

In addition to differentiating the specific perceptions of ability for theoretical reasons, one may assume that behaviour and motivation can be explained better by situation-specific perceptions. This has been shown by a series of studies we have carried out. In summary, we have found the following:

- Top-level athletes show a high correlation between their specific perception of ability in a particular sport (e.g., running, water-polo) and their perception of ability for sport in general, but only very low correlations between these two perceptions of ability and the general perception of ability (Rethorst, Willimczik, & Zastrow, 1987; see Figure 11.2a).
- Compared to top-level athletes, beginners' perceptions of their sport ability are more general rather than specific because of their lack of information on their abilities in specific situations (see Figure 11.2b).

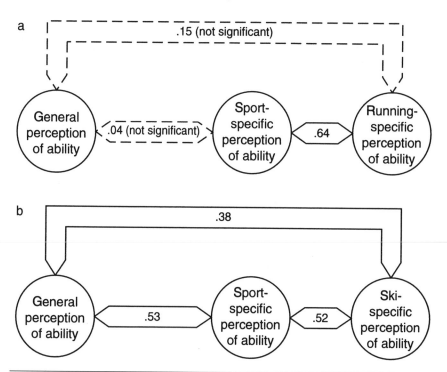

Figure 11.2   Correlations between perception of ability on different levels: (a) top-level runners, (b) skiing beginners.

Note. From 'Begabungskonzept—Generalität versus Spezifik' by S. Rethorst, K. Willimczik and H. Zastrow. In *Handlungskontrolle und soziale Prozesse im Sport* (pp. 226-235) by J.P. Janssen, W. Schlicht, and H. Strang (Eds.), Köln, Germany: bps. Copyright 1987 by bps-Verlag. Reprinted by permission.

- Women's general perception of ability is considerably lower than that of men, except for sport-specific perceptions such as running ability (see Figure 11.3).
- Boys refer to their specific perceptions of ability for languages, mathematics and sport when they form their general perceptions of ability but not to that for music, but girls do not refer to the perceived ability for sport although they do that for music (Willimczik & Zastrow, 1988).

In studies concerning the learning of new sport skills, the use of the sport-specific perception of ability is preferable to the general perception because the specific perception gives a slightly better prediction of the learning process (Willimczik & Rethorst, 1988b).

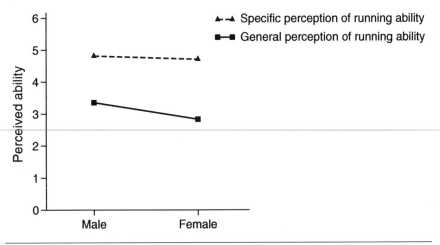

Figure 11.3   Gender differences in perceptions of ability on different levels of specialty. *Note.* From 'Begabungskonzept—Generalität versus Spezifik' by S. Rethorst, K. Willimczik and H. Zastrow. In *Handlungskontrolle und soziale Prozesse im Sport* (pp. 226-235) by J.P. Janssen, W. Schlicht, and H. Strang (Eds.), Köln, Germany: bps. Copyright 1987 by bps-Verlag. Reprinted by permission.

Causal Attributions

People's perceptions of ability have an important influence on the way they attribute causes to an achievement outcome. Although people do not search for the cause of every event, if an outcome is important or unexpected they are likely to ask themselves about the probable causes of the outcome. Causal attributions are central aspects of a cognitive theory of achievement motivation.

The many studies of causal attributions in sport by sport psychologists have focused on the specific causes of success or failure in sport in general or in particular types of sport, and the influence of factors like gender, expectancy of success or specific information on causal attributions in sport.

Classifying Causal Attributions in Sport

The ideas of Weiner et al. (1971) are the basis of most attempts to classify causal attributions. According to their opinion, success and failure in academic settings are predominantly attributed to ability, effort, task difficulty or luck. They systematised these factors in a 2 × 2 scheme (see Figure 11.4) according to the two dimensions of locus and stability.

Later the dimension of controllability was added (see Rosenbaum, 1972; Weiner, 1979). The question whether intentionality and globality have to be considered, as suggested by Weiner (1985) and Abramson, Seligman, and Teasdale (1978) among others, has not yet been answered.

There have been warnings against an uncritical use of the 2 × 2 scheme for studies in the field of sport. The warnings have targeted the inadequacy of the mentioned causes for the field of sport and the difficulty of categorising the various causes into the dimensions in Figure 11.4.

Table 11.1 shows a classification which serves to record the variety of sport-relevant causes and their dimensions. Other efforts at categorisation, mainly centring on certain types of sport, have been undertaken in the context of empirical studies of causal attributions in sport (see, for example, Bierhoff-Alfermann, 1979, 1986).

In the earlier research on attributions a great deal of emphasis was put on the classification of sport-relevant causes. Today this issue has lost much of its interest. Subjective measurements like the CDS are used, in which subjects themselves identify the main reason for the outcome of their actions. Subjects then rate their attributions on the dimensions of locus, stability and controllability.

Most of the studies on attribution in sport have been based on the 2 × 2 scheme and are centred on the influence of outcome and gender differences. For reviews of the current status of attribution theory in sport see Biddle (1993) and McAuley (1992).

Locus / Stability	Internal	External
Stable	Ability	Task difficulty
Unstable	Effort	Luck

Figure 11.4 Dimensions of causal attributions according to Weiner et al.
Note. From '*Perceiving the Causes of Success and Failure*' by B. Weiner, I. Frieze, A. Kukla, L. Reed, S. Rest, and R.M. Rosenbaum, 1971, Morristown, NY: General Learning Press. Copyright 1971 by General Learning Corporation. Reprinted by permission.

Table 11.1   Classification of Sport-Relevant Causal Attributions

	Internal	External
Stable	Talent	Task difficulty
Stable or unstable	Skill, fitness conditions, arousal	Task difficulty, training situation, conditions of competition
Unstable	Effort	Positive or negative influence of competitors, referee, audience, coach, luck etc.

Note. From 'Motivationale Aspekte sportlicher Handlungen' by H. Gabler. In *Einführung in die Sportpsychologie* (pp. 64-106) by H. Gabler, J.R. Nitsch, and R. Singer (Eds.), 1986, Schorndorf, Germany: Hofmann. Copyright 1986 by Hofmann-Verlag. Reprinted by permission.

From another point of view the results of the numerous studies attempting to describe the causes attributed to outcomes in sport can be summarised under the main question, Do athletes use available information in an essentially logical fashion to draw conclusions about causes of outcomes (Nicholls, 1975) or do they make attribution errors? These errors can be explained by the tendency of people to increase or defend their self-esteem by the way they explain an outcome (Nicholls, 1975). Winners would rather attribute the outcome to their own ability whereas losers would rather seek external factors as causes. If a rational attribution took place winners and losers might use similar attributions.

Our results seem to support the self-enhancement theory (Zastrow, Willimczik, & Rethorst, 1987). In a study of 132 handball players, after a match subjects had to rate a set of attributions for their own results as well as for the results of their opponents. For effort and 'form' the result shows a typical enhancement pattern (see Figure 11.5). This is demonstrated by a significant interaction between the factors of outcome and perspective. For playing ability the interaction was not significant. We also found very similar results when comparing the attribution patterns of actors and observers (see Figure 11.6). The self-enhancement tendency can be seen in the fact that observers attribute the causes for losing to a greater extent to internal factors than actors do.

Cognition-Emotion Links

Many emotions following a performance occur as a consequence of cognitions. The first cognitions involved in the process are expectancies concerning the outcome. These are followed by cognitive evaluations of the outcome in terms of either success or failure. The attributions influence which emotions will appear and how

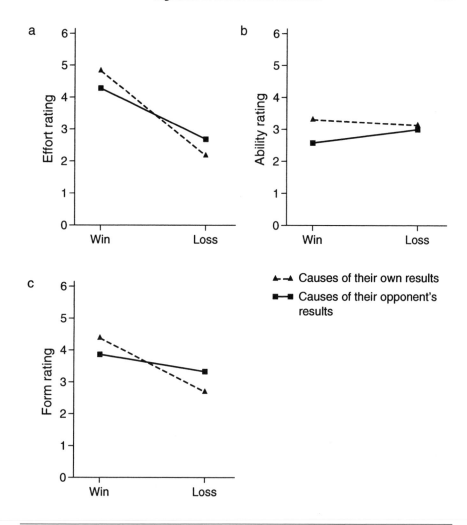

Figure 11.5   Causal attributions of (a) effort, (b) playing ability and (c) form for win and loss and different perspectives (attribution for their own result; attribution for the opponent's result).

Note. From 'Kausalattribuierung—rational oder selbstwerterhöhend?' by H. Zastrow, K. Willimczik, and S. Rethorst. In *Handlungskontrolle und soziale Prozesse im Sport* (pp. 270-279) by J.P. Janssen, W. Schlicht, and H. Strang (Eds.), Köln, Germany: bps. Copyright 1987 by bps-Verlag. Reprinted by permission.

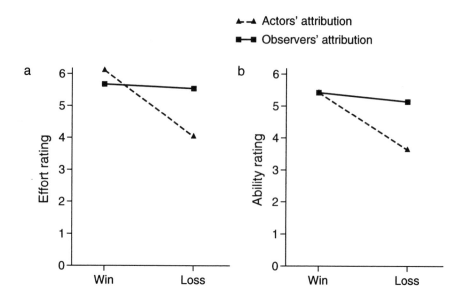

Figure 11.6   Actors' and observers' causal attributions of (a) effort and (b) playing ability for win and loss.

Note. From 'Kausalattribuierung—rational oder selbstwerterhöhend?' by H. Zastrow, K. Willimczik, and S. Rethorst. In *Handlungskontrolle und soziale Prozesse im Sport* (pp. 270-279) by J.P. Janssen, W. Schlicht, and H. Strang (Eds.), Köln, Germany: bps. Copyright 1987 by bps-Verlag. Reprinted by permission.

intense they will be. They decide whether, for example, we will simply feel happy or proud, whether we will be disappointed or ashamed, whether we will be angry and if so, at whom. These emotions will then influence new expectancies and motivation to guide our further actions. Perhaps we will withdraw if we attribute a failure to the internal and stable cause of believing that we lack talent, and feel hopeless.

In order to explain the interplay between cognitions and emotions psychologists have developed various theoretical models, among which Weiner's (1985, 1986) might be the best-known. A discussion of its validity for the processes of cognitions and emotions in the field of sport will be the main focus of the rest of this chapter. It seems necessary, however, first to describe those emotions which are typical and relevant for achievement situations in sport.

Emotions in Sport Achievement Situations

Psychologists have compiled a number of lists of words describing emotions. It is assumed a priori that these are valid for all areas of life and for sport. For English-speaking countries these collections of emotions have been worked out, for example, by Averill (1975); Fuenzalida, Emde, Pannabecker, and Stenberg (1981); Izard

(1971, 1977); Kotsch, Gerbing, and Schwartz (1982). In Germany, Schmidt-Atzert (1980) and Schmidt-Atzert and Strohm (1983) have published lists of emotions. These lists pose two problems. First of all, it must be questioned whether it is possible to draw up such lists in a deductive way. Second, it is doubtful whether some emotions, such as pity, are relevant to the field of sport.

Rethorst (1992), using the scenario technique and providing free responses, interviewed high school students (95 females, 74 males, aged from 14 to 16 years), concerning their emotions following success or failure in 16 different achievement situations in sport. After 8 success situations, 31 emotions were mentioned more often than five times. After failure the number of emotions mentioned more than five times was 38. The overall frequencies of the categorised emotions are presented in Figure 11.7. Results were as follows:

1. Among the emotions mentioned are those also found in the lists drawn up by psychologists and in Weiner's model.
2. Joy and pride after success, and anger and disappointment after failure, are the dominant emotions.
3. The positive emotions that show a high frequency are those that play a central role in Weiner's model. Of the negative emotions, however, shame, which plays a central role in Weiner's theory, is only seldom mentioned.
4. Understandably, positive emotions are stated predominantly after success, negative ones after failure. However, exceptions occur. After success envy, guilt, and anger are also mentioned. After failure optimism sometimes occurs (Rethorst, 1992).

Weiner's Attributional Theory of Emotion in the Field of Sport

Weiner's attributional theory of motivation and emotion, which forms the basis of the following discussion, is a process model which represents cognitions and emotions in the order of their assumed chronological appearance and according to the depth the processing of information has reached. This can be summarised as follows: the outcome of actions (e.g., win or loss) can be rated by the actor as success or failure. This evaluation decides whether there will be either positive (e.g., joy) or negative (e.g., disappointment) emotions. Weiner described these general emotions as being outcome-dependent. If an event is important, unexpected, and/or negative, the actor probably engages in causal search. He or she will perceive the cause according to the causal dimensions of locus, stability and controllability. These perceptions will evoke specific, attribution-linked affects like pride, pessimism, shame or guilt. Figure 11.8 represents Weiner's model developed for achievement situations.

Weiner's model has been tested in various psychological studies (first predominantly by means of the scenario technique; see Weiner, 1986). On the whole, the results support Weiner's theory. For the field of sport, however, only a limited number of studies exist. This is surprising and unfortunate because sport is an activity associated with strong emotions (Biddle, 1988; McAuley & Duncan, 1989;

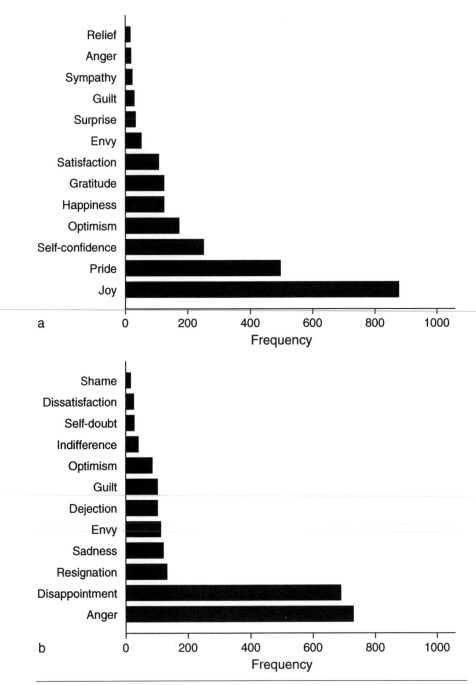

Figure 11.7 Frequencies of mentionings of emotions in (a) 8 success and (b) 8 failure situations (*n* = 169), using free responses.

Note. Adapted from *Kognitionen und Emotionen in sportlichen Leistungssituationen. Eine Überprüfung einer attributionalen Theorie von Emotionen* by S. Rethorst, 1992, Köln, Germany: bps. Copyright 1992 by bps-Verlag. Adapted by permission.

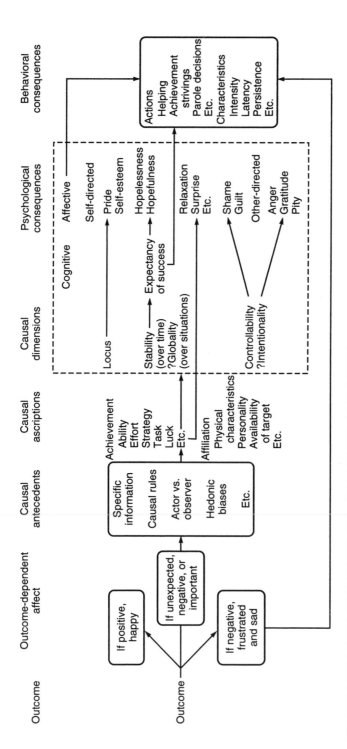

Figure 11.8 Weiner's attributional theory of motivation and emotion.

Note. From *An Attributional Theory of Motivation and Emotion* (p. 16) by B. Weiner, 1986, New York: Springer. Copyright 1986 by Springer-Verlag. Reproduced by permission.

Vallerand, 1983, 1987), and emotions are assumed to play a central role in controlling actions in sport (Nitsch, 1985).

The summary of validation research of Weiner's model in sport in Rethorst (1992) shows that in most cases only single sequences of the complex model have been tested by correlation studies and ANOVA methods. One of the earliest tests of Weiner's assumption regarding the dependence of emotions on certain attribution patterns in situations of sport competition was conducted by McAuley, Russell, and Gross (1983). After a table tennis match, students were asked to rate the positive emotions of satisfaction, pride, confidence and gratitude, and negative emotions of anger, depression, shame and a feeling of incompetence. Also included in the test was the 'neutral' emotion of surprise. Russell's (1982) Causal Dimension Scale served to ascertain the causal attribution dimensions for losing or winning.

The results did not correspond fully to Weiner's model. As had been expected, winners were more satisfied and felt more thankful than losers. Losers were more angry, sad and surprised and showed a greater feeling of incompetence than winners. Contrary to the hypothesis, positive emotions after success were far more dependent on the controllability dimension than on the locus dimension. The negative emotions were only weakly associated with dimensions. Correspondingly, depression was more intense when the causes for failure were internal. Shame was felt more intensively when the causes were uncontrollable. These findings are in accordance with Weiner's later differentiation (1985, 1986) which demands the attribution of internal and uncontrollable causes for the appearance of shame.

We investigated the relationship between attributions and emotions in two studies on achievement situations in sport (Willimczik & Rethorst, 1988a). The first was a field study of 137 German volleyball players from a regional league. After the game the intensity of 14 sport-relevant causal attributions for winning or losing was rated. The attributions were classified into dimensions by the authors. The positive emotions were enthusiasm, pride, contentment and satisfaction, and the negative emotions were anger, disappointment and rage. Among the 'neutral' emotions were indifference and surprise.

The results supported Weiner's thesis according to which pride is linked to the locus dimension. All correlations between pride on one side and four internal causes on the other side (for example one's own effort and form) were significant and higher than 0.40. The correlations between this causal dimension and the outcome-dependent emotion of contentment, however, were, apart from one exception, low and not significant. The results concerning the negative emotions corresponded to the theory too. There were significant correlations between the external attribution of blaming the referee and the dimension-dependent emotions of anger or annoyance. The same accounts for the external attribution of coaching and anger. The correlations, however, between these attributions and the outcome-dependent emotion of disappointment were not significant.

Our second field study investigated male and female high school students in a badminton tournament (Willimczik & Rethorst, 1988a). The outcome was not measured as either a win or loss but as the rank achieved at the end of the tournament. The classification of attributions into dimensions was carried out by the authors as before. The positive emotions of joy, pride and contentment, and the negative emotions of shame, anger and sadness were recorded.

In addition to correlation and analyses of variance, Weiner's hypotheses were tested by means of path analysis. Results are shown in Figure 11.9 and can be summarised as follows. For joy and pride Weiner's model was clearly verified. There was a strong path directly pointing from the outcome to the outcome-dependent emotion of joy. For the dimension-dependent emotion of pride, however, the path ran via the internal attribution. Also in correspondence with the hypothesis there was a strong path from the outcome to the emotion of sadness. The results concerning the emotion of shame were only to a certain degree in accordance with Weiner's model. Although there was a strong path via the attribution there was also a strong direct path. This would suggest some outcome-dependence for this emotion. It should be noted, however, that although the model was confirmed to a high degree, the intensity of pride and shame was quite low. When asked, students affirmed that these were emotions not really likely to be honestly stated even when they appear.

The importance of a good result as a moderator variable for the relation between attributions and emotions was investigated by Biddle and colleagues (Biddle, 1984; Biddle & Hill, 1988, 1992). Weiner sees the importance of a good result as one of the moderator variables that initiate the search for causes (see Figure 11.8).

Biddle and Hill (1988) investigated the relationship between causal attributions and emotions according to their dependence on importance. In a laboratory setting, physical education students took part in a one-versus-one cycle race. Each subject was asked before the race to rate how important it was to do well. After the race the winners were questioned concerning the intensity of 13 positive emotions and the losers concerning the intensity of 13 negative emotions. The categorisation of attributions was done by the researchers.

The results for both winners and losers merely indicated relations between internal attributions and emotions. The influence of importance could not be established for all attribution-emotion links. Importance influenced above all the relation between pride and resignation on the one hand and internal attributions on the other. Very similar findings were gained by Biddle in his field study of 1984. The subjects of this study were school students 16 to 17 years old who were given a questionnaire after a badminton game in physical education classes. In addition to the factor of importance, the probability of success was included as a possible moderator variable. In this study, significant correlations were found almost exclusively between emotions and internal causal attributions. Some of these were, however, only significant when the subjective expectancy of success and the outcome importance had been partialed out. This stresses the likely influence of these moderator variables. The feelings of losers were particularly strong if, before losing, they had thought they had a good chance of winning and when the competition had been very important to them. Biddle and Hill (1992) confirmed the dependence of emotions on internal attributions as well as the influence of importance in a study on students in a simulated fencing competition in a laboratory.

Rethorst (1992) used the scenario technique to interview 122 students concerning their evaluation of the outcome of a competition, their causal attributions and

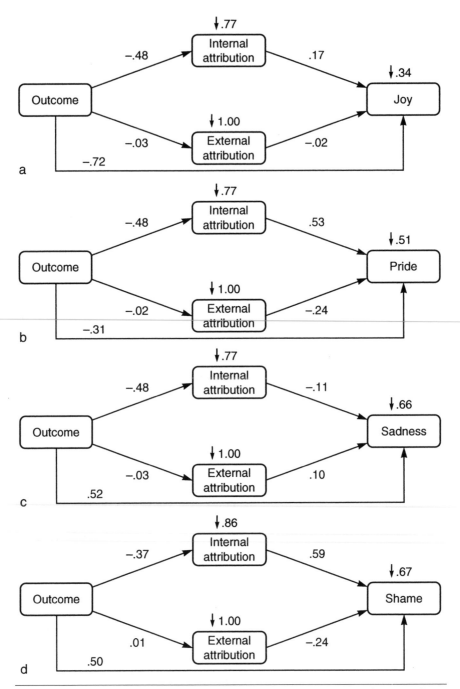

Figure 11.9   Path analyses for attribution-emotion links for (a) joy, (b) pride, (c) sadness and (d) shame. *Note.* From 'Kognitionen als vorauslaufende Bedingungen von Emotionen im Sport' by K. Willimczik and S. Rethorst. In *Proceedings VIIth Congress of the European Federation of Sports* (Vol. 2) (pp. 750-762) by Wissenschaftlicher Rat beim Staatssekretariat für Körperkultur und Sport der Deutschen Demokratischen Republik (Ed.), 1988, Leipzig, Germany: Deutsche Hochscule für Körperkultur.

dimensions (assessed according to Russell [1982]) and those positive and negative emotions that are relevant for sport and for which Weiner had already proposed hypotheses. Results verified the dimension-relatedness of the emotions as Weiner had predicted. Path analyses followed which had the particular purpose of testing processes within Weiner's model.

Figures 11.10 and 11.11 show the results of some path analyses. In each analysis a dimension-dependent and an outcome-dependent emotion are included; these are pride and joy in the first case and guilt and disappointment in the second. The starting point of the cognition-emotion process was descriptions of different competitive situations of success or failure (in a simulation technique). The success and failure results were described to be caused by several reasons that differed in terms of causal dimensions.

The results represented in the top parts of Figures 11.10 and 11.11 show a direct path from outcome evaluation to the emotions of joy and disappointment, while pride is mediated via the locus dimension and guilt via the controllability dimension. These findings support Weiner's theory. When using a different structural model,

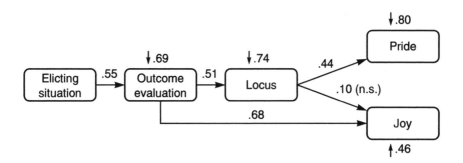

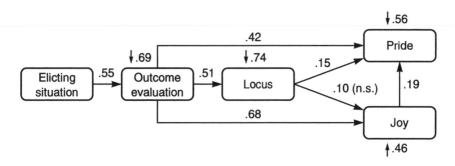

Figure 11.10 Two different models for an explanation of pride by means of path analysis.

Note. From *Kognitionen und Emotionen in sportlichen Leistungssituationen. Eine Überprüfung einer attributionalen Theorie von Emotionen* by S. Rethorst, 1992, Köln, Germany: bps. Copyright 1992 by bps-Verlag. Reprinted by permission.

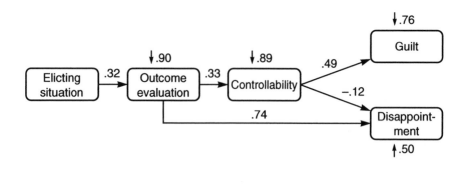

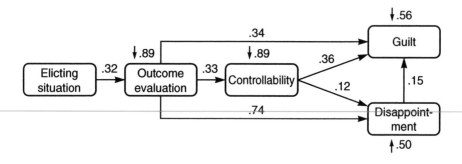

Figure 11.11   Two different models for an explanation of guilt by means of path analysis.
Note. From *Kognitionen und Emotionen in sportlichen Leistungssituationen. Eine Überprüfung einer attributionalen Theorie von Emotionen* by S. Rethorst, 1992, Köln, Germany: bps. Copyright 1992 by bps-Verlag. Reprinted by permission.

however (see foot of Figures 11.10 and 11.11), it can be seen that the dimension-dependent emotions of pride and guilt are also influenced by the outcome evaluation. This is indicated by the coefficient from the outcome evaluation to pride ($\beta_{31} = .42$) and guilt ($\beta_{31} = .34$).

Though our results support the cognition-emotion links proposed by Weiner, it has to be stressed that the explained variance of the emotions in question is often low. This means that the influence of further factors on emotions, and possibly modifications of the model, have to be considered.

Conclusion

Sport is a context with the potential for an intense experience of emotions. Indeed, many people have a strong emotional investment in sport. The relationship between emotions and cognitions is complex, yet a number of possible paths linking cognitions and emotions are now being identified. The framework provided by Weiner appears to have some utility in the sport context, but more needs to be known on how well the model fits sports situations. Given the importance of emotion in sport, further work on cognition-emotion links is warranted.

This chapter has summarised research that sheds some light on the cognition-emotion process with specific reference to the sport situation. Much more needs to be done to achieve a better understanding of cognitions and emotions in sport.

References

Abramson, L.Y., Seligman, M.E.P., & Teasdale, J.D. (1978). Learned helplessness in humans: Critique and reformulation. *Journal of Abnormal Psychology*, **87**, 49-74.

Averill, J.R. (1975). A semantic atlas of emotional concepts. *Catalog of Selected Documents in Psychology*, **5**, 330.

Bandura, A. (1977). Self-efficacy: Toward a unifying theory of behavioral change. *Psychological Review*, **84**, 191-215.

Biddle, S.J.H. (1984). Motivation, attribution and affective consequences of winning and losing. *Journal of Sports Sciences*, **2**, 159-162. (Abstract)

Biddle, S.J.H. (1988). Methodological issues in the researching of attribution-emotion links in sport. *International Journal of Sport Psychology*, **19**, 264-280.

Biddle, S.J.H. (1993). Attribution research and sport psychology. In R.N. Singer, M. Murphey, & L.K. Tennant (Eds.), *Handbook of research on sport psychology* (pp. 437-464). New York: Macmillan.

Biddle, S.J.H., & Hill, A.B. (1988). Causal attribution and emotional reactions to outcome in a sporting contest. *Personality and Individual Differences*, **9**, 213-223.

Biddle, S.J.H., & Hill, A.B. (1992). Relationships between attributions and emotions in a laboratory-based sporting contest. *Journal of Sports Sciences*, **10**, 65-75.

Bierhoff-Alfermann, D. (1979). Ursachenerklärung für Erfolg und Mißerfolg bei einem Schwimmwettkampf: Defensive Attribution und die Bedeutsamkeit des Wettkampfes. In G. Baumler, E. Hahn, & J.R. Nitsch (Eds.), *Aktuelle Probleme der Sportpsychologie* (pp. 91-97). Schorndorf, Germany: Hofmann.

Bierhoff-Alfermann, D. (1986). *Sportpsychologie*. Stuttgart, Germany: Kohlhammer.

Byrne, B.M. (1984). The general/academic self-concept nomological network: A review of construct validation research. *Review of Educational Research*, **54**, 427-456.

Caillois, R. (1960). *Die Spiele und die Menschen. Maske und Rausch*. München, Germany: Langen-Müller.

Carl, K., Kayser, D., Mechling, H., & Preising, W. (Eds.) (1984). *Handbuch Sport (Band 1). Wissenschaftliche Grundlagen von Unterricht und Training*. Düsseldorf, Germany: Schwann.

Covington, M.V., & Omelich, C.L. (1979). Are causal attributions causal? A path analysis on the cognitive model of achievement motivation. *Journal of Personality and Social Psychology*, **37**, 1487-1504.

Deci, E.L. (1975). *Intrinsic motivation*. New York: Plenum.

Försterling, F. (1985). Attributional retraining: A review. *Psychological Review*, **98**, 495-512.

Fox, K.R., & Corbin, C.B. (1989). The Physical Self-Perception Profile: Development and preliminary validation. *Journal of Sport and Exercise Psychology*, **11**, 408-430.

Fuenzalida, C., Emde, R.N., Pannabecker, B.J., & Stenberg, C. (1981). Validation of the differential emotions scale in 618 mothers. *Motivation and Emotion*, **5**, 37-45.

Furnham, A., & Argyle, M. (Eds.) (1981). *The psychology of social situations: Selected readings.* Oxford, England: Pergamon.

Gabler, H. (1972). *Leistungsmotivation im Hochleistungssport.* Schorndorf, Germany: Hofmann.

Gabler, H. (1986). Motivationale Aspekte sportlicher Handlungen. In H. Gabler, J.R. Nitsch, & R. Singer (Eds.), *Einführung in die Sportpsychologie* (pp. 64-106). Schorndorf, Germany: Hofmann.

Göhner, U. (1979). *Bewegungsanalyse im Sport.* Schorndorf, Germany: Hofmann.

Gotlib, I.H., & Olson, J.M. (1983). Depression, psychopathology and self-serving attributions. *British Journal of Clinical Psychology,* **22**, 309-310.

Hägele, W. (1982). Zur Konstitutionsproblematik des Sports. *Sportwissenschaft,* **12**, 195-201.

Halisch, F. (1985). *Operante und respondente Motivmeßverfahren. Ergebnisbericht zum Leistungsmotivationsprojekt am Max-Planck-Institut für Psychologische Forschung.* München, Germany: Author.

Heckhausen, H. (1974). *Leistung und Chancengleichheit.* Göttingen, Germany: Hogrefe.

Heinemann, K. (1989). Der 'nicht-sportliche' Sport. In K. Dietrich & K. Heinemann (Eds.), *Der nicht-sportliche Sport* (pp. 11-28). Schorndorf, Germany: Hofmann.

Hutzlar, J. (1981). This thing that we do: A model for sport and dance. *Quest,* **33**, 87-95.

Izard, C.E. (1971). *The face of emotion.* New York: Appleton-Century-Crofts.

Izard, C.E. (1977). *Human emotions.* New York: Plenum.

Kotsch, W.E., Gerbing, D.W., & Schwartz, L.E. (1982). The construct validity of the differential emotions scale as adapted for children and adolescents. In C.E. Izard (Ed.), *Measuring emotions in infants and children* (pp. 251-278). Cambridge, England: Cambridge University Press.

Kukla, A. (1972). Foundations of an attributional theory of performance. *Psychological Review,* **79**, 454-470.

Loy, J.W. (1968). The nature of sport: A definitional effort. Frames of reference. *Quest,* **19**, 56-71.

Loy, J.W. (1978). The cultural system of sport. *Quest,* **29**, 73-102.

Marsh, H.W., & Richards, G. (1988). The outward bound bridging course for low-achieving high school males: Effect on academic achievement and multidimensional self-concepts. *Australian Journal of Psychology,* **40**, 281-298.

McAuley, E. (1985). Success and causality in sport: The influence of perception. *Journal of Sport Psychology,* **7**, 13-22.

McAuley, E. (1992). Self-referent thought in sport and physical activity. In T.S. Horn (Ed.), *Advances in Sport Psychology* (pp. 101-118). Champaign, IL: Human Kinetics.

McAuley, E., & Duncan, T.E., (1989). Causal attributions and affective reactions to disconfirming outcomes in motor performance. *Journal of Sport and Exercise Psychology,* **11**, 187-200.

McAuley, E., Russell, D., & Gross, J.B. (1983). Affective consequences of winning and losing: An attributional analysis. *Journal of Sport Psychology,* **5**, 278-287.

McClelland, D.C., Atkinson, J., Clark, R., & Lowell, E. (1953). *The achievement motive.* New York: Appleton-Century-Crofts.

Meier, K. (1981). On the inadequacies of sociological definitions of sport. *International Review of Sport Sociology,* **16**, 76-102.

Meyer, W.-U. (1973). *Leistungsmotiv und Ursachenerklärung von Erfolg und Mißerfolg.* Stuttgart, Germany: Klett.

Meyer, W.-U. (1976). Leistungsorientiertes Verhalten als Funktion von wahrgenommener eigener Begabung und wahrgenommener Aufgabenschwierigkeit. In H.D. Schmalt &

W.-U. Meyer (Eds.), *Leistungsmotivation und Verhalten* (pp. 101-135). Stuttgart, Germany: Klett.

Meyer, W.-U. (1981). Leistung, Leistungseinschätzung und Ursachenzuschreibung in Abhängigkeit vom Konzept eigener Begabung. In S.-H. Filipp (Ed.), *Newsletter "Selbstkonzepte"*, *No. 1(4)*. Trier, Germany: University of Trier.

Meyer, W.-U. (1983). Prozesse der Selbstbeurteilung: Das Konzept von der eigenen Begabung. *Zeitschrift für Entwicklungspsychologie und Pädagogische Psychologie, 15*, 1-25.

Meyer, W.-U. (1984). *Das Konzept von der eigenen Begabung*. Bern, Switzerland: Huber.

Mischel, W. (1979). On the interface of cognition and personality: Beyond the person-situation debate. *American Psychologist, 34*, 740-754.

Murray, H.A. (1938). *Explorations in personality*. New York: Oxford University Press.

Nicholls, J.G. (1975). Causal attributions and other achievement-related cognitions: Effects of task outcome, attainment value, and sex. *Journal of Personality and Social Psychology, 31*, 379-389.

Nitsch, J. (1985). Emotionen und Handlungsregulation. In G. Schilling & K. Herren (Eds.), *Angst, Freude und Leistung im Sport. Bericht zum VI. FEPSAC-Kongress 1983* (pp. 37-60). Magglingen, Germany: Published Eidgenössische Turn-und Sportschule.

Rethorst, S. (1991a). Die Kausaldimensionsskala—Eine deutsche Version der Skala von Russell zur Erfassung der subjektiven Dimensionierung von Kausalattributionen. In R. Singer (Ed.), *Sportpsychologische Forschungsmethodik: Grundlagen, Probleme, Ansätze* (pp. 191-197). Köln, Germany: bps.

Rethorst, S. (1991b). *Zwischen Lust und Frust—Die Erlebniswelt von Schülern und Schülerinnen bei den Leichtathletik-Bundesjugendspielen. Bielefelder Beiträge zur Sportwissenschaft, Bd. 13*. Bielefeld, Germany: University of Bielefeld.

Rethorst, S. (1992). *Kognitionen und Emotionen in sportlichen Leistungssituationen. Eine Überprüfung einer attributionalen Theorie von Emotionen*. Köln, Germany: bps.

Rethorst, S., Willimczik, K., & Zastrow, H. (1987). Begabungskonzept—Generalität versus Spezifik. In J.P. Janssen, W. Schlicht, & H. Strang (Eds.), *Handlungskontrolle und soziale Prozesse im Sport* (pp. 226-235). Köln, Germany: bps.

Rosenbaum, R.M. (1972). *A dimensional analysis of the perceived causes of success and failure*. Unpublished doctoral dissertation, University of California, Los Angeles.

Russell, D. (1982). The causal dimension scale: A measure of how individuals perceive causes. *Journal of Personality and Social Psychology, 42*, 1137-1145.

Russell, D., & McAuley, E. (1986). Causal attribution, causal dimensions, and affective reactions to success and failure. *Journal of Personality and Social Psychology, 52*, 1174-1184.

Ryan, E.D. (1980). Attribution and affect. In C. Nadeau, W.R. Halliwell, K.M. Newell, & G.C. Roberts (Eds.), *Psychology of motor behavior and sport—1979* (pp. 49-59). Champaign, IL: Human Kinetics.

Schmidt-Atzert, L. (1980). *Die verbale Kommunikation von Emotionen: Eine Bedingungsanalyse unter besonderer Berücksichtigung physiologischer Prozesse*. Unpublished doctoral dissertation, University of Gießen, Germany.

Schmidt-Atzert, L., & Ströhm, W. (1983). Ein Beitrag zur Taxonomie der Emotionswörter. *Pscychologische Beiträge, 25*, 126-141.

Schuster, B., Försterling, F., & Weiner, B. (1986). Perceiving the causes of success and failure: A cross-cultural examination of attributional concepts. *Journal of Cross-Cultural Psychology, 20*, 191-213.

Shavelson, R.J., Hubner, J.J., & Stanton, G.C. (1976). Validation of construct interpretations. *Review of Educational Research, 46*, 407-441.

Si, G.Y. (1992). *Cognitions and emotions in sport achievement situations. Bielefelder Beiträge zur Sportwissenschaft.* Bielefeld, Germany: University of Bielefeld.

Soares, L.M., & Soares, A.T. (1983, April). *Components of students' self-related cognitions.* Paper presented at the annual meeting of the American Educational Research Association, Montreal.

Spink, K., & Roberts, G.C. (1980). Ambiguity of outcome and causal attributions. *Journal of Sport Psychology, 2,* 237-244.

Vallerand, R.J. (1983). On emotion in sport: Theoretical and social psychological perspectives. *Journal of Sport Psychology, 5,* 197-215.

Vallerand, R.J. (1987). Antecedents of self-related affects in sport: Preliminary evidence on the intuitive-reflective appraisal model. *Journal of Sport Psychology, 9,* 161-182.

Weiner, B. (1979). A theory of motivation for some classroom experiences. *Journal of Educational Psychology, 71,* 3-25.

Weiner, B. (1985). An attributional theory of achievement motivation and emotion. *Psychological Review, 92,* 548-573.

Weiner, B. (1986). *An attributional theory of motivation and emotion.* New York: Springer.

Weiner, B., Frieze, I., Kukla, A., Reed, L., Rest, S., & Rosenbaum, R.M. (1971). *Perceiving the causes of success and failure.* Morristown, NY: General Learning Press.

Weiner, B., Russell, D., & Lerman, D. (1978). Affective consequences of causal ascriptions. In J.H. Harvey, W.J. Ickes, & R.F. Kidd (Eds.), *New directions in attribution research: Vol. 2* (pp. 59-88). Hillsdale, NJ: Erlbaum.

Willimczik, K. (1991). *Theorie der Sportwissenschaft—Die Begründung einer Wissenschaft über ihren Gegenstand. Bielefelder Beiträge zur Sportwissenschaft, Bd. 11.* Bielefeld, Germany: University of Bielefeld.

Willimczik, K., & Rethorst, S. (1988a). Kognitionen als vorauslaufende Bedingungen von Emotionen im Sport. In Wissenschaftlicher Rat beim Staatssekretariat für Körperkultur und Sport der Deutschen Demokratischen Republik (Ed.), *Proceedings of the VI Congress of the European Federation of Sport Psychology* (Vol. 2, pp. 750-762). Leipzig, Germany: DHfK.

Willimczik, K., & Rethorst, S. (1988b). Sportpsychologische Forschungsmethoden im Spannungsfeld von Grundlagen und Anwendungsforschung—ein empirischer Methodenvergleich. In P. Schwenkmezger (Ed.), *Sportpsychologische Diagnostik, Intervention und Verantwortung* (pp. 215-231). Köln, Germany: bps.

Willimczik, K., & Zastrow, H. (1988). *Sportspezifik von Begabungskonzept und Handlungskontrolle.* Unpublished manuscript, University of Bielefeld, Germany.

Winne, P.H., & Marx, R.W. (1981, April). *Convergent and discriminant validity in self-concept measurement.* Paper presented at the annual meeting of the American Educational Research Association, Los Angeles.

Zastrow, H., Willimczik, K., & Rethorst, S. (1987). Kausalattribuierung—rational oder selbstwerterhöhend? In J.P. Janssen, W. Schlicht, & H. Strang (Eds.), *Handlungskontrolle und soziale Prozesse im Sport* (pp. 270-279). Köln, Germany: bps.

12

CHAPTER

Motivation and Goal Perspectives in Children's Physical Education

Athanasios Papaioannou

GREECE

The research reported in this chapter is based on theories developed in North America (Ames & Archer, 1988; Duda, 1992, 1993; Dweck, 1991; Nicholls, 1989), although they also have received some attention in Europe (e.g., Heckhausen, Schmalt, & Schneider, 1985; see also chapter 10). Nevertheless, there are some important differences. First, unlike the American researchers who have concentrated mainly on competitive or recreational sport, in the present chapter research examining students' motivation in physical education lessons is reported. Further, unlike most of the research in North America, which has examined the effects of individual and situational differences on children's achievement mainly in isolation from each other, the perspective adopted here is an initial attempt to examine the interactional effects of person and environment on students' motivation. Finally, the validity of contemporary theories of children's motivation is examined in a culture other than America (namely, Greece).

I started my investigations into children's motivation in physical activities 6 years ago as research student at the University of Manchester, England. At that time there were three general questions that shaped my research. First, since the role of school physical education in public health is widely recognised (e.g., Morrow, 1991) the issue to be addressed was how can we implement physical education in order (a) to motivate students to try their best during the lesson, (b) to make sure that they really learn as much as possible in the lesson, (c) to ensure that they have an enjoyable lesson, (d) to make sure that students develop the most positive attitudes towards exercise, and (e) to be confident that after the end of school, students will continue to exercise, effectively using what they have learned? Obviously, the question was one about students' motivation and achievement.

The second general question was concerned with the way these issues should be examined. Some theories focus primarily on the effects of external or objective conditions on people's behaviours. Others put greater emphasis on internal or subjective conditions and deal primarily with dispositional differences. There are also theories that deal quite effectively with both issues, or better, with the interaction between the person and the external environment. Since the latter appears to be the most comprehensive perspective, a theory and a research methodology sharing this view should be adopted.

The third question was an ethical one. It was whether any existing theory could give effective answers with regard to how we can sustain optimal motivation in all children. In my own country of Greece there are two main characteristics that seem to discriminate students in physical education: gender and level of athletic ability. My experience suggests that gender discrimination to a large extent reflects sport ability-based discrimination (see also Griffins, 1989; Kirk, 1990). Thus a theory should be used whose implications ensure, or at least assist in, optimum motivation in students of all levels of ability.

In support of the argument that the theoretical framework of goals can successfully answer the above questions (Nicholls, 1989; Dweck & Leggett, 1988), the remainder of this chapter reports some findings from my recent studies. Because of space limitations, only a brief description of the theory used in these studies will be presented here. For further reading see Ames (1984a), Ames and Archer (1988), Duda (1992, 1993), Dweck (1991), Dweck and Leggett, (1988), Nicholls (1989) and Papaioannou (1992).

Goal Perspectives Theory and Assessment

According to the theoretical framework of goal perspectives, in achievement situations at least two different classes of goals are identifiable: a task or learning goal and an ego or performance goal.

When a task or learning goal is salient, people are concerned with how to accomplish a meaningful task that will lead to greater personal competence. Since the goal is to gain competence, people see effort as the prime antecedent of achievement and, speaking generally, the major prerequisite of success. Therefore, they try hard to learn new skills, and they value the process of learning itself. No external rewards or threats are necessary in order to motivate task-involved children because the most important rewards are in the accomplishment itself and in the gains in knowledge or skills that imply improvement in competence. In other words, when the goal is the development of competence in a meaningful task, children are always intrinsically motivated.

Because people can infer that their competence has been increased if they evaluate it relative to their personal progress rather than normative criteria such as others' performance, when a learning goal is adopted the criteria of evaluation are personal (i.e., where one's performance stands relative to one's past performances). This implies that when a task or learning goal is salient *success is defined as personal improvement.* When someone is task involved, no actual failure is perceived because any mistake serves as a guide for future improvement in competence. Once an error is identified, the probability of its repetition and the corresponding detrimental effect on future performance are progressively eliminated.

The implications of the theoretical framework of goals extend beyond the achievement domain (e.g., see Duda, Olson, & Templin, 1991; Kelley, Hoffman, & Gill, 1990). For example, since no fear of failure exists in task involvement, people do not hesitate to ask for help from others or to co-operate and to help others, because they see co-operation, help-seeking and help-giving as an effective way towards personal and collective improvement.

When an ego or performance goal is salient people are concerned with how good they are at the particular task (e.g., the goals that a high evaluative environment imposes when, for example, children are told 'We are going to have a race to see who is fastest'). Consequently, people's main interest is to show evidence of their ability in a normative sense. For instance, they try to beat others, or to outperform a high normative performance or to achieve success with little effort. In other words, the criteria of evaluation are normative and children feel successful and satisfied when they are evaluated by others as higher achievers than their group of reference (e.g., children of the same gender, same age, etc.). In contrast, children experience failure and negative emotion when they are evaluated as having lower abilities than most of their reference groups. Thus children feel anxious when they foresee that they will exhibit low abilities and generally they either try to avoid the task or exhibit low effort, which will be used as an excuse for their failure.

The validity of the theoretical framework of goal perspectives has received considerable support in the domain of physical activity (see the reviews of Duda, 1992, 1993). Most of the field studies conducted until now have used questionnaires measuring personal goals in sport. For example, two items from Duda's (1989a) questionnaire state 'I feel most successful in sport when the others can't do as well as me' (ego orientation), and 'I feel most successful in sport when I learn a new skill and it makes me want to practise more' (task orientation).

Adopting the same perspective, in the first study with Greek students (Papaioannou, 1990; Papaioannou & Duda, 1992) a questionnaire measuring individual differences in students' goals (dispositional goals) in sport was completed by 211 adolescents. In addition, they completed a questionnaire measuring students' motives for participation in the physical education lesson (similar to that of Gill, Gross, & Huddleston, 1983) and a questionnaire measuring perceived purposes of physical education (similar to that used by Duda, 1989a).

All questionnaires were analysed by factor analysis. The two-factor solution reflecting task and ego orientation respectively (Papaioannou, 1990) was replicated 2 years later with a sample of 394 Greek students (Papaioannou & Duda, 1992).

Factor analysis also produced five factors for motives for participation (status, fitness development, affiliation, excitement and skill improvement) and five factors for perceived purposes of the physical education lesson (fostering of mastery-coopera- tion, increase of self-esteem, improvement of fitness, increase of status by any means and cultivation of citizens of good character). Analyses using canonical correlation showed that ego orientation was associated with motives for social status while task orientation was associated with motives for skill improvement, fitness development and affiliation.

Furthermore, ego orientation was a positive predictor of the perceived purposes of 'social status by any means' and 'increase of self-esteem', but task orientation was a positive predictor of 'mastery-cooperation', 'increase of self-esteem', 'cultiva- tion of good-character citizens' and 'fitness improvement'.

These results are in accordance with the assumptions of goal perspectives theory and identical to those of Duda (1989a). Further, a useful implication of these findings is that dispositional goals in sport activities can be reliably and validly measured in a Greek population.

Contextual Differences in Students' Perceptions of Their Class

In addition to dispositional differences, contextual differences in goal perspectives exist (for reviews see Nicholls, 1989; Dweck & Leggett, 1988). In the sport domain, most of the studies in this area have been conducted in laboratories (e.g., Jourden, Bandura, & Banfield, 1991). Since many authors have challenged the usefulness of the laboratory's artificial environment (e.g., Martens, 1979), and given that very few field experimental studies (e.g., Burton, 1989) have been conducted in this area, research is lacking on the effects of situational differences in goal perspectives on children's motivation and achievement. This shortcoming, in conjunction with the limited number of studies dealing with motivational issues in physical education (for a review see Papaioannou, 1992), make explicit the reasons why I chose to examine the effects of the physical education environment on students' motivation.

Dealing with the interaction between person and environment, Murray (1938) noticed that there is a difference between the environment perceived by a detached observer and that perceived by the people involved in it. A typical example of the 'objective' approach to the study of the environment is the systematic observation that adopts instruments such as those described in Darst, Zakrajsek, and Mancini's (1989) book. Typical of the 'subjective' research approach are interviews or question- naires measuring students' perceptions of the environment such as those described by Fraser (1986).

According to Fraser (1986), student perceptual measures are more economical and have been found to account for considerably more variance in student learning than observational techniques. Moreover, studying the effects of students' percep- tions of their classes' climates on their motivation and achievement has the advantage of concentrating on both person and situation simultaneously. Indeed, Stern, Stein, and Bloom (1956) distinguished between the idiosyncratic view that each person has of the environment and the shared view that members of a group hold about the environment. As many studies reviewed by Fraser (1986) show, the perceived environment reflects both the idiosyncratic and the shared view of its members.

Based on the theoretical framework of goals, Ames and Archer (1988) have developed a questionnaire measuring the two basic dimensions of classroom climate proposed by this theory: mastery and performance orientations in the classroom. Similarly, a questionnaire measuring mastery- and performance-oriented teams has been developed recently by Seifriz, Duda, and Chi (1992). Ames and Archer (1988) found that perceptions of mastery-oriented classes were strongly related to positive attitudes towards the class, preferences for challenging tasks and effective learning strategies. Seifriz et al. (1992) found that perceptions of a mastery-oriented basketball team were associated with enjoyment in playing basketball and the belief that effort leads to achievement in basketball. On the other hand, perceptions of a performance-oriented team were related to the belief that superior ability causes success in basketball. Thus, there is already some evidence supporting the hypotheses generated by goals theory regarding the effects of the environment on students' motivation.

Learning and Performance Oriented Physical Education Classes Questionnaire (LAPOPECQ)

In order to measure perceptions of physical education classes' goals, I developed a questionnaire ('Learning and Performance Oriented Physical Education Classes Questionnaire'; LAPOPECQ) (Papaioannou, 1994) which consists of five factors. Two of them measure perceptions of class learning orientations and three of them perceptions of class performance orientations. Results from confirmatory factor analysis showed that the questionnaire has a hierarchical structure: the two learning factors are first-order factors of a second higher-order factor named learning, and the three performance factors are first-order factors of a second higher-order factor called performance.

The same five first-order factor solution emerged in three different samples consisting of: (a) 122 students from four physical education classes of students aged 14 and 17 years, (b) 1,393 students from 55 physical education classes (28 classes: students 13 years old; 27 classes: students 16 years old), and (c) 394 students from 16 physical education classes (students' age in 8 classes: 14 years old; students' age in the remaining 8 classes: 17 years old). All students were Greek adolescents.

In addition to the LAPOPECQ, the adolescents from the first two samples were asked whether they perceive that their teacher is mainly satisfied by the success of students who: (a) have high athletic abilities although they do not try very hard, (b) have high athletic abilities and try very hard, (c) try very hard although they lack high athletic abilities. As appears in Table 12.1, the perception of a teacher who is mainly satisfied by high ability but not high effort was positively correlated with the three performance scales but negatively correlated with the two learning scales. In other words, students' perceptions of a teacher who is particularly focused on the issue of normative ability were positively related to the scales measuring perceptions of classes' performance orientation but negatively related to the scales assessing perceptions of classes' learning orientation. On the contrary, as is shown

Table 12.1   Correlations Between Perceptions of Teacher's Satisfaction and Perspectives of Classes' Goals

Teacher's satisfaction with	Teacher-initiated learning orientation	Students' learning orientation	Students' competitive orientation	Students' worries about mistakes	Outcome orientation without effort
high ability low effort	−.27**	−.21**	.18**	.11**	.29**
high ability high effort	.28**	.23**	.02	.01	−.10**
low ability high effort	.38**	.28**	−.07*	−.02	−.08*

*p < 0.01   **p < 0.001

Note. From *Students' Motivation in Physical Education Classes Which Are Perceived to Have Different Goal Perspectives* by A. Papaioannou, 1992, unpublished doctoral dissertation.

in Table 12.1, the perception of a teacher whose main interest is students' effort was positively related to the scales measuring learning orientation.

Although most of these relationships are quite low, they imply that the perception of an emphasis on effort and not on normative ability is inherent in the two learning-oriented scales. On the contrary, the perception of an emphasis on normative ability was inherent in the three performance-oriented scales.

Student Motivation and Achievement

In addition to the LAPOPECQ, the students from the second sample of 1,393 Greek adolescents answered a questionnaire measuring attributions of success and failure to ability, effort, task difficulty and luck (Papaioannou, 1992).

In order to search for differences among profiles of students, eight different groups were created according to their scores on the learning and performance scales and physical perceived competence scale. The learning scale consisted of the items of the 'teacher-initiated learning orientation' and the 'students' learning orientation'. The performance scale was constructed by adding the items of the 'students' competitive orientation' and 'outcome orientation without effort' scales. These two new scales were further split, using as criterion the mean of the physical perceived competence scale. Thus eight new groups were created, differing from one another in terms of learning goals, performance goals and perceived competence (e.g., high learning/high performance with high perceived competence). The sample sizes of all groups varied from 106 to 197 students.

Students in the high learning groups perceived effort as a more important cause of success than students in the low learning groups. These findings are in line with past research (Ames & Archer, 1988) implying that when students perceive their environment as highly learning oriented, irrespective of their perceived competence they define success as competence improvement whose main antecedent is high effort.

However, the results showed that when both learning and performance goals are salient, in addition to effort, children consider ability as an important cause of success. Similar results from experimental studies have been reported in the past (e.g., Ames, 1984b). Although these results are possibly not too important from a practical point of view (the differences were quite small), they imply that students were more likely to focus on issues of ability when they perceived a high performance-oriented class.

Regarding attributions of success to ease of task, the results showed that students in the high learning/low performance group scored significantly lower than students in the other three groups of goal perspectives. Similarly, in terms of success attributions to luck, the most important differences were the lower scores of either high or low perceived competence students in the high learning/low performance group than that of low perceived competence students in the remaining three groups. Despite the small or moderate differences found, these findings suggest that irrespective of students' perceived competence, when they perceive a high learning but low performance-oriented environment, they are less likely to make task or luck attributions.

This conclusion was further supported by findings regarding failure attributions given to task difficulty and luck. Students perceiving high learning and low performance goals made relatively weaker attributions of failure to task difficulty or luck than students perceiving high performance goals.

Since both task and luck ascriptions are external and usually considered uncontrollable and to be avoided (e.g., Weiner, 1985; Rudisill, 1989), the sum of these findings implies that perceptions of both high learning and low performance goals are the most promising for students' motivation and achievement.

A questionnaire developed by Eccles (Eccles, 1983; Midgley, Feldlaufer, & Eccles, 1989), measuring interest in the lesson and perceived usefulness of the lesson, was administered to all three samples (Papaioannou, 1994). Many studies have shown that these factors are strong positive predictors of achievement behaviours (e.g., MacIver, Stipek, & Daniels, 1991; Meece, Wigfield, & Eccles, 1990). Furthermore, the students from the first two samples responded to Harter's (1981) 'preference for challenge' scale from the 'Extrinsic versus Intrinsic Orientation in the Classroom Questionnaire'. All scales had been modified for the physical education lesson. The results showed that intrinsic motivation, interest in the lesson and perceived usefulness of the lesson were strongly associated with the two learning scales. By way of contrast, there were either no correlations or negative correlations among these three variables and the performance scales (see Table 12.2).

Because prior research has found that perceived competence is a positive predictor of both intrinsic motivation (e.g., Harter & Connell, 1984; Weiss, Bredemeier, &

Table 12.2 Correlations of Perceptions of Classes' Goals With Intrinsic Motivation, Interest in the Physical Education Lesson, and Perceived Usefulness of the Lesson

	Teacher-initiated learning orientation	Students' learning orientation	Students' competitive orientation	Students' worries about mistakes	Outcome orientation without effort
Intrinsic motivation	.32***	.44***	−.07*	−.09**	−.22***
Interest in the physical education lesson	.46***	.57***	−.01	−.06	−.13***
Perceived usefulness of the lesson	.45***	.59***	.02	−.02	−.12***

*p < 0.05   **p < 0.01   ***p < 0.001

Note. From *Students' Motivation in Physical Education Classes Which Are Perceived to Have Different Goal Perspectives* by A. Papaioannou, 1992, unpublished doctoral dissertation.

Shewchuk, 1986) and perceived importance of the task (e.g., Meece et al., 1990), hierarchical regression analysis was used in order to examine whether the perceived goal orientation could add further to perceived competence in the prediction of the aforementioned measures. Accordingly, the scores of the learning and performance scales were computed and added into the equation after students' scores on Harter's perceived physical competence scale. The results suggested that irrespective of perceived ability, perceptions of learning goals were strong positive predictors of intrinsic motivation in the lesson, interest in the lesson and perceived importance of the lesson. In contrast, perceptions of performance goals made a small negative contribution to the prediction of students' motivational patterns in physical education.

Developmental Differences in Motivation

Findings regarding developmental differences suggested that junior high school students (aged 13 to 15 years) perceived their classes as more learning oriented than senior high school students (aged 16 to 18 years) (Papaioannou, 1992). Moreover, the younger students had significantly higher scores than the older students on intrinsic motivation, interest in the lesson and perceived usefulness of the lesson (Papaioannou, 1992).

Nevertheless, results from analysis of covariance showed that if students in junior and senior high schools perceived their classes' learning orientation similarly, no difference (at least no considerable difference) would emerge in their intrinsic motivation, interest in the lesson or perceived importance of the lesson. It should be remembered here that results from two different studies did not find any difference between junior high school and senior high school students' dispositional goals (task and ego orientations) (Papaioannou & Duda, 1992). Hence, assuming that the curriculum is a major cause of differences between junior and senior high school students' perceptions of the learning environment, if teachers in senior high schools adopted the learning orientation in their classes that their colleagues in junior high schools do, older students would be intrinsically motivated to the same degree as the younger students. Thus these data seem to suggest that it may not be developmental differences beyond the age of 12 that make Greek students less intrinsically motivated in the physical education lessons, but the differences in the learning environment that affect their motivation negatively.

Perceived Class Goals and Related Variables

According to many theories of attitudes (e.g., Ajzen, 1988) and motivation (e.g., Bandura, 1986), intention is the major determinant of behaviour. Accordingly, the students from the third sample of 394 adolescents, in addition to LAPOPECQ, answered a series of questionnaires measuring intentions for involvement in all physical education lessons, intentions for high effort in all physical education lessons, perceived physical competence and dispositional goals in sport (task and ego orientation). The results (Papaioannou & Theodorakis, 1993) showed that both dispositional goals and perceived classes' goals increased the prediction of intentions beyond that accounted for by perceived competence.

For most theories of human motivation perceptions of control are major determinants of motivation and achievement (e.g., Ajzen 1988; Bandura, 1986; Harter & Connell, 1984). Following Ajzen's (1988) instructions, students' perceptions of control over involvement in all physical education lessons were measured in 394 adolescents (Papaioannou & Theodorakis, 1993). These students had already answered LAPOPECQ, the questionnaire measuring dispositional goals in sport, and Harter's (1982) measure of perceived athletic competence.

The results showed that, in addition to perceived competence, task orientation in sport and perceived learning goals added further to the prediction of perceived behavioral control. In contrast, there was no relationship between ego orientation or perceived performance goals and perceived behavioural control.

Interaction Between the Individual and the Environment

The correlations presented in Table 12.2 show the relationships of each student's total score on each scale of the LAPOPECQ and the three motivational variables. However, these coefficients reflect the combined effects of differences between physical education classes and individual differences in students' views within each class. In order to examine whether the above correlations reflect the effects of actual differences in the environment of the physical education classes or the effects of different perceptions within the same physical education classes, correlations were calculated between the class means (C) of each scale of the LAPOPECQ and the three motivational factors. The results shown in Table 12.3 suggest that, in most

Table 12.3   Correlations of Intrinsic Motivation, Interest in the Lesson, Perceived Usefulness of the Lesson, and Worries About Performance With Means of Classes' Goals (C) and Individual Differences Within Classes (I)

	Teacher-initiated learning orientation	Students' learning orientation	Students' competitive orientation	Students' worries about mistakes	Outcome orientation without effort
Intrinsic	(C) .23***	.26***	−.03	−.04	−.10***
motivation	(I) .24***	.37***	.06*	−.08**	−.20***
Interest	(C) .34***	.36***	−.02	−.03	−.11***
in the	(I) .36***	.48***	−.01	−.07**	−.11***
lesson					
Perceived	(C) .39***	.42***	.02	.03	−.11***
usefulness	(I) .33***	.46***	.02	−.03	−.09***
of the					
lesson					

$*p < 0.05$ $**p < 0.01$ $***p < 0.001$

Note. From *Students' Motivation in Physical Education Classes Which Are Perceived to Have Different Goal Perspectives* by A. Papaioannou, 1992, unpublished doctoral dissertation.

cases, the relationships described previously emerged between classes' mean score (C) on each scale of LAPOPECQ and the other constructs as well.

The next task was to examine the relationships between individual differences within classes and the three motivational variables. To this end, partial correlations were computed between the latter variables and children's perceptions of their classes' goal structure (I) after the variance due to class differences was removed (that is, the means of the classes in each scale of LAPOPECQ were the control variable). Again, each scale of LAPOPECQ showed similar relationships to the other self-related reports as the relationships described for the combined score of each scale of LAPOPECQ with the other self-related constructs.

In sum, these results imply that both between-class differences and within-class differences in the perceptions of classes' goals affect students' motivation. More generally, both situational and dispositional differences in goal perspectives seem to affect students' motivation and achievement.

Determinants of Student Perceptions of Class Goals

Because both between- and within-class differences in the perception of classes' goals affect students' motivation, it is quite important to discover the major determinants of these differences.

To the sample consisting of 394 students from 16 physical education classes with eight different physical education teachers (two classes from each teacher), in addition to LAPOPECQ, questionnaires measuring the following variables were administered: dispositional differences in task and ego orientation in sport, perceived physical competence, attitudes towards exercise, attitudes towards the students' physical education teacher and beliefs about physical education teachers in general (Papaioannou, 1992).

In addition, for each scale of LAPOPECQ two new variables were computed. The first variable was 'teacher' which, for each scale of LAPOPECQ, is the score of the two classes taught by the same teacher. This variable is supposed to measure teacher's contribution to the formation of students' perceptions of their classes' orientation. For example, in the case of the 'teacher-initiated learning orientation' scale, the variable 'teacher' is the mean of the scores on the 'teacher-initiated learning orientation' scale of the two classes belonging to the same teacher. The second variable was 'class' which, for each scale of LAPOPECQ, is the mean score of each class. This variable was created because it was assumed that in addition to the influence of the teacher, between-class differences might remain because of different types of classes taught by the same teacher.

Results implied that the particular teacher and the particular class (both of them represent between-class differences), as well as individual differences in attitudes towards exercise, task orientation in sport, attitudes towards the particular teacher, and beliefs about physical education teachers in general, were positive predictors of a learning orientation. In other words, the above variables determined the way that students perceived their classes' learning orientation.

Regarding the three performance-oriented scales, it was found that the variable 'teacher' and students' ego orientation were positive predictors. Further, perceived competence and attitudes towards the teacher were negative predictors of the 'students' worries about mistakes scale', and the attitudes towards exercise score was a negative predictor of 'outcome orientation without effort' scale.

These findings imply that both the teacher and the students from each particular class are responsible for the creation of the learning orientation of the class. Nevertheless, the within-class differences in the perception of classes' goals appeared to exceed between-class differences. These results question the overemphasis on the observation of teachers' behaviour observable in North American work on sport pedagogy. Further, they suggest that in addition to the teacher, many other factors determining individual differences in goals, attitudes and beliefs should be considered in the study of students' motivation and achievement (e.g., family, friends, media, etc.). Moreover, since many of the findings discussed here suggest that increased perceptions of learning-oriented classes have very positive effects on students' motivation, the most important practical implication of these findings is that teachers may wish to consider adopting a high learning orientation in their classes, and students should become more task oriented, have more positive attitudes towards their teacher and more positive views about teachers and school in general.

Overall, the implications of these findings for teachers, coaches, lecturers, parents, politicians, journalists and anyone who is interested in education, physical education and sport are the same: Create a learning-oriented environment in the class, team, or family; increase adolescents' task orientation in school and sport; strengthen students' positive attitudes and beliefs about their teachers, coaches and school in general. In sum, adopt the policy and behaviours that emphasise learning goals in school, in physical education and in sport contexts.

Determinants of Differences in Goal Perspectives Between Classes

In order to examine whether there were differences in the context of the lesson, in students' involvement in the lesson and in student-teacher interactions in physical education classes differing in goal perspectives, one class of each of eight physical education teachers was observed for three or four consecutive lessons (Papaioannou, 1993). In the study described earlier, two classes of each of these eight physical education teachers had responded to LAPOPECQ (394 students from 16 physical education classes). These answers were used to classify four teachers as having high learning-oriented classes (the classes' score on the learning scale was above the median), and four teachers as having low learning-oriented classes. Results revealed that there were large differences in the learning orientation of the classes taught by these two groups of teachers. Similarly, four teachers were classified as having high performance-oriented classes and four teachers as having low performance-oriented classes. The differences in the performance orientation of the classes taught by these two groups of teachers were also significant.

The observational tools used were the Cheffers Adaptation of Flanders's Interaction Analysis System (CAFIAS; Cheffers, Mancini, & Martinek, 1980) and Academic Learning Time in Physical Education (ALT-PE; Parker, 1989). With respect to the categories of ALT-PE, results revealed that more practice and technique but less game time was observed in high rather than in low learning-oriented classes (see Figure 12.1). Furthermore, in high learning-oriented classes students were more cognitively involved and exhibited less off-task behaviour than in low learning-oriented classes (see Figure 12.2). With regard to the categories of CAFIAS, results suggested that more teacher's verbal instruction and more teacher's verbal orders and directions were recorded in high than in low learning-oriented classes (see Figure 12.3).

The results from both observational systems imply that one very important feature of high learning-oriented physical education classes in Greece is the emphasis placed on instruction and skill development. This is evident from the higher proportion of time spent on skill practice and teaching issues of technique (as recorded by the ALT-PE), and the higher proportion of teacher's verbal instruction and teacher's verbal orders and directions (as recorded by CAFIAS) in high rather than in low learning-oriented classes.

With reference to performance orientation, the only difference from either ALT-PE or CAFIAS emerged in the CAFIAS category 'teacher's verbal orders and directions' which was higher in classes with high performance orientations than in low performance-oriented classes (see Figure 12.4). These results imply that in high

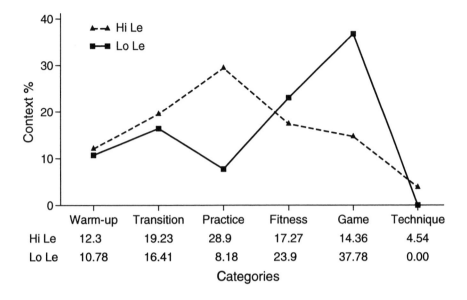

	Warm-up	Transition	Practice	Fitness	Game	Technique
Hi Le	12.3	19.23	28.9	17.27	14.36	4.54
Lo Le	10.78	16.41	8.18	23.9	37.78	0.00

Categories

Figure 12.1   High learning-oriented classes displaying more practice and technique-related behaviours, but less game-related activity, than low learning-oriented classes (Hi = high; Lo = low; Le = learning-oriented class).

Note. From *Students' Motivation in Physical Education Classes Which Are Perceived to Have Different Goal Perspectives* by A. Papaioannou, 1992, unpublished doctoral dissertation.

performance-oriented classes students were given less autonomy by their teachers than in low performance-oriented classes.

Overall, though the observational tools were not the most appropriate for assessing the classes' climate (I believe   that no quantitative observational tool can present an accurate picture of the climate of a class), large differences were observed between classes differing in achievement orientations. The most important were those between high and low learning-oriented classes because there is already a great deal of evidence suggesting that learning orientation is strongly associated with students' motivation. As the above findings suggest, the most prominent characteristic of high learning-oriented physical education classes in Greece is the emphasis on students' skill development. Further, these results imply that Greek teachers should not expect to increase students' motivation in the physical education lesson through the entertainment that the games offer. On the contrary, they can promote students' motivation by focusing their efforts on students' learning and by setting goals for skill and knowledge development. This does not necessarily imply that students should not play games during the physical education lesson. It does suggest, however, that an optimal balance should be adopted between the time devoted to skill practice and the time for playing games.

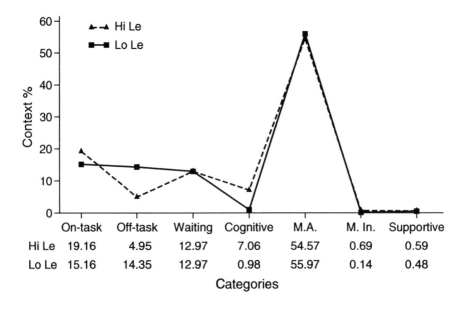

Figure 12.2 High learning-oriented classes displaying more cognitive involvement and less off-task behaviour than low learning-oriented classes (M = motor; A = appropriate; In = inappropriate; Hi = high; Lo = low; Le = learning-oriented class).

Note. From *Students' Motivation in Physical Education Classes Which Are Perceived to Have Different Goal Perspectives* by A. Papaioannou, 1992, unpublished doctoral dissertation.

Differences in Goal Perspectives Between Individuals

As has been suggested, perceived competence and dispositional differences in task orientation are positive predictors of student motivation. On the other hand, dispositional differences in ego orientation do not seem to affect motivation. Indeed, as can be seen in Table 12.4, for the sample consisting of 394 Greek students, intention for participation in all lessons was positively related to perceived competence but weakly related to ego orientation.

However, these relationships concern the whole sample. As I have argued elsewhere (Papaioannou, 1992), there is a hidden cost when we aggregate the data from different individuals and different situations. Moreover, as Nicholls (1989) suggested, students' perceived competence is a stronger predictor of students' motivation when students are ego involved rather than task involved. Accordingly, I divided the whole sample into four different groups: (a) students perceiving high-learning and low-performance goals, (b) students perceiving high-learning and high-performance goals, (c) students perceiving low-learning and high-performance goals and (d) students perceiving low-learning/low-performance goals. In each of these groups, the relationships among intentions for involvement in all physical education lessons and perceived competence and ego orientation were examined.

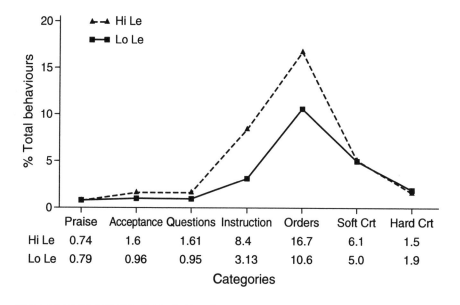

Figure 12.3   Differences in teacher behavior between high and low learning-oriented classes (Crt = criticism; Hi = high; Lo = low; Le = learning-oriented class).
Note. From *Students' Motivation in Physical Education Classes Which Are Perceived to Have Different Goal Perspectives* by A. Papaioannou, 1992, unpublished doctoral dissertation.

A stronger relationship was found between intention and perceived physical competence in the low-learning/high-performance group than in the high-learning/low-performance group. These findings support Nicholls's (1989) arguments that the role of perceived competence in students' motivation and achievement is more prominent when low learning and high performance goals are adopted. This is predictable because when low learning and high performance goals are adopted the main incentive for participation in the lesson is the demonstration of high ability. Hence, the lower the learning goals and the higher the performance ones, the more the high perceived ability students and the less the low perceived ability students intend to take part in the physical education lesson. Accordingly, if we want to maintain equality in educational and sport contexts (i.e., if we want to motivate all students irrespective of how able they are), these results suggest that both high learning and low performance goals should be adopted.

Further, there was a positive relationship between intention and ego orientation in the two low learning groups but almost a zero relationship in the two high learning ones. This is not an unpredictable finding because when students realise that they have no chance to improve their competence by taking part in the lesson an important reason that can possibly motivate them is the satisfaction deriving from demonstrating their abilities to others. On the other hand, the almost zero association between ego orientation and perceived learning goals implies that when the value of all students' improvement is stressed in the class, students cannot derive satisfaction

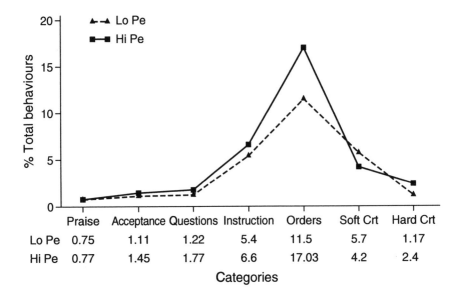

	Praise	Acceptance	Questions	Instruction	Orders	Soft Crt	Hard Crt
Lo Pe	0.75	1.11	1.22	5.4	11.5	5.7	1.17
Hi Pe	0.77	1.45	1.77	6.6	17.03	4.2	2.4

Categories

Figure 12.4 Differences in teacher behaviour in high and low performance-oriented classes (Crt = criticism; Hi = high; Lo = low; Pe = performance-oriented classes). *Note.* From *Students' Motivation in Physical Education Classes Which Are Perceived to Have Different Goal Perspectives* by A. Papaioannou, 1992, unpublished doctoral dissertation.

Table 12.4 Correlations Among Intention for Involvement in all Lessons and Perceived Competence and Ego Orientation in Groups Perceiving Different Goals

			INTENTION		
	Whole sample	High learning, low performance	High learning, high performance	Low learning, high performance	Low learning, low performance
Perceived competence	.34***	.21	.31**	.45***	.28*
Ego orientation in sport	.14**	.04	.04	.28**	.37***

*p < 0.05   **p < 0.01   ***p < 0.001
Note. From *Students' Motivation in Physical Education Classes Which Are Perceived to Have Different Goal Perspectives* by A. Papaioannou, 1992, unpublished doctoral dissertation.

by demonstrating their competence to others. Therefore, high ego-oriented students have no greater incentive than low ego-oriented students to take part in the class.

In sum, although the above results need replication with a larger sample and in different contexts, they suggest that when students perceive differently the goals that are salient in their classes (a difference due both to individual and situational differences), different incentives motivate them and different psychological mechanisms function. Moreover, they offer initial support to the argument that if we want to provide equal motivation for both high- and low-ability students, and to avoid the encouragement of ego orientation, both high learning and low performance goals should be adopted in physical education.

Goal Perspectives and Equality in Physical Education

Some issues about equality and goal perspectives were raised previously and a further elaboration will be attempted here. The focus of discussion is whether we can promote optimum motivation in children of all levels of ability and whether we can eliminate teachers' and students' differential behaviour towards high- and low-ability students. All findings reported below are based on the responses of 1,393 Greek students (Papaioannou, 1992).

Goal Perspectives and Motivation of Students With Different Sport Experiences

Using students' answers regarding their participation in out-of-school sport activities, four different groups were created: the first group was not currently involved in either recreational or organised sport activities on a regular basis (the word 'regular' was defined as participation in any kind of sport activity at least twice a week); the second group was involved in recreational sport activities only; the third group participated in organised sport only; the last group was involved in both recreational and organised sport activities.

Results (Papaioannou, 1992) suggested that students who were not involved in any physical activity in their out-of-school lives scored much lower in intrinsic motivation, interest in the lesson and perceived usefulness of the lesson than students with experience of organised sport. Nevertheless, after adjusting for differences in perceptions of learning goals and perceived competence, the differences in intrinsic motivation and perceptions of the lesson were not of particular importance. These findings suggest that no important differences would emerge in students' motivation as a result of their divergent sport experiences if they did not differ in terms of perceived sport ability and perceptions of learning goals.

It should be noted here that the differences in perceived classes' learning orientation among students with different sport experiences are most probably caused by dispositional differences in task orientation (e.g., Duda, 1989b). Thus, the sum of the above findings suggests that despite students' differences in sport experiences (and correspondingly in sport abilities), if students were involved in activities where perceptions of physical ability had no effects on their personal achievement (as previous findings showed, this is likely in a very high learning and very low performance oriented environment), dispositional task orientation would make the most important difference to their motivation.

Teachers' Differential Behaviour Towards High and Low Achievers

A well-known research area dealing with the issue of equality in education and physical education is that of self-fulfilling prophecies. Major reviews by Brophy (1983), Dusek (1985) and Martinek (1989) suggest that teachers' different behaviour towards high and low achievers affects their expectations for future success as well as future achievement itself.

Since a teacher's different behaviour towards high and low achievers focuses students' attention on issues of ability rather than how to master the task, a positive relationship should exist between performance orientation and teacher's different behaviour towards high and low achievers. When a performance goal is adopted what is most valued in the class is ability, and only students with high normative ability are rewarded. In contrast, when a learning goal is adopted in the class, the issue of normative ability is irrelevant and therefore incompatible with perceptions of different treatment of high and low achievers.

These hypotheses were tested using LAPOPECQ and a modified questionnaire developed by Weinstein (Weinstein, Marshall, Sharp, & Botkin, 1987) in order to measure students' perceptions of their teacher's treatment of high and low achievers (Papaioannou, in press). The latter questionnaire asked students how often their physical education teacher would treat a student who is very able in the manner described by 10 items. A similar question, with the same 10 items was used to measure the teacher's treatment of a student who is not very able. The score resulting from the difference of the two scales measured teachers' differential behaviour. In all 55 classes surveyed, this score indicated that teachers favoured high achievers.

As shown in Table 12.5, the two learning-oriented scales of the LAPOPECQ were positively related to teachers' treatment of low achievers and negatively related to perceptions of differential treatment. In contrast, the three performance-oriented scales were positively related to teachers' treatment of high achievers and positively related to perceptions of differential treatment. These findings suggest that in the physical education context, learning orientation is associated with sustaining equality whereas performance orientation is connected with maintaining inequality.

Students' Intrinsic Motivation and Anxiety
When Participating With High or Low Achievers

One of the most important criticisms that Nicholls (1989) and Dweck (1986) have made of other theories of achievement motivation, such as those of Atkinson (1964) and Weiner (1985), is that they are not applicable to the people who adopt high learning goals.

According to these achievement motivation theorists, students with high perceived ability have higher expectations of success and are therefore more motivated than

Table 12.5 Correlations Among Perceptions of Teacher's Treatment of High and Low Achievers and Classes' Motivational Orientations

	Teacher-initiated learning orientation	Students' learning orientation	Students' competitive orientation	Students' worries about mistakes	Outcome orientation without effort
Teacher's treatment:					
High achievers	−.06	.01	.20**	.26**	.21**
Low achievers	.32**	.31**	.01	−.04	−.02
Differential treatment score	−.27**	−.20**	.15**	.22**	.17**

**p < 0.001

Note. From *Students' Motivation in Physical Education Classes Which Are Perceived to Have Different Goal Perspectives* by A. Papaioannou, 1992, unpublished doctoral dissertation.

students with low perceived ability. Nicholls (1989) argues that this is true when students are concerned about their ability relative to others. However, when students are instead particularly interested in increasing their competence, perceived ability should be irrelevant to their motivation.

Achievement motivation theorists predict that students expect failure when they are forced to become involved in activities that are too difficult for them (e.g., play against more able opponents) and consequently experience anxiety. According to goal perspectives theory, this is true when low learning goals are adopted. However, when the student's goal is improvement in competence, he or she does not worry about failure even when confronted with very difficult tasks.

In order to test these assumptions, in addition to LAPOPECQ and to Harter's (1982) perceived physical competence scale, 1,393 Greek students responded to a modified version of a questionnaire used by Csikszentmihalyi and Larson (1984). Students were asked how they feel when they play or exercise with classmates who are not very able in sport. Factor analysis revealed two stable factors measuring intrinsic motivation and anxiety. A similar factor solution emerged from students' responses to the same questionnaire measuring students' intrinsic motivation and anxiety when they play with classmates who are very good in sport (see Papaioannou, 1992).

Figure 12.5 shows results regarding the intrinsic motivation scores of students extremely high and extremely low in perceived competence for play or exercise with either high or low achievers when they perceive their classes as extremely

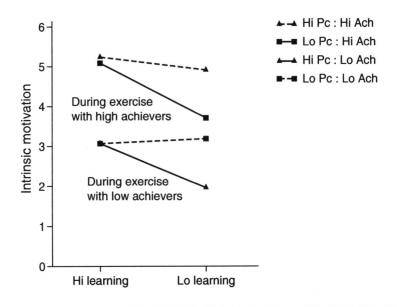

Figure 12.5 Interaction between intrinsic motivation, perceived competence, and perceptions of learning goals (Hi = extremely high; Lo = extremely low; Ach = achievers; Pc = perceived competence).

high or extremely low learning oriented. These results imply that all students are more motivated to play with high rather than low achievers. This finding is hardly surprising because almost every theory of motivation stresses the importance of challenging tasks to the increase of students' intrinsic motivation. For all students, play or exercise with high achievers is a more challenging task than play or exercise with low achievers.

Nevertheless, the most interesting result was an interaction between intrinsic motivation, perceived competence and perceptions of learning goals (see Figure 12.5). This finding implies that when the students' class is perceived as extremely high learning oriented, there is no difference at all between extremely high and extremely low perceived competence students' intrinsic motivation during play or exercise with either high or low achievers. In contrast, when students perceive their class as extremely low learning oriented and play or exercise with high achievers occurs, there is a substantial drop in extremely low perceived competence students' intrinsic motivation but no decrease at all in extremely high perceived competence students' motivation. Moreover, when the class is perceived as extremely low learning oriented, and when exercise or play with low achievers takes place, there is a substantial decrease in extremely high perceived competence students' intrinsic motivation but no decrease at all in extremely low perceived competence students' motivation. Further examination of the results revealed that all the aforementioned differences were very large (see Papaioannou, in press).

The prediction that perceived competence determines students' motivation was true when students perceived low learning goals. However, when extremely high learning goals were adopted, students' intrinsic motivation did not differ in accordance with their perceptions of ability. In other words, when learning goals are strongly emphasised in the class, both high and low perceived competence students prefer difficult, challenging tasks (i.e., play or exercise with high achievers) because this is most likely to lead to further improvement in competence. Importantly, although students may differ in perceptions of competence, they are equally motivated to engage in difficult tasks. Similarly, students are equally motivated during play with low achievers despite the vast differences in their perceptions of competence. Thus, once again, these data suggest that if we want to provide optimum motivation for students of all levels of ability, a learning orientation should be adopted.

Regarding the assumptions about anxiety, the most interesting result was an interaction between anxiety and perceptions of learning goals (see Figure 12.6). The results imply that when play or exercise with high achievers occurs, all students perceiving extremely low learning-oriented classes are more anxious than students perceiving extremely high learning-oriented classes. In contrast, during play or exercise with low achievers, all students perceiving extremely low learning goals are less anxious than students perceiving high learning goals. To express the previous results in a different way, although there is no difference in students' anxiety during

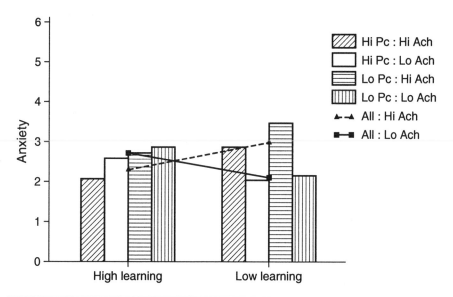

Figure 12.6   Interaction between anxiety and perception of learning goals (Hi = high; Lo = low; Ach = achievers; Pc = perceived competence; All = all students).
Note. From *Students' Motivation in Physical Education Classes Which Are Perceived to Have Different Goal Perspectives* by A. Papaioannou, 1992, unpublished doctoral dissertation.

play or exercise with either high or low achievers when they perceive their classes as high learning oriented, students perceiving extremely low learning-oriented classes are much more anxious when they play with high rather than low achievers.

Overall, when low learning goals are adopted, students perceive the task as relatively difficult (i.e., play or exercise with high achievers), and they experience higher levels of anxiety than when they perceive the task as relatively easy. This is true for either extremely low or extremely high perceived competence students. On the other hand, when high learning goals are adopted there is no difference in students' anxiety due to the level of task difficulty. Students experience the same level of anxiety irrespective of whether they face difficult or easy tasks.

In sum, if we want to increase all students' motivation and to decrease aversive emotions like anxiety, the adoption of high learning goals in the class is recommended. Importantly, taking into consideration the possibility that in the future people will exercise with their wives, husbands, children and friends rather more, that is with people who will have different abilities from their own, the adoption of high learning goals appears to be the best way to motivate adolescents to adopt exercise as a lifestyle habit.

Conclusion

At the beginning of this chapter three general issues were addressed: how we can maximise students' motivation and achievement in the lesson; how we can sustain equality in the class; how we can learn about these issues by adopting a research methodology that considers the interactional effects of dispositional and situational differences.

Overall, the findings presented suggest that the adoption of a high learning- and low performance-oriented environment is the most appropriate in order to maximise motivation and achievement for children of all levels of ability.

With regard to teachers of physical education, it is proposed that they should direct their efforts to how to increase all students' skill learning and not focus on individual differences in athletic ability; spend more time for skill practice, knowledge about skill or fitness development and health promotion; support students' autonomy; consider students' mistakes as a guide for further learning and not as an indication of low ability; provide challenging, difficult tasks for all students; and stress the values of personal progress and cooperation.

References

Ajzen, I. (1988). *Attitudes, personality, and behavior*. Milton Keynes, England: Open University Press.

Ames, C. (1984a). Competitive, cooperative and individualistic goal structures: A motivational analysis. In R. Ames & C. Ames (Eds.), *Research on motivation in education: Vol. I. Student motivation* (pp. 177-207). New York: Academic Press.

Ames, C. (1984b). Achievement attributions and self-instructions under competitive and individualistic goal structures. *Journal of Educational Psychology*, **76**, 478-487.

Ames, C., & Archer, J. (1988). Achievement goals in the classroom: Students' learning strategies and motivation processes. *Journal of Educational Psychology*, **80**, 260-267.

Atkinson, J. (1964). *An introduction to motivation*. Princeton, NJ: Van Nostrand.

Bandura, A. (1986). *Social foundations of thought and action: A social cognitive theory*. Englewood Cliffs, NJ: Prentice Hall.

Brophy, J. (1983). Research on the self-fulfilling prophecy and teacher expectations. *Journal of Educational Psychology*, **75**, 631-661.

Burton, D. (1989). Winning isn't everything: Examining the impact of performance goals on collegiate swimmers' cognitions and performance. *Sport Psychologist*, **3**, 105-132.

Cheffers, J., Mancini, V., & Martinek, T. (1980). *Interaction analysis: An application to nonverbal activity* (2nd ed.). St. Paul, MN: Amidon.

Csikszentmihalyi, M., & Larson, R. (1984). *Being adolescent*. New York: Basic.

Darst, P., Zakrajsek, D., & Mancini, V. (1989). *Analyzing physical education and sport instruction*. Champaign, IL: Human Kinetics.

Duda, J. (1989a). The relationship between task and ego orientation and the perceived purpose of sport among male and female high school athletes. *Journal of Sport and Exercise Psychology*, **11**, 318-335.

Duda, J. (1989b). Goal perspectives, participation and persistence in sport. *International Journal of Sport Psychology*, **20**, 42-56.

Duda, J. (1992). Motivation in sport settings: A goal perspective approach. In G.C. Roberts (Ed.), *Motivation in sport and exercise* (pp. 57-91). Champaign, IL: Human Kinetics.

Duda, J. (1993). Goals: A social cognitive approach to the study of motivation in sport. In R.N. Singer, M. Murphey, & L.K. Tennant (Eds.), *Handbook of research on sport psychology* (pp. 421-436). New York: Macmillan.

Duda, J., Olson L., & Templin T. (1991). The relationship of task and ego orientation to sportsmanship attitudes and the perceived legitimacy of aggressive acts. *Research Quarterly for Exercise and Sport*, **62**, 79-87.

Dusek, J. (Ed.) (1985). *Teacher expectancies*. Hillsdale, NJ: Erlbaum.

Dweck, C. (1986). Motivational processes affecting learning. *American Psychologist*, **41**, 1040-1048.

Dweck, C. (1991). Self-theories and goals: Their role in motivation, personality, and development. In R. Dienstbier (Ed.), *Nebraska symposium on motivation—1990, Vol. 38: Perspectives on motivation* (pp. 199-235). Lincoln: University of Nebraska Press.

Dweck, C., & Leggett, E. (1988). A social-cognitive approach to motivation and personality. *Psychological Review*, **95**, 256-273.

Eccles, J. (1983). Expectancies, values, and academic behaviors. In J. Spence (Ed.), *Achievement and achievement motivation* (pp. 75-146). San Francisco: Freeman.

Fraser, B. (1986). *Classroom environment*. London: Croom Helm.

Gill, D., Gross, J., & Huddleston, S. (1983). Participation motivation in youth sports. *International Journal of Sport Psychology*, **4**, 1-14.

Griffins, P. (1989). Gender as a socializing agent in physical education. In T. Templin & P. Schempp (Eds.), *Socialization into physical education: Learning to teach* (pp. 219-233). Indianapolis: Benchmark Press.

Harter, S. (1981). A new self-report scale of intrinsic versus extrinsic orientation in the classroom: Motivational and informational components. *Developmental Psychology*, **17**, 300-312.

Harter, S. (1982). The perceived competence scale for children. *Child Development*, **53**, 87-97.

Harter, S., & Connell, J. (1984). A model of children's achievement and related self-perceptions of competence, control, and motivational orientation. In J. Nicholls (Ed.), *Advances in motivation and achievement* (Vol. 3, pp. 219-250). Greenwich, CT: JAI Press.

Heckhausen, H., Schmalt, H.Z., & Schneider, K. (1985). *Achievement motivation in perspective.* Orlando, FL: Academic Press.

Jourden, F., Bandura, A., & Banfield, J. (1991). The impact of conceptions of ability on self-regulatory factors and motor skill acquisition. *Journal of Sport & Exercise Psychology,* **13**, 213-226.

Kelley, B., Hoffman, S., & Gill, D. (1990). The relationship between competitive orientation and religious orientation. *Journal of Sport Behavior,* **13**, 145-156.

Kirk, D. (1990). Defining the subject: Gymnastics and gender in British physical education. In D. Kirk & R. Tinning (Eds.), *Physical education, curriculum and culture: Critical issues in the contemporary crisis* (pp. 43-66). London: Falmer Press.

MacIver, D., Stipek, D., & Daniels, D. (1991). Explaining within-semester changes in student effort in junior high school and senior high school courses. *Journal of Educational Psychology,* **83**, 201-211.

Martens, R. (1979). From smocks to jocks. *Journal of Sport Psychology,* **1**, 94-99.

Martinek, T. (1989). The psycho-social dynamics of the pygmalion phenomenon in physical education and sport. In T. Templin & P. Schempp (Eds.), *Socialization into physical education: Learning to teach* (pp. 199-217). Indianapolis: Benchmark Press.

Meece, J., Wigfield, A., & Eccles, J. (1990). Predictors of math anxiety and its influence on young adolescents' course enrollment intentions and performance in mathematics. *Journal of Educational Psychology,* **82**, 60-70.

Midgley, C., Feldlaufer, H., & Eccles J. (1989). Student/teacher relations and attitudes toward mathematics before and after the transition to junior high school. *Child Development,* **60**, 981-992.

Morrow, J. (1991). Physical education's role in the public health: Review and commentary. *Research Quarterly for Exercise and Sport,* **62**, 123-162.

Murray, H.A. (1938). *Explorations in personality.* New York: Oxford University Press.

Nicholls, J. (1989). *The competitive ethos and democratic education.* Cambridge, MA: Harvard University Press.

Papaioannou, A. (1990). *Goal perspectives, motives for participation, and purposes of P.E. lessons in Greece, as perceived by 14 and 17 year old pupils.* Unpublished master's thesis, University of Manchester, England.

Papaioannou, A. (1992). *Students' motivation in physical education classes which are perceived to have different goal perspectives.* Unpublished doctoral dissertation, University of Manchester, England.

Papaioannou, A. (1993, June). Characteristics of physical education classes differing in achievement orientation. In S. Serpa, J. Alves, V. Ferreira, A. Paula-Brito (Eds.) *Proceedings of the 8th World Congress of Sport Psychology,* 799-803. Lisbon: International Society of Sport Psychology.

Papaioannou, A. (1994). The development of a questionnaire to measure achievement orientations in physical education. *Research Quarterly for Exercise and Sport,* **65**, 11-20.

Papaioannou, A. (in press). Differential perceptual and motivational patterns when different goals are adopted. *Journal of Sport and Exercise Psychology.*

Papaioannou, A., & Duda, J. (1992). *Goal perspectives and motives for participation in physical education among adolescent Greek students.* Manuscript submitted for publication.

Papaioannou, A., & Theodorakis, Y. (1993). *Attitudes, values and goals: A test of three models for the prediction of intention for participation in physical education lessons.* Manuscript submitted for publication.

Parker, M. (1989). Academic Learning Time—Physical Education (ALT-PE), 1982 revision. In P. Darst, D. Zakrajsek, & V. Mancini (Eds.), *Analyzing physical education and sport instruction* (pp. 195-205). Champaign, IL: Human Kinetics.

Rudisill, M. (1989). Influence of perceived competence and causal dimension orientation on expectations, persistence, and performance during perceived failure. *Research Quarterly for Exercise and Sport,* **60**, 166-175.

Seifriz, J.L., Duda, J., & Chi, L. (1992). The relationship of perceived motivational climate to intrinsic motivation and beliefs about success in basketball. *Journal of Sport and Exercise Psychology,* **14**, 375-391.

Stern, G.G., Stein, M.J., & Bloom, B.S. (1956). *Methods in personality assessment.* Glencoe, IL: Free Press.

Weiner, B. (1985). An attributional theory of achievement motivation and emotion. *Psychological Review,* **92**, 548-573.

Weinstein, R., Marshall, H., Sharp, L., & Botkin, M. (1987). Pygmalion and the student: Age and classroom differences in children's awareness of teacher expectations. *Child Development,* **58**, 1079-1093.

Weiss, M., Bredemeier, B., & Shewchuk, R. (1986). The dynamics of perceived competence, perceived control, and motivational orientation in youth sport. In M. Weiss & D. Gould (Eds.), *Sport for children and youths* (pp. 89-101). Champaign, IL: Human Kinetics.

13

CHAPTER

Psychology of the Sport Spectator

Pavel Slepicka

CZECH REPUBLIC

Sport spectating is an important social phenomenon. Through viewing sports, spectators can alter the rhythm of a mundane working day. In all historical periods audiences have created their heroes and idols, identifying with them and experiencing their success. Spectators come to the sports ground for the intense emotional experience, excitement and suspense of the match or contest. They also frequently influence the participants of the sport itself.

Enjoyment of the game has always been a strong motive for attending a sporting event. But under the influence of social and situational conditions, common experiences have resulted in negative spectator reactions, sometimes quite serious. The history of sport spectating is accompanied by the paradox of keeping and increasing spectators' interest while managing crowds and preventing hooliganism and violence. These problems still persist and have become the object of interest of sociology, psychology and other branches of the sport sciences (Young, 1991). In writing this chapter I have used both sociological and psychological viewpoints.

For the practice of sport, the most pressing problems are those connected with the negative reactions of spectators watching sport contests. This chapter presents psychological findings concerning the problems of sports spectators and outlines data gained from research at sports grounds in the Czech and Slovak Republics.

The chapter is divided into several relatively independent sections. The first deals with a social psychological view of the visitors to sports grounds. The second part deals with the problem of the spectator as an individual. The third part is concerned with the problem of group behaviour, aggression and violence. In all parts, sociopsychological viewpoints are used when analysing the influence of the spectators' behaviour on sports performance and when explaining the motivation, the attendance rate, and the experience and reactions of spectators. I make here a tentative move towards presenting problems of sports spectating in the context of psychology.

Social Psychological Aspects of Sport Spectators

From a social psychological point of view, it is important to emphasize the influence of the spectator's closest social environment on his or her experience at the sports ground. The reactions of other spectators to dynamic changes and turns in the course of the sport spectacle significantly influence the spectator's actual experience. Also of some significance is the emotional state of the spectator on arrival at the ground and whether this can be changed. The spectator's experience is influenced by a number of sources, and the role of a spectator is one of the multitude of social roles that any sport spectator plays in the course of life. Taking the social psychology point of view lets us study sport spectators as people acting short social roles. This viewpoint joins sociological and psychological approaches, which I consider necessary in analysing spectator responses to sport.

The role of a spectator is influenced not merely by the social environment of the sport itself but also by the overall social environment, including the family and occupational environments. These connections are shown in Figure 13.1.

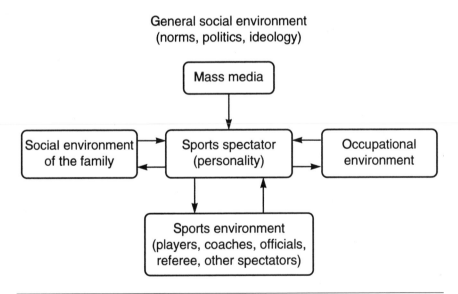

Figure 13.1   Social background of sport spectator.
Note. From *Spectator Reflection of Sports Performance* (p. 15) by P. Slepicka, 1991, Prague, Czechoslovakia: Carolinum. Copyright 1991 by Publishers Carolinum. Reprinted by permission.

The role of a sport spectator is not an isolated phenomenon; it constitutes a network of mutual connections and dependences, a whole based on the social system of the given society.

Modern sport offers a wide variety of sports, each of which creates its own 'fan'. Fans of these different sports do not necessarily represent a homogeneous unit. They differ from one another in their interests, in the intensity of their interests and in their knowledge of the relevant sport (Olivova, 1975).

Sport fans differ in how they express their enjoyment. Football (soccer) fans differ from basketball fans; athletics (track) and tennis fans differ in how they express enjoyment, and they also differ in knowledge, behaviour and interest in the result of the match. One thing common to all sport fans is the desire to spend some of their leisure time watching the sport (Slepicka, 1990). Sport gives them a chance to get away from everyday life and its troubles and difficulties.

To explain spectators' reactions and experiences it is necessary to know what kind of people constitute the audience at matches and whether sport fans of different sports have different social characteristics.

To answer these questions we investigated the social characteristics of sport spectators in the Czech and Slovak republics between 1986 and 1990. The research comprised 6,370 first division spectators, including 3,420 football fans, 856 spectators of basketball, 832 of handball, 832 of volleyball, 200 of athletics and 200 spectators of tennis (Slepicka, 1991).

The social and demographic characteristics studied included the age composition of the spectators, educational level, type of occupation, family status, structure of interests, and participation in active sports and games.

Age

We did not find marked differences in the age distribution of spectators of the different sports (Slepicka, 1991). Football spectators, however, were younger, the highest frequency being the age-group 15 to 18 years (see Figure 13.2).

Young people (22 years and under) constituted a large group of sport spectators. This is relevant to spectators' experience of the contest and their direct reactions to it. Generally it may be said that young people are usually more spontaneous, identifying with sports idols more easily and being more influenced by the atmosphere among the crowd.

Gender

An important factor influencing the social climate among spectators, and their response to the course of the game, might be considered to be the presence of women. Figure 13.3 shows the percentages of male and female spectators at the various sports (Slepicka, 1991).

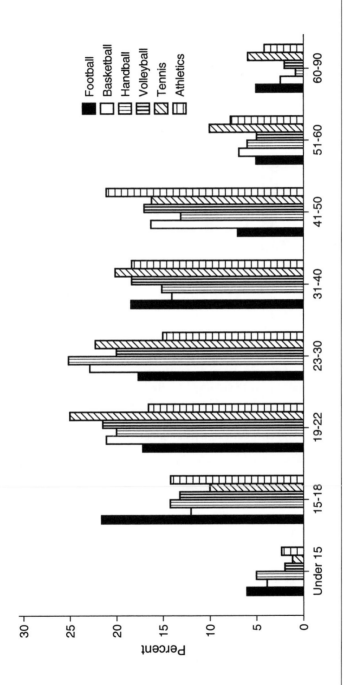

Figure 13.2 Age distribution of sport spectators.

Note. From *Spectator Reflection of Sports Performance* (p. 19) by P. Slepicka, 1991, Prague, Czechoslovakia: Carolinum. Copyright 1991 by Publishers Carolinum. Reprinted by permission.

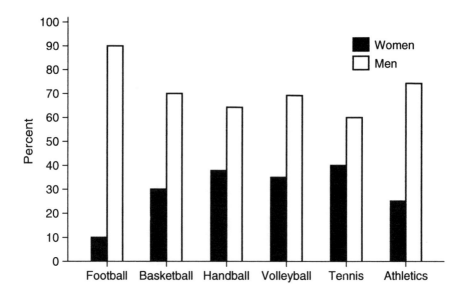

Figure 13.3 Percentage of men and women among spectators of various sports.
Note. From *Spectator Reflection of Sports Performance* (p. 22) by P. Slepicka, 1991, Prague, Czechoslovakia: Carolinum. Copyright 1991 by Publishers Carolinum. Reprinted by permission.

The smaller percentage of women among sport spectators may be attributed mainly to their smaller amount of free time. Women still carry the larger share of domestic responsibilities in most families. Also, women's household duties are more structured and systematic and cannot be shifted in time so easily.

More free time is one reason why spectators of sports contests are mostly men, but there can also be other significant factors, such as men's greater interest in dangerous situations and violence.

Education and Occupation

A very important social characteristic of sport spectators relevant to the spectator experience is education and occupation. Because education is usually a condition of having a certain occupation, the two factors overlap. People with more education may have more demanding and time-consuming jobs than those with less education. The educational composition of fans of different sports is shown in Figure 13.4 (Slepicka, 1991).

The various kinds of sport differ in the educational composition of spectators. The greatest differences are those between football fans and the fans of other sports. This finding is consistent with previous research by Ruchar (1972) and Stollenwerk (1988).

The level of education of football spectators is also associated with age. Many football spectators are under 18, when their university education has not yet started.

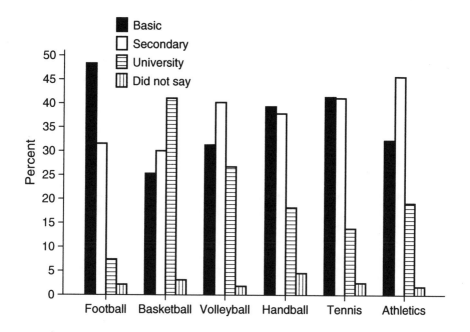

Figure 13.4   Highest achieved education of spectators of various sports.
Note. From *Spectator Reflection of Sports Performance* (p. 24) by P. Slepicka, 1991, Prague, Czecho-slovakia: Carolinum. Copyright 1991 by Publishers Carolinum. Reprinted by permission.

Some authors state that football spectators have traditionally been at a lower educational level and that this is connected with the social origins of the game (Messing & Lames, 1992; Olivova 1975).

Although young people prevail among sport fans, spectators can be divided into two groups. First, there are young spectators: apprentices, students, manual workers, who react more readily to the events of the game and the crowd atmosphere. The second group are adult spectators with a higher educational level. These spectators are mostly married, and they have formed certain social and personal relations in their family and occupation. This polarisation according to age, education and profession is a clearly observable characteristic of the sport audience. Other authors (e.g., Dunning, Murphy, & Williams, 1988) have also considered similar social characteristics of the sport spectators to be important.

Motives and Involvement

Sport fans also differ in the structure of their interests. The majority of Czech and Slovak sport fans (68%) state that sport spectating is an important way to spend their free time. Visiting and watching sport competition evokes a strong emotional response and survives a long time after the match. Football fans especially seem to have this tendency, 29% of them stating that the defeat of their team annoyed them at least until the next match, and some of the fans (19%) stating that the defeat annoyed them for a longer time and that it influenced their behaviour in their family and occupation. Only 15% of spectators of the other sports admitted to such a persistent influence (Slepicka, 1991).

Sport spectators' own sport activity may be a significant influence on their experience and reactions at the sports ground. In their own sport history spectators not only acquire a range of motor skills but also gain information about training and competing. We may suppose that these experiences will be reflected in their evaluation of sport contests and can influence spectators' enjoyment and reactions. Lack of sport participation may have an influence on negative spectator reactions. Research studies (Slepicka 1990; Smith 1983) show that hardly any of the young rowdy spectators are active in some kind of sport. Therefore we think it is important to present the results of a survey of the share of active sport participants among sport spectators (Slepicka, 1991; see Figure 13.5).

These results show that on average about one-third of sport spectators have been active in sport. The greatest share of nonparticipants is among football spectators, with the highest number of participants in basketball and athletics. However, the differences between sports were not great.

To understand spectator reactions it is necessary to pay attention to the most frequent reasons that bring spectators to sport matches. Empirical data (Cechak & Linhart, 1986) show the greatest spectator interest is in games. In such activities, there are elements attracting spectator interest, such as drama, unpredictability of the result and dynamic changes in the course of the event.

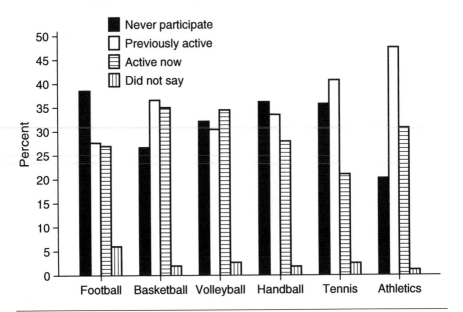

Figure 13.5   Sports activity of spectators of various sports.
Note. From *Spectator Reflection of Sports Performance* (p. 26) by P. Slepicka, 1991, Prague, Czechoslovakia: Carolinum. Copyright 1991 by Publishers Carolinum. Reprinted by permission.

Interest in Sports Events

If we consider interest in sport to be one of the main factors bringing spectators to the arenas, we should bear in mind also the factors influencing the nature, origin and formation of interests. Interests are mostly formed in childhood and adolescence.

If a lasting and deep interest in active sports participation develops in childhood and lasts until the age of about 18 years, it is possible that this will develop into spectator interest. However, interests are the expression of certain dispositions. Their formation and content are related to the subject's social experience, which is often a starting point of educational influences on children's interests. Children of parents who have an active interest in sport are much more likely to develop an interest in sport. In addition, children regularly watching disorderly spectator reactions at sports grounds may start wishing that they too could take an active part in such actions (Melnick, 1986).

A lasting and deep interest in sport is typical of regular sports spectators. Most spectators, however, attend irregularly. What makes these irregular spectators attend sports events? Are they attracted by the expected drama of sport or by the fame of the participating athletes? Are they influenced by the press and television publicity about the matches and races or by outstanding performances? These and similar questions express the most frequent reasons that attract irregular spectators.

Not all spectators, however, could give positive answers to these questions. Certain spectator groups are brought to sports grounds by other reasons (such as starting fights, conflicts with other spectators) that are not always connected with the actual sport itself. These are motivations of only a small group of spectators, but they influence the enjoyment and safety of others, as well as the atmosphere of the event.

When comparing team games with, say, athletics, there appear to be differences in the reasons for attending. In athletic contests the main attraction is often famous athletes in particular track and field events. Stollenwerk (1988) reports that 10% of spectators of track and field contests attend because of a certain athlete and 5% because of interest in a certain event.

The spectator appeal of team games lies in the possibility of identification with one of the teams, the possibility of supporting one's team, in the drama and the resulting excitement and thrill of the game, the possibility of psychological relaxation or maybe in the personalities of players. For the sake of comparison we present a survey (Slepicka, 1991) of the most important reasons spectators give for attending sports events (see Figure 13.6).

It is important to know the basic reasons why spectators go to see a match. Knowledge of these reasons enables, to a certain extent, prediction of their behaviour during a match. This is especially true of the spectators whose reasons do not directly relate to the sports activity itself, such as to be in the group, to find excitement or to provoke other spectators. These people are potential sources of socially unacceptable behaviour (Robins, 1988). The percentage of such spectators in the terraces affects the probability of an outbreak of more extensive undesirable reactions. The danger of such an outbreak is reduced when a higher percentage of spectators come to the match because of their previous sport activity, the individualities of the players or a wish to see a high-quality sport performance.

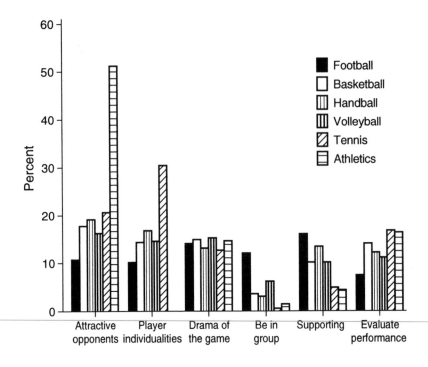

Figure 13.6 Spectators' most important reasons for attending various sports.
Note. From *Spectator Reflection of Sports Performance* (p. 34) by P. Slepicka, 1991, Prague, Czecho-slovakia: Carolinum. Copyright 1991 by Publishers Carolinum. Reprinted by permission.

The Spectator as an Individual

To understand spectator reactions it is necessary to realise that emotions have a multidimensional base, including physiological, neurological and biochemical aspects. Emotions have a mobilising effect on the individual. The dynamics of activation and the sudden increase or decrease of activation level of the spectator depend on external factors (the course of the sport event, the reactions of other spectators, etc.), but also on internal factors based on the spectator's personality and motivation.

Empirical findings (Machac, Machacova, & Hoskovec, 1985) confirm that the anticipated result of the activity being viewed is of great importance. If the match or contest develops according to the spectator's notions, the emotional experience is usually stimulating. On the other hand, emotions can also be negative. If the spectators consider the situation of their own team or athlete to be hopeless, they may experience feelings of hopelessness, depression, apathy and loss of interest in the sports contest itself. Such a situation may cause an increase in emotional feeling in the spectator. Managing this emotion is a complicated matter, depending on the individual. Generally we may say that the situations that are not significant for a person do not generate much of a response. But we have to realise that people differ a great deal in their resistance to emotion.

An important factor is the mental state of the spectator on arrival at the sports ground, especially the spectator's mood (Miksik, 1983). Moods distort the spectator's view and evaluation of the event. Also emotions of higher intensity than mood states affect spectators in a similar way. The spectator who feels the emotion of rage, accompanied by an impulse to behave aggressively is not able to observe and evaluate the event and the surroundings objectively. Strong emotions influence other psychological processes, such as perception, thoughts, memory, attention and volition. The intense emotional state of the spectator establishes a predisposition to a conflict between spectator and environment.

Spectators' emotions may also be greatly increased by stress. Stress may be brought about by any stimuli that occur during the spectator's presence at the sports ground. Adaptation to this stress will depend on the level of resistance and type of temperament of the spectator. Spectators' behaviour in a stressful situation is also connected with the momentary mutual action of their rational and emotional sides. If the emotional aspect prevails a change in the rational process takes place in the evaluation of reality. There appears to be a tendency to make hasty, direct and immediate evaluations, and draw one-sided conclusions. With the increase of emotion comes an increase in suggestibility. This results in an empathy with emotional experiences of others. This increased suggestibility then decreases the rationality of thinking (Miksik, 1983). The absence of rationality, which appears in spectators in various measures, results in concentration on situational stimuli and on development of impulsive behaviours. The spectator, under the influence of emotions, gives up control over behaviour and produces involuntary and uncontrolled behaviour, which is not intentionally regulated. Such behaviour may lead to a partial solution to the stressful situation (e.g., running away from a dangerous spot) but very often it results in a purposeless solution.

Sport spectators may be regarded as individuals who, to a certain extent, intentionally seek strong emotional experiences. For many of them the experience is a considerable psychological load. Sometimes the spectator is not able to cope. It is important to understand what the spectators themselves consider to be the cause of their intense emotional experience. Another important question is what kind of behaviour the spectators are going to produce in these situations. Every person experiences a number of frustrating situations when it is necessary to suppress reactions. This can contribute to the increase of aggression. Smith (1983) confirmed that seeing an event with elements of aggression has a relieving (cathartic) effect.

Not every sports fan watching a sport contest experiences a positive cathartic effect, however. Social influences that affect the fan may be important and the social atmosphere of the sport (McPherson, 1976). The sports fan who has established a system of socially accepted norms of behaviour, who is well adapted to the social conditions and adequately satisfies her or his social needs is probably able to identify with an athlete in an aggressive sport but with a controlled reaction.

Positive Emotions

Looking more closely at emotional experiences in sports spectating, it is evident that some events or aspects induce positive emotional experiences and some induce negative experiences. Presumably, what the spectators appreciate most about sports events is likely to induce positive emotional experiences (see Figure 13.7) (Slepicka, 1991).

As shown in Figure 13.7, the effort the participants exerted in their best possible performance is the aspect most frequently appreciated. Also, the technique of movements of the participants is highly appreciated.

The atmosphere on the terraces is also important, particularly on the terraces of football grounds and is probably connected with social norms which permit a wide range of spectator reactions. If these reactions do not become disorderly they are accepted by the other spectators and positively experienced by a number of them.

Spectators have their favourite sport and favour certain teams. They also have their sports heroes and idols. Their experience of the events involving their favourite teams or participants are often intense. Because they favour one of the teams beforehand, their views are narrowed and aimed at the victory of their own team.

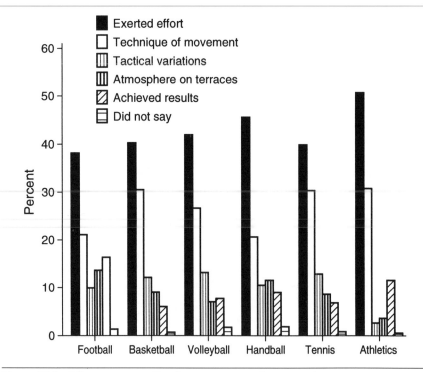

Figure 13.7   What spectators of various sports appreciate most about sports events.
Note. From *Spectator Reflection of Sports Performance* (p. 51) by P. Slepicka, 1991, Prague, Czechoslovakia: Carolinum. Copyright 1991 by Publishers Carolinum. Reprinted by permission.

Their experience in the course of the event differs from the experience of an unbiased spectator (Kershaw, 1988).

Not every fan can be successful in the real world, but through identification with a successful sport participant the spectator may achieve a feeling of success. This is the 'compensatory function' of identification (Helus, 1983). The mechanism of 'envious' identification leads to a substitution for the fan by a famous performer who has fame, authority and admiration; everything that is the object of the fan's desire. This self-realisation in the world of sport, even if in a substitutory form, causes a reduction of the fan's unfulfilled wishes.

Spectators' Views of Their Individual Reactions

The results of our research (Slepicka, 1991) presented in Figures 13.8 and 13.9 show how the spectators themselves describe their reactions to unpunished rough action against a home player and an away player. The graphs present reactions in selected situations typical of sports.

In the sports enabling direct physical contact between players, when a rough action against a home player remains unpunished a minority of spectators react with a loud protest (verbally, with whistling) (see Figure 13.8). Only a small minority react by throwing an object onto the field of play, and it is apparent that such a

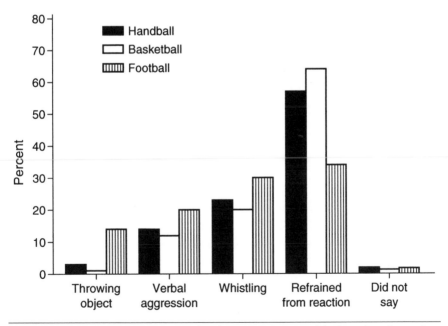

Figure 13.8 Reactions of spectators of various sports to unpunished rough action against a home player.
Note. From *Spectator Reflection of Sports Performance* (p. 63) by P. Slepicka, 1991, Prague, Czechoslovakia: Carolinum. Copyright 1991 by Publishers Carolinum. Reprinted by permission.

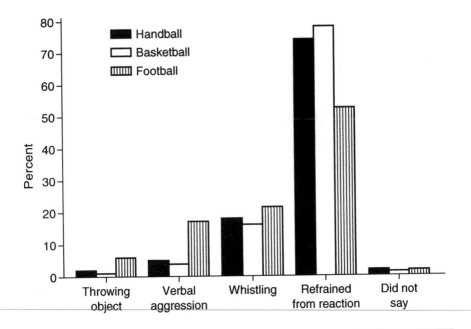

Figure 13.9   Reactions of spectators of various sports to unpunished rough action against an away player.
Note. From *Spectator Reflection of Sports Performance* (p. 63) by P. Slepicka, 1991, Prague, Czechoslovakia: Carolinum. Copyright 1991 by Publishers Carolinum. Reprinted by permission.

reaction is much more frequent at football matches. This suggests that the social norms observed on football terraces are more tolerant of spectator reactions than the norms valid in other sports.

There is also an interesting comparison between the spectator reactions to unpunished rough action against a home player and similar action against an away player. The spectators react to such action against an away player much less with verbal reactions, whistling or throwing an object than they do when the action is against a home player (compare Figure 13.8 and Figure 13.9).

Spectator-Athlete Interaction

Spectators' behaviour significantly involves the process of imitation. The principle of imitation is considered to be part of observation learning. In this connection it is important that the spectator be able to see what the player is doing or what is happening to the player (Smith, 1983). Sport offers visually presented behaviour patterns that are often very effective in creating imitation. The spectator may imitate the player's behaviour either intentionally after previously considering the consequences of the imitation, or unintentionally.

The effect of imitation is greater if the player has high prestige. It is necessary to keep in mind that the spectator may be influenced by the player, either directly on the terraces or by long-term changes in some personality factors. It depends on the intensity of the influence of the observed and imitated object and on the maturity of the spectator's personality.

When considering imitation by spectators, some psychological findings of prior experimentation on imitation learning provide a useful context. There is the classic work of Bandura and Walters (1963), who showed the connection between the imitation of aggressive acts and the previous frustration of the imitator. Then they showed that watching aggressive acts results in imitating such behaviour (learning), but also triggers previously learned cues or behaviors. There was also an important finding that watching quiet or apathetic behaviour by the model lowers the possible aggression resulting from previous frustration of the spectator. Other research (Miksik, 1983) showed clearly that previously suppressed behaviour can be activated again when the model displays aggressive behaviour publicly without negative consequences.

Decisions made by referees also play a vital role. Inconsistent punishment of roughness, dangerous play or provocations of the opponent supply conditions for the activation of similar reactions among the spectators. In general, any individual who in the role of the model successfully breaks certain rules, also breaks the experienced spectator's resistance against the tendency to behave in the same way. Conversely, consistent punishment of any breach of the rules by the model reinforces this resistance (Netik, Neuman, & Vecerka, 1990).

In these situations there does not have to be total and exact imitation of the player's conduct. The spectator does not behave in the same way as, for example, a football player whose aggressive actions the spectator watches, because the spectator is in rather a different situation. But the spectator behaves in the way that he or she thinks corresponds with the player's attitudes. Thus it is the attitude that is often copied. In rough play against the opponent, or in aggressive verbal reactions against the referee, the spectator may see the expression of the player's attitude. Some spectators then imitate the attitude to the referee or to the opponent's fans. The expression of the imitated attitude in behaviour depends on situational circumstances.

Effects of Spectators on Sport Performance

In psychology, the influence of other people on the behaviour of individuals is termed social facilitation. It has been verified that the mere presence or absence of spectators at any sports match creates different sociopsychological conditions for sports performance (Menscikova, 1985). The influence of the presence of spectators on sports performance is a factor often recognised in practice. Research carried out for the most part in laboratory conditions does not, however, yield clear results (Zajonc, 1986). These studies compared the performance without another person present with the same subject's performance in the presence of other people.

Besides studies aimed at general issues of social facilitation, there have also been studies of the influence of sport spectators on performance. One of the first of such studies was by Laird (1923) who found that offensive remarks of spectators lowered the level of motor skills. Conversely, Karpovich (1965) found that performance increased with positive, supportive spectator reactions. Singer (1975) claimed that neither positive nor negative spectator reactions influenced the performance of well-prepared athletes.

Such research shows that the situation is not so simple that performance would improve automatically when spectators are present. Sometimes improvement occurs under the influence of spectators, but sometimes performance deteriorates. How is this apparently contradictory influence of spectators on performance to be explained? One possible explanation is the changes in the activation of the performer under the influence of the presence of spectators. Another is the possible qualitative differences in spectators' influence (agreement, support, disagreement, protest). Yet another is the differences in skill of the players.

The explanation based on the changes in the activation level of the performer holds that sport spectators increase the arousal or activation level of the participants. Moderate increase may improve performance but further increases may raise activation to a level no longer optimal for good performance and may lead to decreased performance (Slepicka, 1991).

The negative reactions of spectators can have considerable importance if the player competes at the opponent's ground. Such reactions are not only negative verbal shouts or commentaries, but also whistling accompanying each action of the player, mocking, mimicry or calling out the player's name. All this brings about an increase in negative psychological stress, directly affecting the quality of performance.

The studies discussed so far show that there can be a connection between spectator reactions and some aspects of activities of both an individual and a whole team. But it cannot be definitely claimed that positive behaviour (supporting, cheering) will act positively in every situation and that negative (antisocial) behaviour will only act negatively.

The Crowd and Group Behaviour

From the point of view of psychology it is not fruitful to study spectator reactions as the reactions of an individual spectator isolated from the behaviour of other spectators or the social environment. An adequate psychological explanation must take these factors into account. On a general level, it is possible to distinguish three types of mutual influence of individuals on the resultant form of social behaviour (Miksik, 1977). The first type is the influence of social convention, such as norms, customs and traditions. It is difficult to study spectator reactions only from the viewpoint of personality traits and situational conditions. It is necessary also to take into account the normatively expected forms of behaviour of the spectator. If spectators have not mastered the behaviour expected in the role of sport spectator, they may either act inadequately or ignore the accepted social norms completely.

In the course of their development, various sports have established norms valid for the spectator, a kind of spectator tradition for each kind of sport. The social environment in which the sport originated had a dominating influence.

The norms valid for the behaviour of spectators are not precisely formulated; they have the form of 'what is done' and 'what is not done'. An example of such a spectator norm is that the spectator should refrain from throwing various objects onto the area of play. Observing this norm, however, depends on several circumstances. It depends on the nature and form of punishments and measures for not keeping to the norm. The reactions of the officials (organisers) are also important because unchecked transgression of these norms strengthens the tendency to observe or not to observe them (Mann, 1979).

The second type of mutual influence on spectators is that of group behaviour, of which at least two basic conditions are of interest. The first one is usually regarded as the existence of the relations of mutual dependence between the members of the group. The behaviour of one member influences the behaviour and activities of any other member. The second condition is the existence of a common set of opinions, values and norms, obligatory for every member of the group, that regulate behaviour. This group ideology is developed and reinforced during common activities and becomes a typical feature of the group, differentiating it from other groups.

The third type of mutual influence of spectators is mass behaviour. According to Miksik (1977), mass behaviour is non-institutionalised (not controlled by any norms and there are no stable ties between the members). It is also a situationally determined behaviour of a group of people subjected to common mass influence of situational variables, which produce extreme psychological load.

Sport spectators are often subjected to the influence of such situational variables. But the behaviour of the spectators who are in such situations cannot be explained only on the basis of such conditions. The spectator's experience and behaviour can differ under the same situational conditions, whether the spectator is alone in these conditions, or inside a large social group. The reactions may also be different according to what kind of people the subject experiences the situation with. In these cases there is a specific quality and intensity of experience and behaviour, which are determined by how the group accepts the given situation, experiences it and reacts to it.

Emotional processes are influenced by the reactions of other spectators. This is the basis of 'emotional infection', which so often appears on the terraces. There is also a considerable influence on volitional processes, where the increased suggestibility of people on the terraces and the possible emotional infection lead to the tendency to follow.

Any activity of a spectator group develops from a certain core. In the background of these actions there are predisposed and motivated individuals or groups who begin the action and later on disappear and become anonymous. Any member of a spectator group is, in conditions of strong emotion, especially receptive to the influence of interaction. A spectator group has, to a large extent, a selective effect on the experience and behaviour of individual spectators.

The people in sports grounds comprise a collection of individuals who depend on one another, although previously there may have been little connection between them. The effect of 'mass character', may be temporarily to homogenise them into a social group. Such homogenisation is mostly based on intense experience of a sports fight, or similar situation provoking strong emotional reactions.

A principal feature of mass spectator behaviour is that there are no previously established relations and social norms. Occasional communication between the spectators is determined by the influence of the situation. Therefore we cannot predict in what form behaviour is going to appear (Krivohlavy, 1986).

Another important feature is the situation itself. Usually it arises suddenly, episodically on certain occasions, for example, an unjust decision of the referee or offensive shouts of the opponents' fans. The concentration of fans face to face around a certain centre of attention, common emotional tuning and a reduction of rational inhibitions create conditions for the realization of commonly directed actions.

Manifestations of mass behaviour do not occur at every match and every sports ground. Most often social interactions go on according to accustomed traditions and norms. Nevertheless, the norms valid for the behaviour in sports grounds are more permissive than, for instance, the norms of behaviour at the theatre. At most sports there is non-adaptive behaviour of a few individual spectators. Their reactions are the result of specific personality dispositions and stress situations the individual has experienced. Spectators groups may also behave in a socially unacceptable manner.

Under the conditions inducing mass behaviour there is a certain reduction in inhibitions that affects the behaviour in current interaction with other people. Let us remember in this connection that interpersonal behaviour is generally determined by some type of mutual interaction. Rationality also plays a significant role, especially from the point of view of the prevailing values. Behaviour and mutual relations are connected in an effort to satisfy certain needs and fulfil certain aims. The purposeful mutual influence results in a common effort to achieve the aims of the group, whether they can be achieved with the help of others or whether other people are a hindrance.

Spectator Aggression and Violence

Violence among some sport spectators is a widely-recognised problem. Psychologists have identified a number of causes of aggression. First, it is necessary to distinguish aggression brought about by an emotional experience climaxing in the feeling of rage or fear, and instrumental aggression, which has no emotional basis and is rational and purposeful. Sources of aggression must also be considered. One source is 'aggressive tuning', or one's sensitivity to situational stimuli, a personal factor predisposing a person to aggressive behaviour. Another source, the feeling of anxiety, also influences sensitivity to situational stimuli. Aggression may result from a combination of these sources with the experience of a situation that directly excites rage. Aggression may also be indirectly provoked by an obstacle that hinders the achievement of a goal and brings about the feeling of frustration.

Psychologists claim that frustration may lead to aggression and that aggression may be caused by frustration (Buss, 1961; Papica, 1975). Smith (1983) has hypothesised that deprivation (e.g., social deprivation) grows into frustration, which may then produce aggression. Research findings (e.g., Berkowitz, 1969), indicate that frustration and rage establish conditions for the development of aggression, although there are also other reactions to frustration.

Aggressive reactions of sport spectators could arise from frustration with the match or from frustration generated prior to entering the sports ground. The reactions that follow are characterised by little adaptation to the situation.

Attacks on people or verbal attacks on the referee, players or organisers are the most typical direct manifestations of aggression among spectators. Sometimes indirect aggression occurs, for example, when spectators attack an empty bus in which the opponents arrived at the match. This type of aggression appears when the aggression cannot be turned against the stimulus that created it. Indirect aggression may produce nonsensical and, for the wider social environment, incomprehensible attacks upon the sports ground facilities, demolition of vehicles or breaking of shop windows. These reactions have the effect of a cathartic outlet. They release the feeling of rage or fear when the true object of aggression is inaccessible.

Frequently so-called postponed aggression occurs, often among football spectators. When the aggression cannot be expressed immediately, the response is suppressed and the aggression is postponed (Machac, Machacova, & Hoskovec, 1985). However, it may appear later. Such a situation is frequent among 'enemy fan groups', who are in separate parts of the grounds and cannot show aggression against the other group directly. They have to suppress their aggression to a 'more suitable' time and place. They will show the aggression when meeting other fans outside the sports ground, in the bus or at the next match.

Spectators' behaviour, therefore, is influenced by their personalities and modified and enriched by the social environment and the prior processes of socialisation. An important question is to what extent a spectator is able to resist the stimuli related to the emotional tension of a match, and to what extent he or she has the ability of rational evaluation and thinking. The spectator's personality, and the quality of prior socialisation, as well as the momentary reinforcement of postponed aggression (a reinforcing factor might be, for example, a spectator's emotional ties to the social group), all directly influence the stress experienced.

Conclusion

This chapter has shown how complex the phenomenon of sport spectating is from a psychological point of view. It has pointed out the sources of spectators' emotions and reactions. It has also pointed to the fact that spectators' reactions to sport performance are influenced by social conditions, by the dynamism of situational changes in the sports arena and by the personality of the spectator (Slepicka, 1993).

Presentation of social demographical characteristics of Czech and Slovak sport spectators illustrates that sport spectators are likely to be conditioned by their social surroundings. Knowledge of social background is very important, because although there have been efforts at social integration there have also been tendencies to assert national identities. Both these tendencies are reflected in sport spectating. Large groups of spectators can travel throughout Europe and their different social, national and political orientation influence their behaviour to a high degree. Sport spectating can become a significant phenomenon in modern Europe. In addition to socio-demographic factors, personal dispositions for aggressive behaviour can be activated by situational circumstances.

In the limited space available in this chapter it is not possible to discuss all psychological aspects of sport spectating. Sport contests attended by spectators are so dynamic that to describe them totally is very difficult. This area calls for further systematic attention to sport spectating from the point of view of psychology. Only further systematic research comparing studies can produce sufficient information to develop methods of influencing sport spectators that might reduce spectator problems and increase spectator comfort and enjoyment.

References

Bandura, A., & Walters, R.H. (1963). *Social learning and personality development*. New York: Holt.

Berkowitz, L. (1969). Simple views of aggression: An essay review. *American Scientist*, **57**, 372-383.

Buss, A.H. (1961). *The psychology of aggression*. New York: Wiley.

Cechak, V., & Linhart, J. (1986). *Sociology of sport*. Prague, Czechoslovakia: Olympia.

Dunning, E., Murphy, P., & Williams, J. (1988). *The roots of football hooliganism*. London: Routledge.

Helus, Z. (1983). *Psychological problems of socialisation*. Prague, Czechoslovakia: SPN.

Karpovich, P.V. (1965). *Physiology of muscular activity*. Philadelphia: Saunders.

Kershaw, T. (1988). The supporters' view. In J. Williams (Ed.), *Proceedings of conference on football in the 1990s* (pp. 44-46). Leicester, England: University of Leicester.

Krivohlavy, J. (1986). *Conflicts among people*. Prague, Czechoslovakia: Avicenum.

Laird, D.A. (1923). Changes in motor control and individual variations under the influence of razzing. *Journal of Experimental Psychology*, **6**, 236-243.

Machac, M., Machacova, H., & Hoskovec, J. (1985). *Emotions and efficiency*. Prague, Czechoslovakia: SPN.

Mann, L. (1979). Sports grounds viewed from the perspective of collective behaviour. In J.H. Goldstein (Ed.), *Sport, games and play: Social and psychological viewpoints* (pp. 337-371). Hillsdale, NJ: Erlbaum.

McPherson, B.D. (1976). Consumer role socialisation: A within-system model. *Sport Science*, **2**, 144-154.

Melnick, M.J. (1986). The mythology of football hooliganism: A closer look at the British experience. International Review for the Sociology of Sport, **1**, 1-21.

Menscikova, A.L. (1985). Spectators and the influencing personality of sportsmen. *Theory and Practice of Physical Culture*, **16**, 5-7.

Messing, M., & Lames, M. (1992, July). *Comparative study of spectators in different sports*. Paper presented at the Olympic Scientific Congress, Benalmadena, Málaga, Spain.

Miksik, O. (1977). *Psychology of group behaviours*. Prague, Czechoslovakia: SPN.

Miksik, O. (1983). *Psychology of resistance*. Prague, Czechoslovakia: SPN.

Netik, K., Neuman, J., & Vecerka, K. (1990). Problems of criminality among youth. *Psychology and Psychopathology of the Child*, **1**, 53-58.

Olivova, V. (1975). *People and games*. Prague, Czechoslovakia: Olympia.

Papica, J. (1975). The aggressive reply to experimental frustration in the groups. *Czechoslovak Psychology*, **5**, 412-428.

Robins, D. (1988). Youth and football in the inner-city. In J. Williams (Ed.), *Proceedings of conference on football in the 1990s* (pp. 22-26). Leicester, England: University of Leicester.

Ruchar, M. (1972). *The problems of psychic and behaviour of the sport spectator*. Prague, Czechoslovakia: Olympia.

Singer, R. (1975). *Motor learning and human performance*. New York: Macmillan.

Slepicka, P. (1990). Sport spectators from social psychological aspects. *Acta Universitatis Carolinae Gymnica*, **26**, 5-22.

Slepicka, P. (1991). *Spectator reflection of sports performance*. Prague, Czechoslovakia: Carolinum.

Slepicka, P. (1993). Personality characteristics of sports spectators and violence in terraces. In S. Serpa, J. Alves, V. Ferreira, & A. Paula-Brito (Eds.), *Proceedings of the 8th World Congress of Sport Psychology* (pp. 757-761). Lisbon, Portugal: Universidade Tecnica de Lisboa.

Smith, M.D. (1983). Violence and sport. Toronto, ON: Butterworths.

Stollenwerk, H. (1988). A close eye on track and field spectators: An empirical analysis. *New Studies in Athletics*, **6**, 27-36.

Young, K. (1991). Sport and collective violence. *Exercise and Sport Sciences Reviews*, **19**, 539-586.

Zajonc, R.B. (1986). Social facilitation. In D. Cartwright & A. Zander (Eds.), *Group dynamics* (pp. 63-73). New York: McGraw-Hill.

IV
PART

RESEARCH ISSUES AND FUTURE DIRECTIONS

In addressing specific themes and topics in this book it is important not to lose sight of issues associated with method and future directions.

Gershon Tenenbaum and Michael Bar-Eli provide a comprehensive critique of trends in the research literature (see chapter 14). They conducted a computer literature search and provide an excellent overview of trends. In addition, they discuss issues of research method that exercise and sport psychologists should be aware of. Their own extensive research experience, often using methods deemed unconventional in exercise and sport psychology (e.g., Rasch and Bayesian approaches), provides the basis for a stimulating and thought-provoking chapter.

Exercise and sport psychologists need to become more aware of different research paradigms and not just discrete methods. Although this point has been made by some in the sport psychology literature, other disciplines seem to be more aware of the deeper issues involved than exercise and sport psychology. For example, it is not just the difference between 'quantitative' and 'qualitative' methods that is the issue here. Whether one adopts a positivist, interpretive or critical paradigm will be determined by the research questions to be answered as well as the ontological and epistemological assumptions associated with the research process. Ontological assumptions are those associated with the nature of existence and the social world we live in. Hence in the scientific paradigm often adopted in exercise and sport psychology, we assume that the social setting is 'real' and made up of 'hard' facts that can be observed and measured.

The epistemological assumptions are those associated with knowledge and the nature of knowledge. In the positivist paradigm such assumptions are centred on the notions of objectivity and dualism. Dualism refers to the separation of mind from the world.

A second issue for exercise and sport psychologists is that we should consider broadening the methods adopted to study the often complex behaviours in question. Although a greater awareness of more qualitative methods is evident in exercise and sport psychology, we also need to consider many other issues, such as the use of case studies, life histories, observational techniques, conversation analysis, etc.

A final methodological issue is the need for more cultural and cross-cultural research. This point is axiomatic given the nature of this textbook and has been made repeatedly elsewhere in this volume.

Additionally, it would be informative to make comparisons, through theoretical or descriptive research, between the physical activity domain and other settings. For example, motivational theories related to children in physical education could easily be compared with classroom settings. Given the importance of some personal and situational cues in physical activity settings which may not appear elsewhere, such as physical effort or physical self-disclosure, a comparison across settings might be informative.

Paul Kunath's commentary on future directions (chapter 15) does not adopt the traditional research review style. Instead, he draws on vast personal experience in international sport psychology and sport science to give his own insight into future issues for our field. I welcome this approach. As a former President of FEPSAC, Dr Kunath is well-placed to review the European scene.

14

CHAPTER

Contemporary Issues in Exercise and Sport Psychology Research

Gershon Tenenbaum
Michael Bar-Eli

ISRAEL

To discuss contemporary issues and postulate future directions in the domain of exercise and sport psychology, one should (a) examine from an historical perspective what has been done in this domain until now, and (b) hypothesise which trends in related domains may influence sport psychology in the future. To satisfy the first requirement, an extensive review of literature in the field of sport psychology has been performed. The state of the art is reviewed in the first section. To satisfy the second requirement, we hypothesise that the most influential trends that will draw the attention of researchers in exercise and sport psychology, will be closely related to integration of biology and psychology (i.e., psychophysiology), cognitive perspectives, health and action-related theories. Psychophysiology advances our knowledge of the relationship between arousal state and motor performance in various tasks. Cognitive components such as attention, memory, concentration, anticipation, problem solving and decision making have been studied extensively in psychology. In sport psychology, our understanding of how knowledge structures are developed is still limited. Also, psychological health benefits related to physical exercise are not sufficiently understood, and much work is still required to arrive at sound conclusions. Action theory, which has been given much attention in Europe, may contribute greatly to the understanding of the integration between cognition, emotion, motivation and organisation of motor behaviour.

All these lines of research should be incorporated in more appropriate methodological designs and measurement devices to advance sport psychology research.

Current Issues in Exercise and Sport Psychology

For a historical review of the field, the Sport Information Resource Center (SIRC) computerised data base (updated until June, 1991) was used to search for descriptors representing most of the issues in sport psychology. We have broken down this search into three time periods: 1975-1980, 1981-1985 and 1986-1991. Furthermore, the search was broken down into three types of publications: basic, intermediate and advanced. The descriptors were broken down by type and year of publication and are presented in Table 14.1.

Psychological variables such as 'motivation', 'attribution', 'arousal', 'anxiety', 'personality' and 'aggression' were very common issues for research in the past. Reviewing the number of publications from 1975-80 to 1986-91 indicates a substantial decrease (55.5%) in publications on personality (47.0% decrease in advanced publications) and aggression (45.5% total and 57.1% in advanced), a smaller drop in publications on anxiety (21.1%) and practically no publications on motivation. The number of publications on arousal also decreased (34.6% total and 42.0% advanced). These trends are even more dramatic, since the number of relevant scientific journals (basic, intermediate and advanced) has increased substantially in the last 5 to 10 years.

The number of publications related to cognition increased (38.7% total and 9.2% advanced), but this increase was most pronounced in 1981-85 (81.7% total and 61.8% advanced). Problem solving and decision making (within the cognitive domain) were not published extensively in the sport psychology literature through the years. Psychological selection of talented youth for sport is a topic on which the number of publications has grown. Despite the low number of publications, the advanced literature has increased substantially on this topic (from 12 to 32 and 31, respectively—158.3%). Both advanced and total publications on social psychology in sport have decreased with time (37.1% and 34.0% respectively), although advanced publications on leadership have remained stable. Health, physical fitness and wellness have gained much attention through the years, and the number of basic, intermediate and advanced publications has increased dramatically (225.2%, 252.9% and 108.9% respectively).

A neglected field is sport psychology in the educational system. Only 26 publications from 1975 to 1991 were advanced articles, an additional 17 being basic and 18 intermediate. Throughout the period, there were 1,396 publications on computers and sports, but only 12 of them were in sport psychology! It seems as though sport psychology is much behind other sport disciplines such as biomechanics, motor learning/control/development, exercise physiology and sports medicine in applying computerised hardware and software in investigations.

Table 14.1　Publications in Sport Psychology by Type and Year of Publication, 1975–June, 1991

| Descriptor | Year | Type of publication | | | |
		Basic	Intermediate	Advanced	Total
Cognition	1975–80	4	13	76	93
	1981–85	9	37	123	169
	1986–91	6	40	83	129
Problem solving	1975–80	19	9	16	44
	1981–85	12	17	13	42
	1986–91	16	4	11	31
Decision making	1975–80	63	51	77	191
	1981–85	39	48	48	135
	1986–91	38	32	67	137
Perception	1975–80	66	103	294	463
	1981–85	45	103	346	494
	1986–91	26	67	248	341
Perception & psychology	1975–80	3	8	11	22
	1981–85	1	16	20	37
	1986–91	3	5	18	26
Selection of talented youth	1975–80	16	23	12	51
	1981–85	48	59	32	139
	1986–91	61	63	31	155
Social psychology	1975–80	34	92	97	223
	1981–85	55	95	102	252
	1986–91	37	49	61	147
Leadership	1975–80	141	97	82	320
	1981–85	151	105	78	334
	1986–91	124	55	79	258
Health, physical fitness, wellness	1975–80	111	85	79	275
	1981–85	239	222	125	586
	1986–91	361	300	165	826
Sport psychology in schools	1975–80	3	10	10	23
	1981–85	12	6	6	24
	1986–91	2	2	10	14
Motivation	1975–80	284	208	298	790
	1981–85	336	330	337	1003
	1986–91	274	204	280	758
Attribution	1975–80	1	11	82	94
	1981–85	2	14	66	82
	1986–91	2	11	49	62

(continued)

Table 14.1 *(continued)*

| Descriptor | Year | Type of publication | | | |
		Basic	Intermediate	Advanced	Total
Arousal	1975–80	11	21	69	101
	1981–85	19	26	58	103
	1986–91	8	18	40	66
Anxiety	1975–80	118	104	200	422
	1981–85	64	100	221	385
	1986–91	27	78	228	333
Personality	1975–80	212	215	389	816
	1981–85	73	160	281	514
	1986–91	65	92	206	363
Aggression	1975–80	40	54	119	213
	1981–85	39	53	75	167
	1986–91	42	23	51	116
Computer	1975–80	112	65	156	333
	1981–85	316	141	119	576
	1986–91	260	112	115	487
Computer & psychology	1975–80	1	1	—	2
	1981–85	3	1	1	5
	1986–91	1	4	—	5
Coaching & psychology	1975-80	193	91	49	333
	1981–85	78	88	21	187
	1986–91	76	47	20	143
Measurement	1975–80	84	212	716	1012
	1981–85	167	293	706	1166
	1986–91	101	165	627	893
Measurement	1975–80	4	16	23	43
& psychology	1981–85	1	12	5	18
	1986–91	1	0	7	8
Method	1975–80	355	540	1111	2006
	1981–85	726	851	1107	2684
	1986–91	174	346	437	957
Method &	1975–80	12	27	59	98
psychology	1981–85	5	31	34	70
	1986–91	2	9	12	23
Culture	1975–80	118	135	133	386
	1981–85	35	83	87	205
	1986–91	44	82	49	175
Cross culture	1975–80	19	30	51	100
	1981–85	2	13	30	45
	1986–91	11	24	46	81
Motor skills	1975–80	143	418	898	1459
	1981–85	128	361	786	1275
	1986–91	77	289	491	857

Note. Data from SIRC data base.

Another neglected field was psychological issues in coaching. Most of the publications in this field were basic and intermediate (573) and only a few were advanced (90).

Measurement and research methods were investigated extensively in all the domains of sports, but ignored dramatically in sport psychology (a total of 35 and 105 advanced publications respectively in 17 years!). Unique methods and techniques are required to measure psychological variables in the sport domain appropriately. Psychological tools designed for other domains are insufficient for sport psychology. More innovative methodologies and tools are required to advance the field of psychology within sport and exercise settings. Finally, cultural and cross-cultural issues have not been given the attention they deserve, despite their importance. It is possible that several publications appeared in the sport sociology literature, but publications on cross-cultural issues in sport psychology are rare.

In this section, we focus on four issues which in our opinion have not yet been satisfactorily investigated within the framework of sport psychology, yet have substantial potential for future research. Starting from the 'classical' arousal-performance relationship, we shall discuss briefly the premises of psychophysiological research (see also chapter 8). Then we shall turn our attention to the cognitive approach, which has revolutionised general psychology, but has not yet done so in sport psychology, despite the recent relative increase in cognitive-oriented investigations in our field (see chapters 10-12). Then the status and future of exercise and health psychology will be considered (also see Part I of this book). Finally, we shall describe Action Theory, which has been given particular attention in European sport psychology and which may have substantial potential for future research, mainly from an integrative point of view.

Psychophysiology

Motor performance has been found to be affected by the psychological arousal state of the athlete (Gill, 1986; Landers & Boutcher, 1986). More specifically, the Inverted-U-Hypothesis (Klavora, 1977; Sonstroem & Bernardo, 1982), claimed that optimal performance is associated with an optimal arousal state, and any deviation from this arousal state negatively alters performance (Sonstroem, 1984).

Intense levels of arousal are frequently accompanied by high anxiety, which is detrimental to motor performance (see, for example, the 'staircase effect'; Cratty, 1989, p. 72). Early theories of anxiety accounted for individual differences in performance by the presence or absence of task-irrelevant responses in subjects' behavioural repertoire (e.g., Sarason, Mandler, & Craighill, 1952). Cognitive-attentional anxiety theory (Wine, 1980, 1982) conceptualises anxiety primarily in terms of cognitive and attentional processes aroused in evaluational settings. According to this approach, cognitive anxiety misdirects attention from task-relevant cues to task-irrelevant self-evaluation or social evaluation cues. Although originally related to test anxiety, this theory applies to other situational states as well (Carver & Scheier, 1988).

Though studies on anxiety and performance have been published extensively in the literature, the inverted-U relationship between performance and arousal has not been consistently established (see chapter 7). In the past, the failure to establish such a relationship was attributed to factors such as the multidimensionality of anxiety, as well as to the situation in which anxiety is evoked. Towards the beginning of the 1990s, the relationship between arousal and performance was still not completely clear (Jones & Hardy, 1990; Landers, 1989). However, some recent scientific developments have advanced its understanding. One substantial contribution in this regard is the taking of psychophysiological measures while athletes perform motor skills.

In the past, arousal was measured by various physiological variables, such as heart rate (HR), galvanic skin response (GSR), systolic blood pressure (SBP), breathing rate and depth, and additional techniques were used as indicators of the sympathetic and parasympathetic nervous systems' arousal state. Unfortunately, no mathematical relationship has been found between these variables. Furthermore, they have not been found to correlate with subjective feelings of the subjects in arousal-evoking situations (Morrow & Labrum, 1978).

A recent publication by Barratt (1987) in which a reformulation of Ashby's personality model (1960) was introduced, may broaden the scope of human behaviour theory. In essence, the model depicts a closed-loop system of an adaptive nervous system. It consists of four categories: biological (the brain nervous system), behavioural, environmental and cognitive. Each of these categories contains its own schemes. These four components are related by a general feedback (FB) loop, as well as by inner separate loops to the brain. Thus, any behaviour should be analysed through integrative concepts, taking into account cognitive, environmental, behavioural and neurological capabilities. Similar ideas were introduced by Action Theory.

Cognitive Perspective

In the cognitive psychology of sport, participants are viewed as active organisms who search, filter, act selectively, organise and process information (Straub & Williams, 1984).

Most sports necessitate an ongoing perceptual analysis, since the perceptually varying situations create an infinite number of problems demanding a solution. The participant's reaction is a visible result of a previous internal plan. The reaction is an indicator of a performance judged later on qualitative and quantitative criteria, but the inherent factors that led to this reaction depend on the perceptual-cognitive system.

Information Processing Models

The psychology of information processing suggests cognitive models describing the flow of information perceived by receptors and stages through which this information passes until a reaction occurs or a decision is made (Simon, 1979).

The athlete perceives information from two sources: external sources of stimuli such as a ball, a goal, an umpire, spectators, players, and internal sources which supply sensory stimuli related to muscle tension and range of movement. According to Singer (1980), every stimulus must pass through a certain stimulus threshold for the athlete to pay attention to it. The peripheral sensation systems transfer the stimuli in the form of neural codes to the sensory memory mechanism (Straub & Williams, 1984). Information below the stimulus threshold does not pass through to the next stage and is forgotten. The function of the sensory memory is to collect the information, to filter and transfer it to the perceptual mechanism.

According to Alderson (1972), the personal perceptual abilities and skills are derived from the central nervous system and are mediators between the variables related to the environment and those related to the performance (acquisition of motor skills), and their quality determines the athlete's skill level.

Although the action performed is influenced by past experience, it must be appropriate to the specific demands of the situation, for example, the direction of a ball flying through the air, the location of opponents, and so on. A skilled athlete is capable of predicting possible environmental conditions and preparing accordingly an action that will shorten the time and nature of the reaction. This advantage takes on a greater significance in an athlete who makes decisions under conditions of pressure, limited time or both. The time required to solve a problem and to make a decision has been found to be a factor affecting the quality of the decision taken (Bronner, 1982).

Exercise and Health Psychology

In recent years the possible psychological benefits of exercise have been extensively examined. Exercising was believed to contribute to physical health, but recent studies show that exercise is also associated with mental well-being (Biddle & Mutrie, 1991; Dishman, 1985, 1986; Morgan & Goldston, 1987; see also chapters 3-4). Aerobic activity has the potential to reduce anxiety (Bahrke & Morgan, 1978; Berger, 1984; Blumenthal, Williams, Needels, & Wallace, 1982; Dishman, 1985; Morgan, 1979; Raglin & Morgan, 1987; Wilson, Berger, & Bird, 1981). Physical activity in the natural environment can be a promising aid for people suffering from mild to moderate depression, anxiety and other disorders (Brown, 1988; Doyne et al., 1987; Dunn & Dishman, 1991; Martinsen, Hoffort, & Solberg, 1989). However, the benefits of exercise for severe depressive disorders are still questionable and ought to be investigated further.

Swimming and yoga were also found to be activities associated with reduced levels of tension, depression, anger, anxiety and confusion (Berger & Owen, 1983). Weight training was associated with increased self-esteem in males (Tucker, 1982, 1984). Despite these psychological benefits, excessive chronic exercise may lead to fatigue, anxiety and depression. It may also lead to feelings of irritability when the obsessive exerciser is forced to stop exercising (Dishman, 1985).

The mechanisms by which exercising produces positive and negative psychological effects are not well understood today. Additional controlled studies are needed to demonstrate the direct and indirect paths through which different exercises are of psychological benefit to human beings. Also undetermined today are the extent, frequency and intensity of exercising that are related to positive as well as negative psychological outcomes. This line of research has much potential for the future.

Action Theory

Action Theory applied to sport psychology has gained substantial attention, particularly in Europe through the work of Nitsch (1981, 1982a, 1982b, 1985, 1986). This concept has also been discussed in relation to various constructs that are of value to sport psychological research and practice (e.g., strain, stress, anxiety and crisis: Bar-Eli, 1984; Bar-Eli & Tenenbaum, 1989c; Hackfort, 1983; Nitsch, 1981; Nitsch & Udris, 1976). Recently, the action theoretical perspective has been applied to the transactions between cognition, emotion and motivation, and to the organisation of motor behaviour (Nitsch, 1988, 1991).

On the basis of previous work, Nitsch (1985) summarises the action-theoretical perspective in a set of four postulates:

1. System postulate: action is an integrative, complex system process.
2. Intentionality postulate: action is a particular form of behavioural organisation, namely, an intentional behaviour; it is not determined by only objective causes, but rather by subjective purposes.
3. Regulation postulate: action as an intentional behaviour cannot be explained by biological regulatory mechanisms, but is to a significant extent regulated psychologically.
4. Development postulate: as a system process, as well as from its intentionality and regulation aspects, action is a phylogenetic, an ontogenetic and a societal-historic phenomenon.

The System Postulate.   Through action, the relationship between person and environment is established and identified, with regard to a task to be fulfilled. Thus, the action situation of a person is determined by personal, environmental and task-related factors, in their objective and subjective senses. To understand one's actions, a simultaneous analysis of these factors should be carried out, with a focus on the 'fit'—both objective and subjective—among them (French, Rodgers, & Cobb, 1974). According to Nitsch and Hackfort (1981), each of these factors can be differentiated into a valence and a competence component, constituting the following action determinants: person (motives and abilities), environment (incentives and opportunities) and task (attractiveness and difficulty). Action theory enables us to describe complex psychological processes (e.g., decision making) by means of logical principles. It should be noted, however, that this theory has a practical orientation and can be easily applied to sport (Holzkamp, 1972). In addition, this theory calls for integration of experimental and field studies with computer simulations, to test not only specific hypotheses, but first and foremost, to investigate their combination in an integrative manner (Kaminski, 1979; Nitsch, 1985).

The Intentionality Postulate. Intention means that every action has a goal, a purpose and a meaning. Action is therefore a specific type of behaviour, which is conscious, intentional and goal-directed. Accordingly, the concept of action is strongly associated with the concept of purpose (Frese & Sabini, 1986; Ginsburg, Brenner, & von Cranach, 1986; Norman & Shallice, 1986). Consequently, actions are linked with motives to be satisfied and with problems to be solved. Both are represented in future expectations of the individual (Fuchs, 1963; Rubinstein, 1971; Tolman, 1967). In other words, actions have explorative, constructive and presentational functions; that is, an individual subjectively explores, constructs and reconstructs reality, and uses actions for purposes of self-presentation and expression (see Goffman, 1959).

The Regulation Postulate. It is assumed that psychological processes require a somatic basis and that somatic processes can be influenced by psychological variables. Accordingly, action is understood as a regulated human behaviour reflecting the simultaneous influence of psychological and somatic processes. This emphasises the integrative, macro nature of action. Regulation is closely associated with the principle of hierarchic-sequential structuring of action organisation. This means, according to Nitsch (1985), that actions such as a long jump are structured in a hierarchy ranging from general (e.g., 'long jump') to specific ('start', 'go', 'take off', 'flight', 'landing', etc.) goals and plans. These are realised step by step in a fixed sequence of operations dominated by respective general goals and plans following the principles of 'from higher to lower levels' and 'from left to right' in the goal-plan pyramid. Despite some problems (see Kaminski, 1973; Oesterreich, 1981; Volpert, 1983, 1984), this principle nevertheless plays a central role in behaviour regulation. In addition, the comparison of desired and actual outcomes is highly important for behaviour regulation. To regulate behaviour, an individual can change the desired outcome and tolerate existing discrepancies, besides changing the actual state. For these purposes, multiple comparisons of goals and results (desired and actual outcomes) are sometimes required (Nitsch, 1985).

The Development Postulate. Action provides a possibility for a person to flexibly adapt to his or her environmental conditions, due to the phylogenetically and ontogenetically higher form of behavioural organisation realised in the concept of action. Human actions also reflect social conditions, which explains the particular emphasis on 'action psychology'. Actions should be considered with reference to the development of both the individual and the personal social context. On these grounds, Nitsch's (1991) recent contribution should be understood as an attempt to present an action-theoretical concept of motor learning and psychomotor development.

Applications in Sport. Regulation mechanisms have been intensively investigated within the framework of sport psychology, making use of action-theoretical principles. For example, the topic of 'naive' psychoregulation applied by athletes and coaches was investigated with regard to the influence of self and others (e.g., Hackfort, 1980; Nitsch & Allmer, 1979). Content analysis of interviews and questionnaire responses from subjects engaged in various sports revealed that 'naive' interventions correspond to the psychoregulative problems presented to the subjects.

The fundamental psychoregulative problems, as perceived by practitioners, may be grouped into two major categories: stabilisation and modification. This differentiation means that if the psychovegetative functional state of an athlete is optimal and perceived as favourable, his or her psychoregulative action is directed to maintain this state (stabilisation). When the psychovegetative functional state of the athlete deviates from the optimal and is perceived as unfavourable, the psychoregulative action consists of altering this state in order to (re-)establish a desirable one (modification).

A further differentiation of psychoregulative problems relates to hypo- and hyper-activation (under- and over-arousal). In the case of hypoactivation, the problem is one of mobilisation, whereas in the case of hyperactivation, the problem is one of relaxation. Mobilisation and relaxation may be further differentiated. A preventive action should be taken in advance when anticipated deviations are expected to occur. A compensatory action is taken if actual deviations are in process, which need to be balanced.

In Action Theory research on crisis, the role of time phases with regard to an individual athlete's psychological performance crisis in competition has been intensively investigated, both on the subjective level (Bar-Eli & Tenenbaum, 1988a, c; Bar-Eli, Tenenbaum, & Elbaz, 1990b) and on the observational level (Bar-Eli & Tenenbaum, 1989b). In team sports such as basketball and team handball Bar-Eli and his colleagues (Bar-Eli, 1984; Bar-Eli & Tenenbaum, 1988a, c; Bar-Eli, Tenenbaum, & Elbaz, 1990b) identified six time phases (three in each half). They found that according to experts' judgments, these phases have a considerable diagnostic relevance regarding an athlete's psychological performance crisis during competition and that athletes are exposed to crisis mainly during the end phase of the game. Previous evidence (Naber, 1972) indicated that athletes' behaviour in competition may correspond quite closely to the predictions of the crisis model. To test this hypothesis, Bar-Eli and Tenenbaum (1989b) observed rule violations of basketball players in competition and found solid evidence for the model's predictions of the role of time phases as crisis indicators.

Wegner and Vallacher (1987) identified five major problems with the concept of action:

1. It is often considered obvious as an explanation.
2. It has a potentially illusory status.
3. It has interpretive ambiguity.
4. It is complex.
5. It suggests a human causal agency.

However, we believe the action concept is of great potential utility. Moreover, the problems identified are the very reasons for action to be further studied (Wegner & Vallacher, 1987). For this purpose, we need a more definite and complete conception of Action Theory because, in many respects, Action Theory is still more of a programmatic, heuristic perspective than a fully formulated model. At present, it is in the process of transition from the programmatic level to that of differentiated elaboration. This, however, implies intensive, demanding and detailed work that goes far beyond using the action concept just because it is 'fashionable' (Nitsch, 1985). For future elaboration of Action Theory, Nitsch (1985) suggests that the following aspects be emphasised:

1. The extension of action control models to processes of social interaction
2. New conceptual and methodological understanding of psychosomatic interrelations
3. More intensive work on processes of generation of goals and plans under uncertain conditions (i.e., in the face of incomplete information on the part of the actor)
4. The development of taxonomies of typical action situations with special reference to constellations of person, environment and task factors of various sports
5. The development of appropriate computer simulation models of action.

Research Designs for Exercise and Sport Psychology

Sport and exercise psychology is unique because sport requires the person to act and behave under constant physical and psychological stress. In general, studies designed and conducted in laboratory settings lack ecological validity. We are frequently uncertain whether behaviours observed in an artificial environment will be reproduced in real field situations. In order to account for more of the 'noise' attributed to the environment (i.e., many factors which affect behaviour, such as spectators, peers, game situation, coach) and the person (arousal state, motivation, physical conditioning), one should apply different approaches to arrive at sound conclusions. The need for single subject and qualitative approaches, in addition to the classical quantitative ones, is discussed in this section. The Bayesian approach, which views behaviours from a probabilistic perspective and is potentially applicable to situations in which more objective measurement is limited, is discussed. Finally, we highlight the need for the integration of data from a substantial number of studies to reach more general and sound conclusions.

Single Subject and Qualitative Methods

Most research on sport is dominated by the natural science paradigm of hypothetico-deductive methodology which assumes quantitative measurement, experimental design and multivariate, parametric statistical analyses.

Despite Smith's (1987) definition of the nature of several approaches of quantitative research in education (interpretive, artistic, systematic and theory driven) and the claim made by Schempp (1988) that methods of investigation should be flexible and not necessarily unique to any of the paradigms, Sparkes (1989) believes that further empirical evidence is needed in the future to advance naturalistic methods for research purposes (also see Sparkes, 1992).

Patton (1980) argues that the choice between qualitative and quantitative methods is, in fact, situation dependent. In the sport setting, where the environment is not fully structured, both paradigms should be applied simultaneously, despite the present limitations of the naturalistic paradigm. In most cases, researchers evaluate their hypotheses in relation to a quantitative theory or a model. However, qualitative data may clarify some aspects that cannot be quantified. Thus qualitative and quantitative methods should be applied simultaneously and more intensively in the sport domain.

An anthropological approach using naturalistic observations and interviews (Naroll & Cohen, 1973; Pelto & Pelto, 1978; Wax, 1971; Williams, 1967) may raise some vital questions not encountered by the hypothetico-deductive methodology. This approach may contribute substantially to the formulation of appropriate questions derived from the sport milieu (Smith, 1988). Athletes' behaviours should be investigated in relation to their conventional environment in order to gain more reliable and valid information than derived from typical pre-post designs. The anthropological approach may also contribute to better understanding and control of intervening variables, which play a substantial role in accounting for experimental results.

Knowing a great deal about a single subject may tell us more than a little information from many cases. A useful strategy in sport psychology is to understand and control the behaviour-environment relationship of the sport domain better. Cooper, Heron, and Heward (1987) introduced several applied behaviour designs termed 'single subject analysis' to gain reliable and internal-external valid generalisation of this relationship. In principle, single subject designs are repeated measures of a subject's behaviour under different conditions of the experiment. Cooper et al. (1987) pointed out that it is necessary that an analysis of pre-intervention data (baseline) be made, decisions be made on objective and subjective measures and flexible designs be tried when unexpected changes occur. Establishing a stable baseline, where many measurements are performed, and sustaining the treatment for a longer period enable a reliable evaluation of behaviour and make the results more conclusive (Baer, Wolf, & Risley, 1968).

Single subject designs are, in fact, experimental tactics aimed at specific questions, but capable of dealing with expected as well as unexpected consequences (Skinner, 1966). Such designs are particularly applicable to sport psychology, since sport settings, such as competitions and practices, have a common framework but different characteristics. Single subject designs may explore the different consequences of such conditions on individual athletes. This may sometimes be more important than calculating means and variations.

More specifically, Cooper et al. (1987) introduced applied behavioural analyses, dividing them into reversal and alternating designs. Reversal designs consist of measuring the dependent variable on several occasions to determine its baseline level (A). Then an intervention is introduced (B). In the third phase, the intervention is withdrawn and baseline is again measured (A). This is a simple A-B-A reversal design. The same intervention may be once again introduced (B) or other interventions made (C), producing reversal designs such as A-B-A-B, A-B-A-C-A-D-A-C-A-C, A-B-C-D-B-D, and others, in which the reversal condition is not necessarily a return to baseline A. Moreover, reversal designs may include combination effects such as A-B-A-B-BC-B-BC where BC is a combination of two interventions that are compared to condition B (but not to A). Thus the additive and interactive effect of treatments should be analysed with some caution. Such designs are applicable and valuable, for example, in examining different mental preparation techniques for athletes. They allow us to take baseline measures and provide each athlete with a different order of techniques, always returning to baseline. These different orders may be applied to various sports and settings, and thus provide sound evidence to both coaches and scientists as to the relevant questions raised earlier: which mental technique is more effective for which athlete in which sport and setting?

Multiple baseline designs and changing criterion designs can also be adopted in the sport psychology domain. A multiple baseline design consists of applying a treatment sequentially to two or more behaviours, the effect on each behaviour being examined at different times. Such designs allow one to analyse the effect of an independent variable across multiple behaviours, settings or subjects, without the necessity of withdrawing the treatment variable. Thus, response measures may be obtained on several subjects across settings (similar behaviours in various settings) and across subjects (similar behaviours in various subjects). Several variations of MBD are discussed in Cooper et al. (1987). For example, one mental preparation technique may be examined on several athletes in various competitive situations that evoke different levels of arousal states. Such a design may also be used when a researcher is interested in investigating the effects of one mental technique on different behaviours such as motivation, anxiety and mental imaging prior to executing an action. The changing criterion design is used to evaluate the effect on a single target behaviour of a treatment applied in graduated or stepwise fashion. Each phase of the design provides a baseline for the following phase. Individual athletes' motivations, outcome attributions and arousal states across competitions can be studied and visually described longitudinally through the MBD and CCD procedures.

The single subject designs are dependent on observational methods, as well as introspective-retrospective questionnaires. The data are collected on each subject separately and presented graphically, using the subject's score in each situation under investigation. Integration of data across situations or subjects is mostly presented by means and standard deviations. Such data, though descriptive in nature, may be very useful not only to practitioners but researchers as well.

Single subject designs should be applied to individual athletes only when controlling all the possible confounding factors (increasing reliability and internal validity) by various control procedures (e.g., double blind technique) and treatment integrity (maximum likelihood between planned and actual treatment). Such steps will give more external and ecological validity to the experimental effect, particularly in field studies. The sport psychology domain is in essence a combination of behaviours in real field situations. Advanced observational techniques are required to increase reliability of the measures of athletic behaviours. Behavioural techniques, together with advanced qualitative and quantitative measures, may advance the sport psychology domain rapidly in the future.

Applying single subject designs in a longitudinal manner results in

1. gain of knowledge of rare and unusual phenomena that cannot be examined through traditional experimental designs;
2. knowledge of observation techniques and their implications;
3. dramatic or persuasive demonstrations of a phenomenon;
4. development of systematic research; and
5. exploration of possible links in real-life interventions too complex for survey or experimental strategies (Guba & Lincoln, 1981; Patton, 1980).

The Bayesian Approach

In some settings, the purpose of data collection is to modify the researcher's degrees of belief in the various situations (hypotheses) that may exist. The researcher starts out with hypotheses about the true situation. These hypotheses are usually mutually exclusive and exhaustive. For various reasons, the researcher may believe in some of these hypotheses more strongly than others, even before data collection. However, as a result of the data, researchers may adjust their beliefs, some being strengthened, some weakened and others remaining unchanged. Thus scientific investigation can be viewed as a process of alteration in researchers' personal probabilities, which continually change in light of accumulating knowledge (data). The probabilistic relations among hypotheses and data are embodied in Bayes's theorem, which was described in 1763 by the Reverend Thomas Bayes. Psychologists were introduced to Bayesian notions by Edwards (Edwards, 1962; Edwards, Lindman, & Savage, 1963).

The Bayesian approach is thoroughly embedded within the framework of decision theory. Its basic tenets are that opinions should be expressed in terms of subjective or personal probabilities, and that the optimal revision of such opinions, in the light of relevant new information, should be accomplished via Bayes's theorem, particularly when it leads to decision making and action (Edwards, 1966). Because of this concern with decision making, the output of a Bayesian analysis is not always a single prediction but rather a distribution of probabilities over a set of hypothesised states of the world. These probabilities can then be used, in combination with information about payoffs associated with various decision possibilities and states of the world, to implement any of a number of decision rules. Bayes's theorem is thus also a normative model. It specifies certain internally consistent relationships among probabilistic opinions and serves also to prescribe, in this sense, how people should think (Rapoport & Wallsten, 1972; Slovic & Lichtenstein, 1971).

The crucial elements of the Bayesian model are conditional probabilities, that is, probabilities with an 'if-then' character ('If so and so is true, then the probability of this event must be such and such'). Thus, Bayes's theorem states that given several mutually exclusive and exhaustive hypotheses, H_i (where i is the number of hypotheses), and a datum, D (a new item of information), their relations are:

$$P(H_i / D) = \frac{P(D/H_i) P(H_i)}{\sum_i P(D/H_i) P(H_i)} \tag{1}$$

This formula has three basic elements:

- Prior probability: The value $P(H_i)$ is the prior probability of hypothesis H_i. It represents the probability of H_i conditional on all information available prior to the receipt of D.
- Posterior probability: $P(H_i/D)$ is the posterior probability that H_i is true, taking into account the new datum, D, *as well as* all previous data.
- Impact of new datum: $P(D/H_i)$ is the conditional probability that the datum D would be observed if hypothesis H_i is true.

For a set of mutually exclusive and exhaustive hypotheses H_i, the values of $P(D/H_i)$ represent the impact of the datum D on *each* of the hypotheses. Suppose, for example, that a university decides to try out a new placement test for admitting students to a particular course. In such a case, two exclusive and exhaustive hypotheses may be defined: H_1—'student passes the course', and H_2—'student does not pass the course'. Prior to the introduction of the new test (D), the proportion $P(H_1)/P(H_2)$ had reflected the chances of each student passing or not passing the course—on the basis of all previous tests that have been conducted (therefore, the term 'prior'). After the introduction of the new test (D), the chances of each student passing or not are reflected by the proportion $P(H_1/D)/P(H_2/D)$, which takes into account the results of the new test, *as well as* the old ones (therefore the term 'posterior'). It is crucial, however, also to know the probability of a particular score in the test (D), given the fact that the student passed or did not pass the course, $P(D/H_1)/P(D/H_2)$; that is, if he or she passed or did not pass the course, which score did he or she probably get? This proportion actually reflects the impact of the new test on both hypotheses.

The denominator in equation (1) serves as a normalising constant. Although equation (1) is appropriate for discrete hypotheses, it can be rewritten, using integrals, to handle a continuous set of hypotheses and continuously varying data. It is, however, often convenient to form the ratio of equation (1) taken with respect to two hypotheses, H_i and H_j:

$$\frac{P(H_i / D)}{P(H_j / D)} = \frac{P(D / H_i)}{P(D / H_j)} \cdot \frac{P(H_i)}{P(H_j)} \tag{2}$$

For this ratio form, new symbols are introduced:

$$\Omega_1 = LR \cdot \Omega_0 \tag{3}$$

where Ω_1 represents the posterior odds, LR is the likelihood ratio, and Ω_0 stands for the prior odds.

Bayes's theorem can be used sequentially to measure the impact of several data. The posterior probability computed for the first datum is used as the prior probability when processing the impact of the second datum, and so on. Thus the terms 'prior' and 'posterior' are relative, depending upon where one is in the process of gathering information. However, the order in which data are processed makes no difference to their impact on posterior opinion. The final posterior odds, given n items of data, are

$$\Omega n = \prod_{k-1}^{n} LR_k \cdot \Omega_o \qquad (4)$$

Equation (4) shows that data affect the final odds multiplicatively. The degree to which the prior odds change upon receipt of a new datum is dependent upon the likelihood ratio for that datum. Thus, the likelihood ratio is an index of data diagnosticity (or importance, analogous to the weights employed in regression models; see Rapoport & Wallsten, 1972; Slovic & Lichtenstein, 1971). This may become clearer when we think about hypotheses such as 'sick' (H_1) and 'healthy' (H_2), on a particular symptom (D) diagnosed by a medical doctor. In a similar way, we could think about events (hypotheses) such as 'it will or will not rain tomorrow' (given that the weather forecast has been such and such, and that 'the Dutch soccer team will or will not win' (given that the star player Marco Van Basten is in such and such shape).

The Crisis Model. Athletes in competition frequently experience psychological stress, which may raise their arousal levels and negatively affect their performance. Under extreme levels of arousal, the athlete may enter a 'psychological performance crisis', a state in which the ability to cope adequately with competitive requirements substantially deteriorates. According to Bar-Eli and Tenenbaum (1989c), a crisis develops when a system (athlete) is no longer characterised by stability (Phase A), but is progressively under- or overcharged and thus, is characterised by lability (Phase B). In the case of extreme lability, failure of coping and defense mechanisms may lead to crisis (Phase C). If we define events C ('crisis') and $\bar{C}$ ('no crisis') as mutually exclusive and exhaustive, then $P(C) + P(\bar{C}) = 1$. In Phase A, $P(C) \ll P(\bar{C})$; in Phase B, $P(C) < P(\bar{C})$ or $P(C) \approx P(\bar{C})$ or $P(C) > P(\bar{C})$; and in Phase C, $P(C) \gg P(\bar{C})$. Finally, the probabilities of all these phases sum to 1 (for a detailed explanation, see Bar-Eli & Tenenbaum, 1989c). This model can be used to diagnose the development of an athlete's psychological performance crisis in competition. The probabilistic measure of diagnostic value used here for this purpose is based on the Bayesian approach. H_i and H_j in equation (2) are replaced by the two following mutually exclusive and exhaustive hypotheses:

- C – The athlete is in a psychological performance crisis during the competition.
- $\bar{C}$ – The athlete is not in a psychological performance crisis during the competition.

Equation (2) then takes the form of:

$$\frac{P(C/D)}{P(\bar{C}/D)} = \frac{P(D/C)}{P(D/\bar{C})} \cdot \frac{P(C)}{P(\bar{C})} \qquad (5)$$

When a total problem is fractionated into a series of structurally related parts, and experts are asked to assess these fractions, processes such as judgment and decision making are substantially improved (Armstrong, Denniston, & Gordon, 1975; Gettys, Michel, Steiger, Kelly, & Peterson, 1973). In case of only two hypotheses, H_i and H_j, people estimate $P(D/H_i)$ and $P(D/H_j)$ values, which are integrated across data and across hypotheses by means of Bayes's theorem (see equation 2). After all the relevant data have been processed, the resulting output is a ratio of posterior probabilities, $P(H_i/D)/P(H_j/D)$. In this way, a probabilistic diagnosis may be substantially facilitated (Edwards, 1962; Slovic & Lichtenstein, 1971).

A diagnosis of crisis requires that diagnostic factors be identified. Through these factors, the problem of diagnosing an athlete's psychological performance crisis in competition is fractionated. Each such factor includes several components (i.e., Bayesian data), which can be separately assessed by experts with regard to their probability of occurrence when a crisis $[P(D/C)]$ or a non-crisis $[P(D/\overline{C})]$ occurs. Later on, the ratio of $P(C/D)/P(\overline{C}/D)$ can be computed by Bayes's rule (equation 3). So far several such factors have been identified for several sports, such as basketball, team handball and tennis. Pre-start susceptibility to crises, with which the athlete enters competition, was investigated by Bar-Eli, Tenenbaum, and Elbaz (1989). Athletes' ability to cope with psychological stress and their competitive motivation were assessed for their effect on motor performance and psychological crisis. A number of factors operating during competition have been investigated. These include time phases (e.g., Bar-Eli & Tenenbaum, 1988a, c; Bar-Eli, Tenenbaum, & Elbaz, 1990b) and athletes' perceived team performance in competition in terms of 'event expectancy' (expected, unexpected event), 'direction of lead' (one's own team, opposing team) and 'momentum' or 'game tendency' (positive, negative). These variables determine 'game standings', which have a considerable diagnostic relevance for crisis development in competition (Bar-Eli & Tenenbaum, 1989a; Bar-Eli, Tenenbaum, & Elbaz, 1991). Bar-Eli and colleagues have also studied task-related behaviour (performance) and rule- and norm-related behaviour ('fairness' and 'sanctions by officials'), which are highly relevant to an athlete's crisis vulnerability in competition (Bar-Eli, Taoz, Levy-Kolker, & Tenenbaum, 1992; Bar-Eli & Tenenbaum, 1988b; Bar-Eli, Tenenbaum, .& Elbaz, 1990a). Athletes' perceptions of social factors, such as teammates' behaviour in competition, have been found to be highly relevant for crisis development (Bar-Eli, Tenenbaum, & Levy-Kolker, 1992).

At this point the Bayesian model, as presented in equation (5), can be used as follows. Upon exposure to information about the existence of a particular datum (i.e., a component of one of the diagnostic factors), the ratio of probabilities concerning the occurrence of the two events, C and $\overline{C}$, is revised, all previous data being taken into account. For this purpose, however, the technical hurdle of computerising such a diagnosis process must be overcome. Furthermore, posterior probabilities should preferably be associated with practical measures aimed at coping with players' psychoregulative problems at each phase of crisis development during competition (Bar-Eli & Tenenbaum, 1989c). It should be noted that the model presented here needs validation on other behavioural levels beyond experts' estimations (i.e., observational and psychophysiological). Thus far, observations of behavioural rule violations, grouped within time phases and used as crisis indicators in basketball competitions, have been encouraging in supporting the model (Bar-Eli & Tenenbaum, 1989b). Such investigations should be continued, including additional factors (e.g., further social psychological variables), as well as additional sport disciplines. In addition, the Bayesian approach can be applied to other problem areas, in which measures such as the psychophysiological ones remain limited to date (mainly for technical reasons), and therefore, investigators must rely on subjective expert judgments to effectively cope with them.

Research Integration: Meta-Analysis

The scientific literature is overloaded with a substantial number of studies on almost every issue on which scientists are engaged. This 'positive' inflation increases the necessity to develop methods that enable researchers to integrate findings beyond single studies that are assumed to be sufficiently well executed from both theoretical and methodological perspectives. Glass (1976) first introduced a method of research synthesis which enabled the calculation of the average effect of treatments on outcome variables across a large number of studies. He termed his method 'meta-analysis' to distinguish it from first and secondary analyses which were single studies. Meta-analysis is not aimed at designing a single study, but rather at summarising the results of many studies. In essence, it yields a single value representing the findings of series of studies, and, at the same time, explains the variation among these findings (Meir, 1987). In individual research studies raw data are subjected to primary and secondary analyses, but meta-analysis is applied to standardised differences, correlations and significance levels of variables in an integrative, meaningful manner. It calculates a single integrating value termed by Glass (1976) 'effect size' (ES), which he defined as the standardised mean difference between a treatment group and a control group in terms of an outcome variable. The ESs are averaged to obtain a single representative value which is used mainly to draw conclusions about the issue under study.

In order to encourage the use of research integration in the sport and exercise psychology domain, we intend to introduce briefly the main approaches to meta-analysis.

The first and oldest method of research integration was performed through the use of significant values (p's) commonly reported in single studies. Rosenthal (1984) described the Stouffer method in which the probability p is transformed to a Z score. The Z scores are summed across all studies selected and divided by the square root of the k studies. Thus, the simple computation is

$$p_i \rightarrow Z_i$$

in each single study and then

$$Z_{(overall)} = \Sigma \, Z_i \, / \, \sqrt{k}$$

Of course, $Z_{(overall)}$ can be transformed back to an overall value:

$$Z_{(overall)} \rightarrow P_{(overall)}$$

The main problem with such a technique is the sample size associated with each of the p values. When combining small samples, the overall N is inflated and significance emerges easily. Second, this technique ignores the distribution of p's which is required to identify and investigate possible sources of variations among the studies on the one hand and to prohibit the possibility that extreme but opposite effects will cancel each other and be summed to zero, and be ignored. Also, Z transformed from p and vice-versa does not indicate a magnitude of treatment effect. However, an additional procedure may take into account this missing information by calculating tests of variation followed by assessing homogeneity (Rosenthal, 1984, p. 77).

$$\chi^2 = \Sigma \, (Z_i - Z)^2$$

$$df = k - 1$$

Also, the effect size r (a simple correlation) can be obtained by $r = Z_{overall} \, / \, \sqrt{N}$, where N is the total sample size (Rosenthal, 1984, p. 31).

The most popular use of meta-analysis is through the combination of ESs drawn from experimental studies in which an experimental group is compared to a control group, where their means (m), standard deviations (s) and sample sizes (n) are known. The ES is, in fact, an index that is an estimation of the strength of the relationship between the treatment and the outcome variable. Most t-test and ANOVA's can easily be transformed to effect size 'g' which reflects the magnitude of difference between two groups in standardised terms (Cohen, 1977). In fact 'g' is identical to a 'z' which is an indicator of a standardised location in the normal distribution, but here it represents a magnitude of a treatment effect. The procedure is very simple. Glass (1976) proposed the simplest computation procedure (equation 6) where

$$g = (m_e - m_c) \, / \, s_c \tag{6}$$

in which m_e is the mean experimental group, m_c is the mean control group and s_c is the standard deviation of the control group. Later, some preferred to use the pooled standard deviation of the two groups (s_p) rather than the s_c:

$$s^2 = (\, (n_c - 1) \, (s_e)^2 + (n_c - 1) \, (s_c)^2 \, / \, (n_e + n_c - 2).$$

Hedges and Olkin (1985) showed that 'g' is biased as a consequence of small sample size. Thus the biased 'g' was corrected by multiplying g by $(1 - (3/4 \cdot N - 9) \,)$ termed d (equation 7):

$$d = (1 - (3/4n - 9) \cdot g \tag{7}$$

This procedure is applied to studies in which a single mean, m, is reported. In designs in which an experimental group is compared to a control group prior to and after treatment, the gain ES is presented in equation 8:

$$(g_e - g_c) \, / \, s_{yp} = [(y_e - y_c) - (X_e - X_c)]/s_{yp} \tag{8}$$

when e is the experimental group, c is the control group, y is the posttest mean, X is the mean pretest score and g is the unbiased estimator of the population parameter effect size. 'g' is corrected for sample bias and transformed to 'd' by the procedure described above.

Although several techniques are offered to combine effect sizes from a series of experiments, the most accepted one was that offered by Hedges and Olkin (1985) termed 'random effects model'. The variation of observed ESs can indicate the population ESs. Differences in treatments, sample characteristics, measurement tools, may account for some of the total variation. Thus, similarly to ANOVA procedure, variation of effect sizes may be attributed partly to population parameters and partly to sampling error of the estimator about the parameter value (Hedges & Olkin, 1985). The population variance (V_p) is computed by subtracting the sample error (V_s) variance from the observed variance (equation 9):

$$V_p = V_o - V_s \tag{9}$$

As described by Schwarzer (1989), the percentage of observed variance made up by sampling error can be computed by equation 10:

$$\% = V_s \cdot 100 / V_o \tag{10}$$

which illustrates the degree of homogeneity or heterogeneity of the data set. If 100% of the observed variance is explained by the sampling error, the data are homogeneous. This procedure enables us to consider moderator variables such as study characteristics, measurement tools and others to account for systematic variation.

Also, correlations derived from several studies pertaining to two or more variables can be subjected to meta-analytic procedures. Each r is transformed to Fisher's Z. The Z's are averaged (Z) and then transformed back to average r (F) (Hedges & Olkin, 1985; Hunter, Schmidt, & Jackson, 1982). Similarly to the case of 'd' corrected for sampling bias, correlations of large n's are more representative of the population 'rho' than r's obtained on small samples. Therefore, when averaging correlations, one also averages the sampling errors. The Schmidt-Hunter technique gives a good approximation of the sampling error variance s_e^2 (equation 11) by

$$s_e^2 = ((1 - r^2)^2 \cdot k) / N \tag{11}$$

where r^2 is the squared weighted mean of the effect sizes, k the number of studies, and N the total sample size (Hunter, Schmidt, & Jackson, 1982). When s_e^2 is known, the population variance s_{res}^2 can be easily calculated by subtracting sample error s_e^2 from the observed variance s_r^2 (equation 12):

$$s_{res}^2 = s_r^2 - s_e^2 \tag{12}$$

s_{res}^2 is also termed 'residual variance', and its square root is termed residual standard deviation s_{res}. It is desired that observed variance s_r^2 be accounted for by the sampling error s_e^2, the residual variance s_{res}^2 then becoming zero. Only then is observed variance fully accounted for by sampling error—an indication of homogeneity. When this is not the case, one should bear in mind to search for moderator variables.

Prior to applying the mathematical properties of meta-analytical procedures, one should consider very seriously the requirements for selection of studies to be entered to the final integrative analysis. The requirements are

- a clear definition of the issue and variables;
- a systematic screening process (library information centre and data bases, resources, but also others, such as dissertations, conferences, reprints, etc.);
- use of quantitative methods;
- exclusion of studies containing serious limitations and methodological flaws; and
- a systematic consideration of moderator variables such as samples, age, gender, type of activity, type of instrumentation, type of treatment.

When the meta-analysis results in a significant homogeneity index, further analysis is required to obtain 'groups' of studies (clusters) which share similar effects. Such studies should be examined for common features that differentiate them from the effect found in other studies (the search of moderator post facto).

Meta-analysis techniques were introduced to the sport sciences literature by researchers such as Thomas and French (1986), but have gained relatively minor attention in sport psychology, probably because sport psychology is quite a young discipline for research integration. However, several recent studies applying meta-analysis have produced sound results, for example, in the field of exercise psychology. Petruzzello, Landers, Hatfield, Kubitz, and Salazar (1991) examined the anxiety-reducing effects of acute and chronic exercise. They concluded that only aerobic forms of exercise are associated with anxiety reduction independently of age and health status of the subjects. Furthermore, training programmes need to exceed 10 weeks before significant changes in trait anxiety occur, and exercise of at least 21 min seems necessary to achieve reductions in state and trait anxiety. Similarly, North, McCullagh, and Tran (1990) investigated the effect of exercise on depression, Gruber (1986) examined the relationship between physical activity and self-esteem development in children, and Crews and Landers (1987) reviewed the relationship between aerobic fitness and reactivity to psychosocial stress. Finally, McDonald and Hodgdon (1991) base the whole of their book on the results of their meta-analysis of the psychological outcomes of aerobic fitness training. The use of meta-analytic techniques in exercise psychology is reviewed by Salazar, Petruzzello, Landers, Etnier, and Kubitz (1993).

In meta-analyses in sport psychology, Feltz and Landers (1983) and Oslin (1987) have examined the effects of mental practice on motor skill learning and performance, and Smith-Fortune (1987) has studied the effect of anxiety on sport performance. More recently, Lirrg (1991) has reviewed gender differences in self-confidence related to involvement in physical activity. The sound conclusions of such analyses contribute much to the understanding of psychological processes in the domain of sport and exercise, and similar analyses should be encouraged in future research.

Measurement of Psychological Characteristics in Exercise and Sport Psychology

Theoretical approaches and statistical designs discussed earlier enable us to understand, predict and control human behaviours in different situations. However, none of the theoretical models and none of the statistical or research procedures is sufficient without applying appropriate measures. Psychological measurement has caused many problems and much ambiguity in the past. Recently, new directions termed 'latent traits models' have been applied to the domain of psychology. The desire for precise linear quantification of psychological variables, such as physical properties, is the basic assumption of one such model called the Rasch Model. In this section we describe the main assumptions of the model and introduce one example from sport psychology.

Thurstone (1928) and Guttman (1944) desired to construct opinion-attitude scales manifesting characteristics of physical measurement. This desire led them to the notion of unidimensionality which classifies persons in an unequivocal order. Transitivity in ordering persons along the continuum with certainty was desired, but not obtained, particularly because the mathematical models and the response distinction assumption they demanded were not sufficient to validate the concepts they strived for. Andrich (1981) further argued that the concept of psychological scaling developed by Guttman (1950) and Thurstone (1959) is adequately dealt with by the Rasch model.

The Rasch Model

Measurement is designed to discriminate among the persons who differ in some property. The test items should differ mainly in difficulty and discrimination levels. Therefore, person $_v$ with ability β_v is expected to solve correctly problems that his or her ability enables him or her to do. From a certain point on the linear continuum, this person is expected to make mistakes. Item $_i$ with difficulty δ_i (its location on the linear continuum) should determine how far along the variable we can expect correct responses to that item to occur. Thus, the simplest representation of person $_v$ taking item $_i$ responding X_{vi} is governed by nothing else than his or her ability β_v and item's difficulty δ_i. To measure a person, estimation of β_v is needed, and to calibrate an item, estimation of δ_i is required. In other words, the difference between β_v and δ_i ($\beta_v-\delta_i$) governs the probability to respond correctly or wrongly to a dichotomously scored item. The difference ($\beta_v-\delta_i$) governs the response X_{vi}. This difference can vary from $-\infty$ to $+\infty$, while the probability of successful response should always remain within the 0-1 limits. Therefore, the difference ($\beta_v-\delta_i$) is treated as an exponent of the natural constant e = 2.71828 and as $e^{(\beta_v-\delta_i)} = \exp(\beta_v-\delta_i)$. Still, this expression has limits between 0 to $+\infty$, and to limit these boundaries to 0-1, the expression is transformed into a ratio:

$$\exp(\beta_v - \delta_i) / [1 + \exp(\beta_v - \delta_i)]$$

This expression has an ogive shape and is used to define the Rasch Model (equation 13):

$$P(X_{vi} = 1; \beta_v, \delta_i) = \exp(\beta_v - \delta_i) / [1 + \exp(\beta_v - \delta_i)] \tag{13}$$

a logistic function that is useful to make both linearity and generality of measure possible (Wright and Stone, 1979). Where $P(X_{vi} = 1; b_v, d_i)$ is the probability of person v encountering item i to respond 1 (out of two possibilities: 0 or 1) given his or her ability level β_{vi} and item difficulty level δ_i. The mathematical formulation to estimate β_v and δ_i independently from each other was suggested by Rasch (1961, 1967), Andersen (1973), and Barndorff-Nielsen (1978).

A person's ability β_v and an item's difficulty δ_i are measured in units termed 'logits' in the Rasch Model. A 'logit' is defined by Wright and Stone (1979, p. 17) accordingly:

> A person's ability in logit is their natural log odds for succeeding on items of the kind chosen to define the 'zero' point on the scale. An item's difficulty in logits is its natural log odds for eliciting failure from persons with 'zero' ability.

Any variable we have defined is on an interval scale. The unit, which we may as well call a 'logit', is constant over the range of the variable, in the sense that one logit implies the same tendency to produce a breakdown across all situations. The Rasch model further develops the mathematical properties that enable the examination of matching between the predicted values and the actual data observed. Following the estimation of β_v and δ_i, the residuals of the model are calculated by estimating from β_v and δ_i the value of each X_{vi} predicted by the model, and subtracting this expected value from the observed X_{vi}. For further formulations and examples of fit statistics which are so essential to detect unexpected patterns of a person's responses and item's positions (values) and to the reliability and validity of measurements, see Wright and Stone (1979, pp. 66-88) and Wright and Masters (1982).

The relatively new terminology associated with the Rasch approach views persons as objects for measurement, the numbers for the persons are 'measures', and the items in the instrument are 'calibrations'. Since measures are made on a linear line, each item on this line has a 'position'. The positions of the items on that line enable the measurement of how much one is 'more' or 'less' than the other. Graphically, we desire to establish a tool (questionnaire) in which a sufficient number of items share positions along the line, so that each person can be precisely measured, as shown in Figure 14.1 with anxiety. The items in the questionnaire are located along the line with respect to how 'easy' or 'difficult' it is to rate them 'high' or 'low'.

Conceptually, when such a scale is established, it enables one to determine how anxious athlete β_2 is compared to athletes β_1, β_3 or β_4 and 'how much' will be expressed in 'logits', similarly to physical quantification.

The main advantage of such an approach over the traditional approach is that it enables us to operationally define the variable on a linear continuum, to measure persons on that continuum, estimate the differences among them, identify their unexpected responses and generalise the finding beyond one sample. It enables the detection of misfit items objectively and with less error than the traditional approach; therefore scale construction and reconstruction are easier and more valuable.

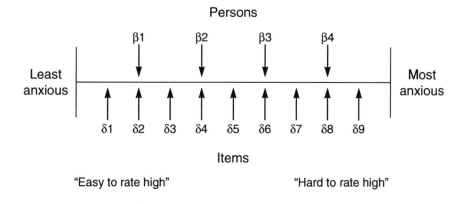

Figure 14.1 A desired linear continuum of anxiety measure, with items' calibration (δ's) and persons measured (β's).

Anxiety Scale Refinement

The Rasch Analysis procedure was applied to the state and trait anxiety questionnaire (STAI; Spielberger, Gorsuch, & Lushene, 1970) in competitive situations (Tenenbaum, Furst, & Weingarten, 1985). Since item values are expressed in logits (linear transformation of probabilistic values), their locations on the linear conceptual anxiety continuum were calculated. In the state anxiety questionnaire (Figure 14.2), items 3, 1 and 5 share the same location and so do items 19 and 10; 20 and 14; 2 and 11; 9 and 16; 12 and 17; 6 and 4. In the trait anxiety questionnaire (Figure 14.3), similar locations on the continuum were shared by items 1, 11; 6, 4, 10, 7; 16, 20; 13, 9; 5, 18.

Figures 14.2 and 14.3 indicate that items were not spread equally along the continua of the state and trait anxiety scales, so that an additional effort should be made to add items discriminating athletes with very high and very low state and trait anxiety levels. The boxes around 9 and 6 of the 20 items in the state and trait anxiety scales, respectively, indicate that these items elicit unexpected responses from athletes who were asked to rate them. Some of the items elicited equal ratings by most of the responders, despite the difference in their anxiety level, and others elicited reversed responses, such that highly anxious athletes rated them 'low' ('1' and '2'), while low anxiety athletes rated them 'high' ('3' and '4').

The state and trait anxiety questionnaires can be used as just one example that emphasises the need to improve psychological tools by consistently examining scale items. The better the tools applied in the sport psychology domain, the more precise the measures will be and the more pronounced the research conclusions. Future studies in the domain of exercise and sport psychology in which psychological scales are applied (especially scales adapted from other environments than sport and exercise), should be encouraged to reexamine the scales' psychometric properties. This procedure will minimise the measurement error on the one hand and provide more conclusive results on the other.

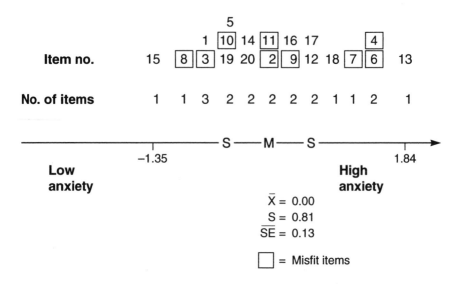

Figure 14.2   Item distribution (in 'logits') on the state anxiety variable and misfit items.

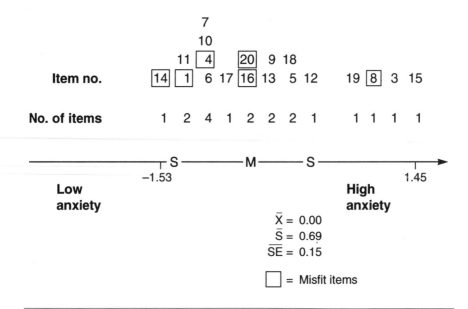

Figure 14.3   Item distribution (in 'logits') on the trait anxiety variable and misfit items.

Conclusion

Our discussion indicates several directions in which future research in exercise and sport psychology should develop.

The Action Theory framework, which regards people as acting like a complex system, demands an integrative approach to the study of human behaviour in sport and physical activity. Such an approach requires psychologists to co-operate with scientists from other disciplines, such as neurologists, computer experts, exercise physiologists and scientists in the domain of motor control. An integrative approach would produce findings of greater ecological validity.

In order to produce more reliable and valid measures, new measurement devices and more appropriate methods need to be developed for sport and exercise psychology, where quantitative psychometric methods have dominated. Qualitative methods should also be developed, along with single subject approaches and anthropological methods, which have rarely (if ever) been applied to sport psychology.

Sport psychology is quite behind other disciplines in applying new methods of measurement. One such approach (Rasch Model), which perceives psychological measures similarly to physical measures, makes it possible to take measures that are generalisable beyond the specific sample under study.

The number of publications on computer applications in sport shows that the discipline of sport psychology has not yet satisfactorily integrated the computer into its repertoire in ways that other disciplines have. Use of the computer to examine cognitive as well as attitudinal variables might dramatically advance our understanding of sport and exercise behaviour.

The Bayesian approach, in which probabilistic judgments are broken down by criterion variables, and then integrated to explore the behaviour as a whole, has been neglected in sport psychology and deserves more attention in the future.

Studies applying meta-analytic approaches have concluded that there is still a long way to go to develop theories that remain consistent across situations and time. More attempts in this direction are desirable.

Finally, although exercising has been shown to be a healthy activity, its psychological benefits have not yet been explored to the same extent as the physical. Further controlled studies in this field are necessary, along with research on the value of physical exercise as a useful alternative to psychological treatment. Sound empirical evidence on these issues may contribute to a mentally healthier society.

References

Alderson, G.J. (1972). Variables affecting the perception of velocity in sports situations. In H.T.A. Whiting (Ed.), *Readings in sport psychology* (pp. 116-155). London: Henry Kimpton.

Andersen, E.B. (1973). Conditional inference for multiple choice questionnaire. *British Journal of Mathematical and Statistical Psychology*, **26**, 31-44.

Andrich, D. (1981, March). *Rasch's models and Guttman's principles for scaling attitudes.* Paper presented at the International Conference on Objective Measurement, Chicago.

Armstrong, J.S., Denniston, W.B., & Gordon, M.M. (1975). The use of the decomposition principle in making judgments. *Organizational Behavior and Human Performance,* **14,** 257-263.

Ashby, W. (1960). *Design for a brain.* New York: Wiley.

Baer, D.M., Wolf, M.M., & Risley, T. (1968). Current dimensions of applied behavior analysis. *Journal of Applied Behavior Analysis,* **1,** 91-97.

Bahrke, M.S., & Morgan, W.P. (1978). Anxiety reduction following exercise and meditation. *Cognitive Therapy and Research,* **2,** 323-333.

Bar-Eli, M. (1984). *Zur Diagnostik individuelle psychischer Krisen im sportlichen Wettkampf: Eine wahrscheinlichkeits orientierte, theoretische und empirische Studie unter besonderer Berucksichtigung des Basketballspiels.* Unpublished doctoral dissertation, Deutsche Sporthochschule, Koln, Germany.

Bar-Eli, M., Taoz, E., Levy-Kolker, N., & Tenenbaum, G. (1992). Performance quality and behavioral violations as crisis indicators in competition. *International Journal of Sport Psychology,* **23,** 325-342.

Bar-Eli, M., & Tenenbaum, G. (1988a). The interaction of individual psychological crisis and time phases in basketball. *Perceptual and Motor Skills,* **66,** 523-530.

Bar-Eli, M., & Tenenbaum, G. (1988b). Rule- and norm-related behavior and the individual psychological crisis in competitive situations: Theory and research findings. *Social Behavior and Personality,* **16,** 187-195.

Bar-Eli, M., & Tenenbaum, G. (1988c). Time phases and the individual psychological crisis in sports competition: Theory and research findings. *Journal of Sports Sciences,* **6,** 141-149.

Bar-Eli, M., & Tenenbaum, G. (1989a). Game standings and psychological crisis in sport: Theory and research. *Canadian Journal of Sport Sciences,* **14,** 31-37.

Bar-Eli, M., & Tenenbaum, G. (1989b). Observations of behavioral violations as crisis indicators in competition. *Sport Psychologist,* **3,** 237-244.

Bar-Eli, M., & Tenenbaum, G. (1989c). A theory of individual psychological crisis in competitive sport. *Applied Psychology,* **38,** 107-120.

Bar-Eli, M., Tenenbaum, G., & Elbaz, G. (1989). Pre-start susceptibility to psychological crises in competitive sport: Theory and research. *International Journal of Sport Psychology,* **20,** 13-30.

Bar-Eli, M., Tenenbaum, G., & Elbaz, G. (1990a). Psychological performance crisis in high arousal situations: Diagnosticity of rule violations and performance in competitive team-handball. *Anxiety Research,* **2,** 281-292.

Bar-Eli, M., Tenenbaum, G., & Elbaz, G. (1990b). Psychological strain in competition: The role of time phases. *Sportwissenschaft,* **20,** 182-191.

Bar-Eli, M., Tenenbaum, G., & Elbaz, G. (1991). A three-dimensional crisis-related analysis of perceived team performance. *Journal of Applied Sport Psychology,* **3,** 160-175.

Bar-Eli, M., Tenenbaum, G., & Levy-Kolker, N. (1992). A three-dimensional crisis-related analysis of perceived teammates' behavior in competition. *Journal of Sport Behavior,* **15,** 179-200.

Barndorff-Nielsen, O. (1978). *Information and exponential families in statistical theory.* New York: Wiley.

Barratt, E.S. (1987). Impulsiveness and anxiety: Information processing and electroencephalograph topography. *Journal of Research in Personality,* **21,** 453-463.

Berger, B.G. (1984). Running away from anxiety and depression: A female as well as male race. In M.L. Sachs & G.W. Buffone (Eds.), *Running as therapy: An integrated approach* (pp. 138-171). Lincoln: University of Nebraska Press.

Berger, B.G., & Owen, D.R. (1983). Mood alteration with swimming: Swimmers really do "feel better." *Psychosomatic Medicine*, **45**, 425-433.

Biddle, S.J.H., & Mutrie, N. (1991). *Psychology of physical activity and exercise: A health-related perspective*. London: Springer-Verlag.

Blumenthal, J.A., Williams, R.S., Needels, T.L., & Wallace, A.G. (1982). Psychological changes accompany aerobic exercise in healthy middle-aged adults. *Psychosomatic Medicine*, **44**, 529-536.

Bronner, R. (1982). *Decision making under time pressure*. New York: Lexington Books.

Brown, D.R. (1988). Exercise, fitness, and mental health. In C. Bouchard, R.J. Shephard, T. Stephens, J.R. Sutton, & B.D. McPherson (Eds.), *Exercise, fitness, and health* (pp. 607-626). Champaign, IL: Human Kinetics.

Carver, C.S., & Scheier, M.F. (1988). A control-process perspective on anxiety. *Anxiety Research*, **1**, 17-22.

Cohen, J. (1977). *Statistical power analysis for the behavioral sciences*. New York: Academic Press.

Cooper, J.O., Heron, T.E., & Heward, W.L. (1987). *Applied behaviour analysis*. Columbus, OH: Merrill.

Cox, T., Gotts, G., Boot, N., & Rerr, J. (1988). Physical exercise, employee fitness and the management of health at work. *Work and Stress*, **2**, 71-77.

Cratty, B.J. (1989). *Psychology in contemporary sport* (3rd ed.). Englewood Cliffs, NJ: Prentice Hall.

Crews, D.J., & Landers, D.M. (1987). A meta-analytic review of aerobic fitness and reactivity to psychosocial stressors. *Medicine and Science in Sports and Exercise*, **19**(Suppl. 5), S114-S120.

Dishman, R.K. (1985). Medical psychology in exercise and sport. *Medical Clinics of North America*, **69**, 123-143.

Dishman, R.K. (1986). Mental health. In V. Seefeldt (Ed.), *Physical activity and well-being* (pp. 303-341). Reston, VA: American Alliance of Health, Physical Education, Recreation and Dance.

Doyne, E.J., Ossip-Klein, D.J., Bowman, E.D., Osborn, K.M., McDougall-Wilson, I.B., & Neimeyer, R.A. (1987). Running versus weight-lifting in the treatment of depression. *Journal of Consulting and Clinical Psychology*, **55**, 748-754.

Dunn, A.L., & Dishman, R.K. (1991). Exercise and the neurobiology of depression. *Exercise and Sport Sciences Reviews*, **19**, 41-98.

Edwards, W. (1962). Dynamic decision theory and probabilistic information processing. *Human Factors*, **4**, 59-73.

Edwards, W. (1966). *Nonconservative probabilistic information processing systems* (Report No. ESD-TR-66-404). Wright Patterson Air Force Base, OH: U.S. Air Force Decision Sciences Laboratory.

Edwards, W., Lindman, H., & Savage, L.J. (1963). Bayesian statistical inference for psychological research. *Psychological Review*, **70**, 193-242.

Feltz, D.L., & Landers, D.M. (1983). Effects of mental practice on motor skill learning and performance: A meta-analysis. *Journal of Sport Psychology*, **5**, 25-57.

French, J.R.P., Rodgers, W., & Cobb, S. (1974). Adjustment as person-environment fit. In G.V. Coelho, D.A. Hamburg, & J.E. Adams (Eds.), *Coping and adaptation* (pp. 316-333). New York: Basic Books.

Frese, M., & Sabini, J. (Eds.) (1986). *Goal directed behavior: The concept of action in psychology*. Hillsdale, NJ: Erlbaum.

Fuchs, R. (1963). Funkionsanalyse der Motivation. *Zeitschrift feur angewandte und experimentelle Psychologie*, **10**, 626-645.

Gettys, C.F., Michel, C., Steiger, J.H., Kelly, C.W., & Peterson, C.R. (1973). Multiple-stage probabilistic information processing. *Organizational Behavior and Human Performance*, **5**, 374-387.

Gill, D.L. (1986). *Psychological dynamics of sport*. Champaign, IL: Human Kinetics.

Ginsburg, G.P., Brenner, M.J., & von Cranach, M. (Eds.) (1986). *Discovery strategies in the analysis of action*. New York: Academic Press.

Glass, G.V. (1976). Primary, secondary and meta-analysis of research. *Educational Researcher*, **5**, 3-8.

Goffman, E. (1959). *The presentation of self in everyday life*. New York: Doubleday.

Gruber, J.J. (1986). Physical activity and self-esteem development in children: A meta-analysis. *Academy Papers—American Academy of Physical Education*, **19**, 30-48.

Guba, E.G., & Lincoln, Y.S. (1981). *Effective evolution*. San Francisco: Jossey-Bass.

Guttman, L. (1944). A basis for scaling qualitative ideas. *American Sociological Review*, **9**, 139-150.

Guttman, L. (1950). In problem of attitude and opinion measurement. In E. Stouffer (Ed.), *Measurement and prediction* (pp. 32-54). New York: Wiley.

Hackfort, D. (1980). Techniken der Angstkontrolle von Trainern. *Leistungssport*, **10**, 104-110.

Hackfort, D. (1983). *Theorie und Diagnostik sportbezogener Aegstlichkeit. Ein Situationsanalytisc her Ansatz*. Unpublished doctoral dissertation, Deutsche Sporthochschule, Koln, Germany.

Hedges, L.V., & Olkin, I. (1985). *Statistical methods for meta-analysis*. New York: Academic Press.

Holzkamp, K. (1972). *Kritische Psychologie. Vorbereitende*. Frankfurt, Germany: Fischer.

Hunter, J.E., Schmidt, F.L., & Jackson, G.B. (1982). *Meta-analysis: Cumulating research findings across studies*. Beverly Hills, CA: Sage.

Jones, J.G., & Hardy, L. (Eds.) (1990) *Stress and performance in sport*. Chichester, England: Wiley.

Kaminski, G. (1973). Bewegungshandlungen als Bewaeltigung von Mehrfachaufgaben. Rahmentheoretische Voraussetzungen einer Untersuchung an Skilaufaenfangern. *Sportwissenschaft*, **3**, 233-250.

Kaminski, G. (1979). Die Bedeutung von Handlungskonzepten fuer die Interpretation sportpaedagogische Prozesse. Handlungstheoretische Grundlagen. *Sportwissenschaft*, **9**, 9-28.

Klavora, P. (1977). An attempt to derive inverted-U curves based on the relationship between anxiety and athletic performance. In D.M. Landers & R.M. Christina (Eds.), *Psychology of motor behavior and sport* (pp. 369-377). Champaign, IL: Human Kinetics.

Landers, D.M. (1989). Controlling arousal to enhance sport performance. In G. Tenenbaum & D. Eiger (Eds.), *Proceedings of the Sport Psychology Section of the Scientific Congress of the 13th Maccabiah Games* (pp. 7-27). Netanya, Israel: Wingate Institute.

Landers, D.M., & Boutcher, S.H. (1986). Arousal-performance relationship. In J.M. Williams (Ed.), *Applied sport psychology* (pp. 163-184). Palo Alto, CA: Mayfield.

Lirrg, C.D. (1991). Gender differences in self confidence in physical activity: A meta-analysis of recent studies. *Journal of Sport and Exercise Psychology*, **13**, 194-310.

Martinsen, E.W., Hoffort, A., & Solberg, O. (1989). Comparing aerobic and nonaerobic forms of exercise in the treatment of clinical depression: A randomized trial. *Comprehensive Psychiatry*, **30**, 324-331.

McDonald, D.G., & Hodgdon, J.A. (1991). *Psychological effects of aerobic fitness training: Research and theory.* New York: Springer-Verlag.

Meir, E. (1987). Meta-analysis of the relationship between congruence and well-being measures. *Journal of Vocational Behavior, 31,* 319-332.

Morgan, W.P. (1979). Anxiety reduction following acute physical activity. *Psychiatric Annals, 9,* 141-147.

Morgan, W.P., & Goldston, S.E. (Eds.) (1987). *Exercise and mental health.* Washington, DC: Hemisphere.

Morrow, G.R., & Labrum, A.H. (1978). The relationship between psychological and physiological measures of anxiety. *Psychological Medicine, 8,* 95-101.

Naber, F. (1972). Verteilung der Fouls waehrend der Dauer eines Basketballspiels. In M. Volkamer (Ed.), *Experimente in der Sportpsychologie* (pp. 66-69). Schorndorf, Germany: Hofmann.

Naroll, R., & Cohen, R.A. (1973). *A handbook of methods in cultural anthropology.* New York: Columbia University Press.

Nitsch, J.R. (1982a). Analysis of action and functionalistic approaches in sport psychology. In E. Geron (Ed.), *Handbook of sport psychology: Vol. I. Introduction to sport psychology* (pp. 58-75). Netanya, Israel: Wingate Institute.

Nitsch, J.R. (1982b). Handlungspsychologische Ansaetze im Sport. In A. Thomas (Ed.), *Sportpsychologie. Ein Handbuch in Schluesselbegriffen* (pp. 26-41). Muenchen, Germany: Urban & Schwarzenberg.

Nitsch, J.R. (1985). The action-theoretical perspective. *International Review for the Sociology of Sport, 20,* 263-282.

Nitsch, J.R. (1986). Zur handlungstheoretischen Grundlegung der Sportpsychologie. In H. Gabler, J.R. Nitsch, & R. Singer (Eds.), *Einfuehrung in die Sportpsychologie Teill: Grundthemen* (pp. 188-270). Schorndorf, Germany: Hofmann.

Nitsch, J.R. (1988). Kognition und ihre Wechselbeziehungen zur Emotion und Motivation aus planungstheoretischer Sicht. In P. Kunath, S. Mueller, & H. Schellenberger (Eds.), *Proceedings of the 7th Congress of the European Federation of Sports Psychology 1987 (FEPSAC),* (Vol. 1, pp. 39-71). Leipzig, Germany: DHfK.

Nitsch, J.R. (1991, September). *The organization of motor behaviour: An action-theoretical perspective.* Paper presented at the 8th Congress of the European Federation of Sports Psychology (FEPSAC), Cologne, Germany.

Nitsch, J.R. (Ed.) (1981). *Stress.* Bern, Switzerland: Huber.

Nitsch, J.R., & Allmer, H. (1979). Naive psychoregulative Techniken der Selbstbeeinflussung im Sport. *Sportwissenschaft, 9,* 143-163.

Nitsch, J.R., & Hackfort, D. (1981). Stress in Schule und Hochschule: Eine handlungspsychologische Funktionsanalyse. In J.R. Nitsch (Ed.), *Stress* (pp. 263-311). Bern, Switzerland: Huber.

Nitsch, J.R., & Udris, I. (Eds.) (1976). *Beanspruchung im Sport.* Bad Homburg, Germany: Limpert.

Norman, D.A., & Shallice, T. (1986). Attention to action: Willed and automatic control of behavior. In R.J. Davidson, G.E. Schwartz, & D. Shapiro (Eds.), *Consciousness and self-regulation* (Vol. 4, pp. 1-18). New York: Plenum.

North, T.C., McCullagh, P., & Tran, Z.V. (1990). Effect of exercise on depression. *Exercise and Sport Sciences Reviews, 18,* 379-415.

Oesterreich, R. (1981). *Handlungsregulation und Kontrolle.* Muenchen, Germany: Urban & Schwarzenberg.

Oslin, J.L. (1987). *A meta-analysis of mental practice research: Differentiation between intent and type of cognitive activity utilized.* Unpublished master's thesis, University of Oregon, Eugene.

Patton, M.Q. (1980). *Qualitative evaluation methods.* Beverly Hills, CA: Sage.

Pelto, P.J., & Pelto, G.H. (1978). *Anthropological research: The structure of inquiry* (2nd ed.). Cambridge, England: Cambridge University Press.

Petruzzello, S.J., Landers, D.M., Hatfield, B.D., Kubitz, K.A., & Salazar, W. (1991). A meta analysis on the anxiety-reducing effects of acute and chronic exercise: Outcomes and mechanisms. *Sports Medicine,* **11,** 143-182.

Raglin, J.S., & Morgan, W.P. (1987). Influence of exercise and quiet rest on state anxiety and blood pressure. *Medicine and Science in Sports and Exercise,* **19,** 456-463.

Rapoport, A., & Wallsten, T.S. (1972). Individual decision behavior. *Annual Review of Psychology,* **23,** 131-176.

Rasch, G. (1961). On general laws and the meaning of measurement in psychology. In *Proceedings of the 4th Berkeley Symposium on Mathematical Statistics and Probability* (Vol. IV, pp. 321-334). Berkeley: University of California Press.

Rasch, G. (1967). An informal report on the state of a theory of objectivity in comparisons. In L.J. Van der Kamp & C.A.J. Viek (Eds.), *Proceedings of the NUFFIC International Symposium Summer Session in Science at 'Het Oude Hof'* (pp. 34-65). Leiden, The Netherlands: Elsevier.

Rosenthal, R. (1984). *Meta-analytic procedures for social research.* Beverly Hills, CA: Sage.

Rubinstein, S.L. (1971). *Grundlagen der Allgemeinen Psychologie.* Berlin: Volk und Wissen.

Salazar, W., Petruzzello, S., Landers, D., Etnier, J., & Kubitz, K. (1993). Meta-analytic techniques in exercise psychology. In P. Seraganian (Ed.), *Exercise psychology: The influence of physical exercise on psychological processes* (pp. 122-145). New York: Wiley.

Sarason, S.B., Mandler, G., & Craighill, P.G. (1952). The effects of differential instructions on anxiety and learning. *Journal of Abnormal and Social Psychology,* **47,** 561-565.

Schempp, P.G. (1988). Exorcist II: A reply to Siedentop. *Journal of Teaching in Physical Education,* **7,** 79-81.

Schwarzer, R. (1989). *Meta-analysis.* Berlin: Free University of Berlin.

Simon, H.A. (1979). Information processing models of cognition. *Annual Review of Psychology,* **30,** 363-396.

Singer, R.N. (1980). *Motor learning and human performance.* New York: Macmillan.

Skinner, B.F. (1966). Operant behavior. In W.K. Honig (Ed.), *Operant behavior: Areas of research and application* (pp. 12-32). New York: Meredith.

Slovic, P., & Lichtenstein, S. (1971). Comparison of Bayesian and regression approaches to the study of information processing in judgment. *Organizational Behavior and Human Performance,* **6,** 649-744.

Smith, M.L. (1987). Publishing qualitative research. *American Education Research Journal,* **24,** 173-184.

Smith, M.L. (1988). The logic and design of case study research. *Sport Psychologist,* **2,** 1-12.

Smith-Fortune, J.A. (1987). *The effect of anxiety on sport performance: A meta-analysis.* Unpublished master's thesis, University of Oregon, Eugene.

Sonstroem, R.J. (1984). An overview of anxiety in sport. In J.M. Silva & R.S. Weinberg (Eds.), *Psychological foundations of sport* (pp. 104-117). Champaign, IL: Human Kinetics.

Sonstroem, R.J., & Bernardo, P.B. (1982). Intraindividual pregame state anxiety and basketball performance: A re-examination of the inverted-U curve. *Journal of Sport Psychology,* **4,** 235-245.

Sparkes, A.C. (1989). Paradigmatic confusions and the evasion of critical issues in naturalistic research. *Journal of Teaching in Physical Education*, **8**, 131-151.

Sparkes, A.C. (Ed.) (1992). *Research in physical education and sport: Exploring alternative visions.* London: Falmer Press.

Spielberger, C., Gorsuch, R., & Lushene, R. (1970). *STAI manual for the State-Trait Anxiety Inventory.* Palo Alto, CA: Consulting Psychologist Press.

Straub, W.F., & Williams, J.M. (1984). Cognitive sport psychology: Historical, contemporary, and future perspectives. In W.F. Straub & J.M. Williams (Eds.), *Cognitive sport psychology* (pp. 3-10). Ithaca, NY: Sport Science Associates.

Tenenbaum, G., Furst, D., & Weingarten, G. (1985). A statistical reevaluation of the STAI anxiety questionnaire. *Journal of Clinical Psychology*, **41**, 239-244.

Thomas, J.R., & French, K.E. (1986). The use of meta-analysis in exercise and sport: A tutorial. *Research Quarterly for Exercise and Sport*, **57**, 196-204.

Thurstone, L.L. (1928). The measurement of opinion. *Journal of Abnormal and Social Psychology*, **22**, 415-430.

Thurstone, L.L. (1959). *The measurement of values.* Chicago: University of Chicago Press.

Tolman, E.C. (1967). *Purposive behavior in animals and men.* New York: Appleton-Century-Crofts. (Original work published 1932)

Tucker, L.A. (1982). Effect of a weight-training program on the self-concepts of college males. *Perceptual and Motor Skills*, **54**, 1055-1061.

Tucker, L.A. (1984). Physical attractiveness, somatotype, and the male personality: A dynamic interactional perspective. *Journal of Clinical Psychology*, **40**, 1226-1234.

Volpert, W. (1983). An den Grenzen des Modells der Hierarchischen sequentiellen Handlungsorganisation. *Berliner Hefte zur Arbeits und Sozialpsychologie*, **3**, 1-89.

Volpert, W. (1984). Maschinen-Handlungen und Handlungs-Modelle: Ein Plaedoyer gegen die Normierung des Handelns. *Gestalt Theory*, **6**, 70-100.

Wax, R.H. (1971). *Doing fieldwork: Warnings and advice.* Chicago: University of Chicago Press.

Wegner, D.M., & Vallacher, R.R. (1987). The trouble with action. *Social Cognition*, **5**, 179-190.

Williams, I.R. (1967). *Field methods in the study of culture.* New York: Holt, Rinehart & Winston.

Wilson, V.E., Berger, B.G., & Bird, E.I. (1981). Effects of running and of an exercise class on anxiety. *Perceptual and Motor Skills*, **53**, 472-474.

Wine, J.D. (1980). Cognitive-attentional theory of test anxiety. In I.G. Sarason (Ed.), *Test anxiety: Theory, research and applications* (pp. 349-385). Hillsdale, NJ: Erlbaum.

Wine, J.D. (1982). Evaluation anxiety: A cognitive-attentional construct. In H.W. Krohne & L. Laux (Eds.), *Achievement, stress and anxiety* (pp. 207-219). Washington, DC: Hemisphere.

Wright, B.D., & Masters, G.N. (1982). *Rating scale analysis.* Chicago: Mesa Press.

Wright, B.D., & Stone, M.H. (1979). *Best test design.* Chicago: Mesa Press.

15

CHAPTER

Future Directions in Exercise and Sport Psychology

Paul Kunath

GERMANY

In this chapter, I shall discuss what exercise and sport psychology is, or can be in the future, when exercise and sport psychology will be relevant to more sport activities of more people than ever before.

Although the first psychological essays on athletic behaviour and sport appeared at the turn of the century in France, Germany (e.g., Schultze, 1897) and Russia, exercise and sport psychology is a young specific discipline within the fields of psychology and sport science. Sport psychology attracted little attention during the 1920s, but after 1945 an upswing could be seen. Its development, however, has been quite different in various countries.

In 1963, Antonelli (Italy), Olsen (Norway) and I (Germany—former GDR) discussed the formation of an international body of psychologists dealing with sport. Antonelli, in Rome in 1965, organised the first congress in this field, at which the International Society of Sport Psychology (ISSP) was established. European sport psychologists started their formal international communications in 1968 in Varna, Bulgaria. The Fédération Européenne de Psychologie des Sports et des Activités Corporelles (FEPSAC—European Federation of Sport Psychology) was founded in 1969 in Vittel, France. In September 1991, FEPSAC held its Eighth Congress in Cologne, Germany.

These international bodies, relationships and meetings have stimulated the development of sport and exercise and sport psychology in many countries. We might estimate that perhaps 2,500 scientists are working on sport and exercise psychology in countries all over the world, although there are no data to confirm this.

Not all of these scientists have formal qualifications in psychology. There are also many physicians, psychiatrists, neurologists, paediatricians, sociologists, physical educators and coaches, who are interested in, or who are dealing with, psychological findings and issues in sport and exercise. Differences in various countries may be explained by their traditions and the different development of psychology, sport science and sport and exercise in general in these countries.

To my mind, exercise and sport psychology should be a specific discipline with defined qualifications, and exercise and sport psychologists need a specific 'licence'. International associations, like ISSP and FEPSAC, can help national groups achieve comparable standards. This is particularly important and topical in Europe given the changing nature of the European Union (EU) and the increased professional mobility between EU countries.

Sport and Sport Science

Currently, all over the world, sport and exercise have become more central to human interests and activities as they come to play a central role in leisure time, commercial life and health promotion. Sport and exercise are also increasingly important for older people, women and other groups previously often excluded or underrepresented.

> The desire of Man to live in a world without wars, to realise himself, to develop the powers inherent in his nature and to use his possible chances, as well as the fact that scientific-technological progress has penetrated the working process and all spheres of life, have resulted in a social and individual upgrading of both the role and significance of physical education and sport. . . . More and more women and men of all age groups are regularly engaged in physical activity and sport in order to preserve their health, maintain their performance capacity, increase their physical, mental and social well-being, find pleasure and manifold experiences, and, finally, improve recreation in the freedom of nature by means of communication and social interaction. With the aid of physical activities, people are enabled to better adapt themselves to modified contents and conditions of work and the impact of related risks, such as lack of physical exercise, one-sided loading, malnutrition, and misbehaviour can be reduced. (*FEPSAC Manifesto on Sports Psychology*, 1987, p. 3)

With such a broad conception of sport, three interrelated factors may be distinguished. First, there is the desire of some to improve their physical and mental health through exercise and sport. This area of sport science has shown a significant increase of interest in recent years. Second, there has been much activity associated with assisting the preparation of talented people and the best athletes for enhanced success in competition. Third, an increasing number of people of all ages and both genders have come to appreciate the value and advantages of sport and exercise participation for health, well-being, quality of life and fun.

Sport science, including sport psychology, explores ways of increasing the positive impact of sport activities on individual life and the relationships between peoples of different countries, religions and races. The findings from sport psychology are largely dedicated to practical problems that can be solved by various approaches.

Thematic aspects of three main trends of sports can be identified. Nitsch (1989) wrote about three functional perspectives of sports and exercise activity, each of them comprised of two subclasses. First, he identified the purposes and effects of sports. Here performance, health or quality of life may be a purpose or an effect of sport participation, or both.

Secondly, Nitsch argues that the main purpose of some sport and exercise activities may be to improve health or to present oneself as healthy and fit, such as in 'impression management'.

A third perspective identified by Nitsch refers to the involvement of the individual and society in sport activity. That is, performance, health or quality of life may be seen relative to the interests of the individual or society or of both.

At present two other tendencies can be observed in the development of sport science. On the one hand there is a process of specialisation and development of further subdisciplines, and on the other hand there is a tendency towards integration. Both are needed, but there is also a need to bring the findings of the specific disciplines of sport science together in a systematically integrated set of theories.

Sometimes the specific disciplines of sport science are considered to be components of pedagogy. Historically this has been the case. In the early stages of the development of sport science most disciplines were educationally orientated. However, in my view, sport pedagogy is a specific discipline of sport science. What is needed is not a discussion of all the disciplines of sport science and the pedagogical disciplines, but a comprehensive theory of sport. Central to this concept should be a concept of sport science (singular), rather than of sport sciences. More integration of different propositions based on research in the specific disciplines of sport science is badly needed.

Sport psychologists have to learn to co-operate better with all other specialists, bringing into the co-operative effort the psychological principles of 'action control' in sport activities. Psychological principles of mental or psychological control of sport activities can be understood by other specialists and can be transferred from one field of sports to another. In this respect, research and applications are centred on the three psychological aspects of sport and exercise mentioned earlier.

Specific Trends in Exercise and Sport Psychology

Historically, sport and exercise psychology began its progress through involvement with the development of competitive sports. It was expected that psychologists could assist coaches and athletes to be more successful in training and competition.

In Canada, Germany, USA and some other countries there have been many applications of psychology, combined with learning theories and aspects of motor learning to the development of effective physical education. In this respect, contemporary exercise and sport psychology can address

- the mental control processes of motor learning in physical education classes;
- emotional control procedures, particularly with respect to anxiety; and
- social-psychological interactions in exercise and sport groups, especially classes and teams.

Sport and exercise psychologists have been less active in, and so know less about, areas such as participation in leisure time sports, exercise for people with disabilities, and health-related exercise or fitness, although some of these areas of study are now expanding. Exercise and sport psychology has concentrated the activities of individuals practising sport and associated effects on personal well-being, performance capacity, mental health and the development of the whole personality. Those who agree with such a conception of exercise and sport psychology must also have to accept that it has to be a distinctive scientific discipline of psychology and sport science in the strict sense of having its own specific topics, aims, tasks and methods. Exercise and sport psychology is one specific science dealing in and with exercise and sports. As Figure 15.1 shows, the research, teaching and practice of exercise and sport psychology must link with general psychology, and the various subfields of the parent discipline, other disciplines of sport and exercise science, such as pedagogy, as well as different types of branches of sport.

Five main aims and tasks of exercise and sport psychology at present, according to a statement from FEPSAC, are:

The different components inciting to active involvement in sport activities (convictions, ideals, needs, attitudes, motives); the effective organization of sport exercises and training with a view to support personality development; the improvement of the experiential capacity and the sense of responsibility for one's own body; the socialisation of individuals on the basis of the cooperative and communicative demands of sport activities, including a comparison of performances in competitions; the optimal level of psychic strain and the resistance to strain in people practising sport. (*FEPSAC Manifesto on Sports Psychology*, 1987, p. 4)

Over the last 20 to 30 years, exercise and sport psychology has received a fresh impetus. Its development has been supported considerably by the constantly rising popularity of sport all over the world. This progress has also been influenced by the fact that other disciplines, such as biology, sociology, pedagogy, economics, philosophy and the theory of training, started to grow in importance in physical education and sport.

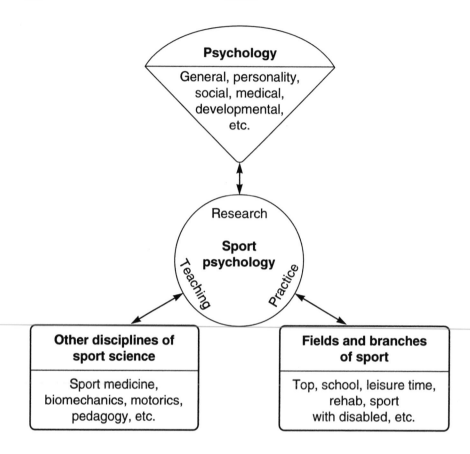

Figure 15.1   The relationship of sport psychology to sport, sport science and psychology. *Note*. From 'Future Trends in Sport Psychology and Sport Sciences' by J.R. Nitsch. In *Proceedings of the 7th World Congress in Sport Psychology* (pp. 200-204), 1989, Singapore: Singapore Sports Council. Reprinted by permission of the author.

Exercise and Sport Psychology as a Profession

More recently, the question has been asked 'What is a sport psychologist?' or 'Who can become a professional sport psychologist in the field of physical education or sport?'

In Europe, the discussion started in 1974 during an international meeting in Magglingen, Switzerland. In the USA, several articles (e.g., Danish & Hale, 1981; Harrison & Feltz, 1979) have considered the problems of limiting the field of sport psychologists through legal credentials. In the British Association of Sports Sciences (BASS; now changed to the British Association of Sport and Exercise Sciences; BASES) Code of Conduct for Sport Psychologists in the United Kingdom, first written in 1988, it was stated: 'BASS will keep a register of suitably qualified sport psychologists . . . Those listed on the register will be known as "Registered Sport Psychologists" (RSPs). The National Coaching Foundation (NCF) and BASS will recommend sport psychological services to be delivered only by RSPs. All RSPs, by being accepted onto the register, automatically consent to abide by the code of conduct.' (Biddle, 1989, p. 26)[1]. BASS can be an example for the future and be used as an international standard. 'Sport psychologist' can no longer be only a name or title. The profession of sport psychology must be based on a specific educational qualification. According to Nitsch (1989),

> we should intensively deal with concepts of education and graduate education
> in sport psychology. In 1986, the national society of sport psychology in the
> former FRG, Arbeitsgemeinschaft fur Sportpsychologie (ASP), in collabora-
> tion with the Association of German Psychologists (BDP), developed a curricu-
> lum for graduate education in sport psychology, including 270 lessons in total.
> Similar programmes are needed for basic education in sport psychology both
> for students in sport science and coaches. (p. 202)

In the eastern part of Germany—the former GDR—the study of sport psychology was organised in two ways. First, psychologists, after 5 years full-time study in an organised postgraduate programme at the German Academy of Physical Culture (former DHfK) of Leipzig (now the Faculty of Sport Science of the University of Leipzig), received a qualification in various disciplines of sport science, with certification. Second, physical educators and coaches, and particularly some athletes, received a psychological qualification after 4 years full-time study, or the equivalent in courses at some selected Institutes of Psychology at various universities.

Conclusion: The Future of Exercise and Sport Psychology

Since 1971, more than 100 books, 7,000 articles and many reports of research in sport psychology have been published (Kunath & Schellenberger, 1991). It is not possible to analyse all of this literature, but some trends can be highlighted. First, sport psychologists are in search of a theoretical basis for their specific discipline. Until now, theoretical research work has not been popular. But data alone allied to techniques found in the natural sciences cannot explain events properly without a theoretical background. Data are neutral—they become important in relation to a theoretical system.

A second trend in the international literature is for sport psychologists to use more functional models in their research. The conception of 'Action Psychology' could be such a functional model. It may be a promising new development in sport psychology, providing a framework for interpretation of psychological phenomena or qualities of personality and global concepts of human behaviour. It is appropriate, however, that sport psychologists utilise different models or concepts in their re-search. Whatever model is adopted, it seems useful to rely less than in the past on descriptive classification models 'which are based on dichotomous distinctions like introversion/extroversion, fear of failure/hope for success, action orientation/state orientation, concentrated attention/distributive attention, open-loop control/closed-loop control. Such global distinctions neglect dynamic processes, complex interrelations and the time perspective' (Nitsch, 1989, p. 203).

In summary, we have to consider the whole system of psychological states and mental control of athletes to really understand the details of inner actions or processes of psychoregulation. With respect to this the construct of the 'bio-psycho-social entity of man' (Kunath & Kunath, 1989) can be helpful to consolidate the theoretical foundation of sport psychology. Athletic activities are resultants of human capacities, structures and functions, mental images, and processes interacting with the situation including the effects and conditions of the social environment, in ways that reflect these three facets of human existence at the same time. If we agree on this, limitations become obvious, since, from this point of view, they are present in the three dimensions of humans—the biological, psychological and sociological.

The following questions, therefore, should be answered in future research:

- Which level of physical perfection and athletic efficiency is thought to be necessary and possible for the individual under these changing conditions during the main stages of his or her life?
- What differences in quality, quantity and effect of athletic engagement result from genetic heritage; how can these differences be found, measured and evaluated?
- Under which conditions, and in what way, can athletic activity affect health, physical capability, and mental, physical and social well-being?
- How can top performances be developed during a long-term complex process?

Currently we cannot state explicitly from a scientific point of view how, where, and under what conditions biological, mental and social factors function interdependently in different sport activities and at various levels of performance. The three strata are temporally, structurally and functionally interrelated although various requirements or situations induce a temporal dominance of one or the other factor at times which must be determined. Any unilateral approach, stressing only one factor in a complex process, risks overestimating the direction and level of action of other factors or giving them insufficient scientific study. One example is the neglect of genetic differences in individuals' biological performance potential. Another is the failure to consider the positive and negative effects of psychological processes mediating between social and biological factors.

The effectiveness for an individual of participation in sport depends on many factors, such as his or her own aims, intentions and motives for taking part in sport, the place of sport in the individual's values and life, the satisfaction experienced during sport activities, and the programmes available to help him or her to meet the requirements of various sport situations.

References

Biddle, S.J.H. (1989). Applied sport psychology: A view from Britain. *Journal of Applied Sport Psychology*, **1**, 23-34.

Danish, S.J., & Hale, B.D. (1981). Toward an understanding of the practice of sport psychology. *Journal of Sport Psychology*, **3**, 182-190.

European Federation of Sports Psychology (FEPSAC). (1987). *Manifesto on sports psychology*. Bad Blankenburg, Germany: Author.

Harrison, R.P., & Feltz, D.L. (1979). The professionalization of sport psychology: Legal considerations. *Journal of Sport Psychology*, **1**, 182-190.

Kunath, H., & Kunath, P. (1989). The bio-psycho-social entity of man: The efficiency of social factors. *Sport Science Review*, **12**, 52-57.

Kunath, P., & Schellenberger, H. (1991). *Tatigkeitsorientierte Sportpsychologie*. Frankfurt/Main, Germany: Deutsch.

Nitsch, J.R. (1989). Future trends in sport psychology and sport sciences. In *Proceedings of the 7th World Congress in Sport Psychology* (pp. 200-204). Singapore: Singapore Sports Council.

Schultze, E. (1897). *Uber die Umwandlung willkurlicher Bewegungen in unwillkurliche*. Unpublished doctoral dissertation, University of Freiburg, Germany.

Notes

[1]A revision of the British scheme is now in place and 'registered sport psychologists' are now referred to as 'accredited sport psychologists'. A full version of the revised BASES Code of Conduct is available from the British Association of Sport and Exercise Sciences, 114 Cardigan Road, Headingley, Leeds LS6 3BJ, UK.

Index

Contributors

Dr **Stuart J.H. Biddle** is a Senior Lecturer in the School of Education at the University of Exeter in the south-west of England where he is Course Director for the MSc degree in Exercise and Sport Psychology. He has a BEd degree in physical education, MSc in the psychology of sport and physical activity and PhD in psychology. He is a Chartered Psychologist of the British Psychological Society, an Accredited Exercise and Sport Psychologist of the British Association of Sport and Exercise Sciences and Fellow of the Physical Education Association of Great Britain and Northern Ireland.

Dr Biddle's research interests focus on motivation and social psychology, primarily in health-related exercise and physical education settings. In 1991 he was co-author, with Nanette Mutrie, of the exercise psychology textbook *Psychology of Physical Activity and Exercise: A Health-Related Perspective* (London: Springer). He has published extensively in exercise and sport psychology, health-related exercise and physical education. Dr Biddle is President of the European Federation of Sport Psychology and International Associate Editor for the journal *The Sport Psychologist*.

Dr **Erwin Apitzsch** is a Lecturer in the Department of Applied Psychology at Lund University in Sweden. He is Director of Research Studies and Course Director for sport psychology. He has BSc and MSc degrees in psychology and a PhD in applied psychology. He is a Licensed Psychologist of the Swedish Psychology Association. Dr Apitzsch is Secretary General of FEPSAC, Secretary of the Research and Education Committee of the International Student Sport Federation, Secretary of the Forum for Sport Research at Lund University and Vice President of the Swedish Student Sport Federation.

Dr **Michael Bar-Eli** is a senior researcher in the Ribstein Centre for Research and Sport Medicine Sciences in the Wingate Institute for Physical Education and Sport, Israel. He has a BA in behavioural sciences, MA in psychology and a PhD in sport psychology. He is a chartered psychologist of the Israel Psychological Association. Dr Bar-Eli is President of the Israel Society of Sport Psychology and Sociology and is one of Israel's two representatives in the European Federation of Sport Psychology. He is on the Editorial Board of the *International Journal of Sport Psychology*.

Dr **Philippe Brunel** is with the Department of Sciences et Techniques des Activités Physiques et Sportives (STAPS) at the University of Nantes in France where he teaches graduate courses in sport psychology. He received his doctoral degree in STAPS from the University of Clermont-Ferrand.

Dr **David Collins** is a Senior Lecturer in the Alsager Faculty of the Manchester Metropolitan University in England. He is the chair of the psychology section of the British Association of Sport and Exercise Sciences (BASES) and an Accredited Sport Psychologist of BASES and the British Olympic Association. Previously he was a professional soldier in the Royal Marines and a physical education teacher.

Dr **George Doganis** has a Diploma in physical education and MA in the psychology of sport from the University of Birmingham and a PhD in physical education (Psychology of Sport). He is currently an elected Assistant Professor of Sport Psychology in the Department of Physical Education and Sport Science at the Aristotle University of Thessaloniki.

Hanspeter Gubelmann studied physical education at the Swiss Federal Institute of Technology (ETH) in Zurich, Switzerland, and applied psychology and journalism at the University of Zurich. Currently he works as a research assistant in the Division of Physical Education at the ETH.

Dr **Graham Jones** is a Senior Lecturer in the Department of Physical Education, Sports Science and Recreation Management at Loughborough University. He has a BA (Hons) in physical education, an MSc in motor learning and a PhD in psychology. He is a Chartered Psychologist of the British Psychological Society and an Accredited Sport Psychologist of the British Association of Sport and Exercise Sciences (BASES).

Professor Dr **Paul Kunath** has a BEd and an MSc in education, and a PhD in pedagogy from the University of Leipzig. He is an Accredited Sport Psychologist of the German Arbeitsgemeinschaft für Sportpsychologie (ASP) and a Fellow of the International Society of Sport Psychology. In 1958 Dr Kunath became a lecturer at the Germany Academy of Physical Culture (DHFK Leipzig) and in 1967 was appointed Professor of Sport Psychology. Dr Kunath is a co-founder of the ISSP and Past President (1983-1991) of FEPSAC.

Dr **Egil W. Martinsen** has a PhD in psychiatry. He is the Medical Director of the Psychiatric Clinic in Forde, a small town in western Norway. Dr Martinsen's research interests focus on the treatment of mental disorders (especially anxiety and depression) with exercise.

Dr **Nanette Mutrie** is a Senior Lecturer in Physical Education and Sports Science at the University of Glasgow and has a PhD from the Pennsylvania State University. Her main teaching responsibilities lie in the area of sport and exercise psychology, and she is the postgraduate co-ordinator for taught master's degrees in physical education, sport and exercise science.

Dr **Athanasios Papaioannou** has a BEd in physical education from the Aristotle University of Thessaloniki. He has an MPhil degree in the psychology of physical activity, and a PhD in education and psychology from the University of Manchester. Dr Papaioannou is now a lecturer at the Democritus University of Thrace in Komotini, Greece.

Dr **Sabine Rethorst** is Assistant Professor in Sport Science at the University of Bielefeld in Germany. She has studied sport science, mathematics, psychology and pedagogy, and has master's degrees in mathematics and physical education. She has a PhD in sports science.

Dr **Guido Schilling** is a Lecturer in the Physical Education Department of the Swiss Federal Institute of Technology in Zurich. He holds degrees in physical education and psychology, and is an Accredited Psychologist of the Federation of Swiss Psychologists. Dr Schilling is a Past President of FEPSAC (1975-1983).

Dr **Pavel Slepicka** is Professor in the Faculty of Physical Education and Sport at Charles University, Prague. He is head of the Department of Pedagogy and Psychology of Sport. Dr Slepicka has an MSc in physical education, a PhD in philosophy and a DSc in pedagogical science. He is a member of the Czech Psychological Society and Czech Association of Sport Psychologists.

Dr **R. Andrew Smith** is a Director of Kerland Management Services, whose clinical interests include a sport science and medicine clinic. He has a BA in sport and recreation studies and a PhD in exercise psychology from the University of Exeter. He is Secretary of the British Association of Sport and Exercise Sciences.

Dr **Gershon Tenenbaum** is the former Director of the Ribstein Centre for Research and Sport Medicine Sciences at the Wingate Institute in Israel. He is a graduate of the Zinman College of Physical Education and has a BA and an MA from the University of Tel Aviv. He has a PhD in measurement, evaluation and statistical analysis from the University of Chicago. Dr Tenenbaum has most recently taken up an appointment in the Department of Psychology at the University of Southern Queensland, Australia.

Dr **Yannis Theodorakis** is a Lecturer in the Department of Physical Education and Sports Science at the Democritus University of Thrace, in Komotini, Greece. He has a BEd in physical education and sports science and a PhD in sport and exercise psychology. Dr Theodorakis is a committee member of the Greek Society of Sport Psychology.

Dr **Edgar E. Thill** is Professor in the Department of Psychology at the Blaise Pascal University of Clermont-Ferrand. He has a degree in physical education and a PhD in psychology. Dr Thill's research interests focus on motivation (primarily on learning strategies and motivation), in both classroom and physical education settings.

Dr **Klaus Willimczik** is a Professor of Sport Science at the University of Bielefeld, Germany. He has studied philosophy, history, geography, physical education and sports science. He has a PhD. He is Past President of the German Association of Sport Science (1979-1985) and of the Committee for German Physical Educators (1982-1985).